ENGINEERING ECONOMY FOR ENGINEERING MANAGERS

≡T⋀⋀ WILEY SERIES IN ENGINEERING & TECHNOLOGY MANAGEMENT

Series Editor: Dundar F. Kocaoglu

PROJECT MANAGEMENT IN MANUFACTURING AND HIGH TECHNOLOGY OPERATIONS
Adedeji B. Badiru, University of Oklahoma

MANAGERIAL DECISIONS UNDER UNCERTAINTY: AN INTRODUCTION TO THE ANALYSIS OF DECISION MAKING
Bruce F. Baird, University of Utah

INTEGRATING INNOVATION AND TECHNOLOGY MANAGEMENT
Johnson A. Edosomwan, IBM Corporation

CASES IN ENGINEERING ECONOMY
Ted Eschenbach, University of Missouri–Rolla

MANAGEMENT OF RESEARCH AND DEVELOPMENT ORGANIZATIONS: MANAGING THE UNMANAGEABLE
Ravinder K. Jain, U.S. Army Corps of Engineers
Harry C. Triandis, University of Illinois

STATISTICAL QUALITY CONTROL FOR MANUFACTURING MANAGERS
William S. Messina, IBM Corporation

KNOWLEDGE BASED RISK MANAGEMENT IN ENGINEERING: A CASE STUDY IN HUMAN-COMPUTER COOPERATIVE SYSTEMS
Kiyoshi Niwa, Hitachi, Ltd.

MANAGING TECHNOLOGY IN THE DECENTRALIZED FIRM
Albert H. Rubenstein, Northwestern University

MANAGEMENT OF INNOVATION AND CHANGE
Yassin Sankar, Dalhousie University

PROFESSIONAL LIABILITY OF ARCHITECTS AND ENGINEERS
Harrison Streeter, University of Illinois at Urbana–Champaign

ENGINEERING ECONOMY FOR ENGINEERING MANAGERS

TURAN GÖNEN

California State University, Sacramento
Sacramento California

WILEY

A WILEY-INTERSCIENCE PUBLICATION

JOHN WILEY & SONS

NEW YORK   CHICHESTER   BRISBANE   TORONTO   SINGAPORE

Library of Congress Cataloging in Publication Data:

Gönen, Turan.
    Engineering economy for engineering managers / Turan Gönen.
        p.   cm. -- (Wiley series in engineering and technology
    management)
    "A Wiley-Interscience publication."
    Bibliography: p.
    Includes index.
    1. Engineering economy.   2. Engineering--Management.   I. Title.
    II. Series.
    TA177.4.G66   1990
    658.15--dc20   89-34112
    ISBN 0-471-62163-3   CIP

Printed in the United States of America

10 9 8 7 6 5 4 3 2 1

To an excellent engineer,
a great teacher, and a dear friend,
DR. HAROLD A. COWLES
and

*To my wife **NILÜFER** and my daughter **SEVIL ESEN***
for their limitless patience and understanding

A man knocked at the heavenly gate
His face was scarred and old.
He stood before the man of fate
For admission to the fold.
"What have you done," St. Peter asked
"To gain admission here?"
"I've been an engineer, Sir," he said
"For many and many a year."
The pearly gates swung open wide;
St. Peter touched the bell.
"Come in and choose your harp," he said,
"You've had your share of hell."

AUTHOR UNKNOWN

It's a story about four people named Everybody,
Somebody, Anybody, and Nobody. There was an
important job to be done and Everybody was asked
to do it. Everybody was sure Somebody would do it.
Anybody could have done it, but Nobody did it.
Somebody got angry about that, because it was
Everybody's job. Everybody thought Anybody could
do it, but Nobody realized that Everybody wouldn't
do it. It ended up that Everybody blamed Somebody
when Nobody did what Anybody could have done.

AUTHOR UNKNOWN

Life is the summation of confusions. The more
confused you are, the more alive you are. When
you are not confused any longer, you are dead!

TURAN GÖNEN

PREFACE

Today, business continues to become more technical. Therefore, engineers play an increasingly important role in management. More and more decision making in industry and government is done by engineers or engineering managers. Thus, engineering managers play a dual role as the linkage between management and technical expertise. As succinctly put by Cleland and Kocaoglu [21]:[†]

Such managers allocate resources, work through people, and make and implement decisions while simultaneously formulating technical strategies. We believe that the time has come for the identification of engineering management as a distinct professional discipline. Individuals who manage engineering organizations find it necessary to understand both the technology involved and the management process through which that technology is applied. Management literature contains very little material that deals with the dual role of the engineering manager—a technologist and a manager.

Presently, there are many excellent textbooks dealing with topics in engineering economy. Some of them are considered to be classics. However, unfortunately, they do not particularly address, nor concentrate on, topics dealing with engineering management or the needs of engineering management or the needs of engineering managers. Therefore, the intention here is to fill the vacuum, at least partially, that has existed so long in engineering management literature.

[†]Cleland and Kocaoglu [21], Copyright McGraw-Hill Book Company, New York, 1981. Used with permission of McGraw-Hill Book Company.

This book has evolved from the content of courses given by the author at the Engineering Management Department of the University of Missouri at Rolla and at the Industrial Engineering Department of the Iowa State University. It has been written for senior-level undergraduate and beginning-level engineering management and/or industrial engineering graduate students, as well as practicing engineers and engineering managers in industry. It can serve as a text for a two-semester course or, by a judicious selection, the material in the text can also be condensed to suit a single-semester course.

The book includes topics on the role of engineering economy in engineering management, cost concepts and managerial accounting, discrete and continuous compounding and interest formulas, comparison of investment alternatives, rate of return and incremental analyses, breakeven and sensitivity analyses, depreciation and depletion, income tax considerations, replacement analysis, inflation and deflation, economic decision making under risk and uncertainty, capital budgeting considerations, and computer-aided capital expenditure analyses and examples of computer applications.

This book has been particularly written for students, practicing engineers or engineering managers who may want to teach themselves. Each new term is clearly defined when it is first introduced; also a glossary has been provided. Basic material has been explained carefully and in detail with numerous examples. Special features of the book include ample numerical examples and problems designed to use the information presented in each chapter. A special effort has been made to familiarize the reader with the vocabulary and symbols used by the industry. The addition of the appendixes and other back matter makes the text self-sufficient. A complete solutions manual is available for the instructors.

The author is most grateful to numerous colleagues for educating the author, particularly Dr. Harold A. Cowles, Dr. Gerald W. Smith, Dr. Keith L. McRoberts, Professor Jean C. Hempstead, Professor Loran E. Mohar, and Professor Richard C. Vaughn of the Iowa State University, and Dr. John Stowe of the University of Missouri at Columbia. Also acknowledged are Dr. Yildirim Omurtag, Dr. Henry A. Weibe, and Professor Bernard R. Sarchet of the University of Missouri at Rolla, Dr. Haluk Bekiroglu of the Boston University, Dr. Fred Choobineh of the University of Nebraska, Dr. Bobbie L. Foote of the University of Oklahoma, Dr. John Krobock, Dr. Joan Al-Kazily, and Professor William R. Neuman of the California State University, Sacramento.

A special thank you is extended to my editor, Mr. Frank J. Cerra of John Wiley & Sons, Inc. and to series editor, Dr. Dündar F. Kocaoglu of the Portland State University, for their support and encouragement.

The author is also indebted to numerous students who studied portions of the book at the Iowa State University and the University of Missouri at

Rolla and made countless contributions and valuable suggestions for improvements.

Finally, the author's deepest appreciation goes to his wife, Nilüfer, and to his daughter, Sevil Esen, for their limitless patience and understanding.

TURAN GÖNEN

Sacramento, California

CONTENTS

1 A Brief Review of Engineering Management and the Role of Engineering Economy 1

1.1 Introduction, 1

1.2 A Brief History of Engineering Management in the United States, 3

1.3 The Engineer in Transition to Management, 4

1.4 Types of Candidates for Engineering Management, 5

1.5 The Functions of Engineering Management, 6

1.6 The Art of Motivation, 7

1.7 The Art of Leadership, 9

1.8 The Required Managerial Skills, 10

1.9 The Role of Engineering Economy, 11

2 Cost Concepts and Managerial Accounting 15

2.1 Introduction, 15

2.2 Cost Concepts and Terminology, 15

    2.2.1 Life-Cycle Costs, 16

    2.2.2 Future and Opportunity Costs, 16

    2.2.3 Past and Sunk Costs, 16

    2.2.4 Direct, Indirect, and Overhead Costs, 17

    2.2.5 Fixed and Variable Costs, 17

2.3 Brief Review of Accounting Principles, 17

2.4 Balance Sheet, 18

2.5 Income Statement, 20

2.6 Cash Flow Generation and Application, 21

2.7 Cost Accounting, 23

2.8 Ratio Analysis of the Financial Position of a Firm, 23

2.9 Liquidity Ratios, 26

    2.9.1 Current Ratio, 27

    2.9.2 Acid-Test Ratio, 27

    2.9.3 Inventory Turnover Ratio, 28

2.10 Debt Ratios, 28

    2.10.1 The Debt-to-Net-Worth Ratio, 28

    2.10.2 Ratio of Total Debt to Equity, 29

2.11 Profitability Ratios, 29

    2.11.1 Profitability with Respect to Sales, 29

    2.11.2 Profitability with Respect to Investment, 30

    2.11.3 Turnover and Earning Power, 31

    2.11.4 Coverage Ratios, 31

    Problems, 34

3 Interest and Interest Formulas   **37**

3.1 Time Value of Money, 37

3.2 Interest Calculations, 38

    3.2.1 Simple Interest, 38

    3.2.2 Compound Interest, 39

3.3 Cash Flow Diagram, 39

3.4 Discrete Compound Interest Formulas, 41

    3.4.1 Notation Used, 42

    3.4.2 Single-Payment Compound Amount Factor (Finding F, Given P), 42

    3.4.3 Single-Payment Present Worth Factor (Finding P, Given F), 45

3.5 Uniform-Series Compound Amount Factor (Finding F, Given A), 49

3.6 Uniform-Series Sinking-Fund Factor (Finding A, Given F), 53

3.7 Uniform-Series Present Worth Factor (Finding P, Given A), 54

3.8 Uniform-Series Capital Recovery Factor (Finding A, Given P), 56

3.9 The Levelizing Process of a Non-Uniform-Series Cash Flow, 61

3.10 Summary of Discrete Compounding Interest Factors, 63

3.11 Arithmetic Gradient Series, 64

    3.11.1 Factor to Convert an Arithmetic Gradient Series to Future Worth (Finding F, Given G), 64

    3.11.2 Factor to Convert an Arithmetic Gradient Series to Present Worth (Finding P, Given G), 67

    3.11.3 Factor to Convert an Arithmetic Gradient Series to a Uniform Series (Finding A, Given G), 69

3.12 Relationships among Compound Interest Factors, 71

3.13 Geometric Gradient Series, 75

3.14 Limits of Compound Interest Factors, 81

    Problems, 83

4 Continuous Compounding and Continuous Interest Factors   **87**

4.1 Nominal and Effective Interest Rates, 87

4.2 Continuous Compounding, 92

4.3 Continuous Compounding Interest Formulas, 93

    4.3.1 Interest Formulas for Continuous Compounding and Discrete Cash Flows, 93

    4.3.2 Interest Formulas for Continuous Compounding and Continuous Cash Flows, 93

    Problems, 106

5 Comparison of Investment Alternatives   **109**

5.1 Decision-Making Process, 109

5.2 Types of Investment Alternatives, 111

5.3 The Minimum Attractive Rate of Return, 112

5.4 Selection of Proper Study Period, 114

5.5 Methods for Comparing Investment Alternatives, 117

5.6 Present Worth Method, 117

5.7 Infinite Study Period—Capitalized Worth Method, 123

5.8 Annual Worth Method, 126

5.9 Capital Recovery Calculations, 127

5.10 Future Worth Method, 134

5.11 Payback Period Analysis, 140

5.12 Valuation of Bonds, 142

5.13 Valuation of Stocks, 143

5.14 Life-Cycle Cost Comparisons, 144

    Problems, 149

6 Rate of Return and Incremental Analysis   **158**

    6.1 Introduction, 158

    6.2 Rate of Return Method, 159

    6.3 Choosing the ROR Before a Trial-and-Error
        Calculation, 164

    6.4 Evaluation of Investment Projects with Multiple
        Rates of Return, 166

    6.5 Incremental Rate of Return Analysis, 168

    6.6 Incremental Rate of Return Analysis Using Smith's
        Network Diagram Method, 171

    6.7 Some Comments on Criteria for Ranking Projects, 174
        Problems, 178

7 Breakeven and Sensitivity Analyses   **184**

    7.1   Introduction, 184

    7.2   Some Comments on the Use of Breakeven Analysis, 187

    7.3   Some of the Possible Application Areas of the
        Breakeven Method, 188

    7.4   Improved Breakeven Analysis, 189

    7.5   Some Comments on Breakeven Point Problems in
        Production, 189

    7.6   Analysis of Make-or-Buy Decisions, 193

    7.7   Analysis of Lease-or-Buy Decisions, 194

    7.8   Profit Margin and Concept of Dumping, 195

    7.9   Utilization of Capacity, 196

    7.10 Sensitivity Analysis, 197
        Problems, 198

8 Depreciation and Depletion   **201**

    8.1   Introduction, 201

    8.2   Depreciation Accounting, 202

    8.3   Depreciation Calculation Fundamentals, 203

    8.4   Depreciation Methods, 204

    8.5   Straight-Line Method, 204

    8.6   Sum-of-Years' Digits Method, 208

    8.7   Declining-Balance Method, 210

    8.8   Sinking-Fund Method, 214

    8.9   Comparison of Depreciation Methods, 217

    8.10 Units of Production Method, 218

8.11 Accelerated Cost Recovery System Method, 218

8.12 Recapture Provisions of the ACRS Method, 224

    8.12.1 Recapture, 224

    8.12.2 Recapture of Investment Tax Credit, 225

8.13 Tax Reform Act of 1986, 227

    8.13.1 Alternative Depreciation System, 230

    8.13.2 Comments on the Modified ACRS Method, 230

    8.13.3 Comments on Averaging Conventions, 231

    8.13.4 Expensing Instead of Cost Recovery, 231

    8.13.5 Investment Tax Credit, 231

8.14 Depletion, 231

8.15 Depreciation of Group Properties, 232

    Problems, 233

9 Income Tax Considerations　　　　**237**

9.1 Introduction, 237

9.2 Types of Taxes, 238

9.3 The Tax Reform Act of 1986, 239

9.4 Individual Federal Income Tax, 239

9.5 Corporation Federal Income Tax, 242

9.6 Income Tax Rates for Corporations, 244

9.7 After-Tax Cash Flow, 245

9.8 Combined Federal and State Income Taxes, 248

    Problems, 252

10 Replacement Analysis　　　　**256**

10.1 Introduction, 256

10.2 Reasons for Replacement, 257

10.3 Optimum Economic Life, 259

10.4 The Concept of Defender versus Challenger, 261

10.5 Sunk Cost, 264

10.6 Outsider Viewpoint, 265

10.7 Replacement by Leasing, 265

10.8 After-Tax Replacement Analysis, 268

10.9 Retirement Patterns for Group Properties, 273

    Problems, 281

11 Inflation and Deflation　　　　**284**

11.1 Introduction, 284

11.2 Inflation and Interest Rates, 285

11.3 Inflation and Price Indexes, 286

11.4 Effects of Inflation on Debtors and Creditors, 288

11.5 The Methods for Taking into Account Inflation or Deflation, 288

11.6 Inflation and Combined Interest–Inflation Rate, 289

11.7 Deflation and Combined Interest–Deflation Rate, 290

11.8 The Effects of Inflation on After-Tax Calculations, 293

11.9 Present Worth of Escalating Series, 295

11.10 Some Further Notes on Inflation, 297

      11.10.1 Demand-Pull Inflation, 297

      11.10.2 Cost-Push Inflation, 297

      11.10.3 Structural Inflation, 298

      11.10.4 Possible Remedies, 298

      Problems, 299

12 Economic Analysis of Projects in the Public Sector   301

12.1 Introduction, 301

12.2 The Role of Point of View in Public Projects, 302

12.3 Financing of Public Projects, 303

12.4 The Interest Rate Selection for Public Projects, 304

12.5 Benefit–Cost Ratio Analysis, 304

12.6 B/C Analysis for Multiple Alternatives, 307

12.7 Some Comments on the B/C Ratio Analysis, 309

12.8 Multipurpose Public Projects, 309

12.9 A Systematic Procedure for Comparison of Multiple Alternatives, 310

12.10 Cost-Effectiveness Analysis, 310

12.11 Public Utilities, 310

      Problems, 314

13 Economic Decision Making under Risk and Uncertainty   316

13.1 Introduction, 316

13.2 Brief Review of Basic Probability Theory,

13.3 Expected Value and Variance,

13.4 Brief Review of Probability Distributions,

      13.4.1 Beta Distribution,

      13.4.2 Normal Distribution,

13.5 Sensitivity Analysis under the Conditions of Uncertainty,

13.6 Monte Carlo Simulation, 338

13.7 Decision Tree Analysis, 343

13.8 Decision Making under Complete Uncertainty, 345

    13.8.1 Payoff Matrix, 345

    13.8.2 Dominance Criterion, 346

    13.8.3 The Laplace Rule or Principle, 346

    13.8.4 Maximin and Minimax Rules or Principles, 347

    13.8.5 Maximax and Minimin Rules or Principles, 347

    13.8.6 Hurwicz Rule or Principle, 348

    13.8.7 Minimax Regret Rule or Savage Principle, 349

13.9 Solution Methods for Multiple Objectives and Criteria, 350

    Problems, 350

14 Capital Budgeting Considerations   **355**

14.1 Introduction, 355

14.2 Types of Investment Projects, 356

14.3 Capital Rationing, 357

14.4 Effects of Capital Budgeting, 360

14.5 Factors Affecting Capital Budgeting, 365

14.6 Capital Budgeting under Risk and Uncertainty, 366

    Risk and Uncertaint, 366

    Problems, 367

Appendix A   Interest Tables   **371**

Appendix B   Computer-Aided Capital Expenditure Analyses   **413**

    B.1 Introduction, 413

    B.2 Organization of IFPS/Plus, 415

Appendix C   Examples of Computer Applications   **418**

    Problems, 426

Appendix D   Statistical Tables   **435**

Appendix E   Glossary   **440**

References   **446**

Index   **451**

ENGINEERING ECONOMY FOR ENGINEERING MANAGERS

___1
A BRIEF REVIEW OF ENGINEERING MANAGEMENT AND THE ROLE OF ENGINEERING ECONOMY

Those who know how can always get a job,
but those who know why, may be your boss!
AUTHOR UNKNOWN

Now that I'm almost up the ladder,
I should, no doubt, be feeling gladder.
It is quite fine, the view and such,
If just it didn't shake so much.
RICHARD ARMOUR

Michelangelo was asked, How do you produce statues that are so
full of life? He responded: The marble already contains the statues;
it is just a matter of extracting them. Like marble, children are
rough material: you can extract gentlemen, heroes, even saints.
ALBINO LUCIANI, *Catechism in Crumbs,* 1949

To fail to plan is to plan to fail.
A. E. GASGOIGNE, 1985

1.1 INTRODUCTION

Engineering management can be defined as the art and science of planning, organizing, allocating resources, and directing and controlling activities that are either technical and/or industrial in character in an organization.

1

As engineers advance through their professional careers, they progress in terms of professional positions with increasingly higher levels of technical responsibilities. Inevitably, these steps bring them closer to the managerial responsibilities of the organization. It is generally accepted as a fact that many engineers encounter serious problems when they reach this stage in their career that marks the transition from engineer to manager. Many engineers consider such transition as trouble or a crisis rather than an opportunity.[†] They frequently find it very hard to overcome difficulties resulting from the lack of conpatibility between the totally technical tasks of the engineering and the nontechnical requirements of management. Therefore, this can cause engineers as managers to have difficulties in communicating with others due to their lack of knowledge of other disciplines as a result of their narrow technical backgrounds and due to their inner conflict between their role as an engineer and their role as a manager. Most of these problems are caused by the change of working environment from one of precision and predictability of physical problems of engineering to one of uncertainty and rapid change of conditions of management, as illustrated in Figure 1.1. The figure depicts the characteristics and the boundary condi-

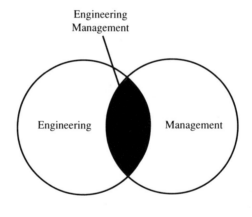

Well-defined problems	Undefined problems
Materials subsystem	Human subsystem
Complete certainty	Uncertainty
Continuity assumption	Discontinuities
Well-developed data bases	Lack of data
Analytical decisions	Intuitive decisions

Figure 1.1 Illustration of the intersection between engineering and management and the overlap between the two fields. (From *Engineering Management* by D. I. Cleland and D. F. Kocaoglu [21], 1981. Used with permission. © McGraw-Hill Book Company, 1981.)

[†]It is interesting to note that in Chinese the word for *crisis* is also the word for *opportunity*.

tions of engineering and management fields, as well as engineering management as the overlap between the fields of engineering and management.[†]

1.2   A BRIEF HISTORY OF ENGINEERING MANAGEMENT IN THE UNITED STATES

Historically, the management of technical activities by technically competent people is not new. For example, Frederick W. Taylor (1856–1915), the father of scientific management, and Henry Fayol (1841–1925), the father of administrative theory, were engineers. However, until recently it has been customary for such people to define themselves as either engineers or managers subject to their work surroundings. The emerging of engineering management as a separate division of academic discipline has taken place after World War II. For example, graduate-level courses in Research Administration were offered at Illinois Institute of Technology, New York University, and the University of Pennsylvania in the late 1940s and early 1950s. Also, engineering management graduate programs offering the master's degree were begun at various universities including New Jersey Institute of Technology, Rensselaer Polytechnic Institute, the University of California in Los Angeles, and George Washington University. Since 1965, however, there has been a rapid growth in the number of educational programs offering engineering management degrees in the United States. For example, today, over 100 universities offer such programs at B.S., M.S., and Ph.D. levels. It is also interesting to note that approximately 20 to 25% of such students enrolling in such programs have an M.S. or even a Ph.D. in their technical backgrounds before they get involved in an engineering management program.

Further, since 1965, there has been a rapid growth of professional organizations in terms of society committees or divisions, or separate societies, that are concerned with engineering management. For example, the Institute of Electrical and Electronics Engineers (IEEE) organized the IEEE Engineering Management Society, and the American Society for Engineering Education (ASEE) established its Engineering Management Division. Other examples include the Institute of Management Sciences (TIMS) College on Engineering Management and similar divisions in a number of other engineering professional societies. Furthermore, in 1979, a group of interested professionals from government, industry, and universities established the American Society for Engineering Management.

[†]For excellent treatment of the subject, see Cleland and Kocaoglu [21] and Cleland and King [20].

1.3   THE ENGINEER IN TRANSITION TO MANAGEMENT

In today's world, engineering practice dictates the exercise of managerial skills as well as possession of technical competence, but conventional engineering education seldom prepares engineers to appreciate the managerial aspects of engineering, let alone to develop their managerial skills required to manage engineering projects or organizations. Today, most engineers start their careers at positions that can be described as the task-oriented part of the engineering function. As their careers progress, usually within 3 to 7 years after graduation, they become less technically oriented as they are given more and more responsibility and authority for staff and other resources. Of course, with such managerial or administrative responsibilities, they are given associated higher financial rewards, status, and some other material and psychological rewards. They become increasingly managerially oriented in their tasks until they cross the boundary into functional management. This means that early in their careers, young engineers reach a point where they have to decide whether or not to remain in their chosen technical field (as technical specialists or technical experts in design, research and development, or in advisory positions) or alternatively become engineering managers with progressively greater administrative responsibilities. At this transitional stage, engineers become primarily managers. Therefore, they have to act accordingly. Unfortunately, not all engineers can make such transition. According to Amos and Sarchet [4], the reasons are: (1) the feeling of insecurity and fearfulness in making wrong decisions in their new managerial positions versus the feeling of confidence, success, and outstanding reputation in engineering that they left behind; (2) the change in points of view from that of a professional engineer to that of company points of view so that they can help to achieve the company's goals and objectives; (3) the change in their roles from that of doers (having direct control over their previous work as engineers) to that of supervisors (being at the mercy of their subordinates and their inefficiencies); (4) the change in their full-time activities from that of engineering to that of being bureaucrats and paper shufflers applying techniques of management and being seen by engineers as obstacles in the way of engineers trying to do their work; and (5) the change in their working environment from one governed by certainties and physical laws to one that deals with intangibles, with man-made rules and regulations, and uncertainties.

If they are successful in the traditional nonproject organizations, the next stage of promotion for such functional managers is to move into general management positions. Thus, they become responsible for the management of resources for the company as a whole. At such top management positions they are involved in multidisciplinary management, and, therefore, in the process they have moved almost totally away from their previous technical roles. Usually, only a limited number of engineers can achieve such success in reaching to such top management positions without having a formal engineering management education in their background. On the other hand, in project-management-oriented organizations, engineers can play the role as general managers at basically the level of functional managers. Therefore, they come across the problems of multidisciplinary management at a much earlier stage in their professional development.

As mentioned, when engineers first become functional managers they go through a period of self-identity conflict in terms of their roles within their organizations. Even though they are in management now, they tend to still see themselves as engineers rather than as managers. Of course, such attitudes result in internal stress and can harm their performance as the functional manager. In the event that such attitudes continue, they end up spending more time in the task-oriented engineering roles and less time in the managerial roles. This, in turn, can cause interpersonal problems with both project management and the engineers under the functional manager. Eventually, though, they can learn to spend more time with people, as opposed to spending the time on the details of the technical work. Of course, this is more assured if they have a formal engineering management education in their backgrounds [44, 47].

1.4 TYPES OF CANDIDATES FOR ENGINEERING MANAGEMENT

It can be said that engineering management is the management of engineering activities, projects, systems, or organizations. According to Kocaoglu [50], this may include the following areas: (1) management of engineers and scientists, (2) management of engineering and R&D projects, (3) management of technical organizations, (4) management of technological systems, and (5) management of critical resources.

Among the engineers working for such organizations, not all of them like to have managerial roles or duties. Therefore, the organization should recognize that some engineers will make their most effective contribution in the science and technology of engineering rather than through management of engineering resources. Thus, organizations should be designed to be sure that such contributions are optimized and given appropriate status and rewards. However, those engineers with the right disposition toward managerial tasks and responsibilities should be encouraged and motivated. According to Bayton and Chapman [9], in their well-known studies for NASA, there are basically three types of engineers that are motivated for management: (1) the *type I engineer* who has strong managerial motivation and is active in moving to managerial roles, generally demonstrating a high degree of success in management; (2) the *type II engineer* who has a specialist motivation at the beginning, but once in a managerial role finds such roles satisfying and challenging; and (3) the *type III engineer* who if forced into managerial roles becomes the classic case of *good engineer but poor manager.*[†]

The results of the study suggest that engineering education should provide for two types of engineers for the organizations: (1) the technical specialist engineer and (2) the management-oriented engineer. Of course, early recognition and selection of the two types of engineers, in order to develop proper educational, training, and professional programs, would result in greater performance and efficiency in engineering management of the organization in addition to the additional benefits such as prevention of personal frustrations and improvement in employee satisfaction.

1.5 THE FUNCTIONS OF ENGINEERING MANAGEMENT

The primary functions of engineering management is basically the same as the basic functions of management. According to Fayol [28], a French mining engineering manager, the basic managerial functions are: (1) planning, (2) organizing, (3) staffing, (4) motivating, and (5) controlling.

The function of *planning* includes tasks such as setting objectives for the organization, determining rules and procedures, and scheduling and forecasting materials. In essence, to Fayol, *managing means looking ahead*, and foresight is an essential element of management. Thus, a good plan of action should have the characteristics of *unity* (i.e., one *overall plan* followed by specific plans for each activity); *continuity* (in terms of both short range and long range); *flexibility* (to compensate for unexpected events); and *precision* (so that much of the guesswork is eliminated.) According to Cleland and Kocaoglu [21], technical objectives and goals of an organization are determined based on its technological capabilities:

> The value structures of the managers, the needs for engineering services and the opportunities, and the outside environment play important roles in the development of objectives. Once the objectives are determined, the strategies are developed to achieve them within the limitations imposed upon the engineering organization by the external conditions. [21]

The function of *organizing* involves activities of grouping and assigning, and delegating authority to subordinates, and so on. Thus, it includes provisions for structuring of activities, and training of personnel. According to Fayol [28], organizing means to provide the organization with everything necessary to its functioning, including capital, personnel, equipment, and raw materials. Further, it is the duty of management to see that the human and material organization is consistent with the objective, resources, and requirements of the organization.

[†]The cliche, "We took a good engineer and made a lousy manager," is prevalent because of the organization's expectations that people will learn by experience.

The function of *staffing* is concerned with selecting, hiring, and training employees, determining the personnel requirement, and establishing standards to measure the performance of employees. Succinctly put, staffing in an engineering organization is finding the technical qualities and knowledge in people to fill all levels of the organization.

The function of *motivating* involves activities such as guiding employees to meet the established performance standards, maintaining morale, specifying the objectives to employees, and rewarding those employees with high achievements. In general, engineers and scientists, by their education and training, are self-motivated people. They are self-starters and perform objectively and logically in their tasks.

The function of *controlling* includes activities such as monitoring the actual performance of personnel, comparing it against the set standards, and taking corrective measures. Succinctly put, control is the verification of whether or not everything takes place in conformity with the plan adopted, the directives issued, and the principles established. An effective control stimulates better planning, simplifies and strengthens the engineering organization, increases the efficiency of command, and facilitates coordination.

1.6 THE ART OF MOTIVATION

Engineering managers have the tasks of overcoming a large number of difficulties involved in getting their personal and group performances from people and organizations to achieve the objectives that are set for them or by them. Most of the time, such achievement is a function of their ability to motivate and to lead the people working for them as well as the realities of the organizational settings and restrictions. In general, it is a well-known fact that engineers, scientists, as well as others *can be motivated* if management shows that it values them and cares about them. Therein lies the problem! How does management accomplish this? To answer this question, researchers have written literally thousands of articles and books on theories of how to motivate people and conducted a large number of experiments to find out what motivates people under a given set of circumstances.[†]

For example, Maslow [56] developed a needs hierarchy, as shown in Figure 1.2. He explained that human needs basically are of two kinds: (1) primary needs and (2) secondary or higher-order needs; and, that the higher-order needs can not be fulfilled until the lower needs have been substantially satisfied.

McGregor [57] developed a set of assumptions called *Theory X* and *Theory Y*. In brief, *Theory X* assumes that people dislike work, will avoid it if possible, and that they must be coerced, controlled, directed, and

---

[†]For further information see Bekiroglu and Gönen [11–13].

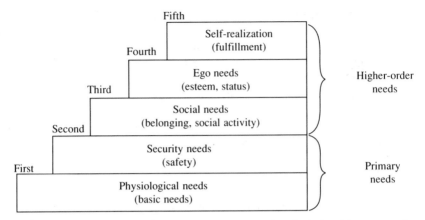

Figure 1.2 Maslow's need hierarchy showing the order of priority of human needs.

threatened to get them to expend effort toward organizational goals. *Theory Y*, conversely, assumes that work is as natural as play, that people will exercise self-direction and self-control in the service of objectives to which they are committed, and that commitment to objectives is a function of inherent rewards associated with their achievement.

Albrook [2] analyzed management systems and explained that the democratic approach to corporate management works well in areas of rapid change, but that it cannot be universally applied. He discussed the work of Likert [23] and his methods for diagnosing of management styles [51].

Herzberg [41] dealt with motivating via KITA, which literally means kick-in-the-pants. He spoke of negative, physical, and psychological KITA, concluding that only the one administering the kick is motivated.

Most of the *human relations* experts, along with Argyris [6–7], indicate that American business management has downgraded the position of the employee to the point where no meaningful work exists. Distrust caused by basic company policy has moved them so far down the hierarchy that employees are concerned only with money, cannot even make friends, and probably cannot function as well as a monkey could in the same work situation. Management is pictured almost as badly. Although most of their needs are satisfied and self-actualization should be the goal, management personnel are full of "separateness, alienation, and frustration." They distrust each other and are afraid to function as well as they probably could.

Therefore, to be successful, management must use those techniques of good human relations that appeal to the basic needs of people, and thus prove to be good motivators. Here, the basic needs of people are defined to include recognition, opportunity, security, and belonging. Of course, such motivational techniques used must also be accompanied by appropriate supervisory styles.

1.7   THE ART OF LEADERSHIP

Leadership begins with a desire to achieve, to achieve goals he must plan;
To plan he must analyze and to implement he must organize;
To organize he must delegate and to delegate he must administrate;
To administrate he must communicate and to communicate he must motivate;
To motivate he must share and to share he must care;
To care he must believe;
To believe he must set goals that inspire belief and desire to achieve;
Thus, the process of leadership begins and ends with goals.

AUTHOR UNKNOWN

Ideally speaking, management positions, especially below general management level, with responsibility for professional engineering work should be filled on merit by qualified and experienced engineers. Other professionals usually do not have the knowledge, skills, or professional competence required for the leadership and management of professional engineering work.

In order to be successful, an engineering manager has to provide the leadership necessary for establishing an effective managerial team and organizational environment. An effective engineering manager, as a leader, should become skillful in various managerial styles that are applicable for different situations because not all management styles or strategies are rightfully applicable for each person or group [22]. For example, the authoritarian style may be more consistent with traditional organizations, whereas the participative management style may provide better results with matrix organizations. Therefore, a successful engineering manager has to be conscious of his or her real managerial style and be able to change styles when it is necessary. The leadership capabilities of the engineering manager are fundamental to the development of a successful group. Thus, the perception and the ability of the engineering manager to detect and solve group problems are essential. Succinctly put, a leader is the one that others will follow willingly and voluntarily. In general, putting it in practical terms, people will follow the person they feel (1) can be believed; (2) knows where he or she is going; (3) knows how to get there; (4) makes the mission appear to be important, exciting, and possible to accomplish; (5) makes their roles in the mission appear to be important; (6) makes them feel capable of doing their roles; (7) has the courage and persistence; will not back off from danger, opposition, or discouragement; and (8) can be trusted not to sell out their cause for his own personal advantage [52]. Of course, for a group to maximize its effectiveness, the engineering manager cannot always fulfill all of the leadership tasks in every situation. Hence, individual team members have to help each other with proper leadership. Therefore, in general, the behavior of the team is not only affected by the leadership qualities of the engineering manager but also the attitude, knowledge, skills, and capabilities of the individual team members as well as by the characteristics of the departments and/or the companies involved.

Furthermore, according to Fayol [28], there are 14 general principles that a leader must follow to be an effective manager:

1. *Division of Work*: Foster specialization for productivity.
2. *Authority*: The right to give orders and the power to extract obedience. Authority is made up of personal authority and official authority.
3. *Discipline*: Obedience, energy, and respect mutually accorded.
4. *Unity of Command*: Receive orders from one superior only.
5. *Unity of Direction*: One plan to reach one set of objectives.
6. *Subordination of Individual Interest to the General Interest*: No favoritism or personal gain.
7. *Remuneration*: Fair and satisfactory to company and employee.
8. *Centralization*: One central brain except in very large companies.
9. *Line of Authority*: Appropriate channels of authority up, down, and across.
10. *Order*: A place for everyone and everyone in his or her place.
11. *Equity*: Fairness and justice.
12. *Initiative*: Maintain freedom to propose and inspire action.
13. *Esprit de Corps*: Harmony and union among employees and managers.
14. *Span of Control*: Supervison that is appropriate to the job.

1.8   THE REQUIRED MANAGERIAL SKILLS

In general, managing is a task or an activity that can be considered as a *process* requiring the performance of several *functions* through the possession of a specific set of professional *skills* employing certain *techniques*. Therefore, an engineering manager must have or develop various other managerial skills, in addition to leadership skills, to perform his or her duties successfully. Such skills include the following:

1. *Technical Skills*: The ability of the engineering manager to employ the required technical knowledge and procedures in doing his or her work tasks. The need for them depends on the level of engineering management. They are required more in the low-level management positions.

2. *Interpersonal Skills*: The ability of the engineering manager to get along with other people and lead them.

3. *Organizational Skills*: The ability of the engineering manager to understand the function of each group and/or department in the organizational structure as well as the ability to develop such organizations.

4. *Communication Skills*: The ability of the engineering manager to provide written or oral information within the organization. It is important to recognize that without communication skills none of the other skills has a chance to show.

5. *Analytical Skills*: The ability of the engineering manager to employ analytical techniques and/or tools in analyzing work-related problems.

6. *Decision-making Skills*: The ability of the engineering manager to make decisions that are associated with the organization and ability to know when to reject perfectionism in favor of action.

7. *Entrepreneural Skills*: The ability of the engineering manager to sell ideas and promote new ideas or products and the ability to examine the worse consequences before taking risks.

8. *Administrative Skills*: The ability of the engineering manager to manage in terms of organizing, planning, directing, and controlling. They also represent the ability to balance direction of subordinates with subordinate independence by providing training and goals, while avoiding dictating how to meet such goals [65].

1.9 THE ROLE OF ENGINEERING ECONOMY

In general, a given organization will continue to operate in the long run as long as it provides: (1) suitable and reliable products and/or services to its customers, at competitive prices; (2) an effective creative environment for the development of new products and the replacement of existing products at the right time; (3) a satisfying employment for its employees; (4) a sufficient amount of rate of return for the capital invested in the projects; and (5) security for the future of business by maintaining or providing for growth in its capital structure for the expansion of business activities.

Here, it may be interesting to note that, most of the time, a given company itself owns no capital, and therefore it simply uses the capital provided by equity shareholders and lenders, that is, investors. Thus, the managers of a company are merely stewards to the owners and other investors. Therefore, such stewardship also has a legal responsibility for the physical and financial assets of the company. Furthermore, it also has the moral and ethical responsibility to make use of the capital of the investors efficiently and with integrity.[†]

Therefore, engineering managers as well as engineers are required to have an adequate working knowledge of modern quantitative management

---

[†]Note that such moral and ethical responsibility is called *fiducial responsibility*.

techniques, including especially engineering economy, so that they can better assess the risk and uncertainty involved in engineering management's capital expenditure opportunities and in resulting decisions.[†] Of course, the knowledge of engineering economy principles is also required for an engineering manager so that he or she can control the allocation of scarce resources of the company in terms of time, capital, and personnel, as well as other tight constraints [71]. In such a process the engineering manager has to keep in mind the technical and managerial objectives of the company and/or project [72].

At times, it may be required that an engineering manager must be aware of tactical and strategic[‡] considerations involving an economic decision. Figure 1.3 depicts the relationship among various organizational strategic

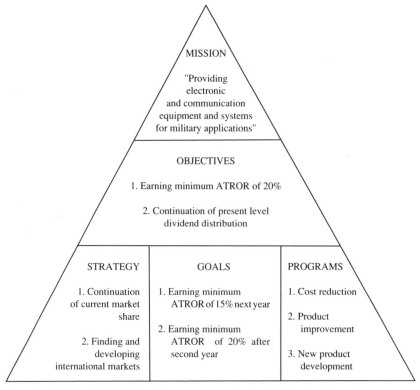

Figure 1.3 Relationship among organizational strategic elements.

[†]It may also be interesting that, in practice, the application of engineering economy is also referred to as *economic analysis, economic decision analysis, financial feasibility analysis,* or simply *economic evaluation.*

[‡]Note that the words *mission, strategy,* and *tactics* historically are military terms, respectively associated with the purpose of a military operation, with its skillful planning and directing provided by the high command, and with the skillful methods (to achieve such results) that are provided by the military echelons.

elements. The top element is the company's mission, which can be defined as the business the company is in. Under the mission there are various objectives that can be defined as the intended future position of the company. Under the objectives there is strategy, goals, and programs. The strategy can be defined as the general direction to follow in achieving the specified objectives. Goals can be defined as the particular targets to be

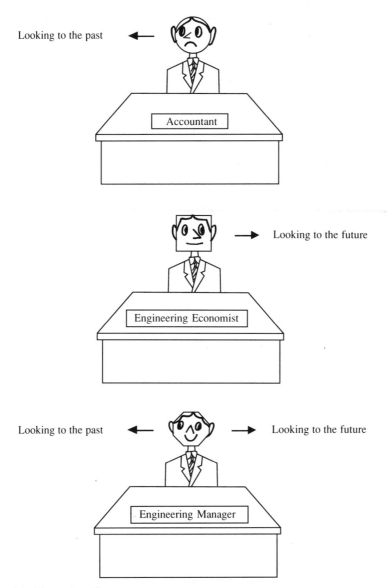

Figure 1.4 Viewpoint differences among accountants, engineering economists, and engineering managers.

reached at the end of specified time periods. Finally, programs (or projects) can be defined as the group of activities that use various resources in the process of achieving specific goals by following specific strategies.[†] Of course, it is one of the challenging tasks for an engineering manager to figure out how to gather such knowledge about these details. However, some of the knowledge may be readily available from the financial information, including those things that top management of the organization might not want to spell out. A successful engineer must learn how to use such information that he or she has successfully obtained to direct his or her group into the areas that should be of concern to the organization, before orders have to come down from the top management.

Finally, it is also interesting to point out that there are differences between the viewpoints of the accountant, engineering economist, and engineering manager, as illustrated in Figure 1.4. An accountant's viewpoint looks to the past because accounting requires analysis and recording of actual data of the *past*. On the other hand, an engineering economist's viewpoint looks to the *future* because for an engineering economy study the past costs are the *sunk costs* and therefore are irrelevant. In that sense accountants are historians, and engineering economists are fortune tellers; whereas an engineering manager learns to look at both directions—looking to the past to learn from the mistakes and looking to the future to fulfill the expectations properly.

[†]For further information, read D. F. Kocaoglu, *Handbook of Technology Management*, Wiley, New York, 1989, and D. F. Kocaoglu, *Management of R&D and Engineering*, Elsevier-North Holland, Amsterdam, 1989.

___2
COST CONCEPTS AND MANAGERIAL ACCOUNTING

There is only one good, knowledge, and one evil, ignorance.
SOCRATES

Many receive advice, few profit by it.
PUBLILIUS SYRUS, 1st Century B.C.

2.1 INTRODUCTION

In general, the decision of investing into a capital investment project must be made based on its profitability as well as its effects on the overall financial strength and position of the company. Obviously, a company that has strength and position will be more willing to invest into new capital projects than one that is weak. The financial strength and position of a company can be determined from its financial statements, including the balance sheet, the income statement, the statement of changes in financial position, and the auditors' report. The balance sheet provides information regarding the financial position of the company and gives a summary of its assets, liabilities, and net worth; whereas the income statement gives an overview of operations and provides information about the associated revenues and expenses of the company for the year. The statement of changes in financial position gives the sources and applications of funds. Finally, the auditors' report is an independent appraisal of the financial statements of the corporation by a team of certified professional accountants.

2.2 COST CONCEPTS AND TERMINOLOGY

In a financial feasibility analysis there are large numbers of cost types that are employed by the engineering economist. Such costs can generally be classified as (1) life-cycle costs, (2) future and opportunity costs, (3) past and sunk costs, (4) direct, indirect, and overhead costs, and (5) fixed and variable costs.

2.2.1 Life-Cycle Costs

The *life-cycle costs* of a prospective alternative, whether it is a system, project, piece of equipment, or product, can be defined as the summation of expenditures associated with such proposal from its inception to its disposal. In general, the life-cycle costs can be categorized as (1) first cost, (2) operating and maintenance costs, and (3) disposal costs, as shown in Figure 5.3. For example, the *first cost* of a piece of equipment is defined as the sum of the initial cost (or investment required) of the equipment, which includes the investment cost, transportation, installation, preparation for service, and other relevant initial expenditures; whereas *operating and maintenance costs* are defined as those costs incurred to operate and maintain the equipment during its useful life. *Disposal costs* are the costs of removing the equipment. There is also salvage value, which can be defined as the cost recovered or that could be recovered from used property when it is removed, sold, or scrapped.

2.2.2 Future and Opportunity Costs

All costs that will take place in the future are defined as the *future costs*. Future costs (as well as future revenues) are subject to uncertainty and risk and therefore have to be estimated. Examples of future costs include investment costs for replacements, future operating and maintenance costs, cost of removal, and so on.

In general, there is more than one opportunity to invest capital. Each time an investor accepts one of these opportunities, the opportunity of investing into others is foregone. Therefore, the *opportunity cost* can be defined as the cost of best opportunity foregone. Alternatively, the opportunity cost can also be defined as the rate of return on the best rejected alternative proposal [58].

2.2.3 Past and Sunk Costs

Past costs are those costs that have taken place in the past and have been included in the accounting records. In other words the past costs are historical costs; whereas, the *sunk costs* are those costs that are incurred, and will continue to be, due to a previous decision and that cannot be changed by present or future decisions. It is the unrecovered balance of an investment. In other words *sunk costs are past costs that cannot be recoverable* by the present or future actions. Therefore, sunk costs are irrelevant in engineering economy applications.

2.2.4 Direct, Indirect and Overhead Costs

Direct costs are those costs that can easily be determined and charged to a specific operation, product, or project; for example, the direct material and labor costs to produce a zubit. On the other hand *indirect costs* are those costs that cannot easily be determined and allocated to a specific operation, product, or project; for example, general and administrative expenses, pensions, and professional services, whereas *overhead* (or *burden*) *costs* are defined as all costs other than direct costs. Therefore, indirect costs are included in the overhead costs.

2.2.5 Fixed and Variable Costs

Fixed costs are those costs that remain constant regardless of the output or activity level. Examples of fixed costs include capital costs, general expenses, management salaries, property taxes and insurance, rent, and building depreciation; whereas *variable costs* are those costs that vary directly with output or activity level. Examples of variable costs include the costs of direct material and direct labor. Many cost items have both fixed and variable components in them. It is also interesting to note that what may be considered fixed cost over one period may be variable cost for another period.

2.3 BRIEF REVIEW OF ACCOUNTING PRINCIPLES

Accounting can be defined as the process of identifying, measuring, and communicating economic information to permit informed judgments and decisions by users of the information. There are various types of accounting used in a corporate environment including (1) management accounting, (2) financial accounting, and (3) cost accounting. The management accounting and financial accounting together are classified as *general accounting*.

The *management accounting* provides summaries, rather than the details, of the operating information of a company to the management (especially to the top management) of the company. Such management accounting information is employed in three management functions: (1) control, (2) coordination, and (3) planning. The term *control* defines the process that management uses to see that the operation of a company is done properly by the employees of the company. Therefore, accounting information is used in such control process as a means of communication, of attention getting, of motivation, and of appraisal. The term *coordination* refers to the process that management uses to have various parts of the company work together to achieve the objectives of the company. Thus, it dictates the requirement that the activities of each unit have to be in coordination with activities of other units. The term *planning* refers to the process of what actions ought to be taken by the company in the future. One of the very important forms of planning is called budgeting. *Budgeting* is defined as the process of planning the overall activity of the organization for a specified period of time, generally a year.

The *financial accounting* is a different form of accounting information intended both for managers of the company and for the use of parties external to the company, including shareholders, bankers, and other creditors, government agencies, and the general public. Of course, such financial accounting includes balance sheet and income statement. Cost accounting is discussed separately in Section 2.7.

2.4 BALANCE SHEET

A *balance sheet* is prepared to show the financial position of an organization as of a specified moment in time, usually at the end of each fiscal year, for example, as of December 31.[†] It is also called a *statement of financial position*. Thus it is a *status* report, rather than a *flow* report. A typical example of a balance sheet is presented in Table 2.1. Such a balance sheet is always based on the following *fundamental accounting equation*:

$$\text{Assets} - \text{Liabilities} = \text{Net worth} \qquad (2.1)$$

or

$$\text{Assets} = \text{Liabilities} + \text{Net worth} \qquad (2.2)$$

Since the net worth is the owners' equity, equation (2.2) can also be expressed as

$$\text{Assets} = \text{Liabilities} + \text{Owners' equity} \qquad (2.3)$$

Assets are the economic resources of a company. They can be of two basic types: (1) current assets and (2) fixed assets. *Current assets* include cash and other assets (as given in Table 2.1) that can be converted into cash or sold, or used within one year or less time period; whereas *fixed assets* include those assets that cannot be converted into cash within one year. Examples are land, building, and equipment and so on.

Liabilities are the obligations (i.e., debt) of a company to pay money or to provide goods or services. In a sense liabilities are claims against the assets of a company. They can also be of two basic types: (1) current liabilities and (2) long-term liabilities. *Current liabilities* are obligations that

---

[†]A balance sheet dated December 31 is implicitly understood to mean "at the close of business on December 31."

TABLE 2.1 Balance Sheet of Zubits Manufacturing Company

Zubits Manufacturing Company
Balance Sheet
December 31, 19xx

Assets			Liabilities and Net Worth		
Current assets			Current liabilities		
Cash	$90,000		Accounts payable	$150,000	
Marketable securities	60,000		Dividends payable	25,000	
Accounts receivable	200,000		Taxes payable	23,000	
Inventories	350,000		Short-term notes payable	18,500	
Prepaid expenses	50,600		Total current liabilities	$216,500	
Total current assets		$750,600			
			Long-term liabilities		
Fixed assets			Long-term notes and bonds payable	$115,000	
Land	$35,000				
Building and equipment	249,400		Total liabilities		$331,500
			Stockholders' equity (net worth)		
Less			Common stock	$349,000	
Accumulated depreciation	(75,000)		Preferred stock	$176,000	
Total fixed assets		$209,400	Retained earnings	103,500	
			Total equity		628,500
TOTAL ASSETS		$960,000	TOTAL LIABILITIES AND EQUITY		$960,000

one expects to paid either by the use of current assets or by the creation of other current liabilities within one year or less time period; whereas *long-term liabilities* are those liabilities that are not due within one year time period. They are also called *noncurrent liabilities* or *long-term debt*. Examples are long-term notes payable and long-term bonds payable.

Net work or *equity* is a summary of the worth of ownership, including outstanding stock issues and earnings retained for expansion. Net worth is also called *owners' equity*, *stockholders' equity*, or *shareholders' equity*.

2.5 INCOME STATEMENT

An *income statement* is prepared to show the results (earnings) of operations for a period of time. It is also called a *profit-and-loss statement*. Thus, it is a *flow* report, rather than a *status* report. A typical income statement is given in Table 2.2. The income statement is based on the following equation:

$$\text{Revenues} - \text{Expenses} = \text{Net income} \tag{2.4}$$

or

$$\text{Revenues} = \text{Expenses} + \text{Net income} \tag{2.5}$$

TABLE 2.2 Income Statement of Zubits Manufacturing Company

Zubits Manufacturing Company
Income Statement
For the Year Ending December 31, 19xx

Sales and other revenues		
Net sales	$650,000	
Interest income	15,000	
Other income	5,000	
Total revenues		$670,000
Costs and expenses		
Cost of goods sold (see Table 2.3)	$155,500	
Selling expenses	17,500	
General and administrative expenses	100,000	
Depreciation	20,000	
Interest expense	14,000	
Total expenses		307,000
Income before taxes		363,000
Income taxes		137,800
Net income		$225,200

TABLE 2.3 Cost of Goods Sold Statement of Zubits Manufacturing Company

Zubits Manufacturing Company
Statement of Costs of Goods Sold
For the Year Ending December 31, 19xx

Raw materials consumed		
Inventory, January 1, 19xx	$10,000	
Purchases during year	35,000	
Less: Raw materials inventory December 31, 19xx	(5,000)	
Cost of raw materials		$40,000
Direct labor		60,000
Manufacturing overhead		50,000
Total manufacturing costs for the period		150,000
Work-in-process inventory January 1, 19xx		15,500
Total manufacturing costs		165,500
Less: Work-in-process inventory December 31, 19xx		(10,000)
Cost of goods sold (see Table 2.2)		$155,500

where *revenues* are the sum of all net sales, interest income, and other income that the company has received in the given accounting period, and *expenses* are the sum of all expenses for the accounting period. Note that some of the expenses are itemized in other statements, including income taxes and cost of goods sold statements. Table 2.3 presents a typical cost of goods sold statement. Also note that if the net income is negative, it represents *net loss*.

2.6 CASH FLOW GENERATION AND APPLICATION

The general nature of flow, or as it is more appropriately called, *cash flow*, generation and application in terms of sources of funds and application of funds is illustrated in Figure 2.1. Note that the after-tax cash flow represents the net funds generated from operations. Therefore, net funds generated from operations, salvage of plant and equipment, new debt and/or equity capital, and other funds are the sources of funds. Thus, their sum is the funds available in terms of *working* capital. Hence, working capital is made up of cash, accounts receivable, and inventory, and less accounts payable. The resulting funds are used for repayment of old debt and equity and for capital expenditures for new plants and equipment. Any remaining funds are set aside as excess funds available for prospective future projects. It may be interesting to note that such cash flows in a company are usually continuous. Finally, Figure 2.2 illustrates the interrelationships among various terms that are used in accounting to generate return on investment.

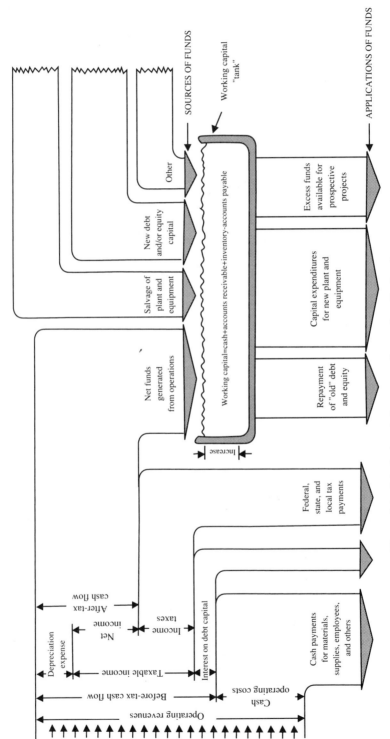

Figure 2.1 A typical cash flow generation and application in a company.

22

2.7 COST ACCOUNTING

Cost accounting is a type of accounting that has a special significance in engineering economy applications (especially in manufacturing companies) because it is the primary source of most of the data that are necessary in such studies. In such a system the cost of each product is accumulated as it flows through the production process, and the amounts involved in the journal entries are obtained directly from the cost records. In such an accounting system items of cost included in the cost of producing a product are called *product costs*. Other items of cost that are matched with revenue in a given accounting period are called *period costs* and are given in the income statement of the period as *selling, general, and administrative expenses*.

According to generally accepted accounting principles[†] (GAAP), the cost of each product includes (1) raw materials cost, (2) labor costs incurred directly in producing the product, and (3) an appropriate portion of other production costs, called *indirect production costs, production overhead*, or simply *burden*.

It is interesting to note that the method a manufacturing company uses to categorize its cost into period costs and product costs can affect its reported net income. Period costs are expenses in the accounting period in which they occur, whereas product costs add to the inventoriable cost of the product and do not affect income until the product has been sold, which may be in a later accounting period than the period in which the costs have taken place. A good cost accounting system is expected to furnish the financial information necessary for making sound decisions in terms of (1) establishing objectives, policies, and future plans for the company; (2) continuing the operations of the company according to such objectives, policies, and plans; and (3) meeting legal, financial, and tax requirements of the company.

2.8 RATIO ANALYSIS OF THE FINANCIAL POSITION OF A FIRM

In order to make rational decisions according to the objectives of the firm, the engineering manager as well as the financial manager must have at their disposal certain analytical tools because the figures that appear on the financial statements are meaningful only in the context of their relationships to the other figures in the financial statements. Therefore, such interpretation and evaluation of financial statement data require familiarity with the primary tools of financial statement analysis. Of course, the type of financial analysis that take place also depends upon the specific interest that the analyst (whether creditor, stockholder, potential investor, government agency, labor leader, or the firm itself) has in the enterprise. The purpose of the firm is not only for internal control but also for better understanding of what

[†]Accounting principles established by the Financial Accounting Standards Board (FASB).

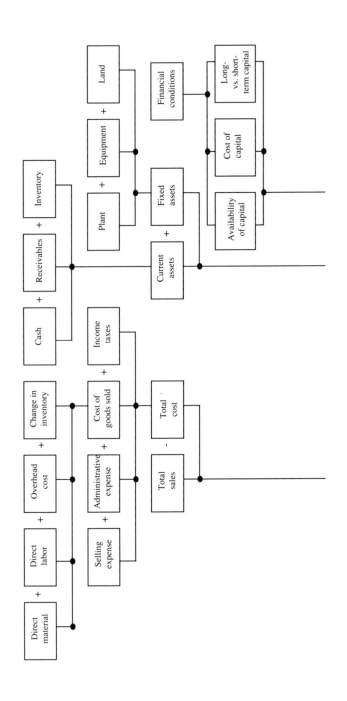

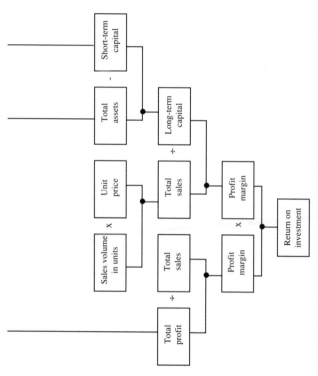

Figure 2.2 Illustration of interrelationships among various terms that are used in accounting.

capital suppliers look for in the way of financial condition and performance from it. Therefore, the management of the firm is necessarily concerned about the composition of its capital structure and about the changes and trends in earnings; whereas a prospective investor is mostly concerned with liquidity, solvency, and profitability of the firm. Here, the term *liquidity* describes the ability of a firm to come up with a sufficient amount of cash to pay off its liabilities as they become due. The term *solvency* defines the long-term ability of a firm to meet its financial obligations, depending on the structure of its debt in relationship to its assets; whereas the term *profitability* refers to the ability of the firm to produce profits.

There are various devices that can be used in the analysis of financial statement data to bring out the comparative and relative significance of any given financial information. Such devices involve ratio analysis, comparative analysis, percentage analysis, and examination of related data. The analysis of financial ratios includes two types of comparison: (1) comparison of a present ratio with past and expected future ratios for the same company and (2) comparison of the ratios of one company with those of similar companies or with industry averages at the same point in time. Of course, such types of comparison provides information about the relative financial condition and performance of the company. However, since reported financial data and the ratios determined using such data are numerical, they must not be taken as precise pictures of a company's real financial position. Often, one may need to go beyond the reported figures (since they may not reflect the actual situation of the company) so that the financial condition and performance of the company can be properly reviewed; for example, such accounting data as depreciation, reserve for bad debts, and other reserves at best are estimates and may not consider economic depreciation, bad debts, and other losses.

In general, financial ratios that are used to analyze the financial position of a company can be classified as liquidity, debt, profitability, and coverage ratios. The first two ratios are determined from the balance sheet; whereas the late two ratios are determined from the income statement and, at times, from both the balance sheet and the income statement. The true financial portrayal of a company cannot usually be determined from a single ratio but from a group of ratios.

2.9 LIQUIDITY RATIOS

The liquidity ratios are used to determine the ability of a company to meet its short-term and current obligations. Liquidity can be determined from the relationship between current assets and current liabilities. One measure of liquidity is the *net working capital*, which is defined as

$$\text{Net working capital} = \text{Current assets} - \text{Current liabilities} \qquad (2.6)$$

The current liabilities (or obligations) are defined as those that are due within one year. If a company does not have significant liquidity, it may not survive the short term. This is why the liquidity is examined first.

2.9.1 Current Ratio

It is one of the most general and most frequently used ratios. However, it is a *broad* measure of liquidity and is defined as

$$\text{Current ratio} = \frac{\text{Current assets}}{\text{Current liabilities}} \tag{2.7}$$

The higher the ratio, the greater the ability of the company to pay its bills. Generally, the current ratio[†] should range between 2 and 3.5. The industry average for this ratio is 2.30, which means that the current assets are 2.30 times as large as the current liabilities; or for every $1.00 of current liabilities, there are $2.30 of current assets. If the current ratio is much smaller than 2, the company can have some difficulty in having sufficient cash in the short term to pay for its short-term liabilities. This is due to the fact that some of its accounts receivables and inventories that are part of the current assets may not be converted into cash in a short time. However, if the current ratio is much greater than 3.5, the company has too large balances of liquid assets with respect to its current requirements. For example, too large inventories may increase the storage costs, or the payments on accounts receivable may be slow, causing both the loss of interest and the risk of default. Therefore, excess cash should be invested in more fixed assets to produce more revenues. A company having current assets made up of primarily cash and current receivables is usually considered as more liquid[‡] than a company whose current assets consist basically of inventories.

2.9.2 Acid-Test Ratio

The acid-test ratio is similar to the current ratio and defined as

$$\text{Acid-test ratio} = \frac{\text{Quick assets}}{\text{Current liabilities}} \tag{2.8}$$

or since the quick assets is the current assets minus the inventories,

$$\text{Acid-test ratio} = \frac{\text{Current assets} - \text{Inventories}}{\text{Current liabilities}} \tag{2.9}$$

[†]Sometimes it is also called the *working capital ratio* because working capital is the excess of current assets over current liabilities.
[‡]*Liquidity* is defined as the ability to realize value in money, that is, the most liquid of assets. Thus, liquidity has two dimensions: (1) the time required to convert the asset into money and (2) the certainty of the amount of money realized [37].

This ratio concentrates on cash, marketable securities, and receivables with respect to current liabilities, and therefore it is considered to be a more accurate measure of liquidity. Since, in general, current assets minus inventories are considered to be *quick assets* that can be converted into cash fast enough to pay off current liabilities, the acid-test ratio is also called the *quick ratio*. In general, an acid-test ratio has to be slightly higher than 1. However, an acid-test ratio of greater than 2 may point out the existence of unused funds.

2.9.3 Inventory Turnover Ratio

The inventory turnover ratio indicates the liquidity of inventory and is defined as

$$\text{Inventory turnover ratio} = \frac{\text{Cost of goods sold}}{\text{Average inventory}} \tag{2.10}$$

Note that the average inventory is the average of the beginning and ending inventories for a given period. The ratio indicates the rapidity with which the inventory is turned over into receivables through sales. Usually, the higher the inventory turnover, the more efficient the inventory management of a company.

2.10 DEBT RATIOS

The debt ratios are used to assess the ability of a company to meet its long-term financial obligations. Here, only two of such ratios will be reviewed, namely, the debt-to-net-worth ratio and the ratio of total debt to equity.

2.10.1 The Debt-to-Net-Worth Ratio

The debt-to-net-worth ratio is calculated by dividing the total debt (i.e., the total liabilities) of the company (including current liabilities) by its net worth. Therefore,

$$\text{Debt-to-net-worth ratio} = \frac{\text{Total debt}}{\text{Net worth}} \tag{2.11}$$

A comparison of the debt ratio for a given company with those of similar companies provides an indication of the creditworthiness and financial risk of the company.

2.10.2 Ratio of Total Debt to Equity

The ratio of total debt to equity takes into account only the long-term capitalization of the company. Thus,

$$\text{Total-debt-to-equity ratio} = \frac{\text{Long-term debt}}{\text{Total capitalization}} \qquad (2.12)$$

Note that the total capitalization, in the denominator, represents all long-term debt and net worth. It provides information about the relative importance of long-term debt in the capital structure of the company. Succinctly put, debt ratios provide information about the financial risk of the company.

2.11 PROFITABILITY RATIOS

In general, profits are the ultimate test of management's effectiveness. The profitability ratios can be classified into two groups: (1) the ones that indicate profitability in relation to sales and (2) the ones that indicate profitability with respect to investment. In summary, profitability ratios provide information about the operational efficiency of the company.

2.11.1 Profitability with Respect to Sales

Profitability with respect to sales are determined either by the *gross profit margin* or by the *net profit margin*. Therefore,

$$\text{Gross profit margin} = \frac{\text{Sales less cost of goods sold}}{\text{Net sales}} \qquad (2.13)$$

and

$$\text{Net profit margin} = \frac{\text{Net profits after taxes}}{\text{Net sales}} \qquad (2.14)$$

Note that the gross profit margin points out the efficiency of operation, whereas the net profit margin indicates the efficiency of operation after considering all expenses and income taxes. The net profit margin is also called the *profit margin*. Another version of the gross profit margin is the *operating margin*. The operating margin is not affected by the means of financing used to generate the sales. It measures the return on sales before expenses, such as interest payments, and taxes are considered. It is similar to the gross profit margin, except that it also takes into account the selling expenses and general and administrative expenses. Thus,

$$\text{Operating margin} = \frac{\text{Operating income}}{\text{Net sales}} \qquad (2.15)$$

where operating income is total revenues (or sales) minus cost of goods sold minus selling expenses minus general and administrative expenses.

2.11.2 Profitability with Respect to Investment

A widely used method of measuring profitability is the *return on assets ratio.*[†]

$$\text{Return on assets ratio} = \frac{\text{Net profits after taxes}}{\text{Total assets}} \qquad (2.16)$$

However, if financial charges are significantly large, it is more appropriate to use net operating profit rate of return.[‡] Therefore,

$$\text{Net operating profit rate of return} = \frac{\text{Income before interest and taxes}}{\text{Total assets}}$$
$$(2.17)$$

Another profitability ratio is the *rate of return* on common stock equity[§]. It is defined as

Rate of return on common stock equity

$$= \frac{\text{Net profit after taxes} - \text{Preferred stock dividends}}{\text{Net worth} - \text{Par value of preferred stock}} \qquad (2.18)$$

It provides information on the earning power on stockholders' book investment and can be used for comparison. Alternatively,

$$\text{Earnings per share} = \frac{\text{Earnings available for common stockholders}}{\text{Average number of shares outstanding}}$$
$$(2.19)$$

Earnings can be retained by the company or paid out to stockholders in the form of cash dividends. The extent to which cash dividends are paid to common stockholders is called the *payout ratio*[¶] and is computed by *dividing dividends* per share by earnings per share. Thus,

$$\text{Payout ratio} = \frac{\text{Cash dividends per share}}{\text{Earnings per share}} \qquad (2.20)$$

[†]It is also called the *return on investment ratio*. For example, some consider a return on investment of 3% or less as poor, 5% as fair, and 10% or more as outstanding.

[‡]It is also called the *return on assets*.

[§]Alternatively, the *return on equity ratio* measures the rate of return on the owners' investment and is computed by dividing net income by total stockholders' equity. If there are large amounts of preferred stock outstanding, a similar ratio may be calculated by dividing income available to common equity by the amount of common equity.

[¶]It is also called the *dividend payout ratio*.

2.11.3 Turnover and Earning Power

The *turnover ratio* relates the net sales to the total assets and is defined as

$$\text{Turnover ratio} = \frac{\text{Net sales}}{\text{Total assets}} \qquad (2.21)$$

It provides information about the relative efficiency with which the company utilizes its resources to generate output. It is affected by the type of company studied. However, it should be used together with other measures of efficiency. Otherwise, a company with equipment that is almost fully depreciated and highly inefficient may have a large turnover ratio but may lose money in reality.

Earning power is also called the *return on assets ratio* and can be obtained by multiplying the asset turnover of the company by the net profit margin. Therefore,

$$\text{Earning power} = \text{Asset turnover} \times \text{Profit margin on sales} \quad (2.22a)$$

$$= \frac{\text{Net sales}}{\text{Total assets}} \times \frac{\text{Net profits after taxes}}{\text{Net sales}} \qquad (2.22b)$$

$$= \frac{\text{Net profits after taxes}}{\text{Total assets}} \qquad (2.22c)$$

Notice that the right-hand side of equation (2.22c) is the same as the right-hand side of equation (2.16).

2.11.4 Coverage Ratios

Coverage ratios are used to associate the financial charges of a company to its ability to meet them. The bond-rating services, such as Moody's Investors Service and Standard & Poor's, use the coverage ratios extensively. There are various types of coverage ratios. The best one is known as the *cash flow coverage ratio* and defined as

$$\text{Cash flow coverage ratio} = \frac{\text{Annual cash flow before interest and taxes}}{\text{Interest} + \text{Principal payments } [1/(1-t)]}$$

$$(2.23)$$

where t is the combined effective income tax rate. Since principal payments on a debt capital are made after taxes, one needs to multiply such a figure by $1/(1-t)$ so that it corresponds to interest payments, which are made before taxes.

There are other coverage ratios that can be used; for example, the *interest coverage ratio*, which is either based on (1) the *overall coverage method*, (2) the *prior deductions method*, or (3) the *cumulative deduction method*. However, the interest coverage ratio, and as well as others, have some shortcomings. For instance, the main shortcoming is the fact that a company's ability to meet debt is related to both interest and principal payments. Further, these payments are not provided by earnings per se, but by cash. Therefore, both the debt ratios and coverage ratios are the crude measures of financial risk of a given company when they are used by themselves. Thus, they should be used *together* to assess the financial risk of the company.

Example 2.1   Consider the balance sheet of Zubits Manufacturing Company given in Table 2.1 and determine:

(a) Net working capital.
(b) Current ratio.
(c) Acid-test ratio.
(d) Debt-to-net-worth ratio.

Solution

(a) Net working capital = Current assets − Current liabilities

$$= \$750,600 - \$216,500 = \$534,100$$

(b) Current ratio = $\dfrac{\text{Current assets}}{\text{Current liabilities}}$

$$= \frac{\$750,600}{\$216,500} = 3.47$$

(c) Acid-test ratio = $\dfrac{\text{Quick assets}}{\text{Current liabilities}}$

$$= \frac{\text{Current assets} - \text{Inventories}}{\text{Current liabilities}}$$

$$= \frac{\$750,600 - \$350,000}{\$216,500} = 1.85$$

(d) Debt-to-net-worth ratio = $\dfrac{\text{Total debt}}{\text{Net worth}} = \dfrac{\text{Total liabilities}}{\text{Net worth}}$

$$= \frac{\$331,500}{\$628,500} = 0.53$$

Example 2.2   Consider the income statement of Zubits Manufacturing Company given in Table 2.2 and determine the following:

(a) Gross profit margin.
(b) Net profit margin.
(c) Operating margin.

Solution

(a) Gross profit margin $= \dfrac{\text{Sales less cost of goods sold}}{\text{Net sales}}$

$= \dfrac{\$650,000 - \$155,500}{\$650,000} = 0.7608 \text{ or } 76.08\%$

(b) Net profit margin $= \dfrac{\text{Net profits after taxes}}{\text{Net sales}}$

$= \dfrac{\$225,200}{\$650,000} = 0.3465 \text{ or } 34.65\%$

(c) Operating margin $= \dfrac{\text{Operating income}}{\text{Net sales}}$

$= \dfrac{\$650,000 - \$155,500 - \$17,500 - \$100,000}{\$650,000}$

$= 0.58 \text{ or } 58\%$

Example 2.3 Consider the balance sheet and the income statement of Zubits Manufacturing Company given in Tables 2.1 and 2.2, respectively, and determine:

(a) Return on assets ratio.
(b) Net operating profit rate of return.
(c) Turnover ratio.
(d) Earning power.

Solution

(a) Return on assets ratio $= \dfrac{\text{Net profits after taxes}}{\text{Total assets}}$

$= \dfrac{\$225,200}{\$960,000} = 0.2346 \text{ or } 23.46\%$

(b) Net operating profit rate of return
$= \dfrac{\text{Income before interest and taxes}}{\text{Total assets}}$

$= \dfrac{\$321,000}{\$960,000} = 0.3344 \text{ or } 33.44\%$

(c) Turnover ratio $= \dfrac{\text{Net sales}}{\text{Total assets}}$

$= \dfrac{\$650,000}{\$960,000} = 0.6771 \text{ or } 67.71\%$

$$\text{(d) Earning power} = \frac{\text{Net sales}}{\text{Total assets}} \times \frac{\text{Net profits after taxes}}{\text{Net sales}}$$

$$= \frac{\$650,000}{\$960,000} \times \frac{\$225,200}{\$650,000} = 0.2346 \text{ or } 23.46\%$$

Of course, the earning power and the return on assets ratio are the same.

PROBLEMS

2.1 Consider the balance sheet of Zubits Manufacturing Company given in Table 2.1 and find its total debt-to-equity ratio.

2.2 Consider the balance sheet and the income statement of Zubits Manufacturing Company given in Tables 2.1 and 2.2, respectively, and determine its inventory turnover ratio.

2.3 Consider the balance sheet and the income statement of Zubits Manufacturing company given in Tables 2.1 and 2.2, respectively, and determine:
(a) Rate of return on common stock equity.
(b) The earnings per share, if the par value of common stock is $1.00.
(c) Payout ratio, if the cash dividend paid per share is $0.10.

2.4 Consider the balance sheet of Cyclones Manufacturing Company given in Table P2.4 and determine the following:
(a) Net working capital.
(b) Current ratio.
(c) Acid-test ratio.
(d) Debt-to-net-worth ratio.
(e) Debt-to-equity ratio.

2.5 Consider the income statement of Cyclones Manufacturing Company given in Table P2.5 and determine the following:
(a) Gross profit margin.
(b) Net profit margin.
(c) Operating margin.

2.6 Consider the balance sheet and the income statement of Cyclones Manufacturing Company given in tables P2.4 and P2.5, respectively and determine its inventory turnover ratio.

TABLE P2.4 Balance Sheet for Problem 2.4

Cyclones Manufacturing Company
Balance Sheet
December 31, 19xx

Assets			Liabilities and Net Worth		
Current assets			Current liabilities		
Cash	$50,000		Accounts payable	$84,650	
Marketable securities	40,000		Dividends payable	15,350	
Accounts receivable	100,500		Taxes payable	17,700	
Inventories	175,600		Short-term notes payable	43,300	
Prepaid expenses	48,900				
Total current assets		$415,000	Total current liabilities		$161,000
Fixed assets			Long-term liabilities		
Land	$52,750		Long-term notes and bonds payable	$129,000	
Building and equipment	168,250				
			Total liabilities		$290,000
Less			Stockholders' equity (net worth)		
Accumulated depreciation	(60,000)		Common stock	$175,940	
Total fixed assets		$220,940	Preferred stock	70,000	
			Retained earnings	100,000	
			Total equity		$345,940
TOTAL ASSETS		$635,940	TOTAL LIABILITIES AND EQUITY		$635,940

35

TABLE P2.5   Income Statement for Problem 2.5

Cyclones Manufacturing Company
Income Statement
For the Year Ending December 31, 19xx

Sales and other revenues		
Net sales	$500,000	
Interest income	3,000	
Other income	7,000	
Total revenues		$510,000
Costs and expenses		
Cost of goods sold	$72,200	
Selling expenses	50,800	
General and administrative expenses	48,000	
Depreciation	15,000	
Interest expense	14,800	
Total expenses		$200,800
		$309,200
Income before taxes		
Income taxes	117,372	
Net income		$191,828

2.7 Consider the balance sheet and income statement of Cyclones Manufacturing Company given in Tables P2.4 and P2.5, respectively, and
determine:

(a) Return on assets ratio.

(b) Net operating profit rate of return.

(c) Turnover ratio.

(d) Earning power.

____3
INTEREST AND
INTEREST FORMULAS

Yesterday is a cancelled check.
Tomorrow is a promissary note.
Today is cash.

AUTHOR UNKNOWN

3.1 TIME VALUE OF MONEY

A dollar now is worth more than a dollar at some future date because of the time value of money. The change in the value of money over time as a result of its *earning power* is called the *time value of money*. The earning power of money can be considered as a cost (rental fee) of using money. Therefore, *interest* can be defined as money paid (or received) for the use of borrowed (or loaned) money.

Another type of time value of money is known as the *purchasing power* of money. It describes the fact that the amount of goods or services that can be purchased for the same amount of money decreases as the time progresses toward the future due to an economical phenomenon known as *inflation*. The effects of inflation on the engineering economy studies will be discussed in Chapter 11.

If a dollar invested now can earn ten cents at the end of one year so that the investor can receive back $1.10, it can be said that the $1.00 today and the $1.10 a year from now are *financially equivalent*, i.e., they are effectively the same.

Therefore, money cannot be shifted through time without changing its value. In general, when it is moved forward through time, its value increases (compounding), and when it is moved backward, its value decreases (discounting). Two separate sums of money can be compared only if they are given at the same point in time. Otherwise, they have to be converted to an equivalent time base. This conversion process involves the use of interest formulas. The factors that affect the equivalence are (1) the amount of the cash flow, (2) the timing of the cash flow, and (3) the interest rate involved.

3.2 INTEREST CALCULATIONS

ANSI Z94.5-1972[†] defines *interest rate* as the ratio of the interest payment to the principal for a given unit of time and is usually expressed as a percentage of the principal. Usually the unit of time is selected to be a one-year period. Interest calculations can be based on interest rates that are either simple or compound.

3.2.1 Simple Interest

Simple interest is calculated by multiplying the principal amount of money by the interest rate per period and by the number of periods involved. Therefore, the interest charge is only based on the principal sum, which does not include the accumulated interest charges. Therefore, the simple interest can be expressed as

$$I = P \times i \times N \tag{3.1}$$

where

I = simple interest charge in dollars,
P = present sum of money in dollars,
i = interest rate per period,
N = number of periods.

Example 3.1   An engineer borrows \$2,000 at a simple interest rate of 10% per year for 5 years. Determine the interest charge that will be paid by the engineer at the end of the 5 years.

Solution   From equation (3.1) the interest charge can be calculated as

$$I = P \times i \times N$$
$$= (\$2,000)(0.10)(5)$$
$$= \$1,000$$

Therefore, the total amount required to be paid at the end of the third year is the principal plus the interest charge, i.e., \$3,000. Note that the interest is paid only on the original principal, i.e., \$2,000 which does not include any accumulated interest charges.

[†]ANSI Z94.5-1972, American National Standard for Industrial Engineering Terminology for Engineering Economy, the American Society of Mechanical Engineers, New York, 1972.

3.2.2 Compound Interest

Compound interest for any given interest period is calculated based on the remaining original principal amount plus any accumulated interest charges up to the beginning of that period. The following example illustrates the effect of compounding.

Example 3.2 Assume that, in Example 3.1, the engineer chooses not to pay any interest charge until the termination of the loan at the end of the fifth year and therefore ends up paying interest on the interest retained. Determine the total amount that has to be paid by the engineer at the end of the fifth year, if the interest is compounded annually.

Solution The calculation of the total amount that has to be paid by the engineer is illustrated in the following table. Therefore, $3,221.02 is required to be paid at the end of the fifth year. The difference of $221.02 is due to the effect of compounding of interest over the 5 years.

Year	Amount Owed at Beginning of Year (A)	Interest Charge for Year (B)	Amount Owed at End of Year $(A) + (B)$
1	$2,000.00	$2,000.00 \times 0.10 = $200.00	$2,200.00
2	2,200.00	2,200.00 \times 0.10 = 220.00	2,420.00
3	2,420.00	2,420.00 \times 0.10 = 242.00	2,662.00
4	2,662.00	2,662.00 \times 0.10 = 266.20	2,928.20
5	2,928.20	2,928.20 \times 0.10 = 292.82	3,221.02

3.3 CASH FLOW DIAGRAM

As the name suggests, cash flow takes place whenever cash or its equivalent (e.g., check, transfer through bank accounts, or some other means) "flows" from one party to another. For example, whenever a given party receives payment, there is a cash flow in: and whenever the party pays out, there is a cash flow out [71].

The cash flow diagram is a graphical illustration of economic transactions. It is employed to indicate the inflows and outflows of cash flow transactions in a given engineering economy study. It has two fundamental segments: (1) the horizontal time line, which includes the complete study period, and (2) the vertical cash flow lines.

The horizontal time line is subdivided into n periods, and each period is labeled to indicate period ends. The periods can be given in years, months, weeks, or days, whichever is appropriate for a given problem, with the progression of time moving from left to right. Zero (0) indicates the beginning of period 1 (or the end of period 0), and it is usually associated with the present time. For the sake of simplicity, it is customary to assume that the cash flows occur at the end of a given period.

The cash flows are illustrated by vertical arrows along the horizontal time line at the time at which they occur. Their magnitudes are usually indicated close to their arrows, rather than drawing them to scale. However, a large cash flow is usually depicted by a longer line than a small cash flow. The direction of the cash flow, i.e., incoming or outgoing, is represented by the direction of the arrow. For example, the outgoing cash flows are represented by downward (i.e., away from the horizontal time line) arrows, and incoming cash flows are represented by upward (i.e., toward the horizontal time line) arrows. In other words receipts are positive (+) cash flows, and therefore they are represented by upward arrows. Whereas, disbursements are negative (−) cash flows, and thus they are represented by downward arrows.

A cash flow diagram is drawn based on the point of view involved. For example, Figure 3.1 shows a cash flow diagram for Example 3.2 from the borrower's (i.e., the engineer's) point of view, whereas Figure 3.2 shows it from the lender's point of view. Therefore, it is always necessary to identify the point of view being taken when drawing cash flow diagrams.

Drawing a cash flow diagram is the first step in the solution process of any engineering economy problem that involves various amounts of cash flows occurring at various points in time. It does not only help to identify the cash flow transaction between the system and the parties external to the system but it also helps to clarify one's point of view for the analysis. Furthermore, it helps to reduce the possibility of errors involved in the analysis through the inspection and review of the data. Finally, the cash flow diagram is an excellent and useful aid in relating and comparing alternatives [16].

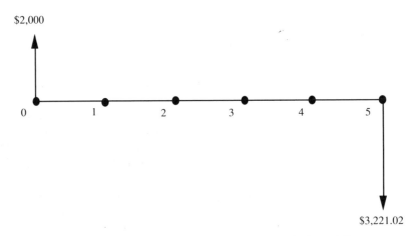

Figure 3.1 Cash flow diagram (from borrower's viewpoint).

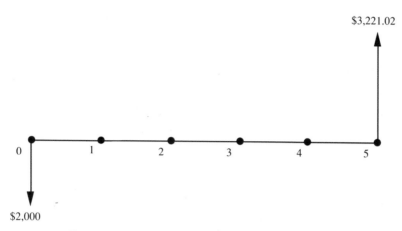

Figure 3.2 Cash flow diagram (from lender's viewpoint).

3.4 DISCRETE COMPOUND INTEREST FORMULAS

As discussed previously, the compounding can be defined as the mathematical process of periodically adding return to principal and thereby increasing the principal upon which future return is based. Therefore, the compounding process can be considered as a mathematical tool by which the future equivalent of a present sum can be found at a particular interest rate. The future equivalent so found is defined as the *future worth* of present sum (amount).

On the other hand discounting can be defined as the mathematical process employed to reduce a principal given at some future time to its equivalent at the present time. Therefore, the discounting process can be considered as a mathematical tool by which the present equivalent of a future sum can be found at a specific interest rate (discount rate). Thus, it is proper to consider the process of discounting as the inverse of compounding process. The present equivalent so found is defined as the *present worth* of a future sum (amount).

In summary, as illustrated in Figure 3.3, the *compounding* process moves amounts forward in time from either the present time or from a near future

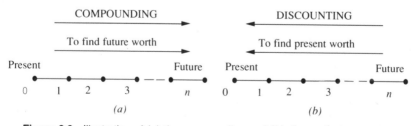

Figure 3.3 Illustration of (a) the compounding and (b) discounting processes.

to a far future, whereas the *discounting* process moves amounts backward in time from a future time to either the present or near present.

3.4.1 Notation Used

The following notation and the notation used throughout this book are suggested by the American National Standard for Industrial Engineering Terminology for Engineering Economy, ANSI Z94.5-1972 [5]:

r = nominal interest rate per period,

i = effective interest rate per period,

N = number of compounding periods,

P = present sum[†] of money, i.e., the equivalent worth of one or more cash flows at a relative point in time defined as the present,

F = future sum of money, i.e., the equivalent worth of one or more cash flows at a relative point in time defined as the future,

A = end-of-period cash flows (or equivalent end-of-period values) in a uniform series continuing for a specified number of periods. Here, the letter A implies annual or annuity.

G = Uniform period-by-period increase or decrease in cash flows or amounts (the arithmetic gradient).

Unless otherwise stated, it is customary to assume that all cash flows are flowing discretely at the end of the given period [8].

3.4.2 Single-Payment Compound Amount Factor (Finding *F*, Given *P*)

If an amount P is deposited now in an account earning an *effective interest rate* of $i\%$ per period compounded per period, then the account at the end of period 1 can be expressed as a future amount of

$$F = P + \text{Interest on } P$$

or

$$F = P + P \cdot i$$
$$= P(1 + i)$$

at the end of period 2

[†]The words *sum, amount, payment, value, worth,* and *equivalent* are used interchangeably in the engineering economy literature to mean the very same thing, e.g., present worth, present value, present sum, etc.

$$F = P(1 + i) + \text{Interest on } P(1 + i)$$
$$= P(1 + i) + P(1 + i)i$$
$$= P(1 + i)(1 + i)$$
$$= P(1 + i)^2$$

and therefore by the end of period N

$$F = P(1 + i)^N \tag{3.2}$$

and its cash flow diagram is shown in Figure 3.4.

Equation (3.2) gives the formula for determining the compound amount, F, that can be obtained in N years from a present amount of P.

From equation (3.2), the *single-payment compound amount factor* can be defined as

$$\frac{F}{P} = (1 + i)^N \tag{3.3}$$

It is also known as the *future worth of a present sum*. Equation (3.3) can also be expressed alternatively as

$$\frac{F}{P} = (F/P, i\%, N) \tag{3.4}$$

It is read as to find F, given P, $i\%$, and N. Therefore, equation (3.2) can be expressed as

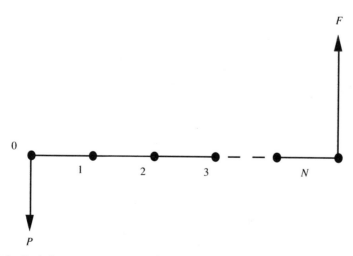

Figure 3.4 Cash flow diagram of the time relationship between single present amount and single future amount.

$$F = P(F/P, i\%, N) \qquad\qquad (3.5)$$

Therefore, the process of using the time-value factors always involve multiplying the quantity that is given by the proper factor to find the quantity that is unknown, i.e.,

$$\frac{\text{Unknown}}{\text{quantity}} = \frac{\text{Given}}{\text{quantity}} \quad \frac{\text{Time-value}}{\text{factor}} \qquad\qquad (3.6)$$

Note that equation (3.5) gives the single-payment compound amount formula in functional notation. The correctness of the functional notation can be checked dimensionally as

$$F = P\left(\frac{E}{P}\right)$$

so that both sides of the equation are found to be the same, i.e., F. This method of dimensional test is especially useful for complicated equations.

The single-payment compound amount factors are precalculated for a wide range of values of $i\%$ and N; see the tables in Appendix A. For the values of $i\%$ and N that are not included in the tables, the factors can be determined by using equation (3.3).

Example 3.3 Repeat Example 3.2 (a) by determining the associated single-payment compound amount factor from the compound interest tables in Appendix A and (b) by calculating the single-payment compound amount factor from equation (3.3).

Solution

(a) The total amount that has to be paid by the engineer at the end of 5 years can be determined from equation (3.5) as

$$F = P(F/P, i\%, N)$$
$$= \$2,000(F/P, 10\%, 5)$$

In order to find the value of $(F/P, 10\%, 5)$: (1) find the table in Appendix A for $i = 10\%$; (2) knowing $N = 5$, locate the proper row in the N column; (3) move horizontally to the right along the $N = 5$ row to the F/P column; and (4) read the value as 1.611. Therefore,

$$F = \$2,000(1.611)$$
$$= \$3,222$$

(b) Alternatively, from equation (3.3)

$$\frac{F}{P} = (1 + i)^N$$

$$= (1 + 0.10)^5$$

$$= 1.10^5$$

$$= 1.6105$$

Therefore,

$$F = P(1 + i)^N$$

$$= \$2,000(1.6105)$$

$$= \$3,221.02$$

Note that there is a slight error introduced in the answer in part (a) due to the round off introduced through the table. However, the error induced is not significant since a great precision is not usually required in interest calculations made for engineering economy analyses.

3.4.3 Single-Payment Present Worth Factor (Finding P, Given F)

From equation (3.2), it can be found that

$$P = F\left[\frac{1}{(1 + i)^N}\right] \tag{3.7}$$

where the resulting factor, $1/(1 + i)^N$, is defined as the *single-payment present worth factor* or the *present worth of a future sum* or simply the *present worth factor* and can be expressed in its functional form as $(P/F, i\%, N)$. It is read as to find P, given F, $i\%$, N. Therefore, equation (3.7) can be expressed in its functional form as

$$P = F(P/F, i\%, N) \tag{3.8}$$

Tabulated values of this factor are given in Appendix A. Note that the single-payment compound amount factor and the single-payment worth factor are reciprocals, i.e.,

$$(F/P, i\%, N) = \frac{1}{(P/F, i\%, N)} \tag{3.9}$$

or better yet, since the $i\%$ and N are kept constant

$$\frac{F}{P} = \frac{1}{P/F} \tag{3.10}$$

or

$$\frac{P}{F} = \frac{1}{F/P} \tag{3.11}$$

Example 3.4   Determine the present amount (P) that when deposited into a savings account for 4 years at an interest rate of 12% compounded annually will have a future worth (F) of $5,000.

Solution   As a first step, the cash flow diagram of the problem is drawn, as shown in Figure 3.5.
    As indicated in Figure 3.5, the only unknown is the present amount P. Therefore, from equation (3.8)

$$P = F(P/F, i\%, N)$$
$$= \$5000(P/F, 12\%, 4)$$
$$= \$5,000(0.6355)$$
$$= \$3,177.50$$

Example 3.5   Determine the number of years that a $10,000 investment, earning 15% annually, must be kept to accumulate $25,000: (a) by using compound interest tables and (b) by using a proper compound interest formula.

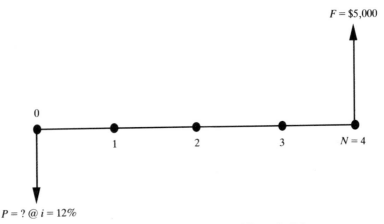

P = ? @ *i* = 12%

Figure 3.5 Cash flow diagram of Example 3.4.

Solution The cash flow diagram of the problem is shown in Figure 3.6.

(a) From equation (3.4),

$$\frac{F}{P} = (F/P, i\%, N)$$

$$\frac{\$25,000}{\$10,000} = 2.5 = (F/P, 15\%, N)$$

From the proper table in Appendix A for $i = 15\%$

$$(F/P, 15\%, 6) = 2.313$$

and

$$(F/P, 15\%, 7) = 2.660$$

Therefore, it is obvious that the real N is somewhere between 6 and 7 years. Thus, by rectilinear interpolation,

$$N = (6 \text{ years}) + \left(\frac{2.5 - 2.313}{2.660 - 2.313}\right)(1 \text{ year})$$

$$= 6 + \left(\frac{0.187}{0.347}\right)(1)$$

$$\cong 6.539 \text{ years}$$

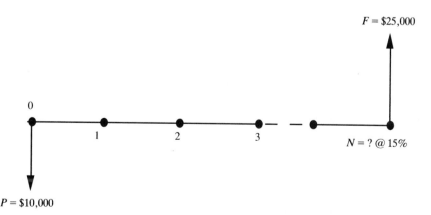

Figure 3.6 Cash flow diagram of Example 3.5.

(b) From equation (3.2)

$$F = P(1 + i)^N$$

$$\$25,000 = \$10,000(1 + 0.15)^N$$

$$2.5 = 1.15^N$$

and therefore

$$N = \frac{\ln 2.5}{\ln 1.15}$$

$$= 6.556 \text{ years}$$

Note the discrepancy between the answers because the relationship is an exponential one and, therefore, by performing a rectilinear interpolation an error has been introduced to the answer in part (a).

Example 3.6   Today, an antique car collector sold a Model-T Ford for $25,000. The car had been purchased for $5,000 fifteen years ago. Determine the annual equivalent compounded interest rate:

(a) By using compound interest tables.
(b) By using the compound interest formula.
(c) By using natural logarithms.

Solution

(a) From equation (3.4)

$$\frac{F}{P} = (F/P, i\%, N)$$

$$\frac{\$25,000}{\$5,000} = 5.00 = (F/P, i\%, 15)$$

From the tables in Appendix A for $N = 15$ years

At $i = 10\%$:	$(F/P, 10\%, 15) = 4.177$
At $i = $ unknown $\%$:	$(F/P, i\%, 15) = 5.00$
At $i = 12\%$:	$(F/P, 12\%, 15) = 5.474$

Therefore, by rectilinear interpolation,

$$i = 10\% + \left(\frac{5.00 - 4.177}{5.474 - 4.177}\right) \times 2\%$$

$$= 10\% + \left(\frac{0.823}{1.297}\right) \times 2\%$$

$$\cong 11.27\%$$

(b) From equation (3.2)

$$F = P(1 + i)^N$$

$$\$25{,}000 = \$5{,}000(1 + i)^{15}$$

$$(1 + i)^{15} = 5.0$$

$$1 + i = 5.0^{1/15}$$

$$1 + i = 1.1133$$

$$i = 0.1133 = 11.33\%$$

(c) From equation (3.3)

$$\frac{F}{P} = (1 + i)^N$$

$$5.0 = (1 + i)^{15}$$

$$\ln 5.0 = 15 \ln(1 + i)$$

$$\ln(1 + i) = \frac{\ln 5.0}{15}$$

$$\ln(1 + i) = 0.1073$$

$$1 + i = e^{0.1073}$$

$$i = 0.1133 = 11.33\%$$

3.5 UNIFORM-SERIES COMPOUND AMOUNT FACTOR (FINDING F, GIVEN A)

Figure 3.7 shows a cash flow diagram having a series of uniform, i.e., equal and equally spaced amounts, cash flows of amount A occurring at the end of each period for N periods with interest at $i\%$ per period. Such a uniform series is often called on *annuity*, and the associated compound interest tables are also known as the *annuity tables*. Note that the equivalent future value, F, of the uniform series occurs at the same time as the last A, which is $N - 1$ periods after the first A amount.

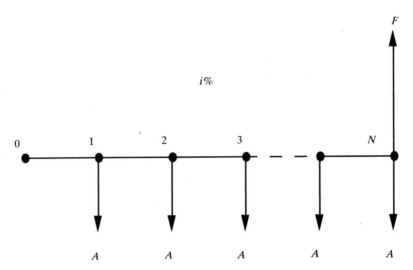

Figure 3.7 Cash flow diagram for uniform series, showing the relationship between A and F.

If an amount A is deposited at the end of each period for N periods in an account earning $i\%$ per period, as shown in Figure 3.7, the future sum F accrued at the end of the Nth period is

$$F = A + A(1 + i) + A(1 + i)^2 + \cdots + A(1 + i)^{N-1} \tag{3.12}$$

by multiplying both sides of the equation by $(1 + i)$,

$$F(1 + i) = A(1 + i) + A(1 + i)^2 + A(1 + i)^3 + \cdots + A(1 + i)^N \tag{3.13}$$

by subtracting equation (3.12) from equation (3.13),

$$F(1 + i) - F = A(1 + i)^N - A$$

and upon solving for F

$$F = A\left[\frac{(1 + i)^N - 1}{i}\right] \tag{3.14}$$

or

$$\frac{F}{A} = \frac{(1 + i)^N - 1}{i} \tag{3.15}$$

The factor given by equation (3.15) is defined as the *uniform-series compound amount factor*, and it can be expressed alternatively as

$$(F/A, i\%, N) = \frac{(1+i)^N - 1}{i} \qquad (3.16)$$

It is read as to find F, given A, $i\%$ and N. Therefore, equation (3.14) can be expressed as

$$F = A(F/A, i\%, N) \qquad (3.17)$$

The uniform-series compound amount factor is also known as the *future worth of uniform series* in the engineering economy literature.

Example 3.7 A 30-year-old engineer wants to establish a tax-sheltered annuity plan for his retirement. His yearly end-of-year premium is $2,000 earning 10% interest, compounding annually. Determine the total savings that will be accumulated after 35 years. He desires the first payment to start at the end of next year.

Solution The cash flow diagram of the problem is shown in Figure 3.8. Note that the last premium is paid at the end of the 35th year, which is the very same time of the equivalent future amount F. Since the premiums are uniform and paid at the end of each year, the equivalent future amount (or the future worth of annuities) can be calculated from equation (3.17) as

$$F = A(F/A, i\%, N)$$
$$= \$2,000(F/A, 10\%, 35)$$
$$= \$2,000(271.024)$$
$$= \$542,048$$

That is, the total savings of $70,000 grows to $542,048 through 10% compounding over 35 years.

Example 3.8 Using the data given in Example 3.7, assume that the engineer has just made his 35th payment today and determine the present worth of his total savings accumulated so far. Note that 15 years ago, i.e., just after his 20th payment, the interest rate was increased to 15%.

Solution As the first step, the worth of the total savings after the 20th payment can be found as

$$F_{20} = \$2,000(F/A, 10\%, 20)$$
$$= \$2,000(57.275)$$
$$= \$114,550 = P_{20}$$

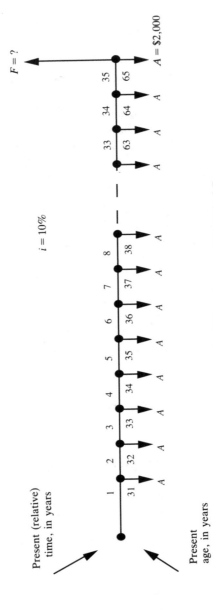

Figure 3.8 Cash flow diagram of Example 3.7.

Therefore, the total savings accumulated, including today's payment, is

$$P = F_{35} = \$114,550(F/P, 15\%, 15) + \$2,000(F/A, 15\%, 15)$$
$$= \$114,550(8.137) + \$2,000(47.580)$$
$$= \$1,027,253$$

3.6 UNIFORM-SERIES SINKING-FUND FACTOR (FINDING *A*, GIVEN *F*)

From equation (3.14), it can be shown that

$$A = F\left[\frac{i}{(1+i)^N - 1}\right] \tag{3.18}$$

and

$$\frac{A}{F} = \frac{(1+i)^N - 1}{i} \tag{3.19}$$

The factor given by equation (3.19) is defined as the *uniform-series sinking-fund factor*, the *uniform-series worth of a future sum*, the *annuity depreciation factor*, or simply the *sinking-fund factor*. It can be expressed alternatively in its functional form as

$$(A/F, i\%, N) = \frac{(1+i)^N - 1}{i} \tag{3.20}$$

It is read as to find *A*, given *F*, *i*%, and N. Therefore, equation (3.18) can also be given as

$$A = F(A/F, i\%, N) \tag{3.21}$$

Example 3.9 The Ozark International Company has just purchased production equipment for $50,000 with a useful life of 10 years (Figure 3.9).

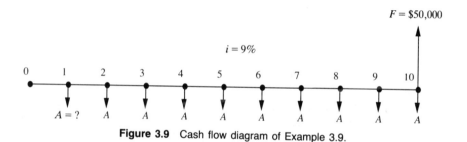

Figure 3.9 Cash flow diagram of Example 3.9.

The management desires to establish a fund to put aside a certain amount from the net income produced by the equipment at the end of each year for the next 10 years in order to replace the equipment at the end of its useful life. (This type of fund is frequently called a sinking fund.) If the fund earns 9% interest, how much should the company deposit at the end of each year?

Solution   From equation (3.21) the sinking fund amount can be found as

$$A = F(A/F, i\%, N)$$
$$= \$50,000(A/F, 9\%, 10)$$
$$= \$50,000(0.06582)$$
$$= \$3,291$$

Example 3.10   In Example 3.7 the total savings of \$542,048 that will be accumulated after 35 years has impressed the engineer. However, he realizes that the purchasing power of those dollars may shrink considerably due to inflation. After studying the consumer price index figures of the last several decades he projects that the average annual inflation rate during the next 35 years will be 7%. Determine the equivalent present work of the future amount, in present dollars.

Solution   From equation (3.8) the present worth of the \$542,048 is

$$P = F(P/F, i\%, N)$$
$$= \$542,048(P/F, 7\%, 35)$$
$$= \$542,048(0.0937)$$
$$= \$50,789.90$$

As can be observed from the result, the future worth in terms of present dollars is much less impressive.

3.7 UNIFORM-SERIES PRESENT WORTH FACTOR (FINDING P, GIVEN A)

Figure 3.10 shows a cash flow diagram that can be used to determine the present worth, P, of a uniform-series cash flow of amount A occurring at the end of each period for N periods when the effective interest rate is $i\%$. For example, in case of installment loan payments (e.g., for cars, appliances, and houses), the value of the end-of-period repayments (i.e., A's) has to be equal to the value of the amount borrowed (P) plus the interest compounded periodically at $i\%$ on the unpaid balance over N periods of

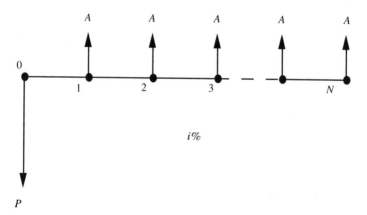

Figure 3.10 Cash flow diagram for uniform series, showing the relationship between A and P.

repayment. Note that the equivalent present value, P, of the uniform series occurs one period before the first A amount.

Since from equation (3.2),

$$F = P(1 + i)^N \qquad (3.2)$$

and from equation (3.14),

$$F = A\left[\frac{(1 + i)^N - 1}{i}\right] \qquad (3.14)$$

by substituting (3.14) into (3.2),

$$A\left[\frac{(1 + i^N - 1)}{i}\right] = P(1 + i)^N$$

from which

$$P = A\left[\frac{(1 + i)^N - 1}{i}\right]\left[\frac{1}{(1 + i)^N}\right]$$

or

$$P = A\left[\frac{(1 + i)^N - 1}{i(1 + i)^N}\right] \qquad (3.22)$$

and

$$\frac{P}{A} = \left[\frac{(1 + i)^N - 1}{i(1 + i)^N}\right] \qquad (3.23)$$

The factor given by equation (3.23) is called the *uniform-series present worth factor* or the *present worth of a uniform series*. It can be denoted as

$$(P/A, i\%, N) = \left[\frac{(1+i)^N - 1}{i(1+i)^N} \right] \qquad (3.24)$$

It is read as to find A, given P, $i\%$, and N. Therefore, equation (3.22) can also be expressed as

$$P = A(P/A, i\%, N) \qquad (3.25)$$

Example 3.11   Determine the present worth of the sinking-fund amount of $3,291 found in Example 3.9 for the next 10 years.

Solution   From equation (3.25) the present worth can be found as

$$P = A(P/A, i\%, N)$$
$$= 3{,}291(P/A, 9\%, 10)$$
$$= 3{,}291(6.418)$$
$$= \$21{,}121.64$$

3.8 UNIFORM-SERIES CAPITAL RECOVERY FACTOR (FINDING *A*, GIVEN *P*)

From equation (3.22) it can be found that

$$A = P\left[\frac{i(1+i)^N}{(1+i)^N - 1} \right] \qquad (3.26)$$

and

$$\frac{A}{P} = \frac{i(1+i)^N}{(1+i)^N - 1} \qquad (3.27)$$

The factor given by equation (3.27) is called the *uniform-series capital recovery factor*, the *uniform-series worth of a present sum*, the *capital recovery factor*, or simply the *amortization factor*. It can be denoted as

$$(A/P, i\%, N) = \frac{i(1+i)^N}{(1+i)^N - 1} \qquad (3.28)$$

It is read as to find A, given P, $i\%$, and N. Therefore, equation (3.26) can also be expressed as

$$A = P(A/P, i\%, N) \qquad (3.29)$$

Example 3.12   Assume that the engineer, in Example 3.7, wants to use the $542,048 savings in the tax-sheltered annuity plan to provide uniform annual payments as an annuity, as the name suggests, for over the next 20 years after his retirement at age 65. Determine the amount of the annuity that he will be receiving at the end of each year (Figure 3.11).

Solution   Note that the future worth, found in Example 3.7, becomes the present worth in the new cash flow diagram. Therefore, from equation (3.29) the amount of the annuity can be calculated as

$$A = P(A/P, i\%, N)$$
$$= \$542{,}048(A/P, 10\%, 20)$$
$$= \$542{,}048(0.11746)$$
$$= \$63{,}669$$

Of course, this annuity will last only for 20 years. In practice, there are also *guaranteed annuities* for an indefinite period of time through an insurance program by sharing the risk of death with others.

Example 3.13   Assume that the projected inflation rate is 7% and determine the present worth of the first annuity found in Example 3.12 in present dollars.

Solution   From Example 3.12 the annuity found was $63,669, which is a future value with respect to the present time. Therefore,

$$F = \$63{,}669$$

Since the engineer will receive the first annuity a year after his retirement, i.e., 36 years from now, by discounting the amount using the projected inflation rate of 7%, the present worth of the annuity can be found as

$$P = \$63{,}669(P/F, 7\%, 36)$$
$$= \$63{,}669(0.0875)$$
$$= \$5{,}574$$

where

$$(P/F, 7\%, 36) = \frac{1}{(1+i)^N}$$
$$= \frac{1}{(1+0.07)^{36}}$$
$$= 0.0875$$

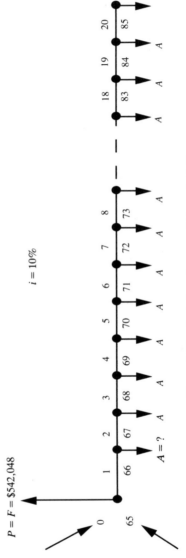

Figure 3.11 Cash flow diagram of Example 3.12.

Example 3.14 In Example 3.12 the engineer determined that his retirement annuity should be $63,669. As it has been calculated previously, in order to receive this annuity starting at the end of the 36th year from today for the next 20 years, he must pay an annual premium of $2,000 at the end of each year for the next 35 years. Instead of doing this, he fantasizes winning a jackpot at a Las Vegas casino today and investing the total amount at a 10% interest rate, compounded annually, and start receiving the same amount of annuity as before, as shown in Figure 3.12. Determine the amount of the jackpot necessary today to achieve this plan. Note that since the payment does not begin until some later date, i.e., the end of 36 years from now, the annuity is called the *deferred annuity*. Whereas, if the first payment of the annuity being made is at the end of the first period, it is called the *ordinary annuity*.

Solution As the first step, the deferred annuity uniform series can be represented by an equivalent present worth at the end of the 35th year as

$$P_{35} = A(P/A, 10\%, 20)$$
$$= \$63,669(8.514)$$
$$= \$542,078$$

Now that P_{35} is known, the next step is to compute the *actual* present worth, i.e., P_0. With respect to P_0, P_{35} is a future worth, and it could be denoted F_{35}. Thus,

$$F_{35} = P_{35}$$
$$= \$542,078$$

Hence, the present worth at time zero is found as

$$P_0 = F_{35}(P/F, 10\%, 35)$$
$$= \$542,078(0.0356)$$
$$= \$19,298$$

Therefore, the necessary amount of the jackpot (ignoring any associated taxes) is $19,298. Alternatively,

$$P = \$63,669(P/A, 10\%, 20)(P/F, 10\%, 35)$$
$$= \$19,298$$

or

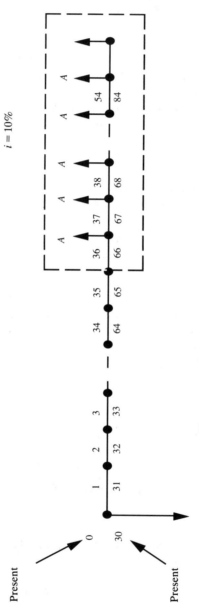

Figure 3.12 Cash flow diagram of Example 3.14.

$$P = \$63,669[(P/F, 10\%, 36) + (P/F, 10\%, 37) + \cdots + (P/F, 10\%, 55)]$$
$$= \$63,669(0.3031)$$
$$= \$19,298$$

or

$$P = \$63,669[(P/A, 10\%, 55) - (P/A, 10\%, 35)]$$
$$= \$63,669(9.947 - 9.644)$$
$$= \$19,292$$

or

$$P = \$63,669(F/A, 10\%, 20)(P/F, 10\%, 55)$$
$$= \$63,669(57.275)(0.0053)$$
$$= \$19,298$$

3.9 THE LEVELIZING PROCESS OF A NON-UNIFORM-SERIES CASH FLOW

The process of converting a given non-uniform-series cash flow to an equivalent uniform-series cash flow is called *levelizing* and involves the following steps:

1. Find the present worth of each cash flow in the series of unequal cash flows by multiplying the amount of the cash flow by the proper single-payment present worth factor.
2. Find the total present worth amount by adding the individual present worth amounts, determined in step 1, together.
3. Finally, find the equivalent uniform series of cash flows by multiplying the calculated total present worth amount by the proper uniform-series capital recovery factor.

The levelizing process is a very useful tool to compare and analyze unequal cash flow schedules.

Example 3.15 Determine the levelized uniform-series cash flow schedule that is equivalent to the non-uniform-series cash flow schedule given in Figure 3.13. Assume that the interest rate is 15%.

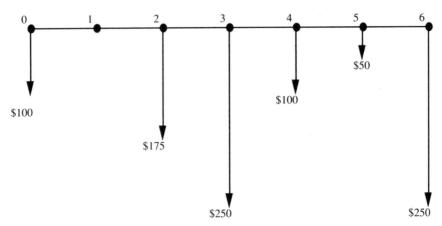

Figure 3.13   Non-uniform-series cash flow schedule.

Solution

Step 1: Find the present worth of each cash flow:
$P_0 = \$100 = \$100(1.0000) = \$100$
$P_1 = \$0 = \$0(0.8696) = \$0$
$P_2 = \$175(P/F, 15\%, 2) = \$175(0.7561) = \$132.32$
$P_3 = \$250(P/F, 15\%, 3) = \$250(0.6575) = \$164.38$
$P_4 = \$100(P/F, 15\%, 4) = \$100(0.5718) = \$57.18$
$P_5 = \$50(P/F, 15\%, 5) = \$50(0.4972) = \$24.86$
$P_6 = \$250(P/F, 15\%, 6) = \$250(0.4323) = \$108.08$

Step 2: Find the total present worth amount:
$$P = \sum_{i=0}^{6} P_i$$
$= \$100 + \$0 + \$132.32 + \$164.38 + \$57.18 + \$24.86 + \$108.08$
$= \$586.82$

Step 3: Find the equivalent uniform-series amount of cash flows:
$A = P(A/P, 15\%, 6)$
$= \$586.82(0.26424)$
$= \$155.06$

Figure 3.14 shows the levelized uniform-series cash flows.

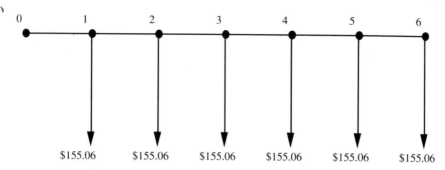

Figure 3.14 Levelized uniform-series cash flow schedule.

3.10 SUMMARY OF DISCRETE COMPOUNDING INTEREST FACTORS

The compound interest factors derived to this point are summarized in Table 3.1. Values of the factors are listed in Appendix A for commonly accruing values of $i\%$ and N. Figure 3.15 illustrates the use of the six basic interest factors. For example, if P, $i\%$, and N are given, the single-payment compound amount can be found by multiplying the P with $(F/P, i\%, N)$ as indicated in Table 3.1.

TABLE 3.1 Summary of Discrete Compounding Interest Factors

To Find	Given	Multiply Given by Factor	Symbol	Name
P	F	$\dfrac{1}{(1+i)^N}$	$(P/F, i\%, N)$	Single-payment present worth factor
F	P	$(1+i)^N$	$(F/P, i\%, N)$	Single-payment compound amount factor
P	A	$\dfrac{(1+i)^N - 1}{i(1+i)^N}$	$(P/A, i\%, N)$	Uniform-series present worth factor
A	P	$\dfrac{i(1+i)^N}{(1+i)^N - 1}$	$(A/P, i\%, N)$	Uniform-series capital recovery factor
F	A	$\dfrac{(1+i)^N - 1}{i}$	$(F/A, i\%, N)$	Uniform-series compound amount factor
A	F	$\dfrac{i}{(1+i)^N - 1}$	$(A/F, i\%, N)$	Uniform-series sinking-fund factor

Key: P = present worth, F = future worth, A = uniform-series amount, i = interest rate per period, N = number of interest periods.

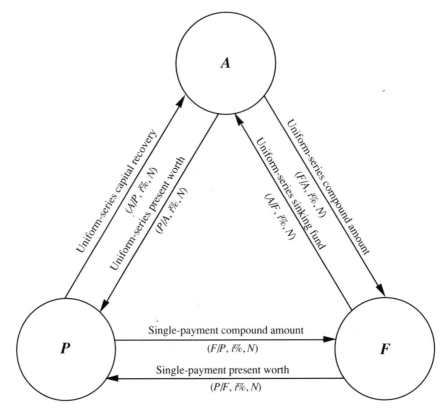

Figure 3.15   The six basic compound interest factors to relate P, F, and A to each other.

3.11   ARITHMETIC GRADIENT SERIES

Some engineering economy problems may involve disbursements or receipts that are projected to increase or decrease by a constant amount from period to period. Typical examples incude (1) maintenance and repair expenses of the mechanical equipment, which often increases as the equipment ages, and (2) depreciation expense calculations using sum-of-the-years-digits method (the annual depreciation charges decrease by a constant amount as the property ages). Figure 3.16 shows a cash flow diagram of a series of end-of-period disbursements increasing at a constant amount of change, G dollars per period. This constant amount is known as the *uniform arithmetic gradient*. It is assumed that the amount G at the end of period one is zero.

3.11.1   Factor to Convert an Arithmetic Gradient Series to Future Worth (Finding F, Given G)

For the sake of convenience, as indicated in Figure 3.16, the gradient series can be the sum of superimposed group of uniform series with end-of-period

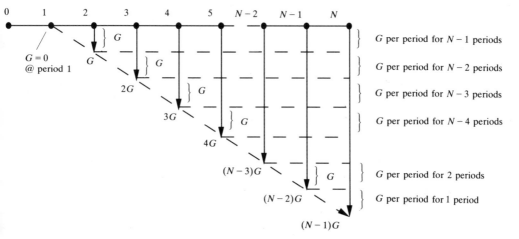

Figure 3.16 Cash flow diagram of an increasing arithmetic gradient series.

payments, each of value A equal to G, but for decreasing time periods starting with $N - 1$. For example, the first series of uniform payments of amount G is started at the end of the second period and continued until the end of the Nth period. Similarly, the second series of uniform payments of amount G is started at the end of the third period and continued until the end of the Nth period, and so on. Therefore,

$$F = G(F/A, i\%, N - 1) + G(F/A, i\%, N - 2) + \cdots + G(F/A, i\%, 2)$$
$$+ G(F/A, i\%, 1) \tag{3.30}$$

Substituting

$$(F/A, i\%, N) = \frac{(1 + i)^N - 1}{i}$$

into equation (3.30),

$$F = G\left[\frac{(1 + i)^{N-1} - 1}{i} + \frac{(1 + i)^{N-2} - 1}{i} + \cdots + \frac{(1 + i)^2 - 1}{i} + \frac{(1 + i) - 1}{i}\right] \tag{3.31}$$

or

$$F = \frac{G}{i}\left[(1 + i)^{N-1} + (1 + i)^{N-2} + \cdots + (1 + i)^2 + (1 + i) - (N - 1)\right] \tag{3.32}$$

Since equation (3.12) is

$$F = A + A(1 + i) + A(1 + i)^2 + \cdots + A(1 + i)^{N-1}$$

or

$$\frac{F}{A} = (1 + i)^{N-1} + (1 + i)^{N-2} + \cdots + (1 + i)^2 + (1 + i) + 1 \qquad (3.33)$$

substituting equation (3.33) into equation (3.32),

$$F = \frac{G}{i}\left(\frac{F}{A} - N\right) \qquad (3.34)$$

From equation (3.15)

$$\frac{F}{A} = \frac{(1 + i)^N - 1}{i}$$

therefore,

$$F = \frac{G}{i}\left[\frac{(1 + i)^N - 1}{i} - N\right] \qquad (3.35)$$

Thus, the factor to convert an arithmetic gradient series to future worth is

$$(F/G, i\%, N) = \frac{1}{i}\left[\frac{(1 + i)^N - 1}{i} - N\right] \qquad (3.36)$$

It is read as to find F, given G, $i\%$, N. Therefore, equation (3.35) can also be expressed as

$$F = G(F/G, i\%, N) \qquad (3.37)$$

Example 3.16   Assume that estimates of certain end-of-year expenses are $0 at the end of the first year, $1,000 for the second year, $2,000 for the third year, and $3,000 for the fourth year, as shown in Figure 3.17. If the interest rate is 10% per year, determine the future worth of the expenses that will be spent by the end of the fourth year (including the fourth year's expense).

Solution   The given data have $0 as the end of the first year expense and $1,000 as the annual gradient. Therefore, from equation (3.37)

$$F = G(F/G, 10\%, 4)$$
$$= \$1,000(6.41)$$
$$= \$6,410$$

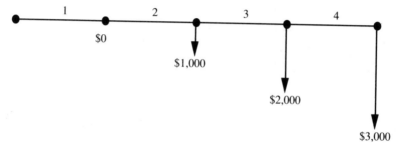

Figure 3.17 Cash flow diagram of Example 3.16.

3.11.2 Factor to Convert an Arithmetic Gradient Series to Present Worth (Finding *P*, Given *G*)

From equation (3.34)

$$F = \frac{G}{i}\left(\frac{F}{A} - N\right)$$

or

$$\frac{F}{G} = \frac{1}{i}\left(\frac{F}{A} - N\right) \tag{3.38}$$

Multiplying both sides of the equation by *P/F* gives

$$\left(\frac{P}{F}\right)\left(\frac{F}{G}\right) = \frac{1}{i}\left[\left(\frac{F}{A}\right)\left(\frac{P}{F}\right) - N\left(\frac{P}{F}\right)\right]$$

and simplifying

$$\frac{P}{G} = \frac{1}{i}\left[\frac{P}{A} - N\left(\frac{P}{F}\right)\right] \tag{3.39}$$

or

$$\frac{P}{G} = \frac{1}{i}\left[\frac{(1+i)^N - 1}{i(1+i)^N} - \frac{N}{(1+i)^N}\right] \tag{3.40}$$

Therefore, the factor to convert an arithmetic gradient series to present worth is

$$(P/G, i\%, N) = \frac{1}{i}\left[\frac{(1+i)^N - 1}{(1+i)^N} - \frac{N}{(1+i)^N}\right] \tag{3.41}$$

It is read as to find *P*, given *G*, *i*%, *N*. Therefore, equation (3.40) can be expressed as

$$P = G(P/G, i\%, N) \tag{3.42}$$

Example 3.17   The operating and maintenance (O&M) costs of a piece of equipment are expected to be $2,000 for the first year, $2,500 for the second year, $3,000 for the third year, $,3500 for the fourth year, and $4,000 for the fifth year. Assume that the interest rate is 12% per year and the costs occur at the end of the given year and determine the equivalent future worth of the arithmetic gradient series.

Solution   The cash flow diagram of the problem is shown in Figure 3.18. Note that it can be resolved into two (subdiagram or subschedule) components. Therefore, the summed future worths of these two subschedules equals the future worth of the original cash flow schedule. Therefore,

$$F = F_1 + F_2$$
$$= A(F/A, 12\%, 5) + G(F/G, 12\%, 5)$$
$$= \$2,000(6.353) + \$500(11.27)$$
$$= \$18,341$$

Note that N equals 5 even though only four positive cash flows are present in the gradient series.

Example 3.18   Using the given data in Example 3.17, determine the equivalent present worth of the given arithmetic gradient series.

Solution   Again, the summed present worths of the two subschedules equals the future worth of the original cash flow schedule. Therefore,

$$P = P_1 + P_2$$
$$= A(P/A, 12\%, 5) + G(P/G, 12\%, 5)$$
$$= \$2,000(3.605) + \$500(6.397)$$
$$= \$10,408,50$$

or alternatively,

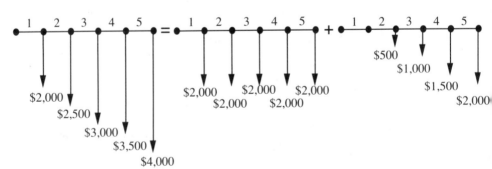

Figure 3.18   Cash flow diagram of Example 3.17.

$$P = F(P/F, 12\%, 5)$$
$$= \$18,341(0.5674)$$
$$= \$10,408.50$$

3.11.3 Factor to Convert an Arithmetic Gradient Series to a Uniform Series (Finding *A*, Given *G*)

From equation (3.38)

$$\frac{F}{G} = \frac{1}{i}\left(\frac{F}{A} - N\right) \qquad (3.38)$$

multiplying both sides of the equation by A/F yields

$$\left(\frac{A}{F}\right)\left(\frac{F}{G}\right) = \frac{1}{i}\left[\left(\frac{F}{A}\right)\left(\frac{A}{F}\right) - N\left(\frac{A}{F}\right)\right]$$

and simplifying

$$\frac{A}{G} = \frac{1}{i}\left[1 - N\left(\frac{A}{F}\right)\right] \qquad (3.43)$$

or

$$\frac{A}{G} = \left[\frac{1}{i} - \frac{N}{(1+i)^N - 1}\right] \qquad (3.44)$$

Therefore, the factor to convert an arithmetic gradient series to a uniform series is

$$(A/G, i\%, N) = \left[\frac{1}{i} - \frac{N}{(1+i)^N - 1}\right] \qquad (3.45)$$

It is read as to find *A*, given *G*, *i%*, *N*. Therefore, equation (3.44) can be expressed as

$$A = G(A/G, i\%, N) \qquad (3.46)$$

Example 3.19 Using the data given in Example 3.17, determine the equivalent uniform annual worth of the given arithmetic gradient series.

Solution Also, the summed equivalent uniform annual worths of the two subschedules equals the uniform annual worth of the original cash flow schedule. Therefore

$$A = A_1 + A_2$$
$$= \$2,000 + \$500(A/G, 12\%, 5)$$
$$= \$2,000 + \$500(1.775)$$
$$= \$2,887.50$$

or alternatively,

$$A = F(A/F, 12\%, 5)$$
$$= \$18,341(0.15741)$$
$$= \$2,887.50$$

Example 3.20 Assume that the O&M costs that were given in Example 3.17 are reversed so that they are $4,000 for the first year, $3,500 for the second year, $3,000 for the third year, $2,500 for the fourth year, and $2,000 for the fifth year, as shown in Figure 3.19. Determine the equivalent uniform annual worth.

Solution Since the original cash flow series can be represented, as shown in Figure 3.19, by the difference in a uniform series of $4,000 and a gradient series of $500, the equivalent uniform annual worth is

$$A = A_1 - A_2$$
$$= \$4,000 - \$500(A/G, 12\%, 5)$$
$$= \$4,000 - \$500(1.775)$$
$$= \$3,112.50$$

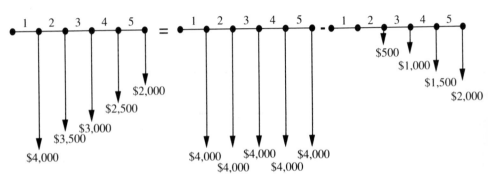

Figure 3.19 Cash flow diagram of Example 3.20.

3.12 RELATIONSHIPS AMONG COMPOUND INTEREST FACTORS

There are certain relationships among the compound interest factors that can be taken advantage of in the engineering economy applications. For example, there are reciprocals such as

$$(F/P, i\%, N) = \frac{1}{(P/F, i\%, N)} \tag{3.47}$$

$$(F/A, i\%, N) = \frac{1}{(A/F, i\%, N)} \tag{3.48}$$

$$(P/A, i\%, N) = \frac{1}{(A/P, i\%, N)} \tag{3.49}$$

Also, multiplication of two time-value factors results in a third time-value factor, e.g.,

$$(P/A, i\%, N)(F/P, i\%, N) = (F/A, i\%, N) \tag{3.50}$$

or

$$(A/F, i\%, N)(P/A, i\%, N) = (P/F, i\%, N) \tag{3.51}$$

Furthermore, there are some special relationships between certain compound factors, e.g.,

$$(A/P, i\%, N) = (A/F, i\%, N) + i\% \tag{3.52}$$

i.e., the uniform-series capital recovery factor equals uniform-series sinking-fund factor plus the interest rate. Also,

$$(P/A, i\%, N) = (P/F, i\%, 1) + (P/F, i\%, 2) + \cdots + (P/F, i\%, N)$$

or

$$(P/A, i\%, N) = \sum_{j=1}^{N} (P/F, i\%, j) \tag{3.53}$$

i.e, the uniform-series present worth factor is simply the sum of the N terms of the single-payment present worth factor.

Also,

$$(F/A, i\%, N) = 1 + (F/P, i\%, 1) + (F/P, i\%, 2) + \cdots + (F/P, i\%, N-1)$$

or

$$(F/A, i\%, N) = 1 + \sum_{j=1}^{N-1} (F/P, i\%, j) \qquad (3.54)$$

i.e, the uniform-series compound amount factor equals one plus the sum of $N-1$ terms of the single-payment compound amount factor.

In addition,

$$(F/P, i\%, N) = (F/P, i\%, N_1)(F/P, i\%, N_2) \ldots (F/P, i\%, N_k)$$

or

$$(F/P, i\%, N) = \prod_{k=1}^{k} (F/P, i\%, N_k) \qquad (3.55)$$

and

$$(P/F, i\%, N) = (P/F, i\%, N_1)(P/F, i\%, N_2) \ldots (P/F, i\%, N_k)$$

or

$$(P/F, i\%, N) = \prod_{k=1}^{k} (P/F, i\%, N_k) \qquad (3.56)$$

where

$$N = N_1 + N_2 + \cdots + N_k$$

Equations (3.55) and (3.56) are especially useful to determine the time-value factors for large values of N that cannot be found in the tables of Appendix A. However, note that the method given is only appropriate to use for the F/P and P/F factors but not for others.

There are also relationships involving the arithmetic gradient series. For example,

$$(P/G, i\%, N) = (A/G, i\%, N)(P/A, i\%, N) \qquad (3.57)$$

$$(P/G, i\%, N) = (P/F, i\%, N)(F/G, i\%, N) \qquad (3.58)$$

$$(F/G, i\%, N) = (A/G, i\%, N)(F/A, i\%, N) \qquad (3.59)$$

$$(F/G, i\%, N) = (F/P, i\%, N)(P/G, i\%, N) \qquad (3.60)$$

$$(A/G, i\%, N) = (A/F, i\%, N)(F/G, i\%, N) \qquad (3.61)$$

$$(A/G, i\%, N) = (A/P, i\%, N)(P/G, i\%, N) \qquad (3.62)$$

Of course, there are reciprocals of the arithmetic gradient factors such as

$$(G/P, i\%, N) = \frac{1}{(P/G, i\%, N)} \tag{3.63}$$

$$(G/F, i\%, N) = \frac{1}{(F/G, i\%, N)} \tag{3.64}$$

$$(G/A, i\%, N) = \frac{1}{(A/G, i\%, N)} \tag{3.65}$$

They can also be found from other relationships, e.g.,

$$(G/P, i\%, N) = (G/A, i\%, N)(A/P, i\%, N) \tag{3.66}$$

$$(G/F, i\%, N) = (G/P, i\%, N)(P/F, i\%, N) \tag{3.67}$$

$$(G/A, i\%, N) = (G/F, i\%, N)(F/A, i\%, N) \tag{3.68}$$

TABLE 3.2 Summary of Discrete Compounding Arithmetic Gradient-Series Interest Factors

To Find	Given	Multiply Given by Factor	Symbol	Name
P	G	$\frac{1}{i}\left[\frac{(1+i)^N - 1}{i(1+i)^N} - \frac{N}{(1+i)^N}\right]$	$(P/G, i\%, N)$	Present worth of gradient-series factor
G	P	$\frac{1}{i}\left[\frac{(1+i)^N - 1}{i(1+i)^N} - \frac{N}{(1+i)^N}\right]$	$(G/P, i\%, N)$	Gradient series of present worth factor
F	G	$\frac{1}{i}\left[\frac{(1+i)^N - 1}{i} - N\right]$	$(F/G, i\%, N)$	Future worth of gradient-series factor
G	F	$\left[\frac{1}{i}\left(\frac{(1+i)^N - 1}{i} - N\right)\right]^{-1}$	$(G/F, i\%, N)$	Gradient series of future worth factor
A	G	$\frac{1}{i} - \frac{N}{(1+i)^N - 1}$	$(A/G, i\%, N)$	Gradient- to uniform-series conversion factor
G	A	$\left[\frac{1}{i} - \frac{N}{(1+i)^N - 1}\right]^{-1}$	$(G/A, i\%, N)$	Uniform- to gradient-series conversion factor

Key: P = present worth, F = future worth, A = uniform-series amount, G = gradient-series amount.

However, the reciprocals of the arithmetic gradient factors are seldom, if ever, used.

The arithmetic gradient-series interest factors derived to this point are summarized in Table 3.2. Values of the factors for P/G, F/G, and A/G are listed in Appendix A for commonly occurring values for $i\%$ and N. The reciprocals of P/G, F/G, and $A.G$ give the G/P, G/F, and G/A. Figure 3.20 illustrates the use of the arithmetic gradient-series interest factors.

Example 3.21 An individual has been promised to receive a series of payments of \$4,000 each 5 years starting today and lasting forever, as shown in Figure 3.21. Assume that the interest rate is 12% and determine the present worth of the series.

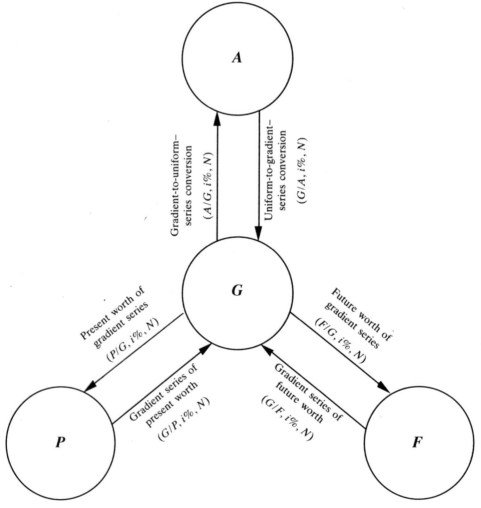

Figure 3.20 Arithmetic gradient-series convention factors.

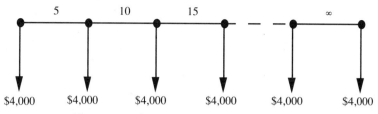

Figure 3.21 Cash flow diagram of Example 3.21.

Solution By adding the present worths of individual cash flows, the total present worth can be found as

$$P = \$4,000[(P/F, 12\%, 0) + (P/F, 12\%, 5) + (P/F, 12\%, 10)$$
$$+ (P/F, 12\% \ 15) + \cdots + (P/F, 12\%, \infty)]$$
$$= \$4,000(1.0000 + 0.5674 + 0.3220 + 0.1827 + \cdots + 0.0000)$$
$$= \$9,247$$

Alternatively,

$$P = \$4,000(A/P, 12\%, 5)(P/A, 12\%, \infty)$$
$$= \$4,000(0.27741)(8.333)$$
$$= \$9,247$$

3.13 GEOMETRIC GRADIENT SERIES

Some engineering economy problems may involve disbursements or receipts that are projected to increase or decrease by a constant percentage (rate) from period to period. Typical examples of the exponential growth patterns may include (1) some maintenance costs, (2) labor costs, (3) material costs, (4) energy costs, and (5) electrical energy consumption. The geometric gradient series can also be used to determine the effects of a constant rate of inflation or deflation. Furthermore, it may also be used to project population growth.[†]

[†]The growth process proceeds in exponential fashion until something restricts the growth process. Shortage of food or resources, natural enemies, and perhaps other limits to growth cannot be ignored. In a realistic environment, no process can or will grow exponentially forever, although it may experience exponential growth for a certain number of periods. A realistic model of g growth would be that of fruit flies in a jar. Assume a fixed amount of air and food are injected daily. The fruit flies would multiply in number, and their growth would be exponential at first, until the air and food became limited resources. Then competition for the resources would leave some flies without the means for survival, and the population would level off, rather than fill the jar completely. Growth would cease rather abruptly since the restraining forces cannot be avoided or altered.

Figure 3.22 shows a cash flow diagram of a series of end-of-period disbursements increasing at a constant $g\%$ per period. The geometric gradient series (or geometric series) can be used to represent a growth (positive g) as well as a decay (negative g). If A_1 is the amount of the cash flow at the end of period 1, it can be observed that the size of the cash flow at the end of each period is $1 + g$ times the cash flow for the preceding period. Therefore, the cash flow at the end of period N can be expressed as

$$A_N = A_{N-1}(1 + g) \qquad N = 2, 3, \ldots \tag{3.69}$$

or

$$A_N = A_1(1 + g)^{N-1} \qquad N = 1, 2, 3, \ldots \tag{3.70}$$

The present worth of the geometric series in Figure 3.22 can be expressed as

$$P = A_1(P/F, i\%, 1) + A_2(P/F, i\%, 2) + \cdots + A_N(P/F, i\%, N) \tag{3.71}$$

or

$$P = A_1(1 + i)^{-1} + A_2(1 + i)^{-2} + \cdots + A_N(1 + i)^{-N} \tag{3.72}$$

Substituting equation (3.70) into equation (3.72)

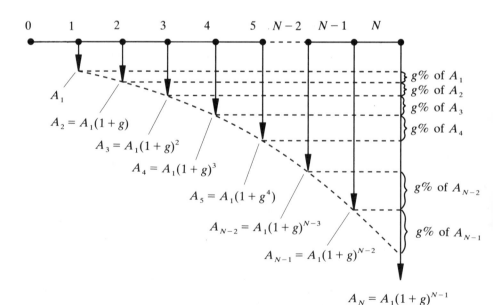

Figure 3.22 Cash flow diagram for geometric series increasing by $g\%$ per period.

$$P = A_1(1+i)^{-1} + A_1(1+g)(1+i)^{-2} + \cdots + A_1(1+g)^{N-1}(1+i)^{-N} \tag{3.73}$$

or

$$P = A_1\left[\frac{1}{1+i} + \frac{1+g}{(1+i)^2} + \cdots + \frac{(1+g)^{N-1}}{(1+i)^N} \right] \tag{3.74}$$

or

$$P = \frac{A_1}{1+g}\left[\frac{1+g}{1+i} + \frac{(1+g)^2}{(1+i)^2} + \cdots + \frac{(1+g)^N}{(1+i)^N} \right] \tag{3.75}$$

Three different formulas are required to determine the present worth of a geometric series. Which one to use depends on the relationship between the constant percentage (g) and the interest rate (i).

Case 1: When $g > i$, let

$$i^* \triangleq \frac{1+g}{1+i} - 1 \tag{3.76}$$

where i^* is defined as a special interest rate so that

$$P = \frac{A_1}{1+i}\left[\frac{(1+i^*)^N - 1}{i^*} \right] \tag{3.77}$$

or

$$P = \frac{A_1}{1+i}\,(F/A, i^*, N) \tag{3.78}$$

Case 2: When $g < i$, let

$$i^* \triangleq \frac{1+i}{1+g} - 1 \tag{3.79}$$

so that

$$P = \frac{A_1}{1+g}\left[\frac{(1+i^*)^N - 1}{i^*(1+i^*)^N} \right] \tag{3.80}$$

or

$$P = \frac{A_1}{1+g}\,(P/A, i^*, N) \tag{3.81}$$

Case 3: When $g = i$, from equation (3.75)

$$P = \frac{A_1 N}{1 + g} \tag{3.82}$$

Alternatively, let

$$x = \frac{1 + g}{1 + i} \tag{3.83}$$

Substituting equation (3.83) into equation (3.73)

$$P = \frac{A_1}{1 + i} (1 + x + x^2 + \cdots + x^{N-1}) \tag{3.84}$$

When $x \neq 1$ or $g \neq i$,

$$1 + x + x^2 + \cdots + x^{N-1} \triangleq \frac{1 - x^N}{1 - x} \tag{3.85}$$

Therefore,

$$P = \frac{A_1}{1 + i} \left(\frac{1 - x^N}{1 - x} \right) \qquad g \neq i \tag{3.86}$$

Similarly, when $x = 1$ or $g = 1$,

$$P = \frac{A_1 N}{1 + i} \qquad g = i \tag{3.87}$$

Substituting equation (3.83) into equation (3.86),

$$P = A_1 \left[\frac{1 - (1 + g)^N (1 + i)^{-N}}{i - g} \right] \qquad g \neq i \tag{3.88}$$

and

$$P = A_1 N (1 + i)^{-1} \qquad g = i \tag{3.89}$$

or

$$P = A_1 \left[\frac{1 - (F/P, g\%, N)(P/F, i\%, N)}{i - g} \right] \qquad g \neq i \tag{3.90}$$

and

$$P = A_1 N (P/F, i\%, 1) \qquad g = i \tag{3.91}$$

Similarly, since

$$F = P(F/P, i\%, N) \tag{3.92}$$

substituting equation (3.90) into equation (3.92), the future worth of the geometric series can be expressed as

$$F = A_1 \left[\frac{(F/P, i\%, N) - (F/P, g\%, N)}{i - g} \right] \qquad g \neq i \qquad (3.93)$$

and

$$F = A_1 N (F/P, i\%, N - 1) \qquad g = i \qquad (3.94)$$

or

$$F = A_1 \left[\frac{(1 + i)^N - (1 + g)^N}{i - g} \right] \qquad g \neq i \qquad (3.95)$$

and

$$F = A_1 N (1 + i)^{N-1} \qquad g = i \qquad (3.96)$$

Example 3.22   The current annual maintenance cost of equipment is given as $5,000, and it is expected to increase at the rate of 15% per year. Assume that the interest rate is 10% and determine the present worth of the maintenance costs over a 10-year period.

Solution   Since $g > i$, using equation (3.77), where

$$i^* \overset{\Delta}{=} \frac{1 + g}{1 + i} - 1$$

$$= \frac{1 + 0.15}{1 + 0.10} - 1$$

$$= 0.0455 \text{ or } 4.55\%$$

so that the present worth of the maintenance costs is

$$P = \frac{A_1}{1 + i} \left[\frac{(1 + i^*)^N - 1}{i^*} \right]$$

$$= \frac{\$5,000}{1 + 0.10} \left[\frac{(1 + 0.0455)^{10} - 1}{0.0455} \right]$$

$$= \$55,986$$

Example 3.23   Repeat Example 3.22, assuming that the maintenance costs are expected to increase at the rate of 10% per year.

Solution   Since $g = i$, using equation (3.82), the present worth of the maintenance costs is

$$P = \frac{A_1 N}{1 + g}$$

$$= \frac{\$5,000 \times 10}{1 + 0.10}$$

$$= \$45,455$$

Example 3.24   Repeat Example 3.22, assuming that the maintenance costs are expected to increase at the rate of 5% per year.

Solution   Since $g < i$, using equation (3.80), where

$$i^* \triangleq \frac{1 + i}{1 + g} - 1$$

$$= \frac{1 + 0.10}{1 + 0.05} - 1$$

$$= 0.0476 \text{ or } 4.76\%$$

then the present worth of the maintenance costs is

$$P = \frac{A_1}{1 + g} \left[\frac{(1 + i^*)^N - 1}{i^*(1 + i^*)^N} \right]$$

$$= \frac{\$5,000}{1 + 0.05} \left[\frac{(1 + 0.0476)^{10} - 1}{0.0476(1 + 0.0476)^{10}} \right]$$

$$= \$37.203$$

Example 3.25   Repeat Example 3.22, using equation (3.90)

Solution   From equation (3.90),

$$P = A_1 \left[\frac{1 - (F/P, g\%, N)(P/F, i\%, N)}{i - g} \right]$$

$$= \$5,000 \left[\frac{1 - (F/P, 15\%, 10)(P/F, 10\%, 10)}{0.10 - 0.15} \right]$$

$$= \$5,000 \left[\frac{1 - (4.046)(0.3855)}{0.10 - 0.15} \right]$$

$$= \$55,973$$

Note that the answer is approximately (due to rounding errors) the same.

3.14 LIMITS OF COMPOUND INTEREST FACTORS

As N goes to infinity, the limits of compound interest factors are

$$\lim_{N \to \infty} (P/F, i\%, N) = \lim_{N \to \infty} \frac{1}{(1+i)^N} = 0 \tag{3.97}$$

$$\lim_{N \to \infty} (F/P, i\%, N) = \lim_{N \to \infty} (1+i)^N = \infty \tag{3.98}$$

$$\lim_{N \to \infty} (P/A, i\%, N) = \lim_{N \to \infty} \frac{(1+i)^N - 1}{i(1+i)} = \frac{1}{i} \tag{3.99}$$

$$\lim_{N \to \infty} (A/P, i\%, N) = \lim_{N \to \infty} \frac{i(i+1)^N}{(1+i)^N - 1} = i \tag{3.100}$$

$$\lim_{N \to \infty} (F/A, i\%, N) = \lim_{N \to \infty} \frac{(1+i)^N - 1}{i} = \infty \tag{3.101}$$

$$\lim_{N \to \infty} (A/F, i\%, N) = \lim_{N \to \infty} \frac{i}{(1+i)^N - 1} = 0 \tag{3.102}$$

$$\lim_{N \to \infty} (P/G, i\%, N) = \lim_{N \to \infty} \frac{1}{i} \left[\frac{(1+i)^N - 1}{i(1+i)^N} - \frac{N}{(1+i)^N} \right] = \frac{1}{i^2} \tag{3.103}$$

$$\lim_{N \to \infty} (G/P, i\%, N) = \lim_{N \to \infty} \left[\frac{1}{i} \left(\frac{(1+i)^N - 1}{i(1+i)^N} - \frac{N}{(1+i)^N} \right) \right]^{-1} = i^2 \tag{3.104}$$

$$\lim_{N \to \infty} (F/G, i\%, N) = \lim_{N \to \infty} \frac{1}{i} \left[\frac{(1+i)^N - 1}{i} - N \right] = \infty \tag{3.105}$$

$$\lim_{N \to \infty} (G/F, i\%, N) = \lim_{N \to \infty} \left[\frac{1}{i} \left(\frac{(1+i)^N - 1}{i} - N \right) \right]^{-1} = 0 \tag{3.106}$$

$$\lim_{N \to \infty} (A/G, i\%, N) = \lim_{N \to \infty} \left[\frac{1}{i} - \frac{N}{(1+i)^N - 1} \right] = \frac{1}{i} \tag{3.107}$$

$$\lim_{N \to \infty} (G/A, i\%, N) = \lim_{N \to \infty} \left[\frac{1}{i} - \frac{N}{(1+i)^{N-1}} \right]^{-1} = i \tag{3.108}$$

Similarly, as $i\%$ goes to zero, the limits of compound interest factors are

$$\lim_{i \to 0} (P/F, i\%, N) = 1 \tag{3.109}$$

$$\lim_{i \to 0} (F/P, i\%, N) = 1 \tag{3.110}$$

$$\lim_{i \to 0} (P/A, i\%, N) = N \tag{3.111}$$

$$\lim_{i \to 0} (A/P, i\%, N) = \frac{1}{N} \tag{3.112}$$

$$\lim_{i\to 0} (F/A, i\%, N) = N \tag{3.113}$$

$$\lim_{i\to 0} (A/F, i\%, N) = \frac{1}{N} \tag{3.114}$$

$$\lim_{i\to 0} (P/G, i\%, N) = \frac{N^2 - N}{2} \tag{3.115}$$

$$\lim_{i\to 0} (G/P, i\%, N) = \frac{2}{N^2 - N} \tag{3.116}$$

$$\lim_{i\to 0} (F/G, i\%, N) = \frac{N^2 - N}{2} \tag{3.117}$$

$$\lim_{i\to 0} (G/F, i\%, N) = \frac{2}{N^2 - N} \tag{3.118}$$

$$\lim_{i\to 0} (A/G, i\%, N) = \frac{N - 1}{2} \tag{3.119}$$

$$\lim_{i\to 0} (G/A, i\%, N) = \frac{2}{N - 1} \tag{3.120}$$

Furthermore, as $i\%$ goes to infinity, the limits of compound interest factors are

$$\lim_{i\to \infty} (P/F, i\%, N) = 0 \tag{3.121}$$

$$\lim_{i\to \infty} (F/P, i\%, N) = \infty \tag{3.122}$$

$$\lim_{i\to \infty} (P/A, i\%, N) = 0 \tag{3.123}$$

$$\lim_{i\to \infty} (A/P, i\%, N) = \infty \tag{3.124}$$

$$\lim_{i\to \infty} (F/A, i\%, N) = \infty \tag{3.125}$$

$$\lim_{i\to \infty} (A/F, i\%, N) = 0 \tag{3.126}$$

$$\lim_{i\to \infty} (P/G, i\%, N) = 0 \tag{3.127}$$

$$\lim_{i\to \infty} (G/P, i\%, N) = \infty \tag{3.128}$$

$$\lim_{i\to \infty} (F/G, i\%, N) = \infty \tag{3.129}$$

$$\lim_{i\to \infty} (G/F, i\%, N) = 0 \tag{3.130}$$

$$\lim_{i\to \infty} (A/G, i\%, N) = 0 \tag{3.131}$$

$$\lim_{i\to \infty} (G/A, i\%, N) = \infty \tag{3.132}$$

PROBLEMS

3.1 What single payment must be made to make available $5,230 at the end of 7 years if the interest rate is $5\frac{1}{2}\%$?

3.2 If after 12 years of annual-end-of-year payments of $420 there was a sum of $7,813.52 available, find the interest rate.

3.3 A man bought a car for $5,985 and make a $1,200 down payment. He financed the balance at 6% with monthly payments of $146. In how many months will he have paid off the debt and how much will the last payment be? All payments are assumed equal except possibly the last.

3.4 How long will it take to double $5,000 if the interest is compounded at 7% annually?

3.5 A man wants to provide a college fund for his child in 13 years. The fund should provide $2,500 per year for 4 years. How much should he deposit annually if the interest rate is $5\frac{1}{2}\%$?

3.6 Management estimates a sheet metal press with a 6-year life has a basic annual maintenance cost of $500 per year, but repair costs tend to increase at about $125 per year with first year's repair costs being $500. Find the annual equivalent end-of-year repair and maintenance costs if the interest is 8%.

3.7 Mr. Smith established a fund to save $8,000 in 10 years by making annual payments with an interest rate of $4\frac{1}{2}\%$ It is now 6 years hence and the interest rate has changed to $5\frac{1}{2}\%$. How much can he reduce his payment by and still meet his goal?

3.8 A sporting goods firm desired to establish a trust fund contributing $5,000 every 4 years to the U.S. Olympic Committee. If the interest rate is 8%, how much must be deposited if the first payment is due in 4 years?

3.9 A firm has bought an old building. Maintenance and repair expenditures are anticipated as follows: $20,000 the 1st year, $5,000 the 5th year, $8,000 the 10th year, and $6,000 the 15th year. If the firm is assuming a 20-year life, what is the annual equivalent year-end cost with 7% interest?

3.10 In Problem 3.5 what would the monthly allotments be if he made a $1,000 initial deposit and continued monthly payments to the last withdrawal?

3.11 A house had been purchased for $31,000 with a 5% down payment and a 20-year mortgage at 8% compounded semiannually. The house is being sold after 3 years. How much of the principal has been paid? Assume payment is made semiannually, interest owed is 4% of outstanding balance each 6 months.

3.12 What sum will be available in 15 years if $1,000 is deposited now, $2,000 in 2 years, $2,500 3 years after that, and $5,000 in 10 years? Let the interest be 6%.

3.13 What is the total amount accrued if $750 is invested at 6% compounded annually for 4 years?

3.14 If $500 is invested annually into a plan that draws 7% interest compounded annually, how much money will be accrued at the end of 5 years?

3.15 How much was initially invested if after 20 years of annual compounding at $5\frac{1}{2}$% the amount accrued is $50,000?

3.16 How much must be deposited initially in order to withdraw $1,000 a year for 7 years when the original deposit is compounded annually at 12%?

3.17 If a machine estimated to cost $25,000 in 7 years will be required in a plant at that time, how much must be invested annually at 6% in order to pay for the machine when it is needed?

3.18 In order for $2,000 to accumulate to $2,500 in 4 years it must be invested at what rate?

3.19 What equal annual payment would be required to pay back a loan of $30,000 at 9% in 20 years?

3.20 If $5,000 a year is expected to be realized from an investment of $40,000 over a 10-year period, at what interest rate must it be invested?

3.21 If an individual plans to retire in 30 years with $60,000 in the bank, how much must he deposit every year if the interest rate is $5\frac{1}{2}$%?

3.22 Assume that you want to have an amount of $100,000 twenty years from now through making annual deposits into a savings account. Assume that the interest rate is 6% compounded annually and that the deposits start now and end 20 years from now. Determine the amount of the uniform annual deposits.

3.23 Assume that, in Problem 3.22, after 11 deposits have been made the interest rate on all funds has been increased to 10% through a special arrangement. Determine the amount of the new uniform annual deposits necessary in the remaining years in order to have the $100,000.

3.24 A man has just sold one of his properties for a profit return on his original investment. Assume that the investment was made 15 years ago. Determine the amount of the original investment, ignoring any tax obligations.

3.25 Assume that the end-of-the-year cash flows of the next 9 years are given as $1,000, $2,000, $3,000, $4,000, $5,000, $4,000, $3,000, $2,000, and $1,000, respectively. If the interest rate is 15%, determine the present worth of the cash flows, using only the uniform-series present worth factors and arithmetic gradient-series factors.

3.26 Repeat Example 3.25, assuming that the O&M cost is $2,000 for the first year but will increase 12% per year for the remaining years.

3.27 In order to save for her son's college expenses, an engineer decides to open a savings account and deposit her annual bonuses for the next 8 years. Her initial bonus is $1,000, and she expects them to grow 10% per year. Assume that the savings account pays 6% interest rate compounded annually. Determine how much there will be in the fund just after the eighth deposit.

3.28 Repeat Example 3.22, assuming that the maintenance costs are expected to increase at the rate of 12% per year.

3.29 Verify the formula given by equation (3.78).

3.30 Verify the formula given by equation (3.81).

3.31 Verify the formula given by equation (3.82).

3.32 Determine the values of the following factors:
(a) $(A/P, \infty\%, 10)$
(b) $(P/F, 0\%, 10)$
(c) $(F/A, \infty\%, 10)$
(d) $(F/A, 0\%, 10)$

3.33 Determine the values of the following factors:
(a) $(F/P, 0\%, 8)$
(b) $(P/G, 0\%, 8)$
(c) $(A/G, 0\%, 8)$
(d) $(A/G, 0\%, 8)$

3.34 Verify the following limit values:
(a) $\lim_{N \to \infty} (P/G, i\%, N) = \dfrac{1}{i^2}$
(b) $\lim_{N \to \infty} (P/A, i\%, N) = \dfrac{1}{i}$

3.35 Verify the following limit values:
(a) $\lim_{i \to 0} (A/F, i\%, N) = \dfrac{1}{N}$
(b) $\lim_{i \to 0} (P/A, i\%, N) = N$

3.36 Expenditures of $2,000 each are required at the end of the fourth, sixth, and eighth years of a 10-year study. Determine the present worth of these expenditures. Assume that the interest rate is 10%.

3.37 Determine the levelized annual cost of the three expenditures given in Problem 3.36, distributed over the 10 years of the study.

3.38 Assume that a company has a 7-year contract that requires end-of-year payments of $6,000 per year for years 1 through 3 an $4,000 per year for the remaining 4 years. Determine the levelized annual cost for this contract. Use i of 10%.

3.39 According to a story, a Dutchman named Mr. Pieter Minuit bought Manhattan Island from the Indians for 60 guilders (that was worth $24) in 1626. Assume that Mr. Minuit, instead of buying the island, invested the $24 at 7% interest compounded annually. Determine the value of such investment in 1991.

3.40 Resolve Problem 3.39 but assume that the interest rate is 5% and compare the results.

_____4

CONTINUOUS COMPOUNDING AND CONTINUOUS INTEREST FACTORS

Delays have dangerous ends.
SHAKESPEARE,
King Henry VI, Part I, Act III

It is double pleasure to deceive the deceiver.
JEAN DE LA FONTAINE, *Fables*, 1668

4.1 NOMINAL AND EFFECTIVE INTEREST RATES

In most engineering economy analyses a great accuracy is not usually required in interest calculations because the data used in the studies are based on forecasts of future costs and future events rather than on certain knowledge. Therefore, it is usually not necessary to differentiate whether the interest is compounded annually, semiannually, quarterly, or continuously. Thus, interest may be accounted for as if compounding occurs once a year, as was done in Chapter 3. However, there may be instances where it is important to take into account the compounding frequency and its effects, especially in finance and banking.

Interest rates are normally stated on an annual basis, e.g., an interest rate may be quoted as 18% compounded quarterly. Here, the 18% understood to be an annual rate, is called the *nominal interest rate*. Since a year is divided into four quarters, the interest rate per interest period is 4.5% per quarter. Therefore, the nominal interest rate is the annual interest rate disregarding the effect of end-of-period compounding where the periods are less than one year. Thus, the nominal (annual) interest rate can be expressed as

$$r = i \times M \tag{4.1}$$

where

r = nominal (annual) interest rate,

i = nominal interest rate per period (or effective interest rate per interest period),

M = number of compounding periods per year.

Therefore, in an example, the nominal interest rate is

$$r = (4.5\% / \text{quarter})(4 \text{ quarters}/\text{year})$$

$$= 18\% \text{ per year}$$

The *effective interest rate* is the annual rate including the effect of compounding at the end of periods shorter than one year. In other words the effective interest rate is the exact annual rate that takes into account the compounding that occurs within the year. Therefore, the effective interest rate is

$$i_{\text{eff}} = (1 + i)^M - 1 \tag{4.2}$$

or alternatively,

$$i_{\text{eff}} = \left(1 + \frac{r}{M}\right)^M - 1 \tag{4.3}$$

Hence, the effective interest rate for the previous example can be calculated either from equation (4.2) as

$$i_{\text{eff}} = (1 + 0.045)^4 - 1$$

$$= 0.1925 \text{ or } 19.25\% \text{ per year}$$

or from equation (4.3) as

$$i_{\text{eff}} = \left(1 + \frac{0.18}{4}\right)^4 - 1$$

$$= 0.1925 \text{ or } 19.25\% \text{ per year}$$

Alternatively, the effective interest rate can be calculated from

$$i_{\text{eff}} = \frac{F - P}{P} \tag{4.4}$$

or

$$i_{\text{eff}} = \frac{F}{P} - 1 \tag{4.5}$$

where

P = present amount,

F = future amount at the end of one year, which includes the principal plus interest.

As a general statement, from equation (3.2)

$$i_{\text{eff}} = \left(\frac{F}{P}\right)^{1/N} - 1 \qquad (4.6)$$

where

P = present amount,

F = future amount at the end of Nth year.

As can be observed from equation (4.3), the effective interest rate is a function of the number of compounding periods per year. As the number of compounding periods per year increases, the effective interest rate becomes greater. Table 4.1 presents the effect of compounding frequency on the effective interest rate for a nominal rate of 18%. Note that the effective (annual) interest rate always equals the nominal rate when compounding occurs annually.

In 1973, the U.S. Congress passed the *Truth-in-Lending Bill* so that the borrowers must be informed of the annual percentage rate corresponding to

TABLE 4.1   Comparisons of Nominal and Effective Rates

Compounding Frequency	Nominal Interest Rate (r) (%)	Number of Periods per year (M)	$i_{\text{eff}} = \left(1 + \dfrac{r}{M}\right)^{M} - 1$	Effective (Annual) Interest Rate (i_{eff}) (%)
Annually	18	1	$\left(1 + \dfrac{0.18}{1}\right)^{1} - 1$	18.0000
Semiannually	18	2	$\left(1 + \dfrac{0.18}{2}\right)^{2} - 1$	18.8100
Quarterly	18	4	$\left(1 + \dfrac{0.18}{4}\right)^{4} - 1$	19.2518
Monthly	18	12	$\left(1 + \dfrac{0.18}{12}\right)^{12} - 1$	19.5618
Weekly	18	52	$\left(1 + \dfrac{0.18}{52}\right)^{52} - 1$	19.6845
Daily	18	365	$\left(1 + \dfrac{0.18}{365}\right)^{365} - 1$	19.7164
Continuously	18	$\to \infty$	$e^{0.18} - 1$	19.7217

the loan transaction. Of course, as illustrated in Table 4.1, the rate is based on the lender's compounding frequency, thus, the percentage rate stated can be either the nominal annual interest rate, the effective annual interest rate, or some other percentage. Therefore, for example, a consumer paying an interest rate of 1.5% per month for a credit card charge account, in reality, pays an effective interest rate of 19.56% compounded annually, even though the annual percentage rate is quoted to be 18%. Thus, for the purpose of comparing different financial alternatives, one should always use the effective annual interest rate as the base.

Example 4.1   Assume that an engineer borrows $1,000 for a 3-year period. The loan will be paid back at the end of its term as a lump-sum payment of $1,643. Determine the effective interest rate involved.

Solution   From equation (4.6)

$$
\begin{aligned}
i_{\text{eff}} &= \left(\frac{F}{P}\right)^{1/N} - 1 \\
&= \left(\frac{1,643}{1,000}\right)^{1/3} - 1 \\
&= 0.18 \text{ or } 18\% \text{ per year}
\end{aligned}
$$

Example 4.2   A senior citizen decides to buy a used car from a friendly car dealer. The price of the car, including tax and other expenses, is $6,000. The down payment requested is $1,000. The car dealer recommends borrowing the remaining amount of $5,000 from the Honest Loaner Credit Agency to be paid in 36 monthly installments. The interest on the loan is 1.75% per month. The credit agency charges $40.00 for the credit investigation fee and requires that the citizen should purchase a 3-year credit risk insurance through its insurance company at a lump-sum cost of $900. Determine the following: (a) the amount of the monthly payments and (b) the annual effective interest rate that the individual will be paying.

Solution

(a) The total loan required can be calculated as

Loan requested =	$5,000
Credit investigation fee =	40
3-year credit risk insurance =	900
Total Loan =	$5,940

Therefore, total interest on the loan is

$$(\$5,940)(36)(0.0175) = \$3,742.20$$

Thus, the total amount borrowed is

$$\$5,940 + \$3,742.20 = \$9,682.20$$

Hence, the monthly installment can be found as

$$A = \frac{\$9,682.20}{36} = \$268.95 \text{ per month}$$

(b) Therefore, from equation (3.29)

$$A = P(A/P, i\%, 36)$$
$$\$268.95 = \$5,000(A/P, i\%, 36)$$

or

$$(P/A, i\%, 36) = \frac{\$5,000}{\$268.95}$$
$$= 18.59$$

From the tables in Appendix A by interpolation

$$i = 4.0135\% \text{ per month}$$

and therefore the annual effective interest rate is

$$i_{\text{eff}} = (1 + 0.040135)^{12} - 1$$
$$= 0.6035 \text{ or } 60.35\%$$

or alternatively

$$i_{\text{eff}} = (F/P, 4.0135\%, 12) - 1$$
$$= 0.6035 \text{ or } 60.35\%$$

Example 4.3 Repeat Example 3.21, using the effective interest rate concept.

Solution As the first step, the 12% annual interest rate can be transformed into the effective interest rate per 5 years as

$$(1 + 0.12)^5 - 1 = 1.7623 - 1$$
$$= 0.7623 \text{ or } 76.23\%$$

then the total present worth of the series of payments of $4,000 each 5 years starting today and lasting forever can be found as

$$P = \$4,000(P/A, 76.23\%, \infty) + \$4,000$$
$$= \$4,000(1.3118) + \$4,000$$
$$= \$9,247$$

where

$$(P/A, i\%, \infty) = \frac{1}{i}$$

so that

$$(P/A, 76.23\%, \infty) = \frac{1}{0.7623}$$
$$= 1.3118$$

4.2   CONTINUOUS COMPOUNDING

From equation (4.3), i.e.,

$$i_{\text{eff}} = \left(1 + \frac{r}{M}\right)^{M} - 1$$

it can be observed that if the number of compounding periods, M, per year continues to increase, then the duration of each period becomes less and less. Therefore, in the limit, the interest may be thought of being compounded infinitely, i.e., continuously. As M approaches infinity, the nominal interest rate per period, i.e., $i = r/M$, approaches zero. Thus, the effective (annual) interest rate can be defined as

$$i_{\text{eff}} = \lim_{M \to \infty} \left(1 + \frac{r}{M}\right)^{M} - 1 \tag{4.7}$$

or

$$i_{\text{eff}} = \lim_{M \to \infty} \left[\left(1 + \frac{r}{M}\right)^{M/r}\right]^{r} - 1 \tag{4.8}$$

Whereas, by definition

$$\lim_{M \to \infty} \left(1 + \frac{r}{M}\right)^{M/r} \overset{\Delta}{=} e \tag{4.9}$$

Substituting equation (4.9) into equation (4.8),

$$i_{\text{eff}} = e^{r} - 1 \tag{4.10}$$

Therefore, when interest is compounded continuously, the effective interest rate is equal to $e^r - 1$, where r is the nominal interest rate. As an example, the effective rate of 18% compounded continuously is 19.7217%, as given in Table 4.1. Note that the effective rates for compounding frequencies of more than 52 times per year show only a slight difference with respect to the continuous compounding.

In this book effective interest rates are denoted by i and are understood as i% per period compounded per period. In cases where the compounding and interest periods are not the same, the associated effective interest rate can be determined, as illustrated in Table 4.1. Further, the compound interest factors derived in Chapter 3 and the tables given in Appendix A are all developed on the basis of effective interest rate, i.e., for an interest rate i stated as *percent per period compounded per period*, e.g., 10% per year compounded yearly, or 4% per quarter compounded quarterly, or 2% per month compounded monthly, and so on. Therefore, whenever the interest period and the compounding period are not agreeable, then the necessary conversion, using equation (4.3) or (4.10), whichever is appropriate, must be made before the interest tables can be employed.

Furthermore, the nominal interest rates with different numbers of annual compounding cannot be compared to one another until they have been converted into the corresponding effective interest rates.

4.3 CONTINUOUS COMPOUNDING INTEREST FORMULAS

In certain economic situations one may be forced to increase the precision in interest calculations by using continuous compounding rather than discrete compounding. This would require having two additional sets of compound interest factors depending on whether the cash flows involved are discrete or continuous.

4.3.1 Interest Formulas for Continuous Compounding and Discrete Cash Flows

If the interest is compounded continuously and the cash flows are occurring at the beginning or end of any period, the continuous compound interest rate may be converted to its equivalent effective (annual) interest rate by using equation (4.10) so that

$$i_{\text{eff}} = e^r - 1$$

Therefore, a new set of interest factors can be found by using a simple substitution process. For example, from equation (3.2), the single-payment compound amount is

$$F = P(1 + i)^N$$

Substituting equation (4.10) into equation (3/2),

$$F = P(1 + i_{\text{eff}})^N$$

or

$$F = P[1 + (e^r - 1)]^N$$

or

$$F = P(e^{rN}) \qquad (4.11)$$

Equation (4.11) gives the formula for determining the compound amount, F, that can be obtained in N years under continuous compounding from a present amount of P.

From equation (4.11), the *single-payment continuous compounding compound amount factor* can be defined as

$$\frac{F}{P} = e^{rN} \qquad (4.12)$$

where r is the nominal annual interest rate. Alternatively, it can be expressed as

$$\frac{F}{P} = (F/P, \, r\%, \, N) \qquad (4.13)$$

It is read as to find F under continuous compounding, given discrete P, $r\%$, and N. Therefore, equation (4.11) can be expressed as

$$F = P(F/P, \, r\%, \, N) \qquad (4.14)$$

Similarly, from equation (4.11), the present worth of a future sum under continuous compounding can be found as

$$P = F\left(\frac{1}{e^{rN}}\right) \qquad (4.15)$$

and therefore the *single-payment continuous compounding present worth factor* can be defined as

$$\frac{P}{F} = \frac{1}{e^{rN}} \qquad (4.16)$$

or

$$(P/F, \, r\%, \, N) = \frac{1}{e^{rN}} \qquad (4.17)$$

It is read as to find P under continuous compounding, given discrete F, $r\%$, and N.

Also, substituting equation (4.10) into (3.13) gives the formula for determining the discrete uniform-series continuous compounding compound amount as

$$F = A\left[\frac{(1 + i_{\text{eff}})^N - 1}{i_{\text{eff}}}\right] \tag{4.18}$$

or

$$F = A\left(\frac{e^{rN} - 1}{e^r - 1}\right) \tag{4.19}$$

where

$$\frac{F}{A} = \frac{e^{rN} - 1}{e^r - 1} \tag{4.20}$$

or

$$(F/A, r\%, N) = \frac{e^{rN} - 1}{e^r - 1} \tag{4.21}$$

is called the *discrete uniform-series continuous compounding compound amount factor*. It is read as to find F under continuous compounding, given discrete uniform-series A, $r\%$, and N.

From equation (4.19) the formula for determining the discrete uniform-series continuous compounding sinking fund amount can be found as

$$A = F\left(\frac{e^r - 1}{e^{rN} - 1}\right) \tag{4.22}$$

where

$$\frac{A}{F} = \frac{e^r - 1}{e^{rN} - 1} \tag{4.23}$$

or

$$(A/F, r\%, N) = \frac{e^r - 1}{e^{rN} - 1} \tag{4.24}$$

is called the *discrete uniform-series continuous compounding sinking-fund factor*. It is read as to find A under continuous compounding, given F, $r\%$, and N.

Similarly, substituting equation (4.10) into equation (3.21) gives the formula for determining the present worth of discrete uniform-series under continuous compounding as

$$P = A\left[\frac{(1 + i_{\text{eff}})^N - 1}{i_{\text{eff}}(1 + i_{\text{eff}})^N}\right] \tag{4.25}$$

or

$$P = A\left[\frac{e^{rN} - 1}{e^{rN}(e^r - 1)}\right] \tag{4.26}$$

where

$$\frac{P}{A} = \frac{e^{rN} - 1}{e^{rN}(e^r - 1)} \tag{4.27}$$

or

$$(P/A, r\%, N) = \frac{e^{rN} - 1}{e^{rN}(e^r - 1)} \tag{4.28}$$

is called the *discrete uniform-series continuous compounding present worth factor*. It is read as to find P under continuous compounding, given discrete uniform-series A, $r\%$, and N.

From equation (4.26) the formula for determining the discrete uniform-series continuous compounding capital recovery amount can be found as

$$A = P\left[\frac{e^{rN}(e^r - 1)}{e^{rN} - 1}\right] \tag{4.29}$$

where

$$\frac{A}{P} = \frac{e^{rN}(e^r - 1)}{e^{rN} - 1} \tag{4.30}$$

or

$$(A/P, r\%, N) = \frac{e^{rN}(e^r - 1)}{e^{rN} - 1} \tag{4.31}$$

is called the *discrete uniform-series continuous compounding capital recovery factor*. It is read as to find A under discrete compounding, given P, $r\%$, and N.

The compound interest factors derived for continuous compounding and discrete cash flows are summarized in Table 4.2. The associated interest tables are not included in this book due to the facts that (1) continuous compounding with discrete cash flows is not frequently used in engineering economy studies and (2) the results obtained using continuous compounding are very close to the results obtained using monthly compounding with a nominal rate r. The interested can easily calculate the desired factors using the given equations in this section.

Example 4.4   Assume that you will be making a uniform-series of year-end deposits of $500 each for the next 10 years at a 10% interest rate compounded continuously. Determine the following:

(a) The effective interest rate.
(b) The present worth of the uniform payments.

TABLE 4.2 Summary of Continuous Compounding Interest Factors for Discrete Cash Flows

To Find	Given	Multiply Given by Factor	Symbol	Name
P	F	e^{-rN}	$(P/F, r\%, N)$	Continuous compounding present worth factor (discrete, single payment)
F	P	e^{rN}	$(F/P, r\%, N)$	Continuous compounding compound amount factor (discrete, single payment)
P	A	$\dfrac{e^{rN}-1}{e^{rN}(e^{r}-1)}$	$(P/A, r\%, N)$	Continuous compounding present worth factor (discrete, uniform series)
A	P	$\dfrac{e^{rN}(e^{r}-1)}{e^{rN}-1}$	$(A/P, r\%, N)$	Continuous compounding capital recovery factor (discrete, uniform series)
F	A	$\dfrac{e^{rN}-1}{e^{r}-1}$	$(F/A, r\%, N)$	Continuous compounding compound amount factor (discrete, uniform series)
A	F	$\dfrac{e^{r}-1}{e^{rN}-1}$	$(A/F, r\%, N)$	Continuous compounding sinking-fund factor (discrete, uniform series)

Key: P = present worth, F = future worth, A = uniform-series amount (occurs at the end of each year), r = nominal interest rate (per year, compounded continuously), N = number of annual periods (years).

Solution

(a) The effective interest rate is

$$i_{eff} = e^r - 1$$
$$= e^{0.10} - 1$$
$$= 0.1052 \text{ or } 10.52\%$$

(b) The present worth of the uniform payments is

$$P = A(P/A, 10.52\%, 10)$$
$$= \$500(6.0104)$$
$$= \$3,005$$

where

$$(P/A, 10.52\%, 10) = \frac{(1 + 0.1052)^{10} - 1}{0.1052(1 + 0.1052)^{10}}$$
$$= 6.0104$$

or alternatively,

$$P = \$500(P/A, r\%, 10)$$
$$= \$500\left[\frac{e^{rN} - 1}{e^{rN}(e^r - 1)} \right]$$
$$= \$500\left[\frac{e^{0.10 \times 10} - 1}{e^{0.10 \times 10}(e^{0.10} - 1)} \right]$$
$$= \$500(6.0104)$$
$$= \$3,005$$

Example 4.5   Use the equation given in Example 4.4 and determine the following:

(a) The future worth of the deposits at the end of the 10th year.
(b) Assume that the first deposit is made now and the remaining nine deposits are made at the end of every year for the next 9 years, and determine the future worth of the deposits at the end of the 10th year.

Solution

(a) The future worth is

$$F = A(F/A, 10.52\%, 10)$$

$$= \$500\left[\frac{(1 + 0.1052)^{10} - 1}{0.1052}\right]$$

$$= \$500(16.3403)$$

$$= \$8,169$$

or

$$F = \$500\left(\frac{e^{rN} - 1}{e^r - 1}\right)$$

$$= \$500\left(\frac{e^{0.10 \times 10} - 1}{e^{0.10} - 1}\right)$$

$$= \$500(16.3403)$$

$$= \$8,169$$

or alternatively,

$$F = P(F/P, r\%, 10)$$

$$= \$3,005(e^{0.10 \times 10})$$

$$= \$8,169$$

(b) The future worth at the end of the 10th year is

$$F = [\$500(F/P, r\%, 9) + \$500(F/A, r\%, 9)](F/P, r\%, 1)$$

$$= \left[\$500(e^{0.10 \times 9}) + \$500\left(\frac{e^{0.10 \times 9} - 1}{e^{0.10} - 1}\right)\right](e^{0.10})$$

$$= \$9,027$$

or alternatively,

$$F = [\$500 + \$500(P/A, r\%, 9)](F/P, r\%, 10)$$

$$= \$9,027$$

4.3.2   Interest Formulas for Continuous Compounding and Continuous Cash Flows

In some economic situations the assumption of continuous cash flows rather than discrete ones may be more realistic. For example, operating and maintenance costs, inventory costs, labor costs, or cash receipts are among the typical examples that can be represented best by a uniform cash flow that flows continuously during a given time period at a uniform rate.

In order to represent such funds that are uniformly distributed continuous cash flows, as shown in Figure 4.1, instead of discrete amounts at one point in time, a new set of continuous compounding interest factors are required. Such factors are also known as the funds flow factors.

The formula for determining the continuous compounding compound amount with continuous uniform payments can be derived as

$$F = \bar{A} \left(\frac{e^{rN} - 1}{r} \right) \tag{4.32}$$

where

F = future worth (single payment),
$\bar{A}$ = amount of money (or equivalent value) flowing continuously and uniformly during each period,
r = nominal annual interest rate,
N = number of annual periods (years).

Therefore,

$$\frac{F}{\bar{A}} = \frac{e^{rN} - 1}{r} \tag{4.33}$$

or

$$(F/\bar{A}, r\%, N) = \frac{e^{rN} - 1}{r} \tag{4.34}$$

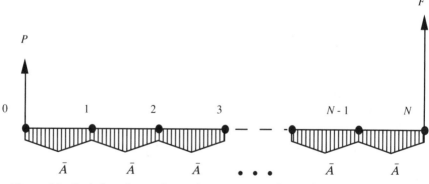

Figure 4.1 Cash flow diagram for continuous compounding uniform cash flow factors.

is called the *continuous uniform-flow continuous compounding compound amount factor*. It is read as to find F under continuous compounding, given continuous uniform payment $\bar{A}$, $r\%$, and N.

From equation (4.32) the formula for determining the continuous compounding sinking-fund amount with continuous uniform payments can be found as

$$\bar{A} = F\left(\frac{r}{e^{rN} - 1}\right) \tag{4.35}$$

where

$$\frac{\bar{A}}{F} = \frac{r}{e^{rN} - 1} \tag{4.36}$$

or

$$(\bar{A}/F, r\%, N) = \frac{r}{e^{rN} - 1} \tag{4.37}$$

is called the *continuous uniform-flow continuous compounding sinking-fund factor*. It is read as to find continuous uniform payment $\bar{A}$ under continuous compounding, given F, $r\%$, and N.

Similarly, the formula for determining continuous compounding present worth of continuous uniform payments can be derived as

$$P = \bar{A}\left(\frac{e^{rN} - 1}{re^{rN}}\right) \tag{4.38}$$

where

$$\frac{P}{\bar{A}} = \frac{e^{rN} - 1}{re^{rN}} \tag{4.39}$$

or

$$(P/\bar{A}, r\%, N) = \frac{e^{rN} - 1}{re^{rN}} \tag{4.40}$$

is called the *continuous uniform-flow continuous compounding present worth factor*. It is read as to find P under continuous compounding, given continuous uniform payment $\bar{A}$, $r\%$, and N.

From equation (4.38) the formula for determining the continuous compounding capital recovery amount with continuous uniform payments can be found as

$$\bar{A} = P\left(\frac{re^{rN}}{e^{rN} - 1}\right) \tag{4.41}$$

where

$$\frac{\bar{A}}{P} = \frac{re^{rN}}{e^{rN} - 1} \tag{4.42}$$

or

$$(\bar{A}/P, \, r\%, \, N) = \frac{re^{rN}}{e^{rN} - 1} \tag{4.43}$$

is called the *continuous uniform-flow continuous compounding capital recovery factor*. It is read as to find continuous uniform payment $\bar{A}$ under continuous compounding, given P, $r\%$, and N.

The compound interest factors derived for continuous compounding and continuous uniform cash flows are summarized in Table 4.3. The associated interest tables are also not included in this book because of the reasons given previously. Again, the interested reader can easily calculate the desired factors using the equations in this section.

TABLE 4.3 Summary of Continuous Compounding Interest Factors for Continuous Uniform Cash Flows

To Find	Given	Multiply Given by Factor	Symbol	Name
P	F	e^{-rN}	$(P/F, r\%, N)$	Continuous compounding present worth factor (discrete, single payment)
F	P	e^{rN}	$(F/P, r\%, N)$	Continuous compounding compound amount factor (discrete, single payment)
P	$\bar{A}$	$\dfrac{e^{rN} - 1}{re^{rN}}$	$(P/\bar{A}, r\%, N)$	Continuous compounding present worth factor (continuous, uniform flow)
$\bar{A}$	P	$\dfrac{re^{rN}}{e^{rN} - 1}$	$(\bar{A}/P, r\%, N)$	Continuous compounding capital recovery factor (continuous, uniform flow)
F	$\bar{A}$	$\dfrac{e^{rN} - 1}{r}$	$(F/\bar{A}, r\%, N)$	Continuous compounding compound amount factor (continuous, uniform flow)
$\bar{A}$	F	$\dfrac{r}{e^{rN} - 1}$	$(\bar{A}/F, r\%, N)$	Continuous compounding sinking-fund factor (continuous, uniform flow)

Key: P = present worth (single payment), F = future worth (single payment), $\bar{A}$ = amount of money flowing continuously and uniformly during each period, r = nominal interest rate (per year compounded continuously), N = number of annual periods (years).

Note that if there is no flow of payments, such as the case with the present worth and compound amount factors, i.e., P/F and F/P, given in Table 4.3, these factors are identical to those for continuous compounding discrete cash flow factors. However, if the payment is a single continuous payment, as shown in Figure 4.2, then the factors are not the same.

Therefore, the formula for determining continuous compounding present worth of a single continuous future payment can be derived as

$$P = \bar{F}\left(\frac{e^r - 1}{re^{rN}}\right) \tag{4.44}$$

where

$\bar{F}$ = future amount of single continuous and uniform payment (payments during the Nth period only),

P = present worth (single payment).

Therefore,

$$\frac{P}{F} = \frac{e^r - 1}{re^{rN}} \tag{4.45}$$

or

$$(P/\bar{F}, r\%, N) = \frac{e^r - 1}{re^{rN}} \tag{4.46}$$

is called the *single continuous uniform-payment continuous compounding present worth factor*. It is read as to find P under continuous compounding, given single continuous uniform payment $\bar{F}$, $r\%$, and N.

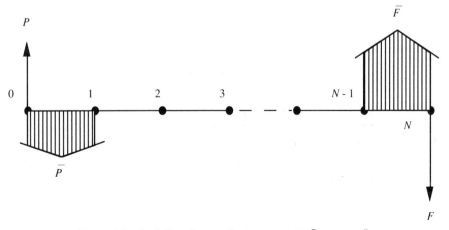

Figure 4.2 Cash flow diagram for factors of $(P/\bar{F})$ and $(F/\bar{P})$.

From equation (4.44) the formula for determining the continuous compounding single uniform-payment amount can be derived as

$$\bar{F} = P\left(\frac{re^{rN}}{e^r - 1}\right) \tag{4.47}$$

where

$$\frac{\bar{F}}{P} = \frac{re^{rN}}{e^r - 1} \tag{4.48}$$

or

$$(\bar{F}/P, r\%, N) = \frac{re^{rN}}{e^r - 1} \tag{4.49}$$

is called the *single continuous uniform-payment continuous compounding compound amount factor*. It is read as to find single continuous uniform payment $\bar{F}$ under continuous compounding, given P, $r\%$, and N.

On the other hand the formula for determining continuous compounding present worth as a single continuous uniform payment from a discrete single future payment is

$$\bar{P} = F\left[\frac{re^r}{e^{rN}(e^r - 1)}\right] \tag{4.50}$$

where

$\bar{P}$ = present amount as a single continuous and uniform payment (payments during the first period only),

F = future amount (single payment).

Therefore,

$$\frac{\bar{P}}{F} = \frac{re^r}{e^{rN}(e^r - 1)} \tag{4.51}$$

or

$$(\bar{P}/F, r\%, N) = \frac{re^r}{e^{rN}(e^r - 1)} \tag{4.52}$$

is called the *single continuous uniform-payment continuous compounding present worth factor*. It is read as to find single continuous uniform payment $\bar{P}$ under continuous compounding, given F, $r\%$, and N.

From equation (4.50) the formula for determining the continuous compounding compound amount as a discrete single future payment from a single continuous uniform payment is

$$F = \bar{P}\left[\frac{e^{rN}(e^r - 1)}{re^r}\right] \tag{4.53}$$

where

$$\frac{F}{\bar{P}} = \frac{e^{rN}(e^r - 1)}{re^r} \tag{4.54}$$

or

$$(F/\bar{P}, r\%, N) = \frac{e^{rN}(e^r - 1)}{re^r} \tag{4.55}$$

is called the *single continuous uniform-payment continuous compounding compound amount factor*. It is read as to find F under continuous compounding, given single continuous uniform payment $\bar{P}$, $r\%$, and N.

Example 4.6 Assume that there will be a uniform series of continuous expenditures totaling $5,000 annually for the next 7 years and that the interest rate will be compounded continuously at 12% per year and determine the equivalent (a) present worth and (b) future worth of the series.

Solution

(a) The equivalent present worth is

$$P = \$5,000(P/\bar{A}, r\%, N)$$

$$= \$5,000\left(\frac{e^{rN} - 1}{re^{rN}}\right)$$

$$= \$5,000\left(\frac{e^{0.12 \times 7} - 1}{0.12e^{0.12 \times 7}}\right)$$

$$= \$23,679$$

(b) The equivalent future worth is

$$F = \$5,000(F/\bar{A}, r\%, N)$$

$$= \$5,000\left(\frac{e^{rN} - 1}{r}\right)$$

$$= \$5,000\left(\frac{e^{0.12 \times 7} - 1}{0.12}\right)$$

$$= \$54,849$$

or alternatively,

$$F = P(F/P, r\%, N)$$

$$= \$23,679(e^{rN})$$

$$= \$23,679(e^{0.12 \times 7})$$

$$= \$54,849$$

PROBLEMS

4.1 What is the effective annual interest rate if the nominal interest rate is 10.5% compounded bimonthly?

4.2 What is the effective interest rate per year when $500 is borrowed at a rate of 2% compounded monthly?

4.3 If you can purchase a garden tractor for $525 cash or for $45 down and $65 a month for 8 months, what is the effective interest rate of the installment payments?

4.4 What is the effective interest rate per year if the rate is 8% per quarter?

4.5 A lender charges $1\frac{3}{4}\%$ per month. What is the simple effective rate of interest charged the borrower?

4.6 A borrower must make a decision between choosing a bank with an interest rate of 0.8% per month and a finance company charging a nominal interest rate of 9% compounded semiannually. Which should she select?

4.7 If $2,000 were deposited now, how much additional interest would accrue after 3 years in a continuously compounding account versus one that compounds interest quarterly? Let 10% be the nominal interest rate.

4.8 What amount has been accrued after 20 years if $2,000 is compounded quarterly at 8% per year?

4.9 If the interest rate is 6%, how long will it take $200 compounded semiannually to grow to $400?

4.10 An engineering student wants to purchase a used car from a local used-car lot. The car dealer offers two different purchasing options: (1) the student can purchase the car for $1,200 paying it in cash or (2) he can purchase the car on credit with a monthly installment plan for 12 months. If the credit purchasing plan is selected, there will be a credit investigation fee of $25 and a 12% interest charge based on a selling price of $1,300. Determine the following:

(a) The amount of the monthly payments.
(b) The actual monthly interest rate.
(c) The annual nominal interest rate.
(d) The annual effective interest rate.

4.11 Assume that a graduate student has purchased a car for $1,800 on a 24-month installment plan with equal monthly payments. The price included taxes and other expenses. The interest rate was 2% per month. The student was required to pay the first installment at the time of the purchase as the down payment. After making 10 monthly payments, she sold the car, on the due date for the 11th payment, for a cash amount of $450. The new buyer also agreed to pay the 11th payment and the remaining payments. Determine the following:

(a) The amount of the monthly payments.

(b) The cost of the car to the new buyer.

4.12 When the purchase of raw materials are made through credit, occasionally the credit terms may involve both the length of the credit period and the discount given. For example, assume that the ABC Company has just received an invoice with the payment terms "2/15, net 45." Here, the terms "2/15, net 45" mean that a 2% discount is given if the bill is paid before the 15th day after the date of invoice; otherwise the payment is due by the 45th day. The credit period, then, is 45 days. Determine the annual effective interest rate that is equivalent to the given discount.

4.13 When he finally started to work on his 25th birthday, Mr. Joe Notsosmarth decided to invest money each month with the objective of becoming a millionaire by the time he reaches his 65th birthday. Assume that the average return on the investments will be 12% per annum, compounded monthly, and determine the monthly amount that he should be investing each month.

4.14 Assume that you are required to pay off a $6,000 loan with uniform monthly payments in 5 years and that the associated nominal interest rate is 18%, compounded monthly. Determine the amount of the monthly payments.

4.15 Assume that a friendly loan shark loans money at 10% per month. Find the associated nominal interest rate and the effective interest rate.

4.16 Assume that a $1,000 deposit has been made today. Determine its future worth at the end of 4 years if the interest rate of 10% is compounded (a) annually, (b) quarterly, (c) monthly, and (d) continuously.

4.17 How many years will it take an investment to quadruple itself if the interest rate is 15% compounded (a) annually and (b) continuously?

4.18 Assume that the interest rate of an investment of $30,000 is 7% compounded continuously, and that $6,500 is received each year. Determine the number of years necessary to recover the investment with the required return.

4.19 Repeat Example 4.4, assuming that the interest rate is 15% and there are five end-of-year payments.

4.20 Repeat Example 4.5, using the data given in Problem 4.19.

4.21 Assume that the ABC Manufacturing Company is considering replacing an aging piece of equipment for $75,000 at the end of the next 10 years. Determine the amount of uniform semiannual deposits into a sinking fund required in order to accumulate the $75,000 at the end of the 10th year at 12% interest compounded continuously.

4.22 Repeat Example 4.4, assuming continuous cash flows.

4.23 Repeat Example 4.5, assuming continuous cash flows.

4.24 Determine the total funds accumulated by each of the following continuous funds:

(a) $1,000 per month in 10 years at 10% compounded continuously.

(b) $12,000 per year in 10 years at 10% compounded continuously.

4.25 Repeat Problem 4.21 with the semiannual deposits given in terms of continuous flow of funds.

4.26 A used-car dealer advertises an "18% loan" for 12 months on "add-on" auto loans. Assume that the loan is $2,000 and determine the following:

(a) The monthly payment.

(b) The nominal interest rate.

(c) The effective interest rate.

____5
COMPARISON OF INVESTMENT ALTERNATIVES

Egyptian Proverb: The worst things:
To be in bed and sleep not,
To want for one who comes not,
To try to please and please not.
FRANCIS SCOTT FITZGERALD,
Notebooks, **1945**

5.1 DECISION-MAKING PROCESS

It is generally accepted that decision making is not a precise activity. For instance, the quantitative disciplines view decision making as a rational process approximating the scientific method. Furthermore, it is often not clear why a decision is needed or whether a decision made was effective. Nevertheless, there are some fundamental principles and logical steps that can be followed to reach a sound decision.

Figure 5.1(*a*) shows the basic steps involved in a typical decision-making process in engineering. The process starts with the recognition of a problem and ends with the determination of the best alternative solution to the problem. The process is further strengthened by inclusion of postaudit of the result and feedback. Figure 5.1(*b*) shows the main steps of a typical decision-making process involved in engineering economy. This process is primarily used for comparing investment alternatives. Of course, the behavioral attitude of the management and the decision maker, the organizational environment for decision making, existing company policies, the amount of information available, the nature of legal and financial restrictions, pressures of competition, limited time for making the decision, and even the social and cultural environment for the decision influence and shape the way that decisions are made in a given organization. By the same token, engineering economics should be considered at best as an aide to sound judgment and not a substitute for it.

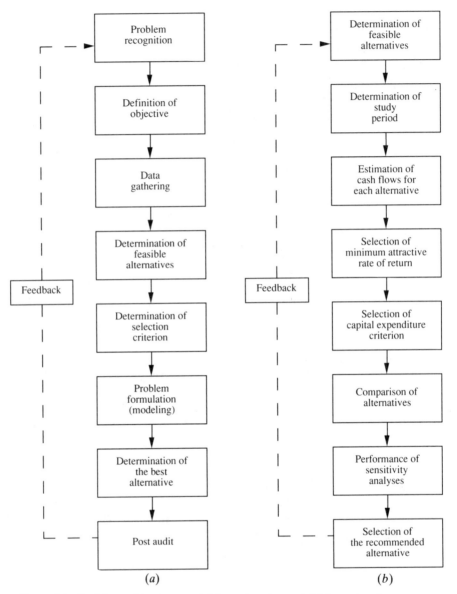

Figure 5.1 Decision-making process (a) in engineering and (b) in engineering economy.

5.2 TYPES OF INVESTMENT ALTERNATIVES

Depending on the circumstances, the feasible investment alternatives may be independent, mutually exclusive, or contingent alternatives.

When the selection of an alternative from a given set of alternatives has no effect on the selection or rejection of any other alternative in the set, the alternative is defined as an *independent alternative*, and such a set is called the set of independent alternatives. For example, assume that there are two projects, namely A and B, in a given set of alternatives and that capital, or funds, are unlimited. The available options are to accept any, all, or none of the alternatives. In a sense each alternative is compared one to one against the *do-nothing*, or *status-quo*, alternative. Independent project alternatives are often descriptively called *opportunities*.

When the selection of an alternative from a given set of alternatives excludes the selection of any other alternative, the alternatives are defined as *mutually exclusive alternatives*. Here, the term *mutually exclusive* signals that an *either–or but not both* situation exists. In other words the investor cannot have the cake and eat it too. For example, on a vacant particular piece of land, there can be a drive-in restaurant or a gas station built, but not both. Most of the problems encountered in engineering economy textbooks are of this type. The student is required to select the best solution from a set of mutually exclusive alternative solutions to a problem. Here, the objective is to minimize costs or maximize profits or savings. For example, if the alternatives involve costs only, then the alternative with lowest equivalent cost is selected. On the other hand, if the alternatives involve both costs and benefits, in terms of revenues or savings, then the alternative that maximizes the net equivalent benefit is selected. Of course, if the do-nothing alternative is available, it should always be taken into account.

When the selection of an alternative is conditional on the choice of one or more other prerequisite investment alternatives, such an alternative is defined as *contingent* or *conditional*. The term is an appropriate one because the selection of a contingent (conditional) alternative is dependent on the selection of some prerequisite alternative. However, the selection of the prerequisite alternative is independent of the contingent alternative. For example, the decision to build a higher stack or to install devices to collect sulfur dioxide after the fuel is burned may be contingent (or conditionally dependent) on the decision to build a coal-fueled power plant.

When alternatives are related to each other in any way that influences the selection process, the alternatives are defined as *dependent* alternatives. The dependence between the alternatives may be economical, technical, or some other type.

At times, due to government regulations, safety considerations, labor union contracts, production requirements, or for some other reasons, selection of one alternative from a set of mutually exclusive alternatives is required (or mandated). Such an alternative is called *mandatory investment*. For example, selection of a pollution control device from a mutually exclusive alternative, i.e., various types of pollution control devices, is a mandatory investment.

5.3   THE MINIMUM ATTRACTIVE RATE OF RETURN

The interest rate or discount rate to be used in comparison and evaluation of investment alternatives is known as the minimum attractive rate of return (MARR). It is a lower limit for investment acceptability set by the firm. The management of the firm would not accept investment proposals yielding less than the MARR even if the capital budget were not exhausted. In other words the management feels that below this cut-off rate the return is insufficient to justify the risk assumed by the company on that investment venture. The minimum attractive rates of return vary widely according to the type of industry, company, and even within the divisions of a given company. However, some companies establish a standard discount rate or MARR to be used in all economy analyses.

It is possible to view the MARR as a rate at which the company can have numerous projects to provide such a return. Therefore, any time an amount of capital is invested into an investment project an opportunity to invest that amount elsewere at the MARR has been foregone. Thus, the MARR can be defined as the *cost of opportunity foregone.*

Capital rationing occurs whenever the funds available for investment are insufficient to allow the company to accept all otherwise acceptable investment proposals. After the available capital allocated to the most favorable proposals, the lowest prospective rate of return within the budget available then becomes the MARR. Under normal circumstances the MARR is set much higher than the cost of capital due to the risk and uncertainty involved. In evaluating investment proposals an MARR should be used even if the funds are provided from internal sources.

The proper determination of the MARR is a controversial subject. Over the years there has been much discussion of how to determine it. The attempts for accurately determining the MARR have not been completely satisfactory so far. In addition to the aforementioned approaches to establish the MARR, there are other methods that have been suggested. For example, White et al. [74][†] give the following approaches:

1. Add a fixed percentage to the firm's cost of capital.
2. Average rate of return over the past five years is used as this year's MARR.

[†]Reprinted from J. A. White, M. H. Agee, and K. E. Case, *Principles of Engineering Economy Analysis.* Copyright © 1977. Used by permission of John Wiley & Sons. Inc.

3. Use different MARR for different planning horizons.
4. Use different MARR for different magnitudes of initial investment.
5. Use different MARR for new ventures than for cost improvement projects.
6. Use a management tool to stimulate or discourage capital investments, depending on the overall economic condition of the firm.
7. Use the average stockholder's return on investment for all companies in the same industry group.

Succinctly put, there is no *one best way* of determining the MARR to use in any given firm. Nor is it possible to express typical MARRs for typical industries with any degree of confidence. The MARR is affected by the availability of money, availability of investment opportunities, business conditions, inflation rates, prime rates, cost of capital of the firm, other economic conditions, business conditions, tax laws, government regulations, management's risk aversion level, the future economic climate as perceived by the management, and the level of risk and/or uncertainty involved.

The minimum attractive rate of return can be an after-tax or before-tax rate or return. The relation between the after-tax MARR and before-tax MARR can be expressed as

$$MARR_{(before-tax)} \cong \frac{MARR_{(after-tax)}}{1-t} \qquad (5.1)$$

where

$MARR_{(before-tax)}$ = before-tax minimum attractive rate of return,
$MARR_{(after-tax)}$ = after-tax minimum attractive rate of return,
t = combined income tax rate (including federal, state, and municipal income tax rates) for a given level of taxable income.

For instance, assume that the after-tax MARR for a given investment project is 15% and that the combined income tax rate is given as 50%.[†] The before-tax MARR that is required from the project can be calculated as

$$MARR_{(before-tax)} \cong \frac{0.15}{1-0.50}$$
$$= 0.30 \text{ or } 30\%$$

The relationship given in equation (5.1) would be exact, rather than an approximate one as it is given, if there are no interest charges on debt capital, i.e., the capital is a 100% equity, and there are no depreciation

[†]Of course, at the present time, the combined income tax rate is much smaller.

expense charges, i.e., the salvage value is equal to the first cost or the useful life of the asset is infinite.

The use of an after-tax rate of return is appropriate since the use of higher before-tax rate of returns causes one to discount the future benefits too greatly and therefore decreases the importance of future dollars. This, in turn, may cause the acceptance of an inferior alternative.

Sometimes, the cost of financing a project is called the *cost of capital* and is usually expressed as an annual rate or percentage. One of the easier ways to calculate the cost of capital is to determine the cost of capital for each individual source of funds, e.g., debt, equity, and so on, and then to combine these costs to find a weighted average or effective cost of capital on the composite capital for the firm. Therefore, the cost of capital can be expressed as

$$i_c = r_d \cdot i_d + (1 - r_d)i_e \qquad (5.2)$$

where

r_d = debt ratio,
   = ratio of debt to total capital,
$1 - r_d$ = ratio of equity to total capital,
i_d = rate of return required on debt capital,
i_e = rate of return required on equity capital.

For example, assume that two-fifths of a firm's capital is borrowed at 15% and that the rest is equity capital earning 12%. The cost of capital can be found as

$$i_c = (\tfrac{2}{5})(0.15) + (1 - \tfrac{2}{5})(0.12)$$
$$= 0.06 + 0.072$$
$$= 0.132 \text{ or } 13.2\%$$

5.4   SELECTION OF PROPER STUDY PERIOD

The study period, or so-called planning horizon, defines the period of time over which the economical analysis is to be carried out. In general, in a given economic analysis, the cash flows that take place before and after the study period are not taken into account, unless they might affect cash flows over the study period. In practice, there may be three different situations involving study periods:

1. The alternatives have equal useful lives.
2. The alternatives have unequal useful lives.
3. The alternatives have perpetual useful lives.

Ideally, alternatives should always be compared over identical time periods. Therefore, if the alternatives have equal useful lives, the common useful life should be used as the study period for the economic analysis. Note that the useful life of an alternative (or asset) is based mainly on economic considerations and is usually shorter than the functional life. In engineering economy studies the term *useful life* defines the economical life.

On the other hand, if the alternatives have unequal useful lives, it would be categorically wrong to compare, e.g., alternative A with cheaper but shorter-lived alternative B without first raising the question of what takes place when alternative B expires. For example, if alternative B must be replaced, then the replacement costs and estimates of other cash flows should be incorporated in the study. Whereas, if the replacement of B is not necessary, perhaps due to a loss of original requirement, then alternative A should be compared on the basis of the shorter useful life provided that its salvage value at the end of the study period is taken into account. In other words the two alternatives should be evaluated on the basis of equal study period, whether it is the longer useful life of alternative A, the shorter useful life of alternative B, or some other appropriate time period. The aforementioned method is known as the study period method and is based on the assumption known as the co-terminated assumption.

Note that the do-nothing alternative does not exist and that the objective is to select either alternative A or B, which have useful lives of 10 to 25 years, respectively.

The second method that can be used to compare alternatives with unequal useful lives is known as the least common-multiple of lives method. It is the most popular method used in the engineering economy literature. It is based on the assumption known as the service continuity assumption or the repeatability assumption, i.e., the assumption that an investment alternative will be replaced by an identical alternative until a least common multiple of lives is reached. For example, if one alternative had a 4-year life and the other a 6-year life, it would be necessary to use a 12-year period as the study period. Therefore, in the associated economic comparison study, the alternatives with the 4-year life and 6-year life would have to be replaced three and two times, respectively. Here, it is assumed that the cash flows that are estimated to happen in the first life cycle will be identical in all succeeding life cycles, if any, for each alternative. However, despite its popularity this method is inadequate in periods of rapid inflation and especially inappropriate in the situations where certain types of technological advances may have happened with replacement alternatives being available other than those originally considered. These disadvantages are particularly paramount when the least common multiple is large.

The least common-multiple of lives method also fails when the alternatives involved have longer useful lives. For example, if alternatives A and B have useful lives of 11 and 17 years, respectively, as shown in Figure 5.2, then the least common multiple of lives is 187 years, which is not so realistic. Therefore, in such situations, the study period should be determined based

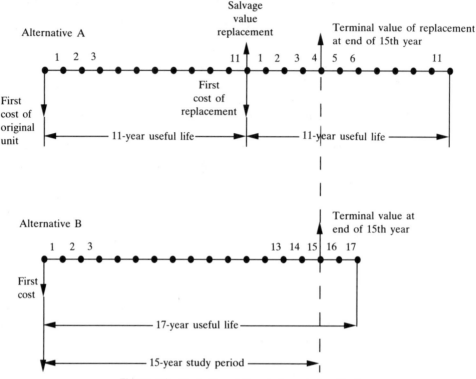

Figure 5.2 Illustration of the study period method.

on the length of time the asset is probably to be needed. Of course, this approach requires that terminal values be estimated for the alternatives at the end of the study period. This terminal value can be determined somewhat arbitrarily by prorating the investment in the asset over its normal useful life and then computing the portion of the unrecovered amount at the time of termination. However, a better estimate can be obtained when it is possible to determine the market value of the asset at that time.

Some prefer to have a *flexible* standard study period. "All of the 'routine' economic analyses would be based on the standard planning horizon of, say, five to 10 years; nonroutine economic analyses would be based on a planning horizon that was appropriate for the situation" [74, p. 135].[†] For example, industries with rapidly changing technologies, such as computer or electronic industries, tend to use very short study periods, whereas industries with more stable technologies may find the use of longer study periods more appropriate. In government studies a very large study period, e.g., 50 years or more, is usually used.

[†] From J. A. White, M. H. Agee, and K. E. Case, *Principles of Engineering Economics.* © 1977, reprinted by permission of John Wiley & Sons, Inc.

Under certain circumstances the comparison of alternatives with unequal useful lives can be performed by calculating the annual worth of one life-cycle costs. However, to do this by using the present worth method would be totally incorrect. Therefore, if the present worth method is employed, the comparison of the alternatives must be done over a common study period that can be determined by the least common-multiple of the unequal lives or the duration of service need.

The case of having alternatives with perpetual useful lives will be discussed in Section 5.7.

5.5 METHODS FOR COMPARING INVESTMENT ALTERNATIVES

The following are the basic methods that can be used to compare investment alternatives:

1. Present worth (PW) analysis
2. Annual worth (AW) analysis
3. Future worth (FW) analysis
4. Payback period analysis
5. Rate of return (ROR) analysis
6. Benefit/cost (B/C) analysis

The methods, with the exception of the fourth method, provide comparable results to measure economic merit or effectiveness of investment alternatives. The fourth method is very popular due to its simplicity and easiness but is not theoretically sound. The first three methods convert all receipts and disbursements, i.e., cash flows, representing an investment alternative into *equivalent* worths at some point or points in time using an interest rate equal to the minimum attractive rate of return. The first four methods will be discussed in this chapter.

It is customary to treat cash flows, in terms of receipts and disbursements, that occur during a year as if they happened at the end of the year. This end-of-year convention makes the necessary compound interest conversions much simpler. Of course, if the use of continuous compounding of interest is necessary, then the cash flows can be assumed to flow uniformly throughout each year.

5.6 PRESENT WORTH METHOD

In the present worth method each individual cash flow is converted to its present worth equivalent at the present, i.e., the beginning of period 1 or the end of period 0, and then the individual present worths are summed.

The interest rate used is usually the minimum attractive rate of return, called the *discount rate*. Because of this, the present worth calculation is often called *discounting*. Therefore, the present worth of a given investment alternative can be expressed as

$$PW(i) = \sum_{t=0}^{N} \frac{A_t}{(1+i)^t} \tag{5.3}$$

or

$$PW(i) = \sum_{t=0}^{N} A_t (1+i)^{-t} \tag{5.4}$$

or

$$PW(i) = \sum_{t=0}^{N} A_t (P/F, i\%, t) \tag{5.5}$$

where

$PW(i)$ = present worth of alternative using MARR of $i\%$,
  A_t = cash flow at the end of period t,
    i = the minimum attractive rate of return,
   N = study period.

If the alternatives are mutually exclusive, they may be ranked according to their (net) present worths. The best alternative is the one with the highest (net) present worth. If only disbursements are considered, then the resultant present worth is defined as *present worth of costs*, and the alternative with the least present cost is preferred. It is customary to drop or neglect the negative sign when cash flow is prevalently composed of disbursements. (Note the fact that a negative net cash flow indicates a negative rate of return on the investment).

If the investment alternatives are independent, then all alternatives with (net) present worths greater than zero satisfy the MARR criterion and, therefore, are economically justifiable. Note that a do-nothing alternative always exists and has a present worth equal to zero.

Example 5.1 An engineer who received a 17-year patent is considering selling it to a particular manufacturing company. She has two options, i.e., either to sell the patent rights for a lump-sum amount of $20,000 or to sell it for an income of $5,000 per year for the first 7 years and then $3,000 per year for the last 10 years. Use an interest rate of 15% and determine the option that should be accepted.

Solution The present worth of the second option can be calculated as

$$PW = \$5,000(P/A, \ 15\%, \ 7) + \$3,000[(P/A, \ 15\%, \ 17) - (P/A, \ 15\%, \ 7)]$$
$$= \$5,000(4.160) + \$3,000[(6.047) - (4.160)]$$
$$= \$26,461$$

or alternatively,

$$PW = \$3,000(P/A, \ 15\%, \ 17) + \$2,000(P/A, \ 15\%, \ 7)$$
$$= \$3,000(6.047) + \$2,000(4.160)$$
$$= \$26,461$$

or

$$PW = \$5,000(P/A, \ 15\%, \ 7) + \$3,000(P/A, \ 15\%, \ 10)(P/F, \ 15\%, \ 7)$$
$$= \$5,000(4.160) + \$3,000(5.019)(0.3759)$$
$$= \$26,461$$

Therefore, the second option should be accepted.

Example 5.2 The XYZ Company is considering installing a solar heating system in its manufacturing plant for space and hot water heating. There are three possible solar system alternatives in addition to the do-nothing alternative. The relevant data for the three alternatives are given in the following table. Note that the possible annual energy savings is a function of the size of the solar system installed. It has been determined that the annual heating cost for the plant is about $10,000. Use an MARR of 10% and determine the best economic alternative.

| | Alternative System | | |
System Data	A	B	C
Solar collector area (ft^2)	2,500	3,500	4,500
Storage tank (gal)	1,500	1,500	3,000
Installed system cost	$20,000	$40,000	$55,000
Annual energy savings	35%	60%	85%
Useful life (year)	20	20	20
Salvage value	0	0	$5,000

Solution   The present worths for alternatives A, B, and C can be calculated as

$$PW_A = -\$20,000 + (\$10,000)(35\%)(P/A, \ 10\%, \ 20)$$
$$= -\$20,000 + \$3,500(8.514)$$
$$= \$9,799$$

and

$$PW_B = -\$40,000 + \$6,000(P/A, \ 10\%, \ 20)$$
$$= \$11,000$$

and

$$PW_C = -\$55,000 + \$8,500(P/A, \ 10\%, \ 20) + \$5,000(P/F, \ 10\%, \ 20)$$
$$= \$18,112$$

Therefore, it can be concluded that the best economic alternative is system C.

Example 5.3   The XYZ Corporation owns a rental property from which it receives $20,000 annually. The property has been leased for 30 years to an industrial company for the same rent. The XYZ Corporation has recently received an offer to sell the property for $170,000. The total annual operating cost, which includes costs of maintenance, insurance, and taxes, is $5,500. It has been estimated that the salvage value of the property at the end of the 30 years will be $50,000 and that the annual expenses and receipts will remain approximately the same over the 30-year period. The MARR used by the XYZ Corporation for similar projects is 10%. Determine whether or not the company should accept the offer.

Solution   The net annual receipts are

$$A = \$20,000 - \$5,500$$
$$= \$14,500$$

Therefore, the present worth of a uniform series of $14,500 receipts over the 30-year period is

$$P = \$14,500(P/A, \ 10\%, \ 30)$$
$$= \$14,500(9.427)$$
$$= \$136,691.50$$

However, this amount does not include the $50,000 salvage value. Therefore, the total present worth is

$$P = \$136,691.50 + \$50,000(P/F, \ 10\%, \ 30)$$
$$= \$139,556.50$$

Since the resultant value is less than the offer, the XYZ should accept the offer.

Example 5.4 Assume that the Blue Skies Airline is contemplating installing computerized fuel allocation systems in all its airplanes. It has been determined that an investment of $10,000 into the computerized system will result in a $1,100 reduction in annual fuel costs over a 12-year period. Assume that the MARR is 10% and determine the following:

(a) The acceptability of the investment.
(b) The acceptability of the investment, if the annual fuel costs increase 7% each year.
(c) Repeat part (b), if the annual fuel costs increase 10% per year.

Solution

(a) From the tables in Appendix A the capital recovery factor for $i = 10\%$ and $n = 12$ years is

$$(A/P, \ 10\%, \ 12) = 0.14676$$

Therefore, the $10,000 investment over 12-year period at 10% rate of return should then yield annually

$$(\$10,000)(0.14676) = \$1,467.60$$

Whereas, the annual fuel costs are only reduced by $1,100. Thus, the return on the investment is insufficient and therefore the investment is not acceptable.

(b) Since the annual fuel costs increase 7% per year after the first year, they can be calculated as

$$F_1 = \$1,100(1.07)^0 = \$1,100$$
$$F_2 = \$1,100(1.07)^1 = \$1,177$$
$$F_3 = \$1,100(1.07)^2 = \$1,259.40$$
$$F_4 = \$1,100(1.07)^3 = \$1,347.55$$
$$F_5 = \$1,100(1.07)^4 = \$1,441.88$$
$$F_6 = \$1,100(1.07)^5 = \$1,542.81$$
$$F_7 = \$1,100(1.07)^6 = \$1,650.80$$
$$F_8 = \$1,100(1.07)^7 = \$1,766.36$$
$$F_9 = \$1,100(1.07)^8 = \$1,890$$
$$F_{10} = \$1,100(1.07)^9 = \$2,022.31$$
$$F_{11} = \$1,100(1.07)^{10} = \$2,163.87$$
$$F_{12} = \$1,100(1.07)^{11} = \$2,315.34$$

Their present worths can be determined as

$$P_1 = \$1,100(P/F, 10\%, 1) \quad = \$1,000.00$$
$$P_2 = \$1,177(P/F, 10\%, 2) \quad = \$\ 972.67$$
$$P_3 = \$1,259.40(P/F, 10\%, 3) = \$\ 946.19$$
$$P_4 = \$1,347.55(P/F, 10\%, 4) = \$\ 920.38$$
$$P_5 = \$1,441.88(P/F, 10\%, 5) = \$\ 895.26$$
$$P_6 = \$1,542.81(P/F, 10\%, 6) = \$\ 870.92$$
$$P_7 = \$1,650.80(P/F, 10\%, 7) = \$\ 847.19$$
$$P_8 = \$1,766.36(P/F, 10\%, 8) = \$\ 824.01$$
$$P_9 = \$1,890.00(P/F, 10\%, 9) = \$\ 801.55$$
$$P_{10} = \$2,022.31(P/F, 10\%, 10) = \$\ 779.60$$
$$P_{11} = \$2,163.87(P/F, 10\%, 11) = \$\ 758.44$$
$$P_{12} = \$2,315.34(P/F, 10\%, 12) = \underline{\$\ 737.67}$$

$$\sum_{i=1}^{10} P_i = \$10,353.98$$

Since the total fuel cost over the 12-year period is greater than the amount of investment required to reduce fuel consumption, the investment is acceptable.

Note that the previous calculation can also be performed using equation (3.80) where

$$i^* \triangleq \frac{1+i}{1+g} - 1$$

$$= \frac{1+0.10}{1+0.07} - 1$$

$$= 0.028 \text{ or } 2.8\%$$

$$P = \frac{A_1}{1+i} \left[\frac{(1+i^*)^N - 1}{i^*(1+i^*)^N} \right]$$

$$= \frac{\$1,100}{1+0.10} \left[\frac{(1+0.028)^{12} - 1}{0.028(1+0.028)^{12}} \right]$$

$$= \$10,073.84$$

The discrepancy in the results is due to the rounding errors involved.
(c) From equation (3.82)

$$P = \frac{A_1{}^N}{1+g}$$

$$= \frac{(\$1,100)12}{1+0.10}$$

$$= \$12,000$$

5.7 INFINITE STUDY PERIOD—CAPITALIZED WORTH METHOD

A special case of the present worth method involves the determination of worth of all cash flows in terms of receipts and/or disbursements over an *infinite* (or *perpetual*) study period. It is defined as the capitalized worth method. This type of evaluation is basically restricted to alternatives with perpetual, or very long, lives. Examples of such situations include economic studies of dams, highways, tunnels, any types of rights-of-way, any other similar type of public works projects, or any circumstances where a service or condition is to be maintained for an infinite period.

In this method, after the actual cash flows are converted into a perpetuity, i.e., a uniform annual worth amount that extends to infinity, they are discounted to the present at some designated interest rate. In other words the capitalized worth is the present worth amount that would be required now at some interest rate to yield the funds necessary to provide the service or whatever continuously. Therefore, it can be shown that

$$\text{Capitalized worth} = PW(i)$$

where $N = \infty$, or

$$\text{Capitalized worth} = A(P/A, i\%, \infty) \qquad (5.6)$$

From equation (3.99), it is known that

$$\lim_{N \to \infty} (P/A, i\%, N) = \frac{1}{i} \qquad (5.7)$$

Therefore,

$$\text{Capitalized worth} = \frac{A}{i} \qquad (5.8)$$

where

A = uniform annual worth of receipts and disbursements,
i = interest rate per period.

When there are no revenues but only disbursements in the cash flow, the result obtained by equation (5.8) is defined as *capitalized cost*.

Alternatively, equation (5.8) can be expressed as

$$A = P \cdot i \qquad (5.9)$$

where

P = capitalized worth of A, i.e., the amount of each of the perpetual payments.

In other words, for a principal amount P, there can be an infinite number of withdrawals as long as the amount of the withdrawals are equal to the interest earned on the principal for that period. Here, of course, the principal remains intact.

If there is a first cost (P) involved in addition to the capitalized cost of uniform annual worth of disbursements (A), the total capitalized cost of the projects can be expressed as

$$\text{Capitalized cost} = \text{First cost} + \frac{\text{Disbursements}}{i}$$

or

$$\text{Capitalized cost} = P + \frac{A}{i} \qquad (5.10)$$

It is important to recognize the fact that the definition of the capitalized cost concept in accounting is different than the one in engineering economy. In accounting sense the term *capitalized cost* is used to describe expenditures that may be allocated (depreciated) over more than one year rather than expensed, i.e., written off, entirely in the year they were made.

Example 5.5 Determine the amount of money required to be deposited into a fund now at an annual interest rate of 12% so that an amount of $10,000 can be withdrawn each year forever.

Solution From equation (5.8) the amount of money required can be found as

$$P = \frac{A}{i}$$
$$= \frac{\$10,000}{0.12}$$
$$= \$83,333.33$$

Example 5.6 A retired engineer who is a graduate of the Ghost City University endowed a million-dolar gift to the university for the construction and continued maintenance of an engineering laboratory. It is estimated that the annual operating cost of the laboratory is $20,000 and that the replacement and/or modernization of the laboratory equipment requires an additional $50,000 every 15 years. The minimum attractive rate of return of this tax-exempt university is 8%. Determine the amount left for the initial construction costs of the laboratory building after funds are allowed for everlasting maintanence and upkeep costs of the laboratory.

Solution From equation (5.10) the total capitalized cost can be expressed as

$$\text{Capitalized cost} = \text{First cost} + \frac{\text{Disbursements}}{i}$$

or

$$\text{First cost} = \text{Capitalized cost} - \frac{\text{Disbursements}}{i}$$
$$= \$1,000,000 - \frac{\$20,000 + \$50,000(A/F, 8\%, 15)}{0.08}$$
$$= \$1,000,000 - \frac{\$20,000 + \$50,000(0.03683)}{0.08}$$
$$= \$1,000,000 - \$273,019$$
$$= \$726,981$$

Note that the interest earned on \$273,019 will pay for all maintenance and upkeep costs forever, assuming that the costs and the interest rate remain constant.

5.8 ANNUAL WORTH METHOD

In the annual worth method all cash flows are converted to an equivalent uniform annual series of cash flows over the study period. Again, the conversion is based on the MARR. Under certain circumstances it may be easier first to calculate the present worth of the original cash flow series and then find its equivalent uniform annual worth by multiplying the resultant present worth by the capital recovery factor. Therefore, the annual worth of a given investment alternative can be expressed as

$$AW(i) = \left[\sum_{t=0}^{N} A_t(P/F, \ i\%, \ t)\right](A/P, \ i\%, \ N) \tag{5.11}$$

or

$$AW(i) = PW(i)(A/P, \ i\%, \ N) \tag{5.12}$$

where

$AW(i) =$ annual worth of alternative using MARR of $i\%$,

$(A/P, \ i\%, \ N) =$ capital recovery factor.

If the alternatives are mutually exclusive, they may be ranked according to their equivalent annual worths. The best alternative is the one with the greatest equivalent annual worth. If only disbursements are considered, then the resultant annual worth is defined as *equivalent uniform annual cost*, and the alternative with the least annual cost is preferred.

If the investment alternatives are independent, then all alternatives with annual worths greater than zero satisfy the minimum attractive rate of return criterion, and therefore, are economically acceptable. Again, note that a do-nothing alternative always exists and has an annual worth equal to zero.

Sometimes, the annual worth method is preferred to the present worth method due to computational convenience that may be present as a result of the characteristic of a given cash flow. Table 5.1 gives some of the typical cash flow patterns that may be encountered in engineering economy studies. It also provides for the necessary compound interest factors to convert them to present annual worth.

5.9 CAPITAL RECOVERY CALCULATIONS

In any investment decision the fundamental question that arises is *will it pay off?*, i.e., whether the investment will provide for a sufficient amount of income to recover the invested capital plus the required rate of return (MARR) on the diminishing investment remaining in the asset at any time during its life. Since returns are distributed over the useful life of the investment, it is convenient to convert the costs of capital recovery to the same base. Thus, the cost of the capital recovery (CR) for an investment is the equivalent uniform annual cost of the capital invested. The capital recovery cost can be calculated in various ways. For example,

$$CR(i) = P(A/P, i\%, N) - F(A/F, i\%, N) \tag{5.13}$$

where

$CR(i) =$ capital recovery cost using MARR of $i\%$,
$P =$ first cost of the asset (investment),
$F =$ estimated salvage value at end of the Nth year,
$i =$ minimum attractive rate of return,
$N =$ study period, or estimated useful life, in years.

Note that the capital recovery cost in equation (5.13) is equal to the annual equivalent of the first cost of the asset less the annual equivalent of the estimated salvage value.
Alternatively, from equation (3.52),

$$(A/P, i\%, N) = (A/F, i\%, N) + i$$

or

$$(A/F, i\%, N) = (A/P, i\%, N) - i$$

by substituting this equation into equation (5.13) and simplifying the resultant equation,

$$CR(i) = (P - F)(A/P, i\%, N) + F \cdot i \tag{5.14}$$

That is, the capital recovery cost is equal to the equivalent annual cost of the repayment of and return on the depreciable portion of the asset plus the interest on the salvage value (nondepreciable portion).
Similarly, by substituting equation (3.52) into equation (5.13) and simplifying,

$$CR(i) = (P - F)(A/F, i\%, N) + P \cdot i \tag{5.15}$$

That is, the capital recovery cost is equal to the annual sinking fund

TABLE 5.1 Typical Cash Flow Patterns and Their Conversion to Annual or Present Worth

Cash Flow Type	Cash Flow Diagram	Example	Annual Worth	Present Worth
1. First cost		Building (or equipment)	$P(A/P, i\%, N)$	P
2. A single deferred cost		Building addition	$F(P/F, i\%, M)(A/P, i\%, N)$	$F(P/F, i\%, M)$
3. Salvage		Resale of building	$F(A/F, i\%, N)$	$F(P/F, i\%, N)$
4. Annual cost		Property tax, maintenance, insurance	A	$A(P/A, i\%, N)$

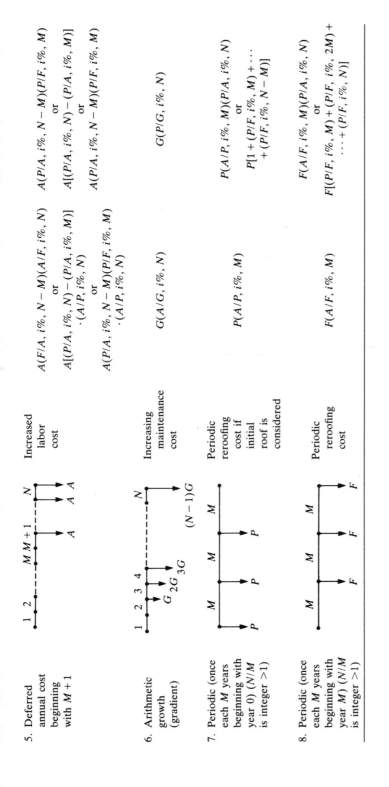

5. Deferred annual cost beginning with $M+1$		Increased labor cost	$A(F/A, i\%, N-M)(A/F, i\%, N)$ or $A[(P/A, i\%, N) - (P/A, i\%, M)]$ $\cdot (A/P, i\%, N)$ or $A(P/A, i\%, N-M)(P/F, i\%, M)$ $\cdot (A/P, i\%, N)$	$A(P/A, i\%, N-M)(P/F, i\%, M)$ or $A[(P/A, i\%, N) - (P/A, i\%, M)]$ or $A(P/A, i\%, N-M)(P/F, i\%, M)$
6. Arithmetic growth (gradient)		Increasing maintenance cost	$G(A/G, i\%, N)$	$G(P/G, i\%, N)$
7. Periodic (once each M years beginning with year 0) (N/M is integer >1)		Periodic reroofing cost if initial roof is considered	$P(A/P, i\%, M)$	$P(A/P, i\%, M)(P/A, i\%, N)$ or $P[1 + (P/F, i\%, M) + \cdots$ $+ (P/F, i\%, N-M)]$
8. Periodic (once each M years beginning with year M) (N/M is integer >1)		Periodic reroofing cost	$F(A/F, i\%, M)$	$F(A/F, i\%, M)(P/A, i\%, N)$ or $F[(P/F, i\%, M) + (P/F, i\%, 2M) +$ $\cdots + (P/F, i\%, N)]$

depreciation charge on the depreciable portion of the asset plus the interest on the full investment.

Also,

$$CR(i) = [P - F(P/F, \ i\%, \ N)](A/P, \ i\%, \ N) \tag{5.16}$$

That is, the capital recovery cost is equal to the repayment and return on the first cost of the asset less the present worth of the salvage value.

Finally,

$$CR(i) = \frac{P - F}{N} + \left[P - \frac{P - F}{N} (A/G, \ i\%, \ N) \right] i \tag{5.17}$$

That is, the capital recovery cost is equal to the uniform repayment (straight-line depreciation) of the depreciable portion of the asset plus return on diminishing investment.[†] Note that the interest rate is equal to the before-tax rate of return rather than the MARR in equation (5.17).

Example 5.7 Assume that the Ghost City council can provide a public service equally well by selecting one alternative out of two possible alternatives and that the service will continue indefinitely. The following estimates have been provided with regard to the alternatives. Use a MARR of 10% and determine the best alternative based on the capitalized costs.

	Alternative	
Data	A	B
First cost	$50,300	$15,700
Useful life	30 years	12 years
Salvage value at end of life	$9,000	0
Annual O&M costs	$2,400	$4,900

Solution

	Capitalized Cost	
	A	B
First cost	$50,300	$15,700
Replacements		
($50,300 − $9,000)(A/F, 10%, 30)/0.10	2,511	
$15,700(A/F, 10%, 12)/0.10		7,341
Annual disbursements		
$2,400/0.10	24,000	
$4,900/0.10		49,000
Total capitalized cost	$76,811	$72,041

[†]See Smith [66], p. 79.

Therefore, alternative B is the best alternative based on the capitalized costs.

Example 5.8 A power and light company is required to serve a newly developed residential area. There are two possible routes for the construction of the necessary power line. Route A is 18 miles long and goes around a lake. It has been estimated that the required overhead power line will cost $8,000 per mile to build and $350 per mile per year to maintain. Its salvage value will be $1,500 per mile at the end of 20 years.

On the other hand, route B is 6 miles long and is an underwater line that goes across the lake. It has been estimated that the required underwater line using submarine power cables will cost $21,000 per mile to build and $1,200 per mile per year to maintain. Its salvage value will be $6,000 per mile at the end of 20 years. Assume that the MARR is 10% and that the annual ad valorem (property) taxes are 3% of the first costs of each power line. Determine the economically preferable alternative.

Solution
Route A: The first cost of the overhead power line is

$$P = (\$8,000/\text{mile})(18 \text{ mile}) = \$144,000$$

and its estimated salvage value is

$$F = (\$1,500/\text{mile})(18 \text{ mile}) = \$27,000$$

From equation (5.13) the equivalent uniform annual cost of capital invested in the line, i.e., its capital recovery cost, can be calculated as

$$CR = \$144,000(A/P, 10\%, 20) - \$27,000(A/F, 10\%, 20)$$
$$= \$144,000(0.11746) - \$27,000(0.01746)$$
$$= \$16,443$$

The equivalent uniform annual cost (EUAC) of the tax and maintenance is

$$(3\%)(\$144,000) + (\$350/\text{mile})(18 \text{ mile}) = \$10,620$$

Therefore, the total equivalent uniform annual cost of the overhead power line is

$$EUAC = \$16,443 + \$10,620$$
$$= \$27,063$$

Route B: The first cost of the submarine power line is

$$P = (\$21,000/\text{mile})(6 \text{ mile}) = \$126,000$$

and its estimated salvage value is

$$F = (\$6,000/\text{mile})(6 \text{ mile}) = \$36,000$$

Thus, its capital recovery cost is

$$CR = \$126,000(A/P, \ 10\%, \ 20) - \$36,000(A/F, \ 10\%, \ 20)$$
$$= \$14,171$$

The associated equivalent uniform annual cost of the tax and maintanance is

$$(3\%)(\$126,000) + (\$1,200/\text{mile})(6 \text{ mile}) = \$10,980$$

Hence, the total equivalent uniform annual cost of the submarine power line is

$$EUAC = \$14,171 + \$10,980$$
$$= \$25,151$$

Therefore, the economically preferable alternative is route B. Of course, if the present worths of costs are calculated, the conclusion would still be the same. For example, the present worths of costs for routes A and B are

$$PW_A = \$27,063(P/A, \ 10\%, \ 20)$$
$$= \$230,414$$

and

$$PW_B = \$25,151(P/A, \ 10\%, \ 20)$$
$$= \$214,136$$

Thus, route B is still the preferred route.

Example 5.9 Assume that you are asked to compare two mutually exclusive equipment alternatives, as shown in Figure 5.2. It has been estimated that the future demand can be met by installing type A or type B equipment. However, if the type A equipment is chosen, then a second unit of type A equipment has to be installed to replace the first unit at the end of its useful life. The financial data for the alternatives are given in the following table:

	A	B
Installed first cost	$40,000	$100,000
Salvage at end of life	$10,000	$6,000
Life	11 years	17 years
Annual operating and maintenance costs	$10,000	$5,000

Use a MARR of 10% and the study period of 15 years and compare the two alternatives, recognizing any terminal values, i.e., unused values, remaining in the equipment at the end of the study period. Assume that there is no cost escalation.

Solution   Based on the equivalent uniform annual costs, the following comparison can be made.

Alternative A: From equation (5.14) the capital recovery cost is

$$CR = (P - F)((A/P, i\%, N) + F \cdot i$$

and therefore

$$EUAC_A = (\$40{,}000 - \$10{,}000)(A/P, \ 10\%, \ 11) + \$10{,}000(0.10) + \$10{,}000$$
$$= \$5{,}619 + \$10{,}000$$
$$= \$15{,}619$$

or alternatively,

$$EUAC_A = [\$40{,}000 - \$10{,}000(P/F, \ 10\%, \ 11) + \$40{,}000(P/F, \ 10\%, \ 11)$$
$$- \$10{,}000(P/F, \ 10\%, \ 22)](A/P, \ 10\%, \ 22) + \$10{,}000$$
$$= \$15{,}619$$

Terminal (unused) value of replacement at the end of the 15th year is

$$\$15{,}619(P/A, \ 10\%, \ 7) = \$27{,}353$$

Alternative B:

$$EUAC_B = (\$100{,}000 - \$6{,}000)(A/P, \ 10\%, \ 17) + \$6{,}000(0.10) + \$5{,}000$$
$$= \$12{,}318 + \$5{,}000$$
$$= \$17{,}318$$

Its terminal value at the end of the 15th year is

$$\$12{,}318(P/A, \ 10\%, \ 2) = \$21{,}384$$

It appears that alternative A is a better alternative. This conclusion can be verified by determining the equivalent present worth of costs for each alternative. Therefore,

$$PW_A = \$15,619(P/A, \ 10\%, \ 15) - \$27,353(P/F, \ 10\%, \ 15)$$
$$= \$112,250$$

and

$$PW_B = \$17,318(P/A, \ 10\%, \ 15) - \$21,384(P/F, \ 10\%, \ 15)$$
$$= \$126,601$$

Thus, alternative A is indeed a better alternative.

5.10 FUTURE WORTH METHOD

In the future worth method all cash flows are compounded forward to a particular point in time designated as the *future* in order to determine the equivalent future worth amount at that future time. The interest rate used is usually the MARR. Therefore, the future worth of a given investment alternative can be expressed as

$$FW(i) = \sum_{t=0}^{N} A_t(1+i)^{N-t} \tag{5.18}$$

or

$$FW(i) = \sum_{t=0}^{N} A_t(F/P, \ i\%, \ N-t) \tag{5.19}$$

or

$$FW(i) = PW(i)(F/P, \ i\%, \ N-t) \tag{5.20}$$

or

$$FW(i) = AW(i)(F/A, \ i\%, \ N-t) \tag{5.21}$$

where

$FW(i) =$ future worth of alternative using MARR of $i\%$,
$PW(i) =$ present worth of alternative using MARR of $i\%$,
$AW(i) =$ annual worth of alternative using MARR of $i\%$.

If the alternatives are mutually exclusive, they may be ranked according to their equivalent (net) future worths. The best alternative is the one with the highest (net) future worth. If only disbursements are considered, then the resultant future worth is defined as the *future worth of costs*, or simply *future cost*, and the alternative with the least future worth cost is preferred. The future worth is also called the *terminal worth*.

If the investment alternatives are independent, then all alternatives with future worths greater than zero satisfy the MARR criterion and, therefore, are economically justifiable. Of course, the do-nothing alternative always exists and has a future worth equal to zero.

In general, the present worth and the annual worth methods are preferred over the future worth method. However, there may be circumstances where the use of this method is required. For example, if the investor expects to sell or otherwise liquidate the investment at a future time, he may be interested in determining an estimate of the net worth or the terminal worth at that future date.

Note the fact that the use of the present worth, annual worth, or future worth methods to compare investment alternatives will always provide the same ranking among the alternatives as long as the MARR and the study period N are kept constant because of the equivalence that exists among the three measures of economic effectiveness. For example, the following relationships will exist among alternatives A and B provided that the MARR and the study period are kept constant:

$$\frac{AW(i)_A}{AW(i)_B} = \frac{PW(i)_A}{PW(i)_B} = \frac{FW(i)_A}{FW(i)_B} \tag{5.22}$$

That is, the ratio that exists between the alternatives remains the same. Alternatively,

$$\frac{AW(i)_A}{PW(i)_A} = \frac{AW(i)_B}{PW(i)_B} = (A/B, i\%, N) \tag{5.23}$$

Example 5.10   The Zubits International Company has already decided to purchase a major production machine to meet the increasing future demand for its zubits. It has been determined that there are two possible alternatives, i.e., the future demand can be met by installing type A or type B machines. However, if the type B machine is selected, a second type B machine has to be installed (in addition to the first unit) 7 years from now to increase the production capacity to its proper level to meet the demand at that time.

The installed first cost of type A machine is $150,000 and has a salvage value of $15,000 at the end of 12 years. Its operating and maintenance costs have been estimated to be $15,000 in year 1 and increasing by $1,500 per year.

On the other hand the installed first cost of type B machine is $80,000 and has a salvage value of $500 at the end of 12 years. Its operating and maintenance costs have been estimated to be $10,000 in year 1 and increasing by $3,000 per year. It has been estimated that the installed first cost of the second type B unit, i.e., the deferred unit, will be the same as the first unit and that it will have a salvage value of $18,000 5 years after its installation. The O&M costs of the second type B unit follow the same pattern as the first unit's. The MARR is 20%. Use a study period of 12 years and compare the alternatives by determining the following:

(a) The present worth of costs for each alternative.
(b) The equivalent uniform annual costs for each alternative.
(c) The future worth of costs for each alternative.

Solution

(a) The present worth of costs for each alternative can be calculated as
    Alternative A: The present worth of the first cost and salvage is

$$\$150,000 - \$15,000(P/F, 20\%, 12) = \$148,317$$

The present worth of the operating and maintenance costs is

$$[\$15,000 + \$1,500(A/G, 20\%, 12)](P/A, 20\%, 12)$$
$$= [\$15,000 + \$1,500(3.484)](4.439)$$
$$= \$89,783$$

Therefore, the total present worth of costs for alternative A is

$$PW_A = \$148,317 + \$89,783$$
$$= \$238,100$$

Alternative B: The present worth of the first cost and salvage for the first unit is

$$\$80,000 - \$500(P/F, 20\%, 12) = \$79,944$$

The present worth of the first cost and salvage for the second unit, i.e., the deferred unit, is

$$\$80,000(P/F, 20\%, 7) - \$18,000(P/F, 20\%, 12)$$
$$= \$80,000(0.2791) - \$18,000(0.1122)$$
$$= \$24,348$$

The present worth of the operating and maintenance costs for the first unit

$$\$10,000(P/A, 20\%, 12) + \$3,000(P/G, 20\%, 12)$$
$$= \$10,000(4.439) + \$3,000(15.467)$$
$$= \$90,791$$

The present worth of the operating and maintenance costs for the deferred unit is

$$[\$10,000(P/A, 20\%, 5) + \$3,000(P/G, 20\%, 5)](P/F, 20\%, 7)$$
$$= [\$10,000(2.991) + \$3,000(4.906)](0.2791)$$
$$= \$12,456$$

Therefore, the total present worth of costs for alternative B is

$$PW_B = \$79,944 + \$24,348 + \$90,791 + \$12,456$$
$$= \$207,539$$

Thus, the economically preferable alternative is alternative B, assuming that the first cost of the deferred unit will remain the same and the MARR will be constant.

(b) The equivalent uniform annual costs for alternatives A and B can be calculated as

$$EUAC_A = (PW_A(A/P, 20\%, 12)$$
$$= (\$238,100)(0.22526)$$
$$= \$53,634$$

and

$$EUAC_B = (PW_B)(A/P, 20\%, 12)$$
$$= (\$207,539)(0.22526)$$
$$= \$45,750$$

Therefore, alternative B is still the preferred alternative. Note that

$$\frac{EUAC_A}{PW_A} = \frac{EUAC_B}{PW_B} = (A/P, 20\%, 12)$$

(c) The future worth of costs for alternatives A and B can be calculated as

$$FW_A = (PW_A(F/P, 20\%, 12)$$
$$= (\$238,100)(8.916)$$
$$= \$2,122,900$$

and

$$FW_B = (PW_B)(F/P, 20\%, 12)$$
$$= (\$207,539)(8.916)$$
$$= \$1,850,418$$

Therefore, alternative B is still the preferred alternative.

Example 5.11   Assume that you are considering the purchase of a major equipment and that there are two possible types of the equipment that can fulfill the technical requirements that are expected from the equipment equally well. The financial data for the alternatives are given in the following table:

	A	B
First cost	$250,000	$100,000
Salvage value, at retirement	$10,000	$2,000
Economic life	10 years	5 years
Operating costs for labor, materials, property taxes, insurance, and maintenance	$12,000 in year 1 and increasing by $1,000 per year	$15,000 in year 1 and increasing by $1,500 per year
Replacement cost escalation	N/A	12% per year
Annual net income	$75,000	$55,000

Use a MARR of 15% and determine the best alternative by calculating:

(a) The net future worth of each alternative.
(b) The net present worth of each alternative.

Solution

(a) The net future worth of each alternative can be calculated as

$$FW_A = \$75,000(F/A, 15\%, 10) - \$250,000(F/P, 15\%, 10)$$
$$+ \$10,000 - [\$12,000 + \$1,000(A/G, 15\%, 10)]$$
$$\times(F/A, 15\%, 10)$$
$$= \$75,000(20.304) - \$250,000(4.046)$$
$$+ \$10,000 - [\$12,000 + \$1,000(3.383)](20.304)$$
$$= \$208,964$$

and

$$FW_B = \$55,000(F/A, 15\%, 10) - \$100,000(F/P, 15\%, 10)$$
$$+ \$2,000(F/P, 15\%, 5) - \$100,000(F/P, 12\%, 5)$$
$$\times (F/P, 15\%, 5)$$
$$+ \$2,000 - [\$15,000 + \$1,500(A/G, 15\%, 5)]$$
$$\times (F/A, 15\%, 10)$$
$$= \$55,000(20.304) - \$100,000(4.046)$$
$$+ \$2,000(2.011) - \$100,000(1.762)(2.011)$$
$$+ \$2,000 - [\$15,000 + \$1,500(1.723)](20.304)$$
$$= \$6,768$$

Therefore, alternative A is the economically preferable alternative.

(b) The net present worth of each alternative can be calculated as

$$PW_A = \$75,000(P/A, 15\%, 10) - \$250,000 + \$10,000(P/F, 15\%, 10)$$
$$- \$12,000(P/A, 15\%, 10) - \$1,000(P/G, 15\%, 10)$$
$$= \$51,690$$

and

$$PW_B = \$55,000(P/A, 15\%, 10) - \$100,000 + \$2,000(P/F, 15\%, 5)$$
$$- \$100,000(F/P, 12\%, 5)(P/F, 15\%, 5)$$
$$+ \$2,000(P/F, 15\%, 10)$$
$$- [\$15,000 + \$1,500(A/G, 15\%, 5)](P/A, 15\%, 10)$$
$$= \$1,671$$

Of course, the net present worths can be found directly from the net future worths as

$$PW_A = FW_A(P/F, \ 15\%, \ 10)$$
$$= \$208{,}964(0.2472)$$
$$= \$51{,}659$$

and

$$PW_B = FW_B(P/F, \ 15\%, \ 10)$$
$$= \$6{,}768(0.2472)$$
$$= \$1{,}673$$

The discrepancies are due to the rounding errors involved in the previous calculations.

5.11 PAYBACK PERIOD ANALYSIS

The payback method (sometimes also called the *payout* or *payoff method*) is a relatively simple and frequently employed analysis method to evaluate the economic merit or effectiveness of investment alternatives. The payback period is defined as the length of time required to recover the first cost of an investment alternative from the net cash flow (benefits or savings) generated by that alternative based on a zero interest rate. Therefore, the payback period is N such that

$$\sum_{t=1}^{N} A_t = P \tag{5.24}$$

or

$$\sum_{t=0}^{N} A_t = 0 \tag{5.25}$$

where

$A_t =$ net cash flow produced by the alternative during period t,
$P =$ first cost of the alternative.

The method ignores the time value of cash flows, the useful life of the project, and all the economic consequences beyond the payback period. It favors short-lived investment alternatives and therefore discriminates against long-lived proposals. Furthermore, it is an approximate rather than an exact calculation, and thus it may cause incorrect ranking among alternatives. Therefore, the use of the payback period as an effectiveness of investment criterion is not recommended. It provides information about the speed with which the investment will be recovered but not about the desirability of the investment proposal.

Nevertheless, the payback period method is a very popular one in industry due to its calculation easiness and its conceptual simplicity. It measures the liquidity of an investment project and therefore indicates the problem of working-capital management when a high degree of uncertainty exists. Therefore, the method, in this or some modified form, is frequently employed in conjunction with other analysis methods.

Example 5.12   Assume that there are three alternative machines that are under consideration to replace an aging production machine. The associated cash flows are given in the following table. Determine the best alternative by using the payback period method.

End of Year	Alternative		
	A	B	C
0	−$5,000	−$7,500	−$5,000
1	2,000	2,000	1,000
2	2,000	2,000	1,000
3	1,000	2,000	1,000
4	0	1,500	1,000
5	0	1,500	1,000
6	0	1,000	1,000
7	0	0	1,000
8	0	0	2,000

Solution   The payback periods can be calculated by using equation (5.25), i.e.,

$$\sum_{t=0}^{N} A_t = 0$$

Therefore, it can easily be seen that the payback periods are 3, 4, and 5 years for alternatives A, B, and C, respectively. Thus, the alternatives can be ranked as A, B, and C, based on the payback periods, where the best alternative is alternative A. However, by using the rate or return method, it can be calculated that the rates of return are 0, 10, and 15% for the alternatives A, B, and C, respectively. Therefore, the ranking of the alternatives is C, B, and A, based on their rates of return. Thus, the best alternative is alternative C based on the rates of return.

5.12 VALUATION OF BONDS

A bond is a certificate of indebtedness (note) representing a long-term obligation of a specific value offering assured interest at an established rate on the par or face value. Bonds are usually issued with par values in multiples of $100 or $1,000. The company promised to pay the bondholders a specific rate (or amount) of interest for a specified length of time and to redeem the bond, i.e., to repay the principal, at some specific maturity date. The specified interest rate is defined as the *bond rate*. The interest payments are defined as the *premiums* and are usually made semiannually or quarterly. The premium is calculated by multiplying the face value of the bond by the bond rate period. Bonds can be classified as *callable bonds* or *noncallable bonds*. The callable bonds have specific terms to allow them to be recalled prior to maturity.

A given bond may be purchased for less than, greater than, or equal to its face value, depending on the economic environment and its overall quality in terms of the perceived ability of the issuing company to pay the obligation involved in insuring the bond. The official opinion by an outside professional service, e.g., Moody's Investor Service, Standard & Poor's Corporation, or Fitch Investor Service, on the credit reputation of a bond issuer and the investment quality of its securities is known as the *bond rating*. The opinion is given in letter values, e.g., AAA or Baa, and so on. The highest rating is AAA (according to the coding system of the Standard & Poor's Corp.) or Aaa (Moody's), which represents bond issuers with an excellent capacity to pay the obligations involved. A slightly lower quality rating is AA (or Aa) and the ratings decrease to D (Standard & Poor's) for issues in default.

A given bond is evaluated based on its size, timing of the periodic premiums, and its maturity date. Therefore, the present worth of the bond is the sum of the present worth of the periodic interest payment cash flows and the discounted face value of the bond. However, when the original owner of a bond wants to sell it before its maturity, the original purchase price and periodic interest payments already collected do not affect its market value. Here, only the future cash flows are important. Therefore, the present worth of a bond can be expressed as

$$PW = A(P/A,\ i\%,\ N) + F(P/F,\ i\%,\ N) \tag{5.26}$$

or

$$PW = P \cdot r(P/A,\ i\%,\ N) + F(P/F,\ i\%,\ N) \tag{5.27}$$

where

A = annual interest payment (annuity),

    = $P \cdot r$

P = face value (par value) of a bond,

r = bond rate per interest period,

F = disposal price or redemption value of a bond,

N = number of periods before maturity,

    i = minimum attractive rate of return (or yield rate) per interest period.

Example 5.13 Assume that a 10-year 12% bond has a face value of $1,000 and that interest is payable semiannually. Determine the present worth of the bond using a nominal interest rate of 20%.

Solution From equation (5.27) the present worth of the bond can be calculated as

$$PW = (\$1,000)(0.06)(P/A, \ 10\%, \ 20) + \$1,000(P/F, \ 10\%, \ 20)$$

$$= \$60(8.514) + \$1,000(0.1486)$$

$$= \$659.44$$

5.13 VALUATION OF STOCKS

A stock is a certificate of a share of ownership in a corporation. Unlike a bond, there is no guarantee of a return to the stockholder, so there is no prior claim on the assets of the corporation as there is with a bond. The types of stock a corporation can issue and sell are stated in the articles of incorporation, i.e., corporate charter. Preferred stock is a class of stock with a claim on the company's earnings before payment made on the common stock and usually given priority over common stock if the company liquidates itself. Therefore, common stockholders have greater risk but usually have the greater control, e.g., voting rights, and have the greater reward in the form of dividends and market price increases.

Stocks may or may not have any par value. If there is a par value, it does not represent the market value of the stock, at any given time. The market value is established in a public stock market by exchanges between willing sellers and willing buyers. However, the market value of a stock is affected by (1) the expected dividends (or earnings), (2) the expected growth in dividends, and (3) the expected future market value.[†]

[†]For further information, see Smith [66], pp. 84–85.

5.14   LIFE-CYCLE COST COMPARISONS

The life-cycle cost for any alternative, whether it is a system, project, or product, can be defined as the summation of expenditures associated with the alternative from its inception to its disposal. Therefore, the economic study that particularly focuses on both direct and indirect cash flows over the life cycle of a project is defined as *life-cycle analysis*, or *life-cycle costing* (*LCC*) *study*. Here, the life-cycle costs may include research and development (R&D) costs, engineering design costs, manufacturing costs, installation and testing costs, operating and maintenance (O&M) costs, and disposal costs, as shown in Figure 5.3.

In a general sense the concept of life-cycle costing is not new. Its origin goes back to 1887 when a civilian engineer, Arthur M. Wellington, analyzed and presented the trade-offs between first cost of railway location and follow-on operating costs in his classic book *The Economic Theory of Railway Location*. Therefore, the life-cycle costing is an extension of well-established engineering economy principles and applications. It is a systematic analytical process of evaluating various alternatives with the objective of optimizing the use of scarce resources. In the 1960s the concept of life-cycle costing was adopted by the U.S. Department of Defense and by other U.S. government agencies as a means of improving the cost effectiveness in a complex system or equipment procurement. As a result of this policy, the *low-bid concept* based on the first cost that was widespread in the past, particularly in the public sector, is being replaced by the life-cycle

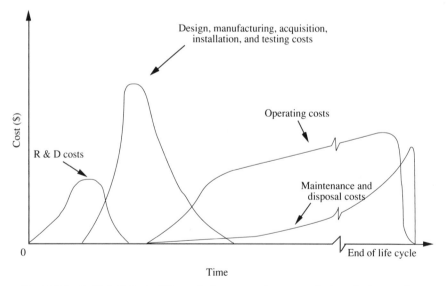

Figure 5.3 Typical phases of life cycle for an asset, e.g., product, project, or system.

costing. Today, the life-cycle costing has moved from public sectors, particularly from defense systems, into private sectors, especially into industrial and commercial sectors. Recent economic events in terms of rapidly increasing energy and labor costs and high inflation rates have enhanced the importance of life-cycle costing. The determination of the life-cycle cost of a system is usually performed by using the present or annual worth methods [15].

Figure 5.4 shows the stages of the life cycle of an asset, which is particularly suitable for a typical defense system. Here, the user, e.g., the U.S. Department of Defense, has complete control over the total life cycle. Figure 5.5 shows the typical stages of the life cycle of an industrial or commercial asset. Note that the asset has two sequential users. Here, each user has control over only a portion of the actual life cycle of the asset. Note that the amount of user discretion decreases as time passes. For example, at

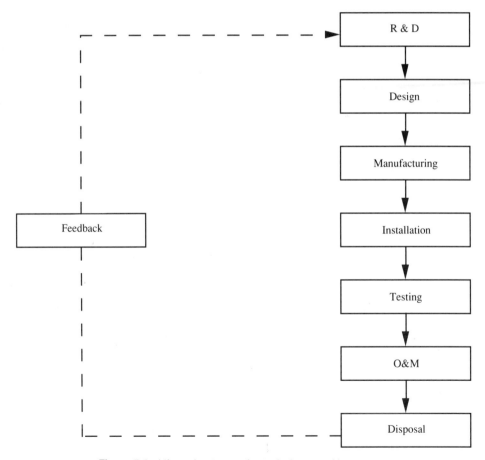

Figure 5.4 Life-cycle stages of a typical asset with one user.

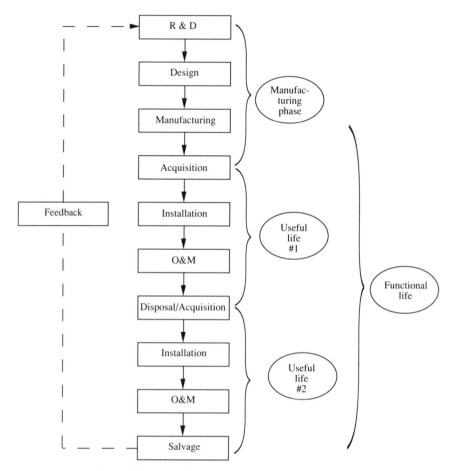

Figure 5.5 Life-cycle stages of an asset with two users.

the beginning stage all options are open, whereas after acquisition the only alternatives left are how to use the asset, at what location and at what capacity level within the restrictions of the design selected. Therefore, all the trade-offs (e.g., better quality versus lower maintenance, or greater complexity versus greater downtime, or higher first cost versus lower operating and maintenance costs) should be considered at the planning stage, and the best alternative should be selected based on the total life-cycle cost over the whole planned or expected life in use. Here, the alternatives available at each stage should be identified and compared in order to develop a plan over that period.

Figure 5.6 shows the key parameters in life-cycle costing. As can be observed from the figure, the life-cycle costing approach may require that certain data be included that have not traditionally been associated with engineering economy. Therefore, the analyst may be forced to interface

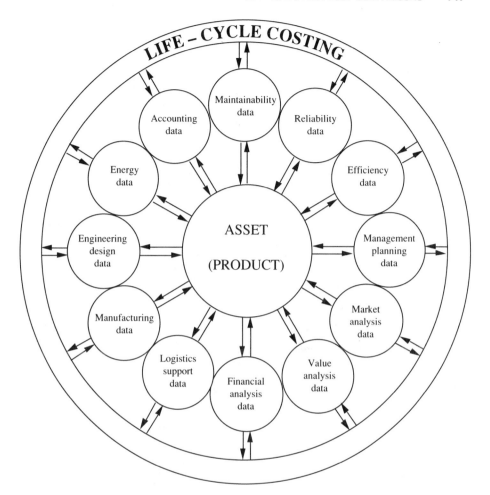

Figure 5.6 Key parameters in life-cycle costing.

with other major activities in the organization. The whole process from manufacturer to user is called *terotechnology*. It is defined as a combination of management, financial, engineering, and other disciplines applied to physical assets in order to achieve the most economic life-cycle costs. It is a concept for use by everyone concerned with the asset (management) leading to better and more economic use of assets.

Another emerging concept is *the design-to-cost* (DTC) concept. It is a different application form of the life-cycle costing concept. In the design-to-cost approach, first a total lifetime cost limit is set; then designers are required to work backward from the disposal stage, to the operating and maintenance expenses, through manufacturing costs, and finally to the beginning design expenses. Sometimes, this process also includes even the research and maintenance expenses.

Blanchard [14] gives the following additional applications of life-cycle cost analysis:

During the early stages of product planning and conceptual design, life-cycle cost analyses can be employed to aid in defining system operational requirements, the maintenance concept, and major program planning objectives. The following questions may arise, and life-cycle costing is an appropriate technique to employ in determining a response that will reflect an efficient use of resources:

A. How should the system or product be distributed and effectively utilized? What is the most cost-efficient approach?

B. How many product distribution centers are required and where should they be geographically located? What is the most cost-efficient approach?

C. How should the system/product be supported throughout its planned life cycle? How many levels of maintenance are necessary, and what logistics support resources are required at each level? What is the most cost-effective approach?

D. What type of program plan is required to satisfy the identified consumer need(s)? What is the most cost-effective approach?

Life cycle cost becomes a significant parameter in the early decision process relative to both management and engineering functions, and realistic LCC/DTC targets can be established with the intent of imparting a high degree of cost consciousness in system/product design.

During preliminary and detailed system/product design, life-cycle costing continues as an iterative process in supporting decisions at a lower level in the system hierarchy. A few typical questions that may arise are noted as follows:

A. Is there an existing design that will fulfill the need? If so, what supplier sources are available, and which source should be selected? What is the most cost-effective approach?

B. If new design is required, which configuration is the most cost-effective in terms of life-cycle cost? Design decisions involving equipment packaging schemes, automatic versus manual functions, diagnostic provisions, etc., have a significant impact on life-cycle cost.

C. Does the selected design configuration incorporate the necessary supportability characteristics to reflect the lowest life-cycle cost (i.e., reliability, maintainability, human factors, etc.)?

D. Are the logistics support requirements identified for the selected design configuration optimal in terms of life-cycle cost? Do the analysis and planning data reflect the correct items of support, at the proper level, and at the right time?

As the system/product design progresses, alternatives may be evaluated using the life-cycle cost technique as a tool to facilitate the decision-making process.

During the production/construction phase of the life cycle, major questions that arise pertain to production rates, production flow, inventory and distribution policies, quality control practices, etc. Since production decisions can significantly impact follow-on system or product operation and support functions, the life-cycle costing technique should be employed in the evaluation of alternatives.

Finally, life-cycle cost analyses are accomplished throughout the operational use and logistics support phase when the system/product is being used in the field by the consumer. The analysis at this stage constitutes an assessment of actual costs based on experience, and use of the life-cycle cost technique serves to identify major problem areas and high cost contributors. Further, life-cycle costing is employed to evaluate the economic impact of potential modifications proposed for the system or product.[†]

PROBLEMS

5.1 Determine the present worth of costs associated with the purchase of the following two machines. Assume that the MARR is 10%.

	Machine A	Machine B
First cost	$11,000	$15,000
Economic life	9 years	9 years
Salvage value	Negligible	Negligible
Annual expenditures	$3,000	$2,500

5.2 Use the present worth method to determine the preferred alternative. Use a MARR of 15%.

	Alternative A	Alternative B
First cost	$600	$1,200
Economic life	4 years	10 years
Salvage value	0	0
Annual O&M costs	$100	$75

5.3 Use the present worth method to determine the preferred alternative. Use a MARR OF 12%.

	Alternative A	Alternative B
First cost	$12,000	$20,000
Economic life, years	10	20
Salvage value	$1,200	$1,000
Annual expenditures	$2,500	$2,000

[†]From B. S. Blanchard, *Design and Manage to Life Cycle Cost*, M/A Press, Portland, OR, 1978. Used with permission of the author.

5.4 A firm is considering starting an additional product line. The management's estimate of the receipts and disbursements follow. Use an interest rate of 8% and determine the present worth of the product line.

End of year	Receipts	Disbursements	Net Cash Flow
0	$0	−$150,000	−$150,000
1	10,000	− 20,000	− 10,000
2	25,000	− 10,000	15,000
3	75,000	− 2,000	73,000
4	75,000	− 1,000	74,000
5	70,000	− 1,000	69,000

5.5 A homeowner has the option of selling her house for $54,000 with an immediate capital gain of $22,000, or renting it. If she rents, her expected cash flows are as follows:

End of Year	0 through 10	11 through 25
Cash Flow	$3,000/year	$2,400/year

If the interest rate is $5\frac{1}{2}$%, should she sell the house? Ignore any tax considerations.

5.6 It has been determined that the roof of the Ghost City hall has to be replaced. The existing roof is made of slate. If the reroofing is done by using slate, it would cost $20 per square foot, and the roof would last 120 years with annual maintenance costs of $500 after the 20th year. Alternatively, the roof can be replaced by using imitation slate tiles. The imitation slate tile roof would cost $10 per square foot, but it would need replacement every 40 years. Its annual maintenance cost would be $400 after the 10th year. The roof is 40,000 square feet. Use an interest rate of 8% and determine the alternative that should be recommended by the city engineer.

5.7 A contractor has a full-time requirement to compact soil with a roller. He can either purchase a self-propelled roller or a towed roller with a crawler tractor. A self-propelled roller costs $30,420 with annual operating costs of $5,850. It has a useful life of 5 years with a salvage value of $4,000. On the other hand a towed roller costs $6,467 with annual maintenance costs of $50 after the third year. It has a 10-year life and no salvage value. A 70-horsepower crawler tractor costs $20,800 with annual operating costs of $2,184. It has a 5-year life and a $2,000 salvage value. Which alternative should the contractor select if the interest rate is 10%?

5.8 Mr. Jones needs to undercoat his automobile. There are three different types of undercoatings available on the market. Their durability and costs follow:

Undercoating	Durability	Cost
A	1 year	$ 35
B	3 years	60
C	5 years	100

If Mr. Jones plans on keeping his automobile for at least 6 years, which undercoating would be the most effective if his interest rate is 6%?

5.9 A 6% $10,000 bond is due in 20 years. Interest is payable semiannually; the first payment is due in 6 months. What should the price of the bond be to return a nominal rate of 9% compounded semiannually?

5.10 Assume that the following cash flow is given.

End of Year	0	1	2	3	4	5
Cash Flow	−$15,000	$4,000	$4,000	$4,000	$5,000	$5,000

(a) Assume that interest is compounded annually. Let the interest rate range from 0 to 15% and plot the present worth as a function of the interest rate.

(b) What conclusion can be drawn from the graph?

5.11 What is the present worth of an initial investment of $40,000, an annual investment of $4,000 a year for 10 years with a total final payment of $20,000 at the end of 10 years if the interest rate is 12%?

5.12 If a grader costs $10,000 with $5,000 annual payments for 2 years, has an annual maintenance requirement of $600, and has a salvage value of $2,500 after 10 years, what is the present worth of the grader if the interest rate is 15%?

5.13 What is the present worth of an initial investment of $2,000, a second investment of $2,000 in 4 years and a third investment of $2,000 in 6 years if the interest rate is 8%?

5.14 What annual disbursement would have to be made to achieve the same present worth as in Problem 5.13 in 6 years if the interest rate is 5%?

5.15 The Ghost City council has recognized the fact that there is a need for a major east–west thoroughfare through their town. They can build an adequate two-lane street now at an initial cost of $250,000 that will require an estimated $4,000 a year in maintenance. Growth predictions indicate that the street will have to be enlarged to four lanes in 15 years. This will cost an additional $200,000 at that time, and then the maintenance requirements will be $5,000 annually for the lifetime of the street. The street is expected to be used for 30 years and the interest rate is 6%. What is the present worth of this street?

5.16   The Ghost City council, in Problem 5.15, has received another bid from another contractor that will construct a four-lane street now for $350,000. The annual maintenance expenditures are expected to be $5,250. With a useful life of 30 years and a rate of return of 12%, which of the two plans has the most attractive present worth?

5.17   What is the present worth of a series of 15 annual payments of $150 each when the first payment will be made 5 years from now if the interest rate is 5%?

5.18   In order to meet the EPA standards on a heating plant a scrubber must be installed or the plant converted to oil. The coversion to oil would cost $10,000, annual maintenance and labor costs would be $2,000 and $8,000, respectively. However, oil would cost $10,000 per year more than coal. Installing a scrubber costs $15,000, annual maintenance and labor costs would be $4,000 and $24,000, respectively. The firm only intends to use the facility another 10 years, and the MARR is 15%. If they did nothing, the EPA would fine the firm $5,000 per year. Which alternative should be selected? Currently, the annual maintenance and labor costs are $4,000 and $24,000, respectively.

5.19   Mr. Smith is being offered a "get rich quick" scheme. The initial one-time payment of $15,000 will be paid back in eight equal yearly payments of $2,700. Determine whether Mr. Smith should consider the proposal, if his MARR is (a) 12% and (b) 8%.

5.20   A road contractor needs an additional 1,000-gallon truck-mounted bituminous distributor. He can rent one with operator for $20 per hour, and he will have to provide an assistant operator at $7 per hour. The distributor will need a major overhaul after 5 years costing $2,000. If his anticipated use of the distributor is 1,000 hours per year and the MARR is 12%, should he rent or buy a distributor?

5.21   A school must provide additional classroom space. It can either place a prefabricated steel structure next to the school or construct a masonry extension matching the existing architecture. The prefabricated structure would cost $100,000, have a 10-year life, and $6,000 salvage value. Maintenance costs are $1,000 per year. The interior and exterior would have to be painted every 5 years at a cost of $1,300. The masonry structure has an initial cost of $180,000 with a

30-year life. Maintenance costs are $800 per year. The interior would have to be painted every 5 years at $750 and the roof replaced after 15 years at $3,000. Which alternative has the lowest equivalent uniform annual cost if the MARR is 10%?

5.22 A land developer built houses adjacent to a stream. She has one lot left within this group of houses. The lot provides the developer access to the stream bed from which she takes sand and gravel for concrete work. She is undecided whether to retain the lot for herself as a means of access to the stream or build a house on it now. A one-family house will return $5,000 in before-tax profit. The real estate tax on the lot is $100 per year. She estimates that the following amount of sand and gravel will be taken out of the stream in the next 5 years: 500 tons in the first year, 400 tons in the second year, and 300, 200, and 100 tons during the third, fourth, and fifth year at a cost of $1.30 per ton. However, she will build a house on the lot at the end of the fifth year and make $5,000. On the other hand, if she builds the house on the lot now, the sand and gravel delivered to the construction sites at the given amounts for the next 5 years would cost $4 per ton. Use a MARR of 10% and determine whether the developer should build on the lot immediately or 5 years later.

5.23 Assume that a new interstate highway must cross a river. Presently, there is a two-lane bridge over the river on a country road. The highway commission has an alternative of building a six-lane bridge now and design it to be expanded to eight lanes in 15 years or construct an eight-lane bridge now. A six-lane bridge would cost $21 million with additional maintenance costs of $800,000 per year. In that case an additional $8 million would have to be spent to expand it to eight lanes, and the maintenance costs would increase by $200,000 per year also. A new eight-lane bridge would cost $25 million with maintenance costs of $1 million per year. Assuming a perpetual life and a MARR of 12%, which alternative should the highway commission select?

5.24 Assume that a facility will have an initial cost of $130,000 and repair and maintenance costs of $8,000 per year for the first 8 years and $10,000 per year thereafter, and that its useful life is 30 years. Use a MARR of 8% and determine the following:

(a) The equivalence uniform annual cost.

(b) The present worth of the facility.

5.25 Assume that two machines that exist currently on the market will accomplish the same task. Machine A costing $150,000 will produce 15 units per hour and have a life of 5 years with no salvage value. Machine B will also produce 15 units per hour but has a 9-year life with $10,000 salvage value and costs $300,000. It has been estimated that the average production will be 30,000 units per year. The operating and maintenance costs for machine B are $4 per hour less than machine A. Determine the preferrred alternative, if the MARR is 12%.

5.26 A photographic equipment manufacturing company is offering the public a movie camera with accessories and projection equipment free of charge, provided that an individual promises to buy one roll of movie film per month from the firm for 5 years. The "free" items have the following value: camera is $124, projector is $210, screen is $50, and additional accessories are $150. A movie film costs $4.25 per roll and $3.00 for developing. Assume a MARR of 6%, equipment life of 10 years, and a 10% salvage value. Also, assume that any developed home-made movie has no monetary value. Determine whether or not the offer is attractive if:

(a) The film is purchased and developed.

(b) The film is purchased and not developed.

5.27 Mr. Jones has discovered a large cave on his property. Since it is a very attractive and interesting cave, he thought he may open it to the public and make some money from his discovery. After doing a complete study, Mr. Jones has estimated that he would need $20,000 for a building, lighting, paths, and so on, and that the annual operating and maintenance costs would be $2,000. The electrical system in the cave would need rewiring every 3 years at $3,000 each time. Advertising costs would be $1,000 initially and then $500 per year thereafter. He estimates that he would charge $1.50 per person to see the cave and half price for children. Furthermore, he estimates that average attendance to be 10,000 people per year with one-fourth of them being children. Use a MARR of 20% and determine the annual before-tax profit if Mr. Jones keeps the venture going for 18 years.

5.28 Assume that the following two machines are being considered for installation in a new plant. Use a MARR of 30% and determine the preferred machine based on the equivalent uniform annual cost method.

	Machine A	Machine B
Installed first cost	$10,000	$13,000
Economic life, years	20	20
Salvage value, at retirement	$100	$2,000
Annual operating costs	$700	$650
Annual maintenance costs	$300	$400

5.29 A cotton mill utilizes electric motors to operate its cording, spinning, and weaving machines. The motors have a first cost of $4,500 each. They have an expected life of 12 to 15 years. If they are replaced after 12 years of service, they have a salvage value of $500. However, the salvage value is reduced to $150 if they are replaced after 15 years. Each motor has annual maintenance cost of $50 for the first year, $150 for the second, and an increase of $100 a year until replaced. Use a MARR of 12% and the annual worth method to determine whether the motors should be replaced in 12 or 15 years.

5.30 Use a MARR of 15% and repeat Problem 5.29. Assume that the annual maintenance costs are $75 for the first year and then increase $75 per year up to 12th year, at which time they remain constant for the next 3 years.

5.31 Assume that a production plant has been in business for the past 40 years. The products have been essentially hand made during that period by the unskilled, low-paid people living in the area. However, because of the increased cost of higher salaries and raw materials, the management is considering automation of the plant. Presently, the costs include average annual salaries and wages of $12,000 per year for 75 employees, the cost of fringe benefits of $1,000 per employee, and plant maintenance of $2,000 per year. It has been estimated that the factory can be automated at a cost of $200,000. The equipment will require a $3,000 per year maintenance expenditure and $800 per year in increased power requirements. It has been estimated that the new automated plant will require only 25 employees at an average salary of $16,000 and that the fringe benefits will be $1,200 per employee. The estimated life of the machinery is 25 years. The salvage value of the machinery is estimated to be $20,000 at the time of retirement. Use a MARR of 20% and determine the economical alternative based on the equivalent uniform annual costs.

5.32 A bulldozer can be purchased from Company A for $60,000. Its estimated useful life is 10 years at which time its salvage value will be $5,000. Annual operating and maintenance costs, at the intended level of usage, are estimated to be $2,000 per year. On the other hand Company B has a bulldozer that can be purchased for $40,000 with an estimated useful life of 10 years at which time its salvage value estimated to be $4,000. It has been estimated that the annual maintenance and operating costs will be $2,500 and $1,500, respectively. Use a MARR of 30% and determine the preferred alternative based on the annual worth method.

5.33 Assume that two alternatives of transporting copper ore from a copper mine over a mountainous terrain are being considered. In the first alternative an overhead conveyor system is to be utilized that will have an installed cost of $200,000. Its operating and maintenance costs will be $20,000 for the first year and will increase by $2,000 per year thereafter. Its estimated salvage value is $18,000 after an estimated useful life of 10 years. The second alternative requires the construction of a road and the purchase of four trucks to transport the ore. The road construction costs are estimated to be $90,000, and it will require $2,000 a year in maintenance costs. Each truck costs $25,000 and has a salvage value of $4,000 after 10 years of operation. The operating and maintenance cost of each truck will be $8,000 for the first year and will increase $800 per year for the last 9 years of operation. Use a MARR of 30% and determine the preferred alternative.

5.34 Repeat Problem 5.33, assuming that the MARR is 15%.

5.35 If $40,000 has been paid for a milling machine over a period of 15 years by annual payments and the rate of return was 12%, what was the equivalent uniform annual cash flow when $6,000 was realized in salvage at the end of the period?

5.36 An investment of $15,000 followed by annual deposits of $500 will yield 15% interest over a 20-year period. A second investment of $15,000 will yield 20% for 15 years. Determine which plan will require the least uniform annual cash flow?

5.37 An extra high voltage transmission line requires periodic maintenance. It has been determined that the end-of-year maintenance expenses follow a 4-year cycle and that they are $7,000 and $10,000 per year for the first 2 years and for the last 2 years, respectively. Use an annual interest rate of 10% and determine the capitalized cost equivalent of these expenses.

5.38 Verify that when there is an arithmetic gradient G involved the capitalized cost can be expressed as

$$\text{Capitalized cost} = \frac{G}{i^2}$$

5.39 Assume that a pipeline requires seasonal maintenance and that it will be in service indefinitely. It has been determined that the seasonal maintennce costs for fall, winter, spring, and summer seasons are $60,000, $50,000, $40,000, and $30,000, respectively. Use an interest rate of 9%, compounded quarterly, and determine the capitalized cost equivalent of the four-season maintenance cycle.

5.40 Assume that a railroad bridge requires a maintenance expense of $15,000 every fourth year forever and that the first expense will be made 4 years from now. If the annual interest rate is 12%, determine the capitalized cost equivalent of the maintenance expenses.

5.41 Assume that your rich uncle decided to give you $4,400 to support you while you are in college. He told you that you can receive the $4,400 in three different ways over the next 4 years. Under the first option you can receive $800 at the end of your freshman year, $1,000 at the end of the sophomore year, $1,200 at the end of the junior year, and $1,400 at the end of the senior year. Under the second option you can receive $1,000 at the end of each year. Finally, under the third option, you can receive $1,400, $1,200, $1,000, and $800 at the end of the first, second, third, and fourth years, respectively. Assume that the interest rate is 6% and determine the following: the best option based on (a) the annual worth method and (b) the present worth method.

_____6
RATE OF RETURN AND INCREMENTAL ANALYSES

The sum which two married people owe to one another defies calculation.
It is an infinite debt, which can only be discharged through all eternity.
JOHANN WOLFGANG VON GOETHE, **1808**

6.1 INTRODUCTION

The *rate of return* is defined as the interest rate at which the net present worth (NPW) of a series of cash inflows (receipts) and cash outflows (disbursements) is zero. Therefore, the rate of return of a project is the specific interest rate i^* that satisfies the following equation

$$\text{NPW} = \sum_{t=0}^{n} F_t(1 + i^*)^{-t} = 0 \tag{6.1}$$

where

   $i^* =$ prospective rate of return from the project,
   $n =$ project life (or study period) in years,
   $F_t =$ positive or negative cash flow in year t.

The method finds some interest rate, initially unknown, that is *internal* to the project and that is the interest earned on unrecovered balance of the project so that the remaining balance is zero at the end of project's life. Such unrecovered balance of a project can be considered as the portion of the initial investment that is left to be recovered. Note that such rate of return is usually calculated based on present worth even though it can also be determined based on annual worth and future worth.

Since the rate of return is found without the assumption of the reinvestment of positive cash flows, it is also called *internal rate of return*. Other names of the method include the *discounted cash flow method*, the *true rate of return method*, the *investor's method*, the *receipts versus disbursements method*, and the *profitability index method*. Regardless of what it is called, it is the rate of interest earned on the unrecovered balance of an investment.

In general, if the rate of return required, either in terms of minimum attractive rate of return (MARR) or before-tax rate of return (BTROR), for a project is known or given, use the PW method given in Chapter 5. Otherwise, employ the rate of return (ROR) method. The selection criterion for a prospective investment project under such ROR method is select the project if i^* (i.e., the ROR) is greater than the company's MARR; otherwise, reject it. The most common forms of the equations used to calculate the ROR's are

$$PW \text{ of revenues} - PW \text{ of costs} = 0 \qquad (6.2)$$

$$PW \text{ of revenues} = PW \text{ of costs} \qquad (6.3)$$

$$\text{Net present worth} = 0 \qquad (6.4)$$

$$\text{EUAB} - \text{EUAC} = 0 \qquad (6.5)$$

$$\frac{PW \text{ of revenues}}{PW \text{ of costs}} = 1 \qquad (6.6)$$

where EUAB and EUAC represent equivalent uniform annual benefits and equivalent uniform annual costs, respectively. However, in practice, the most frequently used form is given by equation (6.2).

6.2 RATE OF RETURN METHOD

The rate of return method is probably the most frequently used exact analysis technique in industry. It is easily understood since it is the interest rate at which the net present worth of the cash flows on a project is zero. Another advantage of this method is that it does not demand the knowledge of a required or minimum rate of interest before calculations can be performed. On the contrary, such calculations themselves provide a percentage figure that can directly be used for comparison with other prospective investment projects or with MARR.

In general, the method of solving for the ROR normally inolves trial-and-error calculation[†] until the specific interest rate (i.e., i^*) is found or can be

---

[†]However, the trial-and-error approach is not the only method of solving for the rate of return. Since the solution for the rate of return of a cash flow with a life of n periods is the solution of an nth degree polynomial, there are various mathematical methods that systematically converge on the roots or values of i (i.e., ROR) that satisfy such a polynomial. Furthermore, in order to minimize the computational time necessary to determine the rate of return, computer programs are often employed to solve such net present worth equations.

interpolated. In such calculations, when both cash inflows and outflows are involved, the convention of using plus signs for cash inflows and negative signs for cash outflows are used. Succinctly put, the method[†] involves finding the $i*$ so that

$$NPW = PW \text{ (of receipts)} - PW \text{ (of disbursements)} = 0$$

Thus, whenever the NPW results in a positive quantity, the next trial should use a greater interest rate to achieve the goal of a zero outcome. On the other hand lowering the interest rate in such NPW calculations will cause the resulting outcome to increase. Usually, a negligible amount of error is caused in the resulting interest rate by the linear interpolation between the factors that are obtained from the adjacent interest tables. In general, interpolated rates of return calculated to the nearest tenth of a percent are sufficient.

Example 6.1   Assume that an investor has purchased a $1,000 bond for $800 and that the bond will mature in 20 years. The bondholder will be receiving an interest payment of $80 per year. Determine the following:

(a) The current yield of the bond.
(b) The yield to maturity of the bond.
(c) Repeat part (b), assuming semiannual interest payments of $40.
(d) Graph the present worth as a function of the interest rate for part (c).

Solution

(a) The current yield of the bond is

$$\frac{\$80}{\$800} = 0.10 \text{ or } 10\%$$

(b) The yield to maturity can be found by calculating the prospective pretax rate of return based on the assumption that the bond will be held until its maturity date. Therefore, the present worth of net cash flow can be expressed as

$$NPW = 0 = -\$800 + \$80(P/A, i\%, 20) + \$1,000(P/F, i\%, 20)$$

[†]It is important to note that the ROR for a given project simply reflects the rate of interest earned on the time-varying unrecovered investment balances for that project with that cash flow. Furthermore, it is independent of the absolute investment of the project. Thus, the investment amount along with other cash inflows must be taken into account. Therefore, a comparison of RORs for two or more investment projects often neglects the absolute investment amounts in the projects.

At $i = 10\%$

$$-\$800 + \$80(8.514) + \$1,000(0.1486) \overset{?}{=} 0$$

$$\$29.70 \neq 0$$

At $i = 12\%$

$$-\$800 + \$80(7.469) + \$1,000(0.1037) \overset{?}{=} 0$$

$$-\$98.80 \neq 0$$

Since the resultant net present worths are positive and negative, the correct rate of return that brackets the value of NPW $= 0$ is somewhere between 10 and 12%. Therefore, a linear interpolation to the correct value of i is found as follows:

i	PW of Net Cash Flow
10%	$29.70
i%	0
12%	$-$98.80

so that the correct $i\%$ can be calculated by solving either

$$\frac{10\% - i\%}{10\% - 12\%} = \frac{\$29.70 - 0}{\$29.70 - (-\$98.80)}$$

or

$$i = 10\% + \left(\frac{\$29.70}{\$29.70 + \$98.80}\right)(2\%)$$

$$= 10\% + \left(\frac{\$29.70}{\$128.50}\right)(2\%)$$

$$\cong 10.5\%$$

Therefore, the yield to maturity of the bond is 10.5%.

(c) If the interest payments are paid semiannually, then the present worth of net cash flow can be expressed as

$$\text{NPW} = 0 = -\$800 + \$40(P/A, i/2\%, 40) + \$1,000(P/F, i\%, 20)$$

At $i = 10\%$

$$-\$800 + \$40(17.159) + \$1,000(0.1486) \overset{?}{=} 0$$

$$\$34.96 \neq 0$$

At i = 12%

$$-\$800 + \$40(15.046) + \$1,000(0.1037) \stackrel{?}{=} 0$$

$$-\$94.46 \neq 0$$

Therefore,

$$i = 10\% + \left(\frac{\$34.96}{\$129.42}\right)(2\%)$$

$$= 10.5\%$$

Note that the yield to maturity of the bond is slightly higher when the interest payments are received semiannually.

(d) Figure 6.1 shows the graph of present worth versus interest rate, i.e, rate of return. Note that the present worth is positive for all values of *i* that are less than 10.5%, and it is negative for all values of *i* that are greater than 10.5%. The calculated yield to maturity of the bond should be compared against the investor's before-tax MARR. Here, the MARR is unknown in *this* example. Therefore, the answer can be given in a conditional way. That is,

If	Decision
MARR < 10.5%	Accept proposed investment
MARR > 10.5%	Reject proposed investment

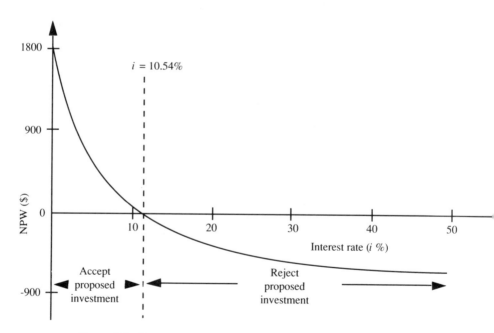

Figure 6.1 Graph of present worth versus rate of return for Example 6.1.

Example 6.2 Assume that Zubits International Corporation is considering issuing 5,000 bonds at 8% to raise capital for the expansion of its production facilities. Each bond has a face value of $1,000. The interest is payable to the bondholders annually at the end of each year, and the bond series matures in 10 years. The corporation has put out the bonds for bid to several underwriters. The highest bid received so far has been $915 less selling expenses of $3.00 per bond. The corporation estimates that there will be handling and clerical expenses of $15,000 per year. Determine the actual cost of this new borrowed capital to the Zubits International Corporation.

Solution   The current market price of the bond is $912 ($915 less $3.00) per bond. The annual expense for the bonds are

Annual interest payments @ 8%

$$($1,000)(5,000)(8\%) = $400,000$$

$$\text{Handling and clerical expenses} = \underline{\$15,000}$$

$$\text{Total} = \$415,000$$

Therefore, the present worth of net cash flow can be expressed as

$$\text{NPW} = 0 = (£912)(5,000) - \$415,000(P/A, i\%, 10)$$
$$- (\$1,000)(5,000)(P/F, i\%, 10)$$
$$= \$4,560,000 - \$415,000(P/A, i\%, 10\%)$$
$$- 5,000,000(P/F, i\%, 10)$$

At $i = 9\%$

$$-\$4,560,000 - \$415,000(6.418) - \$5,000,000(0.4224) \overset{?}{=} 0$$
$$-\$215,470 \neq 0$$

At $i = 10\%$

$$-\$4,560,000 - \$415,000(6,145) - \$5,000,000(0.3855) \overset{?}{=} 0$$
$$\$82,325 \neq 0$$

Therefore, the actual cost of the new borrowed capital would be

$$i = 9\% + \left(\frac{\$215,470}{\$297,795}\right)(1\%)$$
$$= 9.7\%$$

Figure 6.2 shows the graph of present worth versus interest rate.

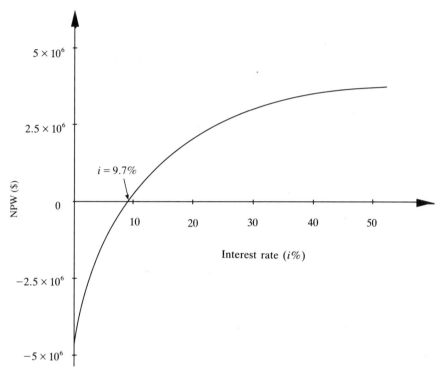

Figure 6.2 Graph of net present worth versus rate of return for Example 6.2.

6.3 CHOOSING THE ROR BEFORE A TRIAL-AND-ERROR CALCULATION

In the process of finding the solution for the unknown ROR by using compound interest methods, it often is necessary to calculate the net present worths (or the net annual worths or the net future worths) at numerous times. Of course, the time required for computation will be greatly reduced if the first interest rate tried is quite close to the correct rate. The simplest and most often used method of approximating a ROR on investment without using compound interest equations is to disregard the timing of revenues and disbursements. The predicted sum of the disbursements, including the original investment, is deducted from the total of the predicted revenues. This excess revenue over disbursements is then converted into an annual amount by dividing by the number of years involved in the study. The ROR is found by dividing the net revenue per year amount by the original investment.

Also, when the salvage value is close to 100% of the amount of the investment, the net annual revenues divided by the amount of the investment provides a good estimate for the interest rate, that is, $A/P \cong ROR$. Furthermore, when the total of the net revenues, at zero interest rate, is about to be equal or twice the investment amount, a good estimate can be obtained for the ROR from $i \cong 72/N$.

Example 6.3   Assume that the ABC Company is considering an investment of $20,000 into a project that will provide a $4,000 salvage value at the end of 5 years. The annual receipts and annual disbursements at the end of each of the next 5 years will be $10,000 and $4,500, respectively. Determine the prospective before-tax rate of return of the project.

Solution   Expressing present worth of the net cash flow:

$$NPW = -\$20,000$$
$$+ (\$10,000 - \$4,500(P/A, i\%, 5) + \$4,000(P/F, i\%, 5) = 0$$

At $i = 15\%$

$$-\$20,000 + \$5,500(3.352) + \$4,000(0.4972) = \$424.80$$

At $i = 18\%$

$$-\$20,000 + \$5,000(3.127) + \$4,000(0.4371) = -\$1,052.10$$

Therefore,

$$i = 15\% + \left(\frac{\$424.80}{\$1,477.90}\right)(3\%) \cong 15.9\%$$

Example 6.4   Consider the data given in Example 6.3 and determine the first trial rate of return by finding annual profit, without regard to the timing of the cash flows, as a percent of the average investment.

Solution   Cash inflow:

$$\text{Annual revenues} = \$10,000 \times 5 = \$50,000$$
$$\text{Salvage} = \qquad\qquad = \$4,000$$
$$\text{Total} = \qquad\qquad\quad \$54,000$$

Cash outflow:

$$\text{Annual disbursements} = \$4,500 \times 5 = \$22,500$$
$$\text{Investment} = \qquad\qquad = \$20,000$$
$$\text{Total} = \qquad\qquad\quad \$42,500$$
$$\text{Net cash inflow (gross profit)} = \qquad\qquad \$11,500$$
$$\text{Average profit per year} = \frac{\$11,500}{5} = \$2,300$$
$$\text{Original investment} = \$20,000$$

Thus,

$$\frac{\text{Average profit per year}}{\text{Original investment}} = \frac{\$2,300}{\$20,000} = 0.115 \text{ or } 11.5\%$$

Therefore, use 12% as the first trial-and-error ROR. The resulting NPW is $2,097.10, which indicates that the interest rate should be increased. Selecting the second trial-and-error ROR as 15% will result in an NPW of $424.80. However, increasing the interest rate to 18%, will result in an NPW of −$1,053.10. Therefore, since the sign of the NPW has changed [i.e., from the plus (+) sign to the minus (−) sign], it is clear that the actual ROR is somewhere between 15 and 18%. Thus, one can then interpolate or have a good base for trying a fourth rate (however, it cannot be done in this case since there are no interest tables for the interests between 15 and 18%) that will be close enough to the actual ROR answer so that interpolation error would then be fairly small. Note that if the equation of $i \cong 72/N$ is used, then the interest rate becomes $(72/5) \cong 14.4\%$ which is rather close to the actual interest rate.

6.4 EVALUATION OF INVESTMENT PROJECTS WITH MULTIPLE RATES OF RETURN

Even though it does not occur often, it is possible to have rare situations in which the case flow pattern may cause multiple solutions, rather than a unique solution, for the ROR. Such multiple ROR solutions may take place when the cumulative cash flow changes signs more than once. This is due to *Descartes' rule of signs*, which gives the maximum number of positive real roots of any polynomial equal to the number of sign changes in the coefficients.

Example 6.5   Assume that a proposed project has the following revenues (+) and disbursements (−). Find the rate of return of the project and determine whether or not to accept the project:

End of Year	Net Cash Flow for the Year	Cumulative Cash Flow
0	−$250	−$250
1	+ 600	+ 350
2	− 359.38	− 9.38

Solution   The cash flow of the proposed project is shown in Figure 6.3(*a*). The number of sign changes in the cumulative cash flow, given in the preceding table, indicates that there can be two solutions for the ROR that satisfy the given cash flow stream. Based on the net present worth method,

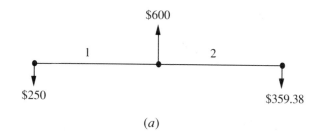

(a)

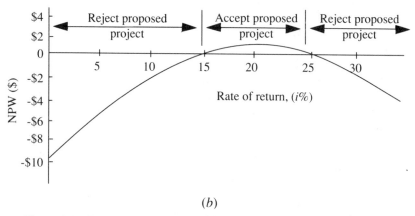

(b)

Figure 6.3 Graph of net present worth versus rate of return for Example 6.5.

$$NPW = -\$250 + \frac{\$600}{1+i} - \frac{\$359.38}{(1+i)} \overset{?}{=} 0$$

from which

$$-\$250(1+i)^2 + \$600(1+i) - \$359.38 = 0$$

or

$$(1+i)^2 - 2.40(1+i) + 1.4375 = 0$$

or

$$[(1+i) - 1.15][(1+i) - 1.25] = 0$$

Solving the last equation for i provides two answers: $i = 0.15$ or 15% and $i = 0.25$ or 25%. Of course, solving by the quadratic equation gives the same results, as does solution by trial-and-error methods.

Figure 6.3(*b*) shows the plot of the net present worth versus the rate of return of the project. The decision of whether or not to accept or reject the project depends on the unspecified MARR (or BTROR). Therefore, accept the project if the MARR is between 15 and 25%. Otherwise, reject the project.

6.5 INCREMENTAL RATE OF RETURN ANALYSIS

The *incremental rate of return* (IROR) can be defined as the rate of return that results due to an additional (i.e., incremental) initial investment when comparing against a lower cost investment. The incremental rate of return and the incremental investment are also called the *marginal rate of return* and *marginal investment*, respectively. The *incremental ROR method* (or simply, *incremental method*) is applicable when one is deciding which one of the two or more *mutually exclusive* alternative projects should be accepted. By doing so, one has to decide whether or not the *differential* (i.e., incremental) costs are justified by the differential benefits. Thus, the two alternatives are related to each other in the following manner:

High cost alternative = Lower cost alternative + Differences between them

Succinctly put, each increment of investment capital must justify itself by generating acceptable ROR on that increment. Furthermore, a higher investment alternative can be compared with respect to a lower investment alternative only if that lower investment alternative is justified. Of course, the underlying assumption is that the company is willing to invest any capital needed as long as the investment is justified by yielding an acceptable ROR on each increment of capital. Such IROR on the incremental investment for any pair of investment alternatives can be determined in one of two ways: (1) find the IROR at which the net present worth (alternatively, the net annual worth or the net future worth) of the net incremental cash flow that due to the differences among the two investment alternatives is zero, or (2) find the IROR at which the net present worth (alternatively, the net annual worth or the net future worth) of the two investment alternatives are equal.

Example 6.6 Consider three mutually exclusive alternative projects, which are given in Table 6.1. Assume that the MARR is 12%. Determine the following:

(a) The alternatives that meet the MARR criterion.
(b) Arrange the alternatives in order of increasing present worth of investment.
(c) The incremental RORs between the alternatives.
(d) Find the best alternative project.

TABLE 6.1 Date for Example 6.6

	Alternative Projects			
	A	B	C	D
First cost	$200,000	$300,000	$400,00	$450,000
Annual net income	56,007	124,275	129,366	73,230
Project life	10 year	10 year	10 year	10 year
Salvage value	0	0	0	0

Solution

(a) Calculating the ROR for each alternative:

$$\text{Alternative A} \quad \$2,000,000 = \$56,007(P/A, i\%, 10)$$

where

$$(P/A, i\%, 10) = \frac{\$200,000}{\$56,007} = 3.571$$

Thus

$$i_A = \text{ROR}_A = 25\%$$

$$\text{Alternative B} \quad \$300,000 = \$124,275(P/A, i\%, 10)$$

where

$$(P/A, i\%, 10) = \frac{\$300,000}{\$124,275} = 2.414$$

Therefore

$$i_B = \text{ROR}_B = 40\%$$

$$\text{Alternative C} \quad \$400,000 = \$129,366(P/A, i\%, 10)$$

where

$$(P/A, i\%, 10) = \frac{\$400,000}{\$129,366} = 3.092$$

Hence

$$i_C = \text{ROR}_C = 30\%$$

Alternative D $450,000 = \$73,230(P/A, i\%, 10)$

where

$$(P/A, i\%, 10) = \frac{\$450,000}{\$73,230} = 6.145$$

Thus

$$i_D = ROR_D = 10\%$$

Since the ROR of alternative D is 10% and less than the MARR (or BTROR) of 12%, alternative D is rejected and dropped from further consideration. However, the RORs of the other three alternatives exceed the MARR.

(b) Table 6.2 gives the remaining alternatives that are in the order of increasing present worth of investment.

(c) Therefore, incremental first cost and incremental annual net incomes between alternatives B and A, respectively, are

$$\Delta \text{first cost}_{B-A} = \$100,000$$

and

$$\Delta \text{annual net income}_{B-A} = \$68,268$$

Thus,

$$\$100,000 = \$68,268(P/A, i\%, 10)$$

where

$$(P/A, i\%, 10) = \frac{\$100,000}{\$68,268} + 1.4648$$

hence

TABLE 6.2 Results of Part (a) of Example 6.6

	Alternative Projects		
	A	B	C
First cost	$200,000	$300,000	$400,000
Annual net income	56,007	124,275	129,366
Rate of return	25%	40%	30%

$$i_{B-A} = \Delta ROR_{B-A} = 66\%$$

Similarly, for the increments between alternatives C and B

$$\Delta \text{first cost}_{C-B} = \$100,000$$

and

$$\Delta \text{annual net income}_{C-B} = \$5,091$$

Therefore,

$$\$100,000 = \$5,091(P/A, i\%, 10)$$

where

$$(P/A, i\%, 10) = \frac{\$100,000}{\$5,091} = 19.6425$$

thus

$$i_{C-B} = \Delta ROR_{C-B} \cong 0\%$$

Since the B–A increment is satisfactory (due to the fact that the additional investment of $100,000 earns a ROR of 66%), alternative B is preferred over alternative A; whereas, the C–B increment is unsatisfactory (due to the fact that the additional investment of $100,000 earns a negligible ROR of almost zero). Thus, alternative B is preferred over alternative C. Therefore, the conclusion is to choose alternative B.

6.6 INCREMENTAL RATE OF RETURN ANALYSIS USING SMITH'S NETWORK DIAGRAM METHOD

If there are a number of mutually exclusive alternative projects and the MARR (either in terms of before-tax or after-tax percentage) is not known, the preferred alternative project can be expressed in a conditional manner. Smith [66] has developed a graphical solution method that is known as the *network diagram method* to simplify the selection process.

In the network diagram method a *n*-sided closed (geometric) figure is drawn. Here, the *n* represents the *n* alternative projects. For example, a triangle represents three mutually exclusive alternative projects, and a square and a pentagon represent four and five mutually exclusive alternatives, respectively. The corners of the figure are arranged clockwise in increasing order of investment. Thus, the first corner drawn always represents the alternative project requiring the lowest capital investment. Therefore, proceeding clockwise around the diagram, each successive corner represents the alternative project requiring the next greater capital investment. The sides between the corners are connected to each other and are tipped with arrows pointing toward the next higher investment corner. Also, each such side is labeled with the associated rate of return on the incremental investment that is involved.

According to Smith's network diagram method, the best alternative project can be found graphically by starting at the first corner representing the lowest capital investment and selecting the path (i.e., line) with the highest IROR originating from that corner. The selected path is indicated by small arrows. If the MARR is greater than the ROR on this "decision path," then the alternative requiring the lowest investment is the better one. Then the path with the greatest IROR is chosen among the paths originating from the second *decision point*. This process is repeated until the largest investment is reached and the last *decision process* is completed for that investment. After the completion of such decision paths for all alternatives involved, a *choice table*, which gives the decision of selecting the best alternative in a conditional manner, is prepared.

If the *do-nothing* (i.e., no investment) alternative is available, the process involved is the same as before. The only difference is that the number of corners involved has been increased by one (which represents the do-nothing alternative). Of course, the process starts at the corner that represents the do-nothing alternative since it has the lowest (i.e., no investment) investment requirement.

Example 6.7   Assume that there are four mutually exclusive alternative projects, which are alternatives A, B, C, and D, as given in Table 6.3. Investment is mandatory, MARR is not known, and sufficient funds are available for all investments, as long as the projects can generate RORs that are equal or higher than the unknown MARR. Alternative projects are listed in the order of ascending investment. However, additional information on operating costs, salvage values, and so forth have been included in

TABLE 6.3   Data for Example 6.7

Alternative Project	First Cost	0 (%)	A (%)	B (%)	C (%)
		IROR			
A	$100,000	17			
B	200,000	8	40		
C	300,000	10	15	33	
D	400,000	−5	6	25	20

the IROR calculations but not given in Table 6.3. The useful life of each investment project is 5 years. Note that alternative 0, the do-nothing alternative (i.e., rejection of all four alternatives), is not allowed in this example (it is simply included in the table for its use in the next example, i.e., Example 6.8). The table is read from left to right so that alternatives in the column on the left are compared to other alternatives in the top row. Values of IROR are given only where a higher cost alternative in the left-hand column can be compared to a lower cost alternative in the top row. For example, on the second row, the $100,000 increment of B above A ($200,000 − $100,000 = $100,000), an IROR of 40% can be earned. (Also, note that the $100,000 increment of B above the do-nothing alternative 0, an IROR of 8% can be earned.) Determine the following:

(a) Draw the network diagram for the example.
(b) Indicate the decision path involved on the network diagram by using small arrows.
(c) Prepare a choice table showing the preferred alternative project at the various MARR possibilities.

Solution

(a) Since there are four alternative projects, the network diagram is represented by a square, as shown in Figure 6.4(a).
(b) The decision path involved has been indicated on the network diagram by using small arrows. Note that the process starts at A since it represents the lowest cost investment alternative. Among the paths that originate at the decision point A, the path AB provided the highest IROR (since 40% is greater than 15 and 6%). The next decision point is point B, which has two paths that originate from it.

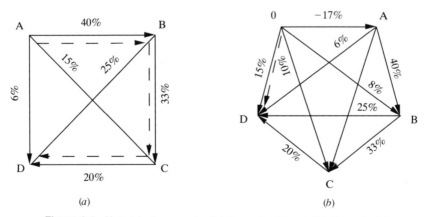

(a)   (b)

Figure 6.4 Network diagrams for (a) Example 6.7 and (b) Example 6.8.

TABLE 6.4   Choice Table for Example 6.7

If	Choose Alternative
$40\% \leq \text{MARR}$	A
$33\% < \text{MARR} \leq 40\%$	B
$20\% < \text{MARR} \leq 33\%$	C
$\text{MARR} \leq 20\%$	D

Selecting the path that provides the greater IROR (i.e., 33 over 25%), the next decision point is point C. Note that at this point, there is only one possible path (i.e., starting from point C to point D), which provides an IROR of 25%. At point D the process ends since there are no paths that originate from that point.

(c) The resulting choice table is given in Table 6.4. It gives the preferred alternative project at the various MARR possibilities.

Example 6.8   Repeat Example 6.7 but assume that the do-nothing alternative is allowable, that is, investment is not mandatory.

Solution

(a) Since there are five alternatives now, the network diagram is represented by a pentagon, as shown in Figure 6.4(b).
(b) The resulting new decision path has been indicated in Figure 6.4(b).
(c) The resulting choice table is given in Table 6.5. It gives the preferred alternative project at the various MARR possibilities.

6.7   SOME COMMENTS ON CRITERIA FOR RANKING PROJECTS

In general, for a given company the funds required to finance all the *capital expenditure projects proposed* almost always exceed the *funds available* for such projects. Of course, whenever such rationing takes place, it is necessary to use some criterion. There are various different critieria for the ranking of discretionary capital projects that have been proposed in the

Table 6.5   Choice Table for Example 6.8

If	Choose Alternative
$15\% < \text{MARR}$	0
$\text{MARR} \leq 15\%$	D

literature of the capital budgeting and engineering economy. For example, such criteria include ranking projects in descending order of the certain value or the expected value of ROR, NPW, NPW/P (where P represents the amount of investment into the project), NAW (i.e., net annual worth of the investment project), NAW/P, and

$$\frac{NPW}{PWC} = \frac{NAW}{AWC} \qquad (6.7)$$

It is interesting to note that in the event of having zero income taxes, equation (6.7) is analogous to the benefit/cost (B/C) ratio (criterion) minus one and can be expressed as

$$\frac{PWR - PWC}{PWC} = \frac{PWR}{PWC} - 1 = \frac{AWR - AWC}{AWC} = \frac{AWR}{AWC} = 1 \qquad (6.8)$$

where

PWR = present worth of revenues,

AWR = annual worth of revenues,

PWC = present worth of costs,

AWC = annual worth of costs.

If the precise cutoff rate of return were known and applied in the above criteria, all would yield the same list but not necessarily the same *ranking* of projects. Thus, if the cost of external funds (less than the cutoff rate of return of capital rationing) is used, the aforementioned criteria will not necessarily yield the same list or ranking. Some engineering economists advocate that one use a *trial* cutoff rate, then successively adjust that rate up or down until funds available just balance the funds required to finance those projects that, at the final trial rate, have a nonnegative value for that NPW or NAW type of criterion.

The proceeding ranking criteria have been applied to four (not so usual type) independent projects that are given in Table 6.6. Project 1 requires investments of $100,000 now and $110,000 at the end of year 1; in return it provides an income of $231,000 at the end of year 1. Project 2 requires investments of $1 now and $100,000 at the end of year 1; in return it provides $111,001.10 at the end of year 1. Project 3 requires an investment of $1 now, but in return it provides $11,001.10 at the end of year 1. And project 4 requires investments of $100,000 now and $1,000 at the end of each year forever, but it provides an annual income of $22,000 at the end of each year forever. It is interesting to note that, based on the aforementioned criteria, the resultant ranking of the projects is substantially different. For example, the ROR criterion ranks projects 2 and 3 as first choice followed by projects 1 and 4, whereas the NAW criterion ranks all of the projects as first choice.

TABLE 6.6 Review of Ranking Method Applications to Four Specific Projects

Project Number	Cash Flow Diagram	ROR	NPW	$\dfrac{\text{NPW}}{P}$	NAW	$\dfrac{\text{NAW}}{P}$	$\dfrac{\text{NPW}}{\text{PWC}} = \dfrac{\text{NAW}}{\text{AWC}}$
1		21%	$10K	0.1	$11K	0.11	0.05
2		1,100,010%	$10K	10,000	$11K	11,000	0.11
3		1,100,010%	$10K	10,000	$11K	11,000	10,000
4		21%	$110K	1.1	$11K	0.11	1.00
Resultant ranking		2 & 3, 1 & 4	4, 1 & 2 & 3	2 & 3, 4, 1	1 & 2 & 3 & 4	2 & 3, 1 & 4	3, 4, 2, 1

Criterion will bias ranking in favor of projects that have

	ROR	NPW	$\dfrac{\text{NPW}}{P}$	NAW	$\dfrac{\text{NAW}}{P}$	$\dfrac{\text{NPW}}{\text{PWC}}$
1. High first cost		X		X		X
2. Long Life		X	X			X
3. High gross profit margin		X				X

In general, the criteria of NPW, NAW, and (NPW/PWC) = (NAW/AWC) will bias ranking in favor of projects that have high first cost. Similarly, the criteria of NPW, NPW/P, and (NPW/PWC) = (NAW/AWC) will bias ranking in favor of projects that have long lives. Further, the criterion of (NPW/PWC) = (NAW/AWC) will bias ranking in favor of projects that have high gross profit margin. Therefore, based on the results, one may conclude that there is no answer for using a specific method over others.

Furthermore, a review of the capital budgeting and engineering economy clearly indicates the differences of opinion among the capital budgeting and engineering economy theorists in the choice of a ranking methodology. In general, all the theorists can be classified under one of three categories with regard to their suggestion of a ranking method. The three categories include (1) those who suggest the use of a single method, (2) those who suggest multiple methods, and (3) those who have avoided discussion in this area. A survey of 27 books has been performed and the results are presented in Table 6.7.

The survey shows that the NPW and ROR methods are most widely accepted as the best methods. For example, it can be seen from the table that 33% of theorists suggested the use of the NPW method either by itself or in combination with the ROR method. It is slightly higher that the acceptance of the ROR method which was 26%. Together, the ROR and NPW methods received acceptance of 41% of all theorists and 80% of all theorists who openly advocated any method. As stated, nearly half of the authors omitted any discussion in the choice of a ranking methodology.

However, there was a unanimous agreement among all of the authors regarding the credibility of the payback period method. All of them discouraged the use of this method due to (1) the noninclusion of the concept of discounting and (2) the noninclusion of receipts beyond the payback period in the analysis.

TABLE 6.7 Results of a Survey of Capital Budgeting Methodology Used

Name of Method(s)	Suggested by Books	
	Number	Percentage
NPW	2	7.4
NPW or NPW/PWC	1	3.7
NPW or NAW	1	3.7
NPW, NAW, or ROR	2	7.4
NPW or ROR	3	11.1
ROR	1	3.7
NPW/P or ROR	1	3.7
B/C ratio	1	3.7
Any method	2	7.4
No discussion	13	48.1

According to some of the advocates of the NPW method, the measure of investment worth that best describes the profit potential of the proposed investment is the net present worth of the cash flows associated with the proposed investment. Advocates of the NPW method also express the opinion that choosing investments with the NPW method maximizes the net present value of the company and this, in turn, implements the goal and maximizes the wealth of the stockholders. Some of the theorists suggest that under capital rationing the NPW method be used and that one continue successive iterations with increasing rates until the funds available match the amounts required.

According to the advocates of the ROR method, the NPW method requires the accurate determination of the rate. However, the advocates of the ROR method immediately point out that (1) the ranking is not sensitive to minor changes in the rate and (2) the ROR method also requires the determination of the cutoff rate in the final choice. Also, these advocates claim the following advantages: (1) computational ease, (2) provides a compact summary measure of the economic evaluation of a given project, and (3) avoids the difficult task of establishing the rate to be used in the study (i.e., MARR).

Furthermore, there are many who advocate the simultaneous use of both the ROR and NPW methods. They recommend the use of the ROR method under *correct circumstances* and, if it produces incorrect results, to decide on the ranking produced by the NPW method. For example, consider two alternative projects A and B. Assume that project A has a ROR of 30% and that project B has a ROR of 100%. Based on the RORs, one is inclined to select project B. But project B gives only $1 profit on a $1 investment, whereas project A provides $3,000 profit on a $10,000 investment. Therefore, the simultaneous use of ROR and NPW methods results in the correct answer. Some theorists even suggest that there is no one single best ranking method to use and that in many situations the optimal set of projects is more important than their ranking.

In summary, one can conclude that the NPW method should be used for the following reasons: (1) it is the most popular method, (2) the ROR method does not always produce correct results, (3) it facilitates the use of multiple rates to study projects, (4) it maximizes the net present worth of the company, and (5) it best meets the goals of the stockholders. However, if the first cost of the projects differ considerably, the NPW method does not give the optimal set of investments. In such a case the NPW/P method could be used to provide additional information.

PROBLEMS

6.1 Assume that you have the choice of buying a 7%, $1,000 at 95 or 10 shares of 10% preferred stock, par valued at $100 per share, at 105.

Perform all necessary calculations to the nearest $\frac{1}{10}\%$ and determine the following:

(a) The effective yield of each investment.

(b) The difference between the yields, in percent.

6.2 How much must be invested in $1,000, 8% bonds to have an annual income from interest of $4,000 if the bonds sell at 85? Assume a brokerage fee of $4 per bond.

6.3 Assume that a 6% preferred stock has a par value of $100 and is selling for $75\frac{3}{4}$. Determine its rate of return.

6.4 Assume that a $1,000, 6% bond is sold for $875 and that the bond will mature in 10 years. Determine the before-tax rate of return if the interest is payable annually.

6.5 An equipment rental firm purchases a wheeled tractor shovel for $18,000. It is hired out to construction contractors for 5 years, and the total receipts and disbursements are as given in Table P6.5.

After the fifth year the tractor shovel is overhauled and sold for $2,000. What was the rate of return on the investment? Was it attractive if the minimum attractive rate of return was 12%?

Table P6.5   Data for Problem 6.5

End of Year	Operating Receipts	Salvage	Operating Disbursements	Overhaul	Net Cash Flow
0			$18,000		−$18,000
1	$10,000		6,200		+3,800
2	11,500		6,000		+5,500
3	11,500		5,900		+5,600
4	10,500		6,000		+4,500
5	9,500	$2,000	6,500	$1,000	+4,000
Total	$53,000	$2,000	$48,600	$1,000	$5,400

6.6 A man invested in 100 shares of mutual funds 5 years ago at $20.10 per share. A year later he bought an additional 20 shares at $14.50. His dividends the first 3 years were $400, $300, and $200, respectively. He was paid $100 in dividends the last 2 years. Since the price of the shares were steadily declining, all 120 shares held were sold at the end of the fifth year at $14.17. Could he have done better by placing his money in a bank at $5\frac{1}{2}\%$ interest? What return did he earn on his mutual fund investment?

6.7 A $5,000, 5% bond matures in 20 years. Interest is paid semiannually with the first payment due in 6 months. The bond currently sells for $4,500. Find the annual interest rate if the buyer holds the bond until maturity.

6.8 The Friendly Postal Loan Company offers public borrowing by mail service. Their newspaper advertisement states a $1,931.47 loan can be paid off with 36 monthly payments of $72 each. The ad claims that the annual interest percentage rate is 20.22% Is it correct? If not, what is the effective interest rate?

6.9 The Ace Shoe Company must purchase a new machine to form synthetic soles. The plant manager is being presented a choice between a manual and semiautomatic machine. The manual machine costs $8,000 and would require full-time operation by a skilled employee at $11,500 per year. The machine would have a 10-year life, no salvage value, and would cost an additional $2,000 per year for repairs, taxes, insurance, and so on. The semiautomatic machine has a first cost of $16,000 but can be operated by unskilled labor for $9,000 per year. It has a 10-year life and a $2,000 salvage value. The semiautomatic machine would cost the firm about $3,000 per year for repairs, taxes, insurance, and so on. If the MARR = 8%, is the additional investment in the semiautomatic machine justified?

6.10 In Problem 5.19 what is the rate of return of Mr. Jones's proposed investment?

6.11 In Problem 5.22 what is the rate of return if the contractor decided to build on the lot and purchase the sand and gravel?

6.12 Plot the present worth of the cash flows as given in Table P6.12 as a function of interest rate. Then determine the rate of return.

TABLE P6.12

End of Year	Net Cash Flow
0	−$1,590
1	+ 3,546
2	− 1,975

6.13 Calculate the rate of return for the cash flows given in Table P6.13.

TABLE P6.13

Year	0	1	2	3	4
Cash Flow	−$1,250	$150	$300	$450	$600

6.14 A firm has three mutually exclusive investment opportunities. The first costs, operating costs, and gross income are given in Table P6.14. If the minimum attractive rate of return is 11%, which alternative should be selected? Assume unlimited funds are available.

TABLE P6.14

	A	B	C
First cost	$20,000	$25,000	$38,000
Operating cost/year	5,000	4,000	3,900
Investment life	5 years	5 years	5 years
Gross income/year	$11,000	$12,000	$12,000

6.15 Nine years ago an investment of $10,000 was made. During the time since the initial $10,000 investment and today, additional annual expenses have been $750 and gross annual receipts have been $1,250. The investment was sold today for $24,000. What was the rate of return?

6.16 An individual has an opportunity to invest $5,000 in a small business venture. It is estimated that he will receive $1,500 at the end of each year for 4 years, and at the end of 4 years he can also withdraw his original investment. What is his expected rate of return?

6.17 If $12,000 is invested at time zero with a return of $1,500 at the end of the first year and an increase of $50 every year, what is the rate of return after 12 years?

6.18 If a $17,000 initial expenditure for an item of construction equipment will return $4,000 annually for 8 years and then have a salvage value of $7,000, what will be the rate of return if annual operation and maintenance costs are $1,500?

6.19 A new car has a sticker price of $4,587, but since you do not have $4,587 cash and because the salesman is your brother-in-law, you can get the car for only $400 down plus $150 for insurance and handling fees, which are necessary in order to finance the balance of the cost at 12% annual interest payable annually for 3 years. You find out later that your neighbor bought the same model and style car for $4,000 cash. What is your actual interest rate? (That is, what penalty has been incurred by not borrowing $3,500 at a bank and paying $4,000 cash for the car?)

6.20 A small shopping complex will cost $250,000. The expected rental receipts will be $26,000 a year, and expected annual disbursements for utilities and maintenance will be $8,000. It is believed that the property can be sold for $200,000 in 15 years. What is the expected rate of return if all of these figures are correct?

6.21 Twenty years ago Peter Jackson invested $5,000 in a company that has in return paid him $350 a year ever since. What has been his rate of return on his investment?

6.22 Referring to Problem 6.21, if Mr. Jackson reinvested his annual dividend in a bank that compounded his money at $5\frac{1}{2}\%$ annually, what was his total rate of return on the original $5,000 after 20 years?

6.23 You can invest $25,000 in a commercial property. This property is expected to provide an annual net income 15% greater than the annual expenses. The expenses have been estimated at $4,000 a year for the first 4 years, $6,000 annually for the next 6 years, and $8,000 for the last 5 years. What is your expected rate of return if the property is sold for $15,000 in 15 years?

6.24 What is the rate of return on an initial investment of $800 when it returns a gradient annual dividend that increases $75 a year for 7 years and the first dividend is $100?

6.25 Assume that there are five mutually exclusive alternative investment projects that are under consideration, as given in Table P6.25. The selection of one of the five projects is mandatory, that is, the do-nothing alternative is not accepted. The MARR is unknown. Determine the following:
(a) Draw the network diagram for the example.
(b) Indicate the decision path involved on the network diagram by using small arrows.
(c) Prepare a choice table showing the preferred alternative project at the various MARR possibilities.

TABLE P6.25   Data for Problem 6.25

| | IROR | | | | |
Alternative	0 (%)	A (%)	B (%)	C (%)	D (%)
A	26				
B	28	9			
C	29	27	4		
D	19	15	21	21	
E	32	2	19	12	8

6.26 Resolve Problem 6.25 but use the data given in Table P6.26.

TABLE P6.26 Data for Problem 6.26

	IROR			
Alternative	0 (%)	A (%)	B (%)	C (%)
A	5			
B	2	8		
C	15	25	18	
D	12	20	3	6

6.27 Resolve Problem 6.26 but assume that the do-nothing alternative is allowable.

___7
BREAKEVEN AND SENSITIVITY ANALYSES

Forgive, O Lord, my little jokes on Thee
And I'll forgive Thy great big one on me.
ROBERT FROST, *In the Clearing,* **1962**

7.1 INTRODUCTION

Despite its many deficiencies, *breakeven analysis* is one of the most popular methods of comparison used by the industry in this country and in those parts of the world (especially in the underdeveloped and developing countries) that are based on *labor-intensive* economies (i.e., labor-using economies) rather than *capital-intensive* (i.e., capital-using economies[†]). It is also called the payback analysis or payout analysis. It is a popular method for comparing investment alternatives because it tells the investor the number of years required to recover the initial cash investment. Therefore, the *breakeven period* (also called the *payback period* or *payout period*) is the ratio of the initial fixed investment over the net annual cash inflows for the recovery period. In other words it is the period of time required for the cumulative profit, or other benefits, from an investment to be equal to the initial cost of the investment. Thus, it represents the number of years required to recover the initial investment based on zero interest rate. Such a relationship may be expressed as a *breakeven point* or *standoff*.

If the breakeven period calculated is less than some maximum acceptable breakeven period, the proposed project is accepted. Otherwise, it is reject-

---

[†]In such countries where capital is extremely limited, the emphasis on quick capital turnover in the breakeven criterion is much more pronounced. It is also popular in centralized socialist societies since it is in harmony with their ideological beliefs concerning the social harm of interest charges.

ed. The breakeven analysis[†] can be used to deal with such affairs as the investment justified by a prospective cost saving, annual hours of operation necessary before a proposed extra investment is profitable, and the period of time in which a proposed investment will *pay for itself*. The reciprocal of a breakeven period is called an effective interest rate, i, or effective rate of return.

Example 7.1 Assume that an investor is considering two mutually exclusive prospective investment alternatives. Alternative A requires an investment of $1,000 now and, in return, it provides a revenue of $1,000 at the end of year 1. Whereas, alternative B requires an investment of $10,000 now and, in return, it provides a uniform annual revenue of $4,000 at the end of the next 5 years. Assume that the salvage values are zero for both alternatives. Determine which alternative is a better investment opportunity based on the breakeven analysis.

Solution For alternative A

$$\text{Breakeven period} = \frac{\text{Investment cost}}{\text{Uniform annual revenue}} = \frac{\$1,000}{\$1,000} = 1 \text{ year}$$

For alternative B

$$\text{Breakeven period} = \frac{\text{Investment cost}}{\text{Uniform annual revenue}} = \frac{\$10,000}{\$4,000} = 2.5 \text{ years}$$

Of course, since the objective involved in such an application of breakeven analysis is to minimize the breakeven period, alternative A is selected. However, at a closer look, one can observe that alternative B has a breakeven period of 2.5 years and provides a uniform annual revenue of 40%.[‡] Its cumulative revenue over the 5-year period is $20,000. Whereas, alternative A, with a breakeven period of 1 year, provides a revenue of 100%, but its cumulative revenue over the 1-year period is only $1,000. In other words its return is merely equal to its investment amount without any profit.

Example 7.2 Assume that an investor has three mutually exclusive investment alternatives. Alternative A requires an investment of $10,000 now and, in return, it provides a uniform annual cash flow of $2,500 at the end of

---

[†]The breakeven analysis is also called *cost–volume–profit analysis* and is often used for financial studies since it is simple and provides useful insights from a minimum amount of data. Of course, such studies take into account production costs and operating policies.

[‡]Note that the inverse of the breakeven period is equal to a uniform annual return (or benefit) of 0.40 or 40%. Thus, the reciprocal of the payback period can be used as a crude measure of the average rate of return on original investments.

each of the next 4 years. Alternative B also requires an investment of $10,000 now and, in return, it provides a cash flow of $4,000, $3,000, $2,000, and $1,000 at the end of years 1, 2, 3, and 4, respectively. Whereas, alternative C also requires an investment of $10,000 now and, in return, it provides a cash flow of $1,000, $2,000, $3,000, and $4,000 at the end of years 1, 2, 3, and 4, respectively. Use the breakeven method and determine the best alternatives.

Solution For alternative A

$$\text{Breakeven period} = \frac{\text{Investment cost}}{\text{Uniform annual revenue}} = \frac{\$10,000}{\$2,500} = 4 \text{ years}$$

For alternative B

$$\text{Breakeven period} = \frac{\$10,000}{\$2,500} = 4 \text{ years}$$

For alternative C

$$\text{Breakeven period} = \frac{\$10,000}{\$2,500} = 4 \text{ years}$$

Note that the amounts of $2,500 for alternatives B and C represent the average annual revenues without taking into account the time values of the cash flows involved. Therefore, from the point of breakeven periods, all three alternatives are equally attractive. In other words these projects would be considered equally desirable despite the fact that the second alternative provides larger returns than do the other two alternatives during the early years in the life of the investment. Thus, alternative B should be the first choice followed by the alternatives A and C as the second and third choices, respectively.

Example 7.3 Assume that there are two mutually exclusive alternatives that are under consideration. Both projects require an investment of $15,000. Alternative A has a uniform annual return of $5,000, at the end of the year, for each of the next 3 years. On the other hand alternative B provides the same amount, that is, $5,000 per year, but *forever*. Use the breakeven method and determine the better alternative.

Solution In both alternatives

$$\text{Breakeven period} = \frac{\$15,000}{\$5,000} = 3 \text{ years}$$

Therefore, these alternatives would be considered equally desirable by the breakeven criterion, despite the fact that the first alternative project provides *nothing* over and above the initial investment, whereas the second alternative project provides a $5,000 return each year *forever* after the end of the payback period.

7.2 SOME COMMENTS ON THE USE OF BREAKEVEN ANALYSIS

The characteristics of the breakeven analysis can be summarized as follows: (1) It is an approximate rather than an exact analysis method. (2) All cash flows, in terms of all expenses and all profits or savings of the investment, before the breakeven period are included without taking into account the differences in their timing. (3) Since it is an approximate analysis method, the method may or may not provide the right answer. (4) It completely ignores all earnings beyond the breakeven period and therefore penalizes projects that have long economic lives in favor of those that provide greater earnings or savings for a relatively short period of time. Thus, it considers only the recovery period as a whole. Therefore, it cannot be used as a measure of profitability.

However, when the business cycle is at a low point and prospective revenues of the existing projects are correspondingly low, the breakeven period becomes more important since a short breakeven period will return the capital to the company for reinvestment in more profitable future projects when the business cycle has improved. The use of the breakeven period method is sometimes justified on the basis that it does afford management limited insight into the risk and liquidity of a prospective project. However, as a measure of investment risk, the breakeven period method is less than satisfactory. It does provide a crude measure of risk in the sense that there is usually less certainty about near-term cash inflows than those in the more distant future. Thus, the shorter the breakeven period, supposedly, the less risk the project, and the greater its *liquidity*. If the company is cash poor, it may find the breakeven method to be very beneficial in measuring the early recovery of the initial investment capital. However, the use of the breakeven period as a measure of investment risk fails to take into account the possible dispersion or variation in cash inflows within each year during the life of the project. Therefore, it cannot be considered an adequate indicator of risk. Hence, when the breakeven method is employed, it should be more appropriately treated as a restriction to be met than as a profitability criterion to be maximized. In general, it is recommended that, in addition to the use of the breakeven method, one of the discounted cash flow methods, preferably the present worth method should be used so that the decision maker can compare alternative projects with respect to both profitability and liquidity.

7.3 SOME OF THE POSSIBLE APPLICATION AREAS OF THE BREAKEVEN METHOD

The possible application areas of the breakeven method are rather large. For example:

1. To determine the cash inflow necessary to equal (breakeven with) the equivalent cash outflow, as done in Chapter 5.
2. To determine the rate of return at which the two alternative projects are equally attractive.
3. To determine the annual sales and production level necessary for two or more alternative production equipment, with different capacity, to be equal in annual equivalent cost.
4. To determine the economic life of an equipment necessary for selection of the associated alternative.
5. To determine the future salvage values of an equipment that will have no effect on timing of the retirement.
6. To determine the level of product promotion expenses justifiable in terms of increased sales.
7. To determine the applicable inflation rate under which the differences between two alternatives will be nil.
8. To determine the best investment alternative for a company that is short of working capital.
9. To determine the future income tax rates at which the differences between two alternatives will be negligible.
10. To determine the best alternative among various alternatives that are subject to rapid technological changes (e.g., lease versus purchase of large-frame computers).
11. To determine the best alternative among various alternatives when it is difficult to establish the MARR.
12. To hedge against possible errors in estimating future cash flows.

Example 7.4 Use a MARR of 15% and resolve Example 7.3 using present worth method.

Solution For alternative A

$$PW_A = -\$15,000 + \$5,000(P/A, 15\%, 3)$$
$$= -\$15,000 + \$5,000(2.283) = -\$3.585$$

For alternative B

$$PW_B = -\$15,000 + \$5,000(P/A, 15\%, \infty)$$
$$= -\$15,000 + \$5,000(6.667) = \$18,335$$

Note that alternative B is clearly a better project from the financial point of view when the present worth method is used. However, when the breakeven method is used, as it has been done in Example 7.3, the two alternatives were found to be equally desirable.

7.4 IMPROVED BREAKEVEN ANALYSIS

Some of the aforementioned deficiencies of the breakeven analysis can be eliminated by taking into account of the time values of the month as well as including any salvage values that exist in the prospective alternatives into the calculations.

Example 7.5   Assume that there are two mutually exclusive and mandatory alternatives that are considered by the Ghost City council. Alternative A requires an investment of $25,000 now and provides an annual income of $10,000 at the end of each of the next N years. Also, it has a salvage value of $1,000 at the end of the N years. Alternative B requires an investment of $35,000 now and, in return, provides an annual income of $14,000 at the end of each of the next N years. Its salvage value will be negligible at that time. Use a MARR of 10% and determine the number of years of operation required to breakeven between the two alternatives.

Solution   Setting

$$NPW_A = NPW_B - \$25,000 + \$10,000(P/A, 10\%, N) + \$1,000(P/F, 10\%, N)$$
$$= -\$35,000 + \$14,000(P/A, 10\%, N)$$

or after simplifying,

$$\$4(P/A, 10\%, N) - (P/F, 10\%, N) = \$10$$

from which the number of years of operation required to breakeven between the two alternatives can be found as 3.287 years. Note that until the breakeven period of 3.287 years, alternative A is preferable; but after the breakeven period alternative B is a better alternative. Therefore, alternative B must be chosen by the Ghost City council.

7.5 SOME COMMENTS ON BREAKEVEN POINT PROBLEMS IN PRODUCTION

In production problems the term *breakeven point* describes the production level of operation at which total revenue is equal to the total cost of production. In general, there are many possible breakeven criteria that can be used to determine the number of hours of operation required: (1) for a prospective investment to become profitable, (2) for the required life of a prospective project to pay for itself, and (3) for an investment to be justified by a prospective cost savings. If the cost and revenue functions can be assumed to be linear, then

$$\text{Total cost} = \text{Fixed cost} + \text{Unit Variable cost} \times \text{Number of units produced}$$

(7.1)

and

$$\text{Total revenue} = (\text{Unit Selling price}) \times \text{Number of units sold} \quad (7.2)$$

Thus, by setting total cost function equal to total revenue function, it is possible to determine the breakeven rate (i.e., level) as

$$\text{Breakeven production units} = \frac{\text{Fixed cost}}{\text{Selling price per unit} - \text{Variable cost per unit}}$$

(7.3)

The best known breakeven model refers fixed and variable costs to revenues for the purpose of profit analysis. Therefore, the name *breakeven chart* refers to the situation at which total revenue and total cost of operations exactly break even. Thus, at such point, one additional unit manufactured or sold would result in a profit. Of course, until such breakeven point is achieved, the manufacturer operates at a loss for the period.

Example 7.6   Assume that the Zubits International Corporation is considering producing a new type of zubit. The total cost of producing 10,000 zubits per month is $25,000. Whereas, the total cost of producing 15,000 zubits per months is $30,000. Assume that variable costs are directly proportional to the number of units produced. Determine the following:

(a) The variable cost per unit.
(b) The total fixed cost per unit.
(c) The fixed cost per unit for the first 1,000 units per month.
(d) The total cost per unit for the first 1,000 units per month.
(e) If the zubit is sold for $6 per unit, how many zubits per month have to be produced for costs to breakeven with revenues?
(f) What is the gross profit or loss to produce and sell 4,000 zubits per month if the zubits are sold for $6 per unit?
(g) What is the gross profit or loss to produce and sell 12,000 zubits per month if the zubits are sold for $6 per unit?

Solution

(a) The variable cost per unit is equal to the slope of the total cost curve. Thus, the variable cost per unit is

$$\text{Variable cost} = \frac{\$30,000 - \$25,000}{15,000 - 10,000} = \$1.00 \text{ per unit}$$

Note that the variable cost per unit is also called the *marginal cost* per unit or *incremental cost* per unit.

(b) Since from equation (7.1) the total cost can be expressed as

$$\text{Total cost} = \text{Fixed cost} + (\text{Unit Variable cost}) \times \text{Number of units produced}$$

Thus, by using the given values for the two production levels,

$$\$25,000 = \text{Fixed cost} + (\$1.00/\text{unit})(10,000 \text{ units}) \qquad (7.4)$$

and

$$\$30,000 = \text{Fixed cost} + (\$1.00/\text{unit})(15,000 \text{ units}) \qquad (7.5)$$

Therefore, from equation (7.4) or (7.5), it can be found that the fixed cost is $15,000.

(c) Since the fixed cost is $15,000, the fixed cost per unit is $15 for the first 1,000 zubits per month.

(d) The total cost per unit for the first 1,000 zubits per month is ($25,000/1,000) = $25 per unit.

(e) From Figure 7.1 the breakeven point can be graphically found to be 3,000 zubits per month. Alternatively, the breakeven point can be found by setting the total cost equation equal to the total income equation. From equation (7.1)

$$\text{Total cost} = \$15,000 + (\$1.00/\text{unit})(x \text{ units/month})$$

and

$$\text{Total revenue} = (\$6/\text{unit})(x \text{ units/month})$$

Therefore,

$$\$15,000 + (\$1.00/\text{unit})(x \text{ units/month}) = (\$6/\text{unit})(x \text{ units/month})$$

Thus, $x = 3,000$ units per month, and 3,000 units have to be produced for costs to breakeven with revenues.

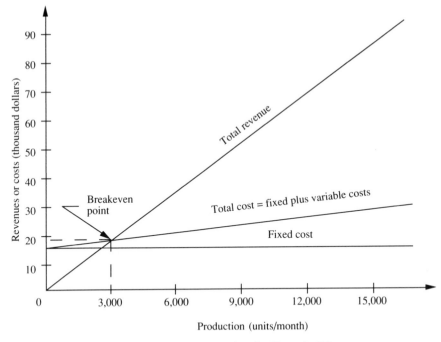

Figure 7.1   Breakeven chart for Example 7.6.

(f) Total cost = \$15,000 + (\$1.00/unit)(4,000 units) = 19,000, and

$$\text{Total revenue} = (\$6/\text{unit})(4,000 \text{ units}) = \$24,000$$

Thus, the gross profit is \$5,000 per month.

(g) Total cost = \$15,000 + (\$1.00/unit)(12,000 units) = \$27,000, and

$$\text{Total revenue} = (\$6/\text{unit})(12,000 \text{ units}) = \$72,000$$

Therefore, the gross profit is \$45,000 per month.

Example 7.7   Assume that the ABC Company is contemplating producing a new product. It is estimated that the necessary production equipment will cost \$150,000, plus its operating and maintenance (O&M) costs will be \$35 per hour. The additional annual overhead cost, as a result of producing the new product, will be \$75,000. The industrial engineer in charge of the project estimates that the necessary production time, based on a time-and-motion study, will be 150 hours to manufacture 1,000 units. Further, it is estimated that the product life is 10 years, and it will be sold \$15 per unit. Use a MARR of 20% and determine the number of units that have to be produced annually to breakeven. Assume that the salvage value will be zero at the end of 10 years.

Solution Let x be the number of units to be produced annually to breakeven. Setting annual worth of costs (AWC) to be equal to annual worth of revenues (AWR) at a MARR of 20%,

$$AWC = AWR$$

where

$$AWC = \$15,000(A/P, 20\%, 10) + \$75,000 + 0.150(\$35)x$$
$$= \$110,778 + \$5.25x$$
$$AWR = \$15x$$

Thus,

$$\$110,778 + \$5.25x = \$15$$

hence,

$$x \cong 11,362 \text{ units}$$

7.6 ANALYSIS OF MAKE-OR-BUY DECISIONS

The decisions of producing (i.e., making) a product internally or purchasing (i.e., buying) the product from an outside supplier (i.e., vendor) are mutually exclusive alternative choices. Thus, one can either produce or purchase the product but cannot do both. Such a make-or-buy decision is often encountered when a product can be made in-house at a lower variable cost than the purchase price for that product from a vendor. Usually, the *fixed costs* (i.e., *overhead costs*) of the plant or operation will exist regardless of whether the product is bought externally or made internally. Therefore, they should be taken into account accordingly; also, qualitative aspects (e.g., legal and/or ethical factors and/or relationships between the company and a vendor or between the company and its labor union).

Example 7.8 Assume that the Zubits International Corporation is producing 120 different types of products. A recently hired engineering manager in charge of production is performing a make-or-buy analysis on 4 of 125 products. Table 7.1 gives variable costs, in terms of direct material and direct labor, for products A, B, C, and D. It also provides fixed costs (i.e., overhead costs) in terms of costs of allocated plant floor space and other

TABLE 7.1   Data for Example 7.7

	Cost Types	Product Types			
		A	B	C	D
Variable costs	Direct labor	$80	$60	$40	$90
Variable costs	Direct material	20	40	100	30
Total variable costs		$100	$100	$140	$120
Fixed costs	Cost of allocated floor space	$50	$4	$10	$10
Fixed costs	Other fixed costs	10	56	10	70
Total fixed costs		$60	$60	$20	$80
Total costs		$160	$160	$160	$200

fixed costs (e.g., administration, repayment and pretax return on investment, property taxes, and insurance). Assume that a vendor is willing to provide the four products (A, B, C, and D) for $140, $170, $130, and $205, respectively. Furthermore, assume that the purchase of any or all four products from the outside supplier will not affect any of the overhead costs of the corporation. Find which, if any, of the four products should be bought rather than made within the corporation.

Solution   Since the fixed costs (i.e., overhead costs) are assumed to exist despite the make-or-buy decision, the only possible savings will be in the total variable costs, made up of direct labor and direct material costs. Therefore, Zubits International should continue to manufacture products B and D but should purchase products A and C. The purchase of products A and C will decrease their costs by $20 and $30, respectively.

7.7   ANALYSIS OF LEASE-OR-BUY DECISIONS

It is similar to the make-or-buy decision. The total cost of purchasing, in terms of first cost (i.e., purchase price, cost of installation, cost of transportation, etc.), has to be added to operating costs when owning an equipment (or a building, etc.) is compared against one that is leased. It is important to note that any fixed cost investment to lower variable costs with regard to a strictly direct cost alternative is subject to the time that is necessary to payback the investment from variable cost savings.

Example 7.9   Assume that the Longlive Cyclons Industries Corporation is considering installing a mainframe computer for its operations. There are two possible alternatives: (1) purchase the computer for $500,000 including its installation and a 1-year warranty or (2) lease the computer for an annual fee of $100,000, which includes its installation and annual O&M expenses. It is estimated that the computer may have an economic life of 10 years. Its net salvage value (which is equal to gross salvage minus cost of removal) at the end of the 10th year will be negligible. If the computer is purchased, its annual O&M expenses are estimated to be $5,000. There are rumors that much more powerful computers will be on the market at reduced prices within a few years. Use a MARR of 10% and determine the breakeven years of use between the two alternatives.

Solution Present worth of purchasing the computer is

$$PW_{purchase} = -\$500,000 - \$5,000(P/A, 10\%, 10)$$

Similarly, the present worth of leasing the computer is

$$PW_{lease} = -\$100,000x$$

where x is the number of years required to breakeven between the purchase and lease alternatives.

$$\$500,000 + \$5,000(P/A, 10\%, 10) = \$100,000x$$

Thus, it can be found that x is 5.3 years. Therefore, if the company's engineering manager is convinced that the recent trends in computer technology will continue into the near future, the company is definitely better off leasing the computer.

7.8 PROFIT MARGIN AND CONCEPT OF DUMPING

The way that a company sees its breakeven point is a function of the specific conditions under which it operates. Thus, a successful company and a struggling company may view the same breakeven point totally different. Therefore, a company that is trying to obtain a market for its products has different concerns than of a company that has already captured a large segment of the market. The struggling company may be troubled with the lack or restriction of working capital whereas a well-established company may have a totally different problem, e.g., maintaining or expanding its market share.

For a company that is struggling or trying to get into foreign markets, the practice of selling a portion of its products at a reduced price may be an acceptable solution. Such a practice is called *dumping* and is achieved by selling to foreign markets at a lower price or by selling the same product (e.g., a television set) at various prices under various brand names. Of course, there may be many possible problems in this approach, but if it is successful, profit will rise due to the enlarged plant utilization. Obviously, an increase in plant utilization will, in turn, decrease the fixed cost per unit produced. This, in turn, causes the overall costs to decrease and net revenues to increase.

7.9 UTILIZATION OF CAPACITY

In all types of industries the utilization of available capacity is an important element in terms of profitability of operations. The primary reason for this is that *idle capacity* is not costless. There are a number of factors that can be applicable depending on the company and the situation at hand.

For example, the ratio of the maximum demand of a system (or an equipment) to the rated capacity of the system (or the equipment) is called the *utilization factor*.[†] Therefore,

$$\text{Utilization factor} = \frac{\text{Maximum demand}}{\text{Rated system capacity}} \qquad (7.6)$$

The ratio of the total actual production (or service) over a designated period of time to the production (or service) level that would have been produced (or served) if the plant (or equipment) had operated continuously at maximum rating is called the *plant factor*, or the *capacity factor*. Therefore,

$$\text{Annual plant factor} = \frac{\text{Actual annual production}}{\text{Maximum plant rating}} \qquad (7.7)$$

For example, such a factor is used in generation studies by electric power utility companies with a slight modification as

$$\text{Annual plant factor} = \frac{\text{Actual annual production}}{\text{Maximum plant rating} \times 8760} \qquad (7.8)$$

Furthermore, the concept of load factor is often encountered in practical applications. The *load factor* is defined as the ratio of average load over a designated period of time to the peak load occurring on that period. Thus,

$$\text{Load factor} = \frac{\text{Average load}}{\text{Peak load}} \qquad (7.9)$$

[†]See Gönen [33], Chapter 2, for additional information.

For example, the electric utility industry uses the annual load factor with a slight modification as

$$\text{Annual load factor} = \frac{\text{Total annual energy}}{\text{Annual peak load} \times 8760} \qquad (7.10)$$

Example 7.10 Assume that the Blueskies Commuter Airline has 10 small airplanes under operation. The combined rated system capacity and maximum (daily) demand, in terms of passengers, are about 200 and 140 passengers, respectively. Also, assume that average and peak (or maximum) numbers of passengers that fly by the airline are 120 and 180 passengers per day, respectively. Determine the following:

(a) The daily utilization factor of the airplanes.
(b) The daily load factor of the airplanes.

Solution

(a) From equation (7.6)

$$\text{Utilization factor} = \frac{140 \text{ passengers per day}}{200 \text{ passengers per day}} = 0.70 \text{ or } 70\%$$

(b) From equation (7.9)

$$\text{Load factor} = \frac{120 \text{ passengers per day}}{180 \text{ passengers per day}} = 0.67 \text{ or } 67\%$$

7.10 SENSITIVITY ANALYSIS

In engineering economy applications the word *sensitivity* describes the relationship between the relative change in forecast of some parameter of the study and the degree of attractiveness of the prospective project involved. In other words sensitivity refers to the relative magnitude of the change in one or more parameters of an engineering economy study required to alter the decision. For example, if one specific parameter can be changed over a broad range of values without affecting the previously resulted conclusion, then such decision is *insensitive* to uncertainties about that parameter. However, if a small change in the estimate of one specific parameter can change the resulted conclusion, then such a decision is *sensitive* to uncertainties about that parameter. Therefore, *sensitivity analysis* helps to determine how sensitive the results of a study are to changes in the values of the estimates. Such sensitivity analysis is performed by changing just one parameter at a time and observing the effect on acceptability of the proposed project. The parameters that may be subject to such sensitivity analysis may include the forecasted investment costs, future costs, revenues, interest rates, salvage values, and tax rates. At times, an engineering manager may observe that, in such studies, large changes in the values of certain parameters may affect the final result or conclusion very little. On the other hand small changes in the values of other parameters may affect the outcome greatly. Succinctly put, such studies provide insights for an engineering manager about (1) the effects of estimation errors that may be involved in the determination of parameters of the study and (2) the effects of such errors on the desirability of the project.[†]

Example 7.11   Assume that there are two mutually exclusive alternatives under consideration. Alternatives A and B require an initial investment of $5,000 and $7,000 and will provide net annual revenues of $2,000 and $3,000, respectively, for the next 5 years. Use a MARR of 10% and the net present worth method and determine:

(a) The better of the two alternatives.
(b) If the initial investment of alternative A is $5,500, which of the two is a better alternative.
(c) If the net annual revenue of alternative A is $2,500, which of the two is a better alternative.
(d) Repeat part (c) with an initial investment of $5,500.

Solution

(a) $NPW_A = -\$5,000 + \$2,000(P/A, 10\%, 5) = \$2,582$
    $NPW_B = -\$7,000 + \$3,000(P/A, 10\%, 5) = \$4,373$
    Of course, alternative B is a better alternative.

(b) $NPW_A = -\$5,500 + \$2,000(P/A, 10\%, 5) = \$2,082$
    Since $NPW_B = \$4,373$, alternative B is better.

(c) $NPW_A = -\$5,000 + \$2,500(P/A, 10\%, 5) = \$4,477.50$
    Since NPW_A is greater than NPW_B, alternative A is better.

(d) $NPW_A = \$5,500 + \$2,500(P/A, 10\%, 5) = \$3,977.50$
    Since NPW_A is less than NPW_B, alternative B is better.

PROBLEMS

7.1   Assume that an investor has three mutually exclusive investment alternatives. Alternative A requires an investment of $20,000 now and, in turn, it provides a uniform annual cash flow of $5,000 at the end of each of the next 6 years. Alternative B requires an investment of $30,000 now and, in return, it provides a cash flow of $5,000,

---

[†]For additional information on sensitivity analysis, see Chapter 13.

$10,000, $15,000, and $15,000 at the end of years 1, 2, 3, and 4, respectively. Alternative C requires an investment of $40,000 now, and in return, it provides a cash flow of $25,000, $15,000, $10,000, and $5,000 at the end of years 1, 2, 3, and 4, respectively. Use the breakeven method and determine the best alternative.

7.2 Resolve Problem 7.1 using the net present worth method. Use a MARR of 10%.

7.3 Resolve Example 7.3 employing the net present worth method. Use a MARR of 10%.

7.4 Assume that the Blueskies Commuter Airline is considering purchasing a small aircraft for $270,000. It is estimated that the associated net year-end cash flow stream will be $50,000 per year for the first 3-year period, $40,000 per year for the next 3-year period, $35,000 per year for the next 2-year period, and followed by $30,000 and $25,000 for year 9 and 10, respectively. It is estimated that the salvage value of the aircraft will be $70,000 at the end of year 10. Find the breakeven period for the investment.

7.5 Consider the data given in Problem 7.4 and use a before-tax MARR of 25% and determine the net present worth of the investment proposal.

7.6 Consider the solution of Example 7.7 and assume that the marketing department of the ABC Company estimates, based on their market research, that the average annual number of units that can be sold is 20,000 units. Determine the following:
(a) The annual worth of costs involved to produce 20,000 units.
(b) The annual worth of revenues from the sale of 20,000 units.
(c) The annual gross profit (or loss) that can result.

7.7 Consider the solution of Example 7.7 and assume that the marketing department of the ABC Company estimates, based on their market research, that the average annual number of units that can be sold is 15,000 units at $12 per unit. Determine the following:
(a) The annual worth of costs involved to produce 15,000 units.
(b) The annual worth of revenues from the sale of 15,000 units.
(c) The annual gross profit (or loss) that can result.

7.8 Consider Example 7.7 and assume that the company has found an alternative production equipment that will cost $200,000, but its O&M costs will be $10 per hour. The necessary production time will be reduced to 100 hours to manufacture 1,000 units. Assume that other things will remain the same and determine the number of units that have to be produced annually to breakeven.

7.9 Consider Example 7.7 and the new data given in Problem 7.8 and assume that the marketing department of the ABC Company estimates, based on their market research, that the average annual number of units that can be sold is 15,000 units. Determine the following:

(a) The annual worth of costs involved to produce 15,000 units.

(b) The annual worth of revenues from the sale of 15,000 units.

(c) The annual gross profit (or loss) that can result.

7.10 Consider Example 7.8 and assume that the corporation is a small company and it is manufacturing only the four products. Assume that the vendor is willing to provide products A, B, C, and D for $150, $170, $140, and $195, respectively. Determine which, if any, of the four products should be bought rather than made within the company.

7.11 Assume that a prospective project requires an investment of $10,000 and is estimated to return net cash flows of $2,000 each year for 8 years. If the MARR is 10%, determine the following:

(a) The breakeven period of the project.

(b) The breakeven rate of return of the project.

(c) The effective rate of return of the project.

(d) Whether or not to accept the project.

7.12 Assume that there are two mutually exclusive alternatives that are under consideration. Both alternatives require an investment of $25,000 now. Alternatives A and B have annual incomes of $8,000 and $9,000, respectively. Alternative A provides a net salvage value of $800 at the end of N years. The salvage value of alternative B is zero. Use a MARR of 15% and determine the following:

(a) The number of years required to breakeven between the two alternatives.

7.13 Resolve Example 7.11 but assume that the life of the project is 10 years.

____8
DEPRECIATION
AND DEPLETION[†]

In everything one must consider the end.
JEAN DE LA FONTAINE, *Fables*, 1668

8.1 INTRODUCTION

Depreciation is defined as a decrease in value of a physical property with use and time. Here, the word *value* may mean *market value* (i.e., the amount that will be paid by a willing buyer to a willing seller for a property) or may mean *value to the owner* (i.e., the amount that is perceived by the owner of the property). The value to the owner is also called *use value*. Also, there are other value concepts that may be encountered in practice, for example, the value estimate of a property that is reasonable and fair to all concerned, based on every proper consideration, is called *fair value*. The value of a property[‡] determined on the basis of what it would cost, usually at the present price level, to replace the property or its service with at least equally satisfactory and comparable property and service is defined as *replacement value*.

The U.S. Supreme Court has ruled that the depreciation allowance represents reduction in value through the wear and tear of depreciable

---

†The material in this book, especially in this and following chapters, illustrates only some selected requirements of the U.S. Internal Revenue Service (IRS) and each state's tax body and others. Of course, it is not advocated that the material in this book be used as the sole basis for the applications of depreciation and tax determinations. While every precaution has been taken in the preparation of this book, the author and the publisher assume no responsibility for errors or omissions. Neither is any liability assumed for damages resulting from the use of information contained herein. If legal advice or other expert assistance is required, the services of a competent professional person (attorney or accountant) should be sought.

‡The term *property* is used in this chapter in a general sense. It includes buildings, machines, goods, and so on.

assets. Therefore, depreciation represents the loss in value of a property (e.g., a production machine or equipment, vehicle, building, or other investment) over a period of time, caused by one or more of the following factors: (1) physical deterioration of the property (or equipment) due to wear and tear resulting from its usage, (2) new and greater production (or service) requirements, (3) reduced (or vanished) production requirements, (4) obsolescence of facilities by technological advances, and (5) development of improved facilities that provide products with higher quality and lower costs at improved safety levels.

8.2 DEPRECIATION ACCOUNTING

Succinctly put, *depreciation* is an annual charge made against annual revenue intended to recover the total original investment in each depreciable property, less net salvage value of the property, over its useful life. Therefore, depreciation, is a *noncash expense* that affects cash flow of a company through its effect upon income taxes. Accountants define depreciation as the *write-off* of an asset's net costs over its life, in a systematic and rational manner. Thus, *depreciation accounting* is an instrument to allocate the depreciable value of a property (i.e., capital net investment) over its depreciable life. Hence, depreciation accounting provides (1) recovery of capital that has been invested in the physical property, (2) an estimate (which approximately may represent market value) of the present value of the depreciable asset, and (3) a maximum depreciation allowance to provide maximum possible tax benefits within the legal boundaries enforced by the IRS. However, since the two aforementioned purposes are substantially different, companies are legally and openly usually permitted to keep two separate books[†] (based on two different methods of depreciation accounting).

As each new property (facility or equipment) goes into service, the original investment is added to the appropriate property account. The new asset is then said to be *capitalized*. This means that the original amount remains *on the books* (i.e., on the accounting department record) as long as it is in service. Each year, an appropriate *depreciation charge* is made against revenue and credited to the *depreciation reserve account*. When a *capitalized asset* (facility or equipment) is retired for any reason, an amount that is equal to the original investment is deducted from both the property account and the depreciation reserve account. The money in the depreciation account, together with retained earnings, deferred taxes, and investment tax credits (if any) is called *internally generated funds* and is reinvested into other projects. The depreciation charge is also called *depreciation*

[†]Some companies keep three separate books: one for tax purposes, one for the internal record keeping purposes, and one for the purpose of reporting to the stockholders of the company.

expense or *capital write-off* and appears as a tax-deductible expense on the income statement of the company.

8.3 DEPRECIATION CALCULATION FUNDAMENTALS

As mentioned before, certain expenses that take place in the production of income are tax deductible, that is, excluded from taxable income. For example, the day-to-day operating expenses of doing business are deductible as they happen. Such expenses include labor, materials, maintenance, insurance, utilities, taxes, and interest charges. However, capital expenditures (i.e., capital investments), which include buildings, machinery, trucks, office equipment, and patents, cannot be expensed; instead they can be depreciated.[†] For the purpose of such depreciation, the following estimates are required: (1) the depreciation base, which is usually equal to the cost of the property; (2) the economic (or useful) life of the property; and (3) the salvage value of the property at the end of its economic life. The *depreciation base* is also called the *first cost*, or the *original cost*, of the property, and it includes not only the cost of the property itself but also costs of transportation, installation, and start-up. The *economic*, or *useful life*, of a property is the time period between purchase when new and disposal of the property. The economic, or useful life,[‡] of a property is usually less than its physical life of the property. The *salvage value* is the amount that will be realized upon disposal of the asset. Net salvage value[§] is the difference between gross salvage value (i.e., the amount for which the property sold for) of an asset and the cost of removal and/or disposal. Therefore,

$$\text{Net salvage value} = \text{Gross salvage value} - \text{Cost of removal} \quad (8.1)$$

The *scrap value* is the amount that the property would bring if sold for junk.

 Book value of a property is the worth of a property as shown on the accounting records of a company. Hence, it is the difference between the first cost of the property and the sum of the amounts that have been charged (i.e., *accrued*) as depreciation expense up to date. Thus,

$$\text{Book value} = \text{First cost} - \text{Depreciation charges made} \quad (8.2)$$

In other words the book value of a property is the remaining unallocated cost of the property.

[†]The IRS has published *Depreciation Guidelines and Rules* to establish the useful life of a property. However, the useful life of such property can be different than the one specified in the IRS guidelines if it can be justifiable. The useful life is also called *write-off* life.

[‡]Note that land is not depreciable since its life is indeterminate. Furthermore, working capital, salvage value residual, and interest lost during construction are also not depreciable.

[§]Usually, it is referred to as simply *salvage value*.

8.4 DEPRECIATION METHODS

There are various depreciation methods that can be used to determine annual *depreciation charges*. They include the following:

1. Straight-line method
2. Sum-of-years' digits method
3. Declining-balance method
4. Sinking-fund method
5. Units of production method
6. Accelerated cost recovery system method
7. Tax Reform Act of 1986 (Internal Revenue Code of 1986)

8.5 STRAIGHT-LINE METHOD

The straight-line (SL) method of computing depreciation is based on the assumption that the loss in value is directly proportional to the age of the asset. It is the simplest method to apply and is the most widely used method of depreciation.[†] The annual depreciation charge allowed at the end of each year t is

$$D_t = \frac{P - E}{N} \tag{8.3}$$

where

P = cost of asset,
F = salvage value,
N = useful life (also called expected life or write-off period in years).

Thus, straight-line rate of depreciation is

$$R_t = \frac{1}{N} \tag{8.4}$$

Hence, the value of the asset on the books of account at the end of year t is called *book value* (BV_t) and it is equal to the undepreciated portion of the cost of asset. Thus,

$$\text{BV}_t = P - \left(\frac{P - F}{N}\right) t \tag{8.5}$$

[†]The SL method is also used in most countries of the world. Its popularity is followed by the declining-balance method and units of production method. Many governments specify applicable declining-balance rates for different assets, e.g., 0.1, 0.2, or 0.3 to be multiplied by the adjusted cost basis.

Example 8.1   Assume that the ABC Company has purchased production equipment for $5,200. The transportation costs (i.e., freight) and installation charges of the equipment are $300 and $500, respectively. The useful life of the equipment is 5 years. Its resale (salvage) value and cost of removal, at that time, are estimated to be $1,200 and $200, respectively. Use the straight-line depreciation and determine the following:

(a) First cost of the equipment.
(b) Net salvage value of the equipment.
(c) Annual depreciation charges for the equipment.
(d) Book value of the equipment at the end of year 4.
(e) Prepare a table giving a depreciation schedule and the corresponding book values for the equipment.
(f) Plot the book value versus useful life of the equipment.

Solution

(a) First cost = Purchase price + freight + installation charges
$$= \$5,200 + \$300 + \$500 = \$6,000$$
(b) Net salvage value = Gross salvage value − Cost of removal
$$= \$1,200 - \$200 = \$1,000$$
(c) Annual depreciation charge for each year is the same and is

$$D_t = \frac{P - F}{N} = \frac{\$6,000 - \$1,000}{5} = \$1,000 \text{ per year}$$

(d) The book value of the equipment at the end of year 4 is determined from equation (8.5) as

$$BV_t = P - \left(\frac{P - F}{N}\right)t \qquad (8.5a)$$

or from

$$BV_t = P - \sum_{j=1}^{t} D_j \qquad (8.5b)$$

where the second term in equation (8.5b) represents the accumulated depreciation charges. Therefore, for year 4, it is

$$BV_4 = \$6,000 - \left(\frac{\$6,000 - \$1,000}{5}\right)4 = \$2,000$$

or

$$BV_4 = \$6,000 - \sum_{j=1}^{4} \$1,000 = \$2,000$$

(e) Table 8.1 gives the complete depreciation schedule and the corresponding book values for the equipment.

(f) Figure 8.1 shows the plot of the book value versus the useful life of the equipment.

Example 8.2 In order to stimulate the economy of the country and encourage investments, from time to time, the IRS may allow 20% to be taken off of the depreciable amount of the asset as the first year's depreciation for the asset and still use the straight-line depreciation method for the remaining years. Assume that it is so, and consider Example 8.1 and determine the following:

(a) Annual depreciation charge of the equipment for the first year.

(b) Annual depreciation charges for the remaining years.

(c) Prepare a table giving depreciation schedule and the corresponding book values for the equipment.

(d) Plot the book value versus useful life of the equipment.

Solution

(a) $D_1 = 2\left(\dfrac{P-F}{N}\right) = 2(\$1,000) = \$2,000$

(b) $D_t = \dfrac{\$4,000 - \$1,000}{4} = \$750$ per year

(c) Table 8.2 gives the complete depreciation schedule and the corresponding book values for the equipment.

(d) Figure 8.2 shows the plot of the book value versus the useful life of the equipment.

TABLE 8.1 Depreciation Schedule and Corresponding Book Values for Example 8.1

End of year t	Depreciation charge for year t	Book value at the end of year t
0	0	$6,000
1	$1,000	5,000
2	1,000	4,000
3	1,000	3,000
4	1,000	2,000
5	1,000	1,000

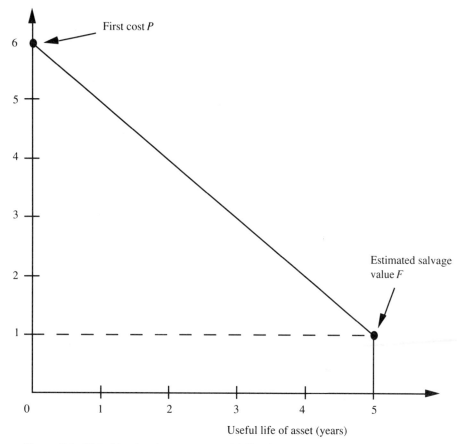

Figure 8.1   Plot of book values versus useful life of equipment in Example 8.1.

TABLE 8.2   Depreciation Schedule and Corresponding Book Values for Example 8.2

End of year t	Depreciation charge for year t	Book value at the end of year t
0	0	$6,000
1	$2,000	4,000
2	750	3,250
3	750	2,500
4	750	1,750
5	750	1,000

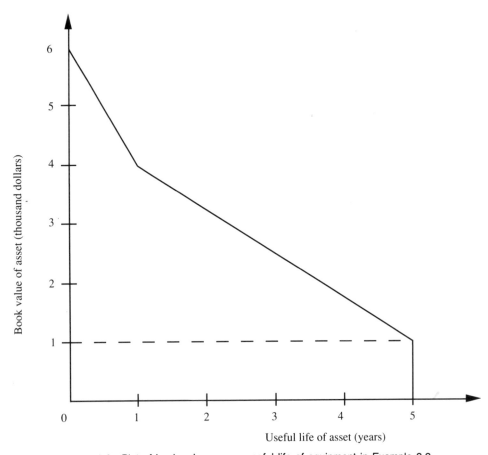

Figure 8.2   Plot of book value versus useful life of equipment in Example 8.2.

8.6   SUM-OF-YEARS' DIGITS METHOD

The sum-of-years' digits (SYD) method is one of several methods of *accelerated depreciation* used to depreciate the cost of an investment faster than by the straight-line method. It provides for depreciation charges that are larger in the early years and smaller in the later years. The primary use for accelerated depreciation methods is related to the calculation of income tax. For example, in the electric power utility industry, the straight-line method is usually used to determine book depreciation rates, and the customer pays for the recovery of the investment on a straight-line basis, whereas, accelerated depreciation is used in the calculation of income tax. Therefore, its use results in paying less tax when an investment in plant or equipment is new and more tax as it gets older. When a new plant or equipment goes into service, the utility company therefore retains the excess tax revenues in a *deferred tax account* for internal use. When the plant or equipment gets older, then *taxes due* exceed *taxes collected*. The deferred tax account then provides the difference needed to pay the tax bill.

The name of this (fast write-off)[†] method is taken from the calculation procedure. The present year's depreciation amount is determined by subtracting the salvage value from the original cost basis of the property and multiplying this quantity by a fraction (i.e., depreciation rate) that differs from year to year. The fraction has a denominator that is constant with time and is equal to the sum of the digits representing the number of years of useful life of the asset. For example, if N is 5 years, then the denominator is equal to $1 + 2 + 3 + 4 + 5 = 15$, whereas, the numerator changes each year and is equal to the number of useful years of life left in the asset at the beginning of the present year. For example, if an asset originally had a useful life of 5 years, at the end of the second year it has 3 years' useful life remaining so that the fraction for the third year would be a $\frac{3}{15}$ or $\frac{1}{5}$. Therefore, the name *sum-of-years' digits* comes from the fact that the sum

$$\text{SYD} = 1 + 2 + 3 + \cdots + (N - 1) = \frac{N(N + 1)}{2} \tag{8.6}$$

where N is the useful life of the asset. Equation (8.6) represents the denominator of the fraction. The numerator of the fraction is equal to $N - t + 1$. Therefore, the annual depreciation charge allowed at the end of year t is

$$D_t = \frac{N - t + 1}{\text{SYD}}(P - F) \tag{8.7}$$

or

$$D_t = \frac{N - t + 1}{N(N + 1)/2} + (P - F) \tag{8.8}$$

The book value of the asset at the end of year t is

$$\text{BV}_t = (P - F)\frac{(N - t)(N - t + 1)}{N(N + 1)} + F \tag{8.9}$$

Example 8.3 Consider the depreciable asset given in Example 8.1. Use sum-of-years' digits method and prepare a table giving the depreciation schedule and corresponding book values for the equipment.

Solution Since

$$\text{SYD} = \frac{N(N + 1)}{2} = \frac{5(5 + 1)}{2} = 15$$

[†]The term *fast write-off* is applicable to any method that permits depreciation at a rate faster than the straight-line method.

TABLE 8.3 Depreciation Schedule and Corresponding Book Values for Example 8.3

End of year t	Depreciation charge for year t	Book value at the end of year t
0	0	$6,000
1	$\frac{5}{15}$($5,000) = $1,666.67	4,333.33
2	$\frac{4}{15}$($5,000) = 1,333.33	3,000
3	$\frac{3}{15}$($5,000) = 1,000	2,000
4	$\frac{2}{15}$($5,000) = 666.67	1,333.33
5	$\frac{1}{15}$($5,000) = 333.33	1,000

the depreciation charge for year 1 can be found from equation (8.7) as

$$D_1 = \frac{N-t+1}{\text{SYD}}(P-F) = \frac{5-1+1}{15}(\$6,000 - \$1,000) = \$1,666.67$$

and the book value at the end of year 1 can be found from equation (8.9) as

$$\text{BV}_1 = (P-F)\frac{(N-t)(N-t+1)}{N(N+1)} + F$$

$$= (\$6,000 - \$1,000)\frac{(5-1)(5-1+1)}{5(5+1)} + \$1,000$$

$$= \$4,333.33$$

Table 8.3 gives the complete depreciation schedule and the corresponding book values for the equipment.

8.7 DECLINING-BALANCE METHOD

The declining-balance (DB) method also produces accelerated depreciation. It can be used for any property with a useful life of at least 3 years. In this method depreciation for any given year t is calculated by multiplying a constant depreciation *rate* by the present basis of the asset. In the declining-balance method,[†] it is assumed that the annual cost of depreciation is a *fixed percentage* of the book value at the beginning of the year. It provides for a fast depreciation write-off during the early years of the life of an asset, with progressively smaller depreciation charges with increasing years.

[†]It is also called the *constant percentage method* or the *Matheson formula*.

Therefore, the depreciation charge[†] for a given year t is

$$D_t = R \times BV_{t-1} \tag{8.10}$$

where

BV_{t-1} = book value of the asset at the end of the previous year (i.e., $t-1$)

R = depreciation rate for declining balance depreciation.

Thus, the book value of the asset at the end of year t is

$$BV_t = BV_{t-1} - D_t \tag{8.11}$$

Substituting equation (8.10) into equation (8.11),

$$BV_t = BV_{t-1} - R \times BV_{t-1} \tag{8.12}$$

or

$$BV_t = (1 - R)BV_{t-1} \tag{8.13}$$

Therefore, using this recursive expression, the depreciation in any given year can be expressed as

$$D_t = R(1 - R)^{t-1}P \tag{8.14}$$

Similarly, the book value at the end of year t can be expressed as

$$BV_t = (1 - R)^t P \qquad \text{as long as } BV_t \geq F \tag{8.15}$$

It is interesting to note that the age t, at which the book value of an asset, BV_t, will be declined to any given future value F, can be found from

[†]Note that equation (8.10) can be expressed as

Annual declining balance depreciation = Declining balance rate × Adjusted basis

where the term *adjusted basis* can be defined as

Adjusted basis = Cost or other basis ± Required adjustments − Cumulative depreciation previously accrued

Note that the terms *book value, tax book value,* or *adjusted basis* may mean the same thing in the United States; and the terms of *diminishing balance, written down value,* or *adjusted basis* may mean the same thing in Canada and Australia [67].

$$t = \frac{\ln(F/P)}{\ln(1 - R)} \qquad (8.16)$$

and the associated rate (i.e., at which $BV_t = F$) can be determined from

$$R = 1 - \left(\frac{E}{P}\right)^{1/t} \qquad (8.17)$$

but it is rarely used in practice. The depreciation rate is usually dictated by the IRS guidelines. Therefore, it is selected with respect to its effects on income taxes.

Furthermore, note that the depreciation charge D_t, in equation (8.10), is found by the book value only and is not affected by the salvage value F (other than the situations where $BV_t - D_{t-1} \geq F$). In this method the book value at the end of the write-off period, N years, will not normally equal the salvage value. Because of this, the taxpayer is generally allowed to switch later to straight-line depreciation for the remaining years.

As mentioned previously, in the declining-balance method, a constant depreciation rate is applied to the book value of the asset. The depreciation rate to use depends on the type of asset and when it is purchased. For example, the three depreciation rates given in the Economic Recovery Tax Act of 1981 are 200, 175, and 150% of the straight-line depreciation rate; whereas the two depreciation rates given in the Tax Reform Act of 1986 are 200 and 150% of the straight-line depreciation rate. Since 200% is twice the straight-line rate, it is called *double-declining-balance* (DDB) rate and is applied to the book value of the asset at the end of the previous year (i.e., the undepreciated balance in the account). Since the IRS permits a switch in any year (without any written permission), the optimum time to switch, of course, is in the year that results in a present worth tax advantage by deferring taxes to later years. For example, the time to switch from double-declining-balance method to straight-line depreciation method is when the straight-line depreciation charge on the undepreciated portion of the asset is greater than the one that can be obtainable by using the double-declining-balance method.

Example 8.4   Consider the depreciable asset given in Example 8.1. Use double-declining-balance method and prepare a table giving depreciation schedule and corresponding book values for the equipment.

Solution   Since the rate is 200%, the depreciation charge for year 1 can be found from equation (8.10) as

$$D_1 = R \times BV_{t-1} = (\tfrac{2}{5})(\$6,000) = 0.40(\$6,000) = \$2,400$$

Note that in this method the depreciation basis is not $P - F = \$5,000$, but it is equal to P of $\$6,000$ (i.e., without subtracting the salvage value of

TABLE 8.4 Depreciation Schedule and Corresponding Book Values for Example 8.4

End of year t	Depreciation charge for year t	Book value at the end of year t
0	0	$6,000
1	$(0.40)(\$6,000) = \$2,400$	3,600
2	$(0.40)(3,600) = 1,440$	2,160
3	$(0.40)(2,160) = 864$	1,296
4	$(0.40)(1,296) = 518.40$	777.60
5	$(0.40)(777.60) = 311.04$	466.56

$1,000). Therefore, the book value at the end of year 1 can be found from equation (8.11) as

$$BV_1 = BV_0 - D_1 = \$6,000 - \$2,400 = \$3,600$$

Table 8.4 gives the complete depreciation schedule and the corresponding book values for the equipment. Note that the book value at the end of year 4 is $777.60, which is less than the estimated salvage value of $1,000. It is interesting that if the salvage value for this equipment had been zero, for this method of depreciation the book value would never reach zero despite the length of time span over which the asset is depreciated. Therefore, adjustments are required to correct the differences between the estimated and calculated book value of the asset. For example, during the fourth year the calculated depreciation charge of $518.40 would, if used, decrease the book value to $777.60, which is less than the salvage value of $1,000. Thus, the fourth year's depreciation is reduced to $296 from $518.40 in order to force the book value to equal the salvage value, F, of $1,000. Therefore, the depreciation method is switched to the straight-line method from the double-declining-balance method starting at year 4, as indicated in Table 8.5. Also, note that the depreciation charge for year 5 is zero. Figure 8.3 shows book value versus useful life of equipment in Example 8.4.

TABLE 8.5 Adjusted Depreciation Schedule and Corresponding Book Values for Example 8.4

End of year t	Depreciation charge for year t	Book value at the end of year t
0	0	$6,000
1	$2,400	3,600
2	1,400	2,160
3	764	1,296
4	296	1,000
5	0	1,000

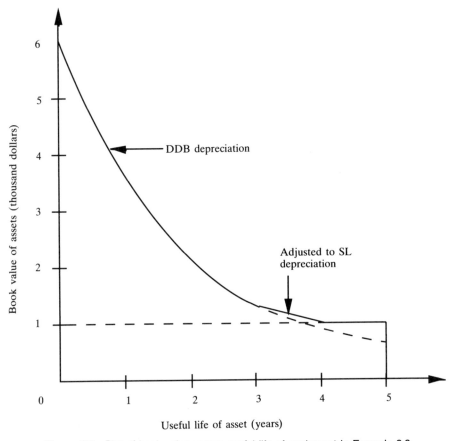

Figure 8.3 Plot of book value versus useful life of equipment in Example 8.3.

8.8 SINKING-FUND METHOD

The sinking-fund (SF) method[†] is based on an *imaginary* sinking fund that is established into which uniform end-of-year deposits (that are depreciation charges) are made. It is assumed that such a fund earns an interest (usually, it is assumed to be equal to the MARR of the company). Therefore, the accumulated annual deposits plus interest will be equal to the accumulated depreciation (i.e., first cost minus salvage) on the asset by the end of the

[†]Today, only a few utility companies still use this method to determine a *fair cost* to charge a customer when the customer wants to purchase an item from the company. It is also used by some government agencies as a realistic representation of public projects that decrease in value slower in early years than the ones in later years. Also, a company with internal financial problems may be ordered by courts to set up a sinking fund for its depreciation reserve. Furthermore, the method is still used in the Professional Engineering examinations.

useful life of the asset.[†] In the sinking-fund method the interest charge increases each year as the fictitious fund increases with depreciation charges. Hence, the depreciation charges are smaller in early years than the ones in later years. Because of this future, it is not often used. Since the sinking fund[‡] pays interest at a rate of $i\%$ and will have a balance that is equal to the total amount to be depreciated (i.e., $P - F$) after N years), the equal annual deposit is

$$A = (P - F)(A/F, i\%, N) \tag{8.18}$$

Thus, the depreciation charge for any year t is the sum of the deposit, A, plus the interest earned on the account. Since the first year's depreciation is A, the second year's $A(1 + i)$, and the tth year's is $A(1 + i)^{t-1}$, which is equal to $A(F/P, i\% \ t - 1)$, the sinking-fund depreciation charge for any given year t is

$$D_t = (P - F)(A/F, i\%, N)(F/P, i\%, t - 1) \tag{8.19}$$

It is also equal to the difference in book value for the previous year $(t - 1)$ and that year (t). Therefore,

$$D_t = BV_{t-1} - BV_t \tag{8.20}$$

Whereas the book value[§] for any year t is the first cost minus the accumulated sinking-fund deposits and interest. Hence, it can be expressed as

$$BV_t = P - (P - F)(A/F, i\%, N)(F/A, i\%, t) \tag{8.21}$$

[†]For example, a well-known electric utility company determines its sinking-fund depreciation factor in the following manner. First it determines the capital recovery factor as

$$\frac{\text{Original investment}}{\text{Sum of PW of plant in service}} = \frac{\$1,400}{\$5,500} = 0.2545$$

Assume that its MARR is 12%. Since

$$\text{Capital recovery factor} = \text{sinking-fund depreciation factor} + \text{MARR}$$

thus

$$\text{Sinking-fund depreciation factor} = \text{Capital recovery factor} - \text{MARR}$$

$$= 0.2545 - 0.12 = 0.1345$$

Therefore, the factor of 0.1345 is used as the fixed charge rate for the depreciation.

[‡]The sinking-fund method is also called the *present worth method*. This is due to the fact that the book value at any time is equal to the present worth of the uniform annual cost of capital recovery for the remaining years of useful life plus the present worth of the future salvage value. Sometimes the sinking-fund is referred to as *interest plus amortization*.

[§]Note that book values with this method are always larger than the ones with the straight-line method. The differences are more paramount if N and $i\%$ are larger. Because of this, if i is 0%, the straight-line method becomes the limiting case of the sinking-fund method.

Example 8.5 Consider the depreciable asset given in Example 8.1. Use the sinking-fund depreciation method and prepare a table showing the depreciation schedule and corresponding book values of the equipment. Assume that a MARR of 10% is used as the interest rate. Prepare a table that gives the depreciation schedule and corresponding book values for the asset.

Solution The depreciation charge for year 1 can be found from equation (8.19) as

$$D_1 + (P - F)(A/F, i\%, N)(F/P, i\%, t - 1)$$
$$= (\$6,000 - \$1,000)(A/F, 10\%, 5)(F/P, 10\%, 0)$$
$$+ \$5,000(0.16380)(1.0) = \$819$$

The book value at the end of year 1 can be found from equation (8.21) as

$$BV_1 = P - (P - F)(A/F, i\%, N)(F/A, i\%, t)$$
$$= \$6,000 - (\$6,000 - \$1,000)(A/F, 10\%, 5)(F/A, 10\%, 1)$$
$$= \$6,000 - (\$5,000)(0.16380)(1.0) = \$5,181$$

or from equation (8.20) as

$$BV_1 = BV_0 - D_1 = \$6,000 - \$819 = \$5,181$$

Table 8.6 gives the complete depreciation schedule and the corresponding book values for the equipment.

TABLE 8.6 Depreciation Schedule and Corresponding Book Values for Example 8.5

End of year t	Depreciation charge for year t	Book value at the end of year t
0	0	$6,000
1	$819	5,181
2	900.90	4,280.10
3	990.99	3,289.11
4	1,090.09	2,199.02
5	1,199.02	1,000

8.9 COMPARISON OF DEPRECIATION METHODS

Figure 8.4 shows the patterns of the book values of the same asset based on the straight-line (SL) method, the sum-of-years' digits (SYD) method, the double-declining-balance (DDB) method, and the sinking-fund method. It can be seen that the book values, especially in the intermediate years are substantially affected by the depreciation method chosen. The amount of taxes paid, in turn, depends on the depreciation charges that can be made. The larger the depreciation charge for a given year, the smaller the taxable income (and therefore, the smaller the taxes) and thus the greater the after-tax cash flow. Note that, in Figure 8.4, the double-declining-balance method provides the largest depreciation charges, and therefore it recovers a large share of the initial investment early in the depreciable life of the

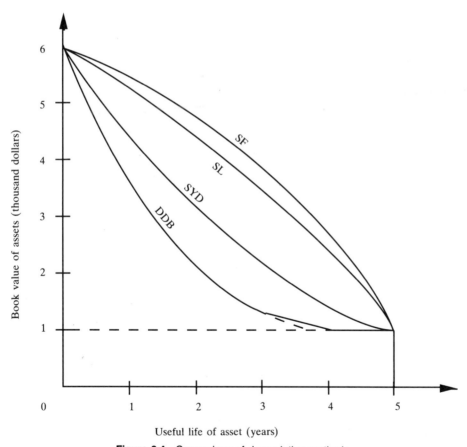

Figure 8.4 Comparison of depreciation methods.

asset. Therefore, from the tax point of view, it is the best method. It is followed by the sum-of-years' digits method. Also, note that the sinking-fund method has the slowest rate of capital recovery.

8.10 UNITS OF PRODUCTION METHOD

The units of production method allows the asset to be depreciated for tax purposes in direct proportion to its use, rather than to time. Therefore, it is used for those assets whose useful lives are defined by the factors of wear and tear, or usage, or the rate of production. Thus, under such circumstances, the depreciation charge of the asset for year t equals the depreciable base of the asset (i.e., $P - F$) times the ratio of the units produced during year t (i.e., U_t) to the total amount of units that can be produced during the estimated useful life of the asset (i.e., U_{tot}). Therefore, the depreciation charge for year t is

$$D_t = (P - F) \frac{U_t}{U_{tot}} \tag{8.22}$$

Example 8.6 Assume that special drilling equipment used in a coal mine has a first cost of $25,000 and salvage value of $1,000 after 500 holes. Determine its first annual depreciation charge and book value after 100 holes.

Solution From equation (8.22) its depreciation charge is

$$D_1 = (P - F) \frac{U_1}{U_{tot}} = (\$25,000 - \$1,000) \frac{100}{500} = \$4,800$$

and its book value is

$$BV_1 = P - D_1 = \$25,000 - \$4,800 = \$20,200$$

8.11 ACCELERATED COST RECOVERY SYSTEM METHOD

The *Economic Recovery Tax Act* of 1981 introduced a new depreciation method called *Accelerated Cost Recovery System* (ACRS) depreciation.[†] In addition to its rules and regulations, it has introduced new accounting phrases. For example, the word *depreciation* is basically replaced by the phrase *accelerated cost recovery system*. The phrase *recovery property* defines any depreciable, tangible property (both real or personal property)

[†]It is called *ACRES* in accounting jargon.

used in business or held for the production of income, whereas the phrase *recovery period* defines the depreciation period of recovery property over which capital cost is recovered (i.e., depreciated). The recovery period is generally less than the useful life of the capital investment to facilitate a faster write-off and therefore stimulate the economy by encouraging capital investment and increasing productivity. The phrase *salvage value* has vanished because there is no provision for including it in the new computations. According to the new rules, the recovery property can typically be depreciated down to zero value. Therefore, the salvage value is not included in depreciation calculations. However, any gain over the depreciated value will be taxed either as capital gains or recapture. In the ACRS method, both new and used property are handled the same.

Under the ACRS method all eligible depreciable assets (i.e., personal property) have statutory recovery periods of 3, 5, 10, and 15 years for tax purposes. Either ACRS tables or straight-line (SL) recovery, with zero salvage value, can be employed to determine depreciation charges, at the discretion of the taxpayer. For personal property ACRS depreciation is determined by using the double-declining-balance method with a switch later to sum-of-years'-digits depreciation method. For real property ACRS depreciation is found by using 175% declining-balance method with the switch later to straight-line depreciation method. Here, the term *personal property* defines anything that is not real estate, for example, machinery and vehicles; whereas the term *real property* defines land and usually anything attached to, growing on, or built on the land. Of course, the land itself is not depreciable. Table 8.7 gives the ACRS classes of depreciable property. It also provides information on investment tax credit for each class. Note that all real estate property is defined as real property in a separate class with a 15-year recovery period.[†] Contrary to the treatment of personal property, there is no investment tax credit for real property. Based on the determination of the property class, the depreciation schedules can be found for personal property and for real property from Tables 8.8 and 8.9, respectively.

It is interesting to note that, for personal property, the ACRS depreciation percentages (which are given in Table 8.8) are based on the double-declining-balance depreciation at the beginning and are switched to sum-of-years' digits depreciation for the rest of the recovery period. It is based on the assumption that the property was obtained in the middle of the first year (using the *half-year convention*), and therefore there is only one-half year depreciation allowance in recovery year 1; whereas for real property (i.e., real estate), the ACRS depreciation percentages (which are given in Table 8.9) are based on 175% declining-balance depreciation at the beginning and are switched to straight-line depreciation for the rest of the recovery period. The recovery percentages provide for the number of months the property is

---

[†]Previously, most real estate property had to be depreciated over a 45-year period.

TABLE 8.7 ACRS Classes of Depreciable Property

Personal Property (All property except real estate)	Property Class	Investment Tax Credit
Autos and light-duty trucks Machinery and equipment used for R&D Special tools and other personal property with an average life of 4 years or less	3-year property	6%
Most other machinery and equipment Office furniture and equipment Heavy-duty trucks Aircrafts Ships	5-year property	10%
Public utility property with a life between 18 and 25 years Railroad tank cars Manufactured homes Real property with a life of 12.5 years or less	10-year property	10%
Public utility property with a life of more than 25 years	15-year public utility	10%

Real Property (real estate)	Property Class	Investment Tax Credit
All buildings	15-year property	—

in service during the first year of the purchase (i.e., first recovery year). Likewise, if the property is sold before the end of the recovery period, then the recovery percentage must include the number of months in the year of disposition.

Example 8.7   Assume that the ABC Company has purchased a light-duty truck for $10,000 in 1985. Determine its ACRS depreciation schedule.

Solution   Since the light-duty truck is considered as a three-year personal property under the ACRS depreciation method and has been purchased in 1985, the associated percentages are found from Table 8.8 and the resulting ACRS depreciation schedule is given in Table 8.10.

Example 8.8   Assume that a duplex has been purchased on April 1, 1981, as an income-bringing property (i.e., to be used as a rental property). The purchase price of the duplex was $125,000. The value of the land has been

TABLE 8.8 ACRS Standard Recovery Percentages for Computing Annual Depreciation for Personal Property under 1981 Tax Act

Recovery Year	Property Acquired During 1981–1984				Property Acquired in 1985				Property Acquired After 1985			
	3-year (%)	5-year (%)	10-year (%)	15-year Public Utility (%)	3-year (%)	5-year (%)	10-year (%)	15-year Public Utility (%)	3-year (%)	5-year (%)	10-year (%)	15-year Public Utility (%)
1	25	15	8	5	29	18	9	6	33	20	10	7
2	38	22	14	10	47	33	19	12	45	32	18	12
3	37	21	12	9	24	25	16	12	22	24	16	12
4		21	10	8		16	14	11		16	14	11
5		21	10	7		8	12	10		8	12	10
6			10	7			10	9			10	9
7			9	6			8	8			8	8
8			9	6			6	7			6	7
9			9	6			4	6			4	6
10			9	6			2	5			2	5
11				6				4				4
12				6				4				3
13				6				3				3
14				6				2				2
15				6				1				1

TABLE 8.9 ACRS Standard Recovery Percentages for Computing Annual Depreciation for Real Property Under 1981 Tax Act

If the Recovery Year is	The Applicable Recovery Percentage			
	Property First Placed in Service by First Day of			
	January	April	July	October
1	12%	9%	6%	3%
2	10	11	11	11
3	9	9	10	10
4	8	8	9	9
5	7	7	8	8
6	6	6	7	7
7	6	6	6	6
8	6	6	5	6
9	6	6	5	6
10	5	6	5	5
11	5	5	5	5
12	5	5	5	5
13	5	5	5	5
14	5	5	5	5
15	5	5	5	5
16	—	1	3	4

estimated to be $25,000. Assume that the house has been sold July 1, 1988. Determine the following:

(a) Find the ACRS depreciation percentages for each of the 8 years involved. Round the results to integer values.
(b) Find the straight-line depreciation for the last half year.
(c) Compare the results calculated in part (a) with the ones given in Table 8.9.
(d) Find the accrued ACRS depreciation charges for each of the 8 years.

TABLE 8.10 Depreciation Schedule for Example 8.7

Year	First Cost	ACRS Percentage	ACRS Depreciation
1	$10,000	29	$2,900
2	10,000	47	4,700
3	10,000	24	2,400
			$10,000

Solution

(a) Since the land is not depreciable, the depreciation base is $100,000. The salvage value is not required since it is not used in the ACRS depreciation. Since it is a real property, its ACRS depreciation is based on 175% declining-balance depreciation with switch to straight-line depreciation.

For year 1: In the year of purchase the property is owned for 9 months. Thus, based on 175% declining-balance depreciation,

$$D_1 = \frac{9}{12} \times \frac{1.75}{15} \, (100\% \text{ of cost} - 0) = 8.75\% \cong 9\% \text{ of cost}$$

For year 2

$$D_2 = \frac{1.75}{15} \, (100\% \text{ of cost} - 8.75\%) = 10.65\% \cong 11\% \text{ of cost}$$

For year 3

$$D_3 = \frac{1.75}{15} \, (100\% \text{ of cost} - 19.4\%) = 9.40\% \cong 9\% \text{ of cost}$$

For year 4

$$D_4 = \frac{1.75}{15} \, (100\% \text{ of cost} - 28.8\%) = 8.31\% \cong 8\% \text{ of cost}$$

For year 5

$$D_5 = \frac{1.75}{15} \, (100\% \text{ of cost} - 37.11\%) = 7.34\% \cong 7\% \text{ of cost}$$

For year 6

$$D_6 = \frac{1.75}{15} \, (100\% \text{ of cost} - 44.44\%) = 6.48\% \cong 6\% \text{ of cost}$$

For year 7

$$D_7 = \frac{1.75}{15} \, (100\% \text{ of cost} - 50.93\%) = 5.73\% \cong 6\% \text{ of cost}$$

For year 8

$$D_8 = \frac{6}{12} \times \frac{1.75}{15} \, (100\% \text{ of cost} - 56.65\%) = 2.53\% \cong 3\% \text{ of cost}$$

Note that the duplex has been sold after 6 months, thus only one-half year's depreciation is permitted.

TABLE 8.11   The ACRS Depreciation Charges for Example 8.8

Year	Cost	ACRS Percentage	ACRS Depreciation
9 months of 1981	$100,000	9	$9,000
1982	100,000	11	11,000
1983	100,000	9	9,000
1984	100,000	8	8,000
1985	100,000	7	7,000
1986	100,000	6	6,000
1987	100,000	6	6,000
6 months of 1988	100,000	3	3,000
			$100,000

(b) The straight-line depreciation for the last half year is

$$D_{SL} = \frac{6}{12} \times \frac{100\% - 56.65\%}{15 \text{ years} - 6.75 \text{ years}} = 2.63\% \cong 3\% \text{ of cost}$$

Both the 175% declining-balance depreciation and the straight-line depreciation give the same amount.

(c) The results, in terms of depreciation percentages, agree with the values that can be obtained from Table 8.9 under the April column. Therefore, there is no need to calculate them as was done in part (a), that is, one can use them directly from the table.

(d) The depreciation charges are given in Table 8.11 for the ACRS depreciation.

8.12   RECAPTURE PROVISIONS OF THE ACRS METHOD

8.12.1   Recapture

The process of taxing income that was not previously taxed due to offsetting deductions is defined as *recapture*. Examples of such *offsetting deductions* include all previous tax deductions due to accelerated capital recovery, investment tax credit, and so on that are more than straight-line depreciation.[†] The term *recapture* can be better understood by the following example. Assume that you own a residential rental property for which you have received tax deductions due to accelerated capital recovery over the years. Now, you have just sold the property for a price that is greater than its depreciated book value. According to the ACRS method, you have to pay an ordinary income tax (i.e., recapture) for the gain that has resulted due to the difference between the ACRS depreciation book value and the straight-

[†]With some exceptions.

line depreciation book value. In addition, if you have kept the property for one year or more, you have to pay capital-gain tax[‡] for any additional gain between straight-line based book value and the selling price.

If a personal property has been depreciated by using the ACRS or SL methods over the years, when it is sold any resulting gain that is in excess of depreciated book value has to be recaptured by taxing the gain as *ordinary income* (instead of capital gain) but only to the extent of any prior depreciation; whereas, any resulting gain due to the difference between selling price and the original purchase price is taxed as *capital gain*.

8.12.2 Recapture of Investment Tax Credit

The investment tax credit is also subject to recapture if a personal property is disposed of at an earlier date that is less than 5 years. Table 8.12 gives the percentages of investment tax credit to be recaptured. The investment tax credit is also applicable to *used* personal property that costs up to $125,000 in 1982 and $150,000 in 1985 and afterward.

Example 8.9 Assume that Mr. Joe Smart has purchased a rental property for $110,000 on January 1, 1981, and has sold for $170,000 on January 1, 1984. If the value of the land is $10,000, determine the following:

(a) Depreciable amount (also called depreciation base) of the property.
(b) Depreciation schedules for the property using both 175% declining-balance and straight-line depreciation methods.
(c) Taxable capital gain.
(d) The amounts of total gain and capital gain.
(e) The amount of recapture to be taxed as ordinary income.
(f) If Mr. Smart is in the 28% tax bracket, find his total tax liability due to the sale.

TABLE 8.12 Percentages of Investment Tax Credit to be Recaptured

Ownership Year in which Sold	Percentage of Investment Tax Credit to be Recovered	
	3-Year Property	Other Property
1	100%	100%
2	67	80
3	33	60
4	0	40
5	0	20

[†]In general, only about 40% of capital gain is taxable at ordinary income tax rates.

Solution

(a) Depreciation base = Purchase price − Cost of land
$$= \$110,000 - \$10,000 = \$100,000$$

(b) Since the property is a real estate property, it has a 15-year recovery period and zero salvage value. Its depreciation schedules for the property using both 175% declining-balance and straight-line depreciation methods are given in Table 8.13. Note that the depreciation charges using 175% declining-balance method have been calculated in this example rather than determined from Table 8.9. Therefore, they have slightly different values.

(c) Taxable capital gain = Selling price − SL depreciated value
− Cost of land
$$= \$170,000 - \$79,999 - \$10,000 = \$80,001$$

(d) In the event of using the 175% declining-balance (DB) method to find the depreciated book value for tax calculations, the difference between SL and 175% DB depreciation is taxed as recapture at ordinary income tax rates. Therefore,

$$\text{Total gain} = \text{Selling price} - 175\% \text{ DB book value}$$
$$= \text{Selling price} - (175\% \text{ DB value} + \text{Land})$$
$$= \$170,000 - (\$68,924 + \$10,000) = \$91,076$$

$$\text{Capital gain} = \text{Selling price} - \text{SL book value}$$
$$= \text{Selling price} - (\text{SL value} + \text{Land})$$
$$= \$170,000 - (\$79,999 + \$10,000) = \$80,001$$

Therefore, taxable capital gain is the difference between the total gain and the capital gain.

TABLE 8.13   Depreciation Schedules for Example 8.9

| Year | 175% Declining-Balance Method | | Straight-Line Method | |
	Depreciation Charge	Book Value at End of Year	Depreciation Charge	Book Value at End of Year
0	—	$100,000	—	$100,000
1	$11,667	88,333	$6,667	93,333
2	10,306	78,027	6,667	86,666
3	9,103	68,924	6,667	79,999

(e) Thus,

$$\text{Recapture taxable as ordinary income} = \text{Total gain} - \text{Capital gain}$$
$$= \$91,076 - \$80,001$$
$$= \$11,075$$

or alternatively,

Recapture taxable as ordinary income = SL book value − 175% DB book value

$$= \$79,999 - \$68,924$$
$$= \$11,075$$

(f) Total tax Liability = 40% of capital gain at ordinary rate

+ Recapture at ordinary rate

Since Mr. Smart is in the 28% tax bracket, the 40% of capital gain at the ordinary rate is

$$0.40 \times \$80,001 \times 0.28 = \$8,960$$

and recapture at ordinary rate is

$$0.28 \times \$11,075 = \$3.101$$

Therefore, the total tax liability is

$$\$8,960 + \$3,101 = \$12,061$$

8.13 TAX REFORM ACT OF 1986

The *Tax Reform Act of 1986*, also called the *Internal Revenue Code of 1986*, has modified the ACRS method by (1) revising the recovery periods and/or rates of recovery and (2) prescribing depreciation methods rather than statutorily prescribed rates. In general, under the modified ACRS system, assets are classified into six groups of personal property based generally on the asset depreciation range (ADR) midpoint life, and into two classes of real property. Each class is assigned a recovery period and a depreciation method, as given in Table 8.14. Note that in the case of the first six classes, recovery is based on the use of the applicable percentage and the declining-balance method over the indicated period, switching to the straight-line method to maximize deductions. The new system is mandatory for all

TABLE 8.14   Modified ACRS Classes of Depreciable Property

Personal Property (All property except real estate)	Property Class
All property with an ADR midpoint of 4 years or less (except for automobiles and light general-purpose trucks) and certain horses.	3-year 200% class
All property with an ADR midpoint of more than 4 and less than 10 years. Also included are automobiles and light trucks, certain technological equipment, semiconductor manufacturing equipment, computer-based central office switching equipment, renewable energy and biomass properties that are small power production facilities, and research and experimentation property.	5-year 200% class
All property with an ADR midpoint of at least 10 and less than 16 years. Also included are railroad track, single-purpose agricultural or horticultural structures, and property having no ADR midpoint and not classified elsewhere.	7-year 200% class
All property with an ADR midpoint at least 16 and less than 20 years.	10-year 200% class
All property with an ADR midpoint of at least 20 years and less than 25 years. Also included are municipal wastewater treatment plants, and telephone distribution plants and comparable equipment used for two-way exchange of voice and data communications.	15-year 150% class
All property with an ADR midpoint of 25 years or more (including municipal sewers), other than real property with an ADR midpoint life of 27.5 years or more.	20-year 150% class

Real Property (Real estate)	
All residential rental property, defined as a building or structure with 80% or more of its rental income from dwelling units.	27.5-year straight-line class
All nonresidential real property, defined as all depreciable real property other than residential and real property having an ADR midpoint life of less than 27.5 years.	31.5-year straight-line class

eligible property, although a taxpayer may choose to employ an alternative system (i.e., the one described in Section 8.13.1), or to use the straight-line method over the asset's recovery period.

The eligible property includes tangible depreciable property (both real and personal) placed in service after December 31, 1986. The eligible property does not include (1) property depreciated under any method not expressed in a term of years (other than the retirement–replacement–betterment method), such as the units of production method; (2) public utility property if the taxpayer does not use a normalization method of accounting; (3) any motion picture film or videotape; (4) certain sound recordings; or (5) any property excluded from ACRS by reason of anti-churning rules or from the modified ACRS system by reason of the extension of those rules, as explained in Table 8.14. The taxpayer may also decide to depreciate property placed in service after July 31, 1986, under the new system, provided that such property is not eligible for the investment tax credit under the transition rules. Note that unlike prior law, taxpayers are now required to compute the applicable recovery percentages, taking into account the recovery method, period, and applicable convention.

Example 8.10   Assume that the ABC Corporation has purchased a light truck, with an ADR midpoint of 8 years, for $50,000. It is assumed that its salvage value will be zero at the end of its useful life. Use the modified ACRS method and prepare a depreciation schedule for the truck.

Solution   From Table 8.14 it can be found that the property belongs to the "5-year, 200%" personal property class. Therefore, double-declining-balance depreciation can be used. Based on the modified ACRS method, for the first and the last years, a half-year convention is used for personal property. Thus, under this convention, property placed in service or disposed of during a taxable year is considered placed in service or disposed of at the midpoint of that year. Therefore, the depreciation charge for the first year is

$$D_1 = \tfrac{1}{2} \times \tfrac{2}{5}(\$50{,}000 - 0) = \$10{,}000$$

Similarly,

$$D_2 = \tfrac{2}{5}(\$50{,}000 - \$10{,}000) = \$16{,}000$$
$$D_3 = \tfrac{2}{5}(\$50{,}000 - \$26{,}000) = \$9{,}600$$
$$D_4 = \tfrac{2}{5}(\$50{,}000 - \$35{,}600) = \$5{,}760$$

Switching to the straight-line depreciation,

$$D_5 = \$5,760$$
$$D_6 = \tfrac{1}{2}(\$5,760) = \$2,880$$

Thus, the depreciation schedule for the property is given in Table 8.15.

8.13.1 Alternative Depreciation System

The alternative depreciation system provides for straight-line recovery without taking into account the salvage value of the property. In general, the recovery period is the property's ADR midpoint life, that is, 12 years for personal property with no ADR midpoint life and 40 years for real property. For this purpose property specifically assigned to a class generally has a special recovery period.

A taxpayer may decide to apply the alternative system for property placed in service during a specific taxable year. The election is irrevocable and applies generally to all property in the modified ACRS class placed in service during that year, except that for residential and nonresidential real property, the election may be made on a property-by-property basis. The alternative system must be used for (1) foreign-use property, (2) tax-exempt property (in which case the recovery period may not be less than 125% of the least term), (3) tax-exempt bond financed property, (4) certain imported property, and (5) mixed-use property used 50% or more for personal purposes. It is also used for purposes of computing earnings and profits.

8.13.2 Comments on the Modified ACRS Method

Under the new system, recovery is usually dependent on the ADR midpoint life assigned to the property, so one must be more aware of that life than under the previous law. Furthermore, the IRS is authorized to monitor and analyze actual experience and to redefine a new ADR midpoint for property. However, an asset specially assigned to a class generally may not be assigned a longer life if placed in service before 1992. Therefore, depreciation periods are subject to change in the future.

TABLE 8.15 Depreciation Schedule for the Property Given in Example 8.10

Year	Depreciation Charge
1	$10,000
2	16,000
3	9,000
4	5,760
5	5,760
6	2,880
	Total = $50,000

8.13.3 Comments on Averaging Conventions

Under both the modified ACRS and the alternative depreciation systems, a half-year convention is generally employed for personal property. Under this convention property placed in service or disposed of during a taxable year is considered placed in service or disposed of at the midpoint of that year. Further, a midquarter convention applies when more than 40% of all property is placed in service during the last quarter of the taxable year. Under that convention property is treated as placed in service, or disposed of, in the middle of the quarter. Furthermore, for residential rental and nonresidential real property, depreciation is based on the number of months the property is in service during the taxable year. Therefore, a midmonth convention is used.

8.13.4 Expensing Instead of Cost Recovery

The expensing choice is still available, with the following restrictions: (1) The amount is increased to $10,000 per year; (2) The $10,000 is reduced dollar for dollar where the cost of qualified property placed in service during the taxable year exceeds $200,000; (3) The amount is further limited to the taxable income derived from any active trade or business. Disallowed costs are to be carried forward. The effective date, generally, is for property placed in service after 1986.

8.13.5 Investment Tax Credit

In the Tax Reform Act of 1986 there is no allowance provided as investment tax credit. The effective date is after December 31, 1985, for property that is placed in service. In general, there are additional transitional rules that apply.

8.14 DEPLETION

Consumption of exhaustible natural resources such as minerals, coal, gas, oil, timber, and other natural deposits as a result of their removal is called *depletion*. Even though the concept of depletion is similar to the concept of depreciation, there is a substantial difference between them. In depreciation an asset is decreasing in value as a result of wear and tear, obsolescence, use, or the passage of time; whereas in depletion a resource (usually a natural resource) is literally being exhausted through its removal. There are two methods to determine depletion allowance: (1) cost depletion and (2) percentage depletion. The taxpayer is permitted a choice, depletion is computed by both methods, and the larger value is taken as the depletion for the year.

The *cost depletion* is a write-off based on units consumed. In this method the cost depletion allowance for a given year is usually calculated by first determining a cost per unit and multiplying it by the number of units sold during that year. The cost per unit is found by dividing the value of the mineral property by the total number of recoverable units (in terms of tons, barrels, board-feet, etc.). The value of the property (which is also called *adjusted basis*) is the original cost less all depletion previously allowed or allowable.

The *percent depletion* for a given year provides an allowance equal to a fixed percentage of the gross income produced from the property during that year. However, the deduction for depletion under this method cannot extend 50% of the taxable income from the property, calculated without the deduction for depletion and loss carry-forward deduction.

The Tax Reform Act of 1986 has caused many changes in application of depletion in various areas. For example, percentage depletion is no longer allowed on bonuses, advance royalties, and other amounts paid without regard to actual production from an oil, gas, or geothermal property; whereas royalty owners are allowed to deduct percentage depletion on coal and iron ore royalties in any taxable year in which long-term capital gains are subject to tax at the same maximum rates as ordinary income.

8.15 DEPRECIATION OF GROUP PROPERTIES

In the depreciation methods reviewed so far, each asset (i.e., property) has been taken into account separately, having its own depreciation method, useful life, and salvage value (if it is available to use). However, with *group-property depreciation* method (also called *multiasset depreciation* method), one account is used to include the investment in all these properties. Thus, each year the depreciation charge is made against the group of properties rather than against the individual property, and the book value at any time is applicable to the whole group. Therefore, the advantage of having a number of properties in the same account is that the group as a whole can be treated as one entity. Hence, some properties in the group (or account) can experience very short lives while others survive much longer, however, together they can be represented by a *normal* life. The possible grouping can be as general as only one single overall composite account for the company or can be in detail with respect to any one or more characteristics, for example, similarity of properties within a given account, data of installation, mortality characteristics, average life, or geographic location. Of course, this depreciation method does not take into account the individual properties that are abandoned early or have unexpectedly long usage. Therefore, properties with the same or different useful lives are grouped in one account for which a single rate of depreciation is employed. There are three types of multiasset accounts, namely group accounts, composite accounts, and classified accounts. A *group account* includes similar properties with approximately the same useful lives. On the other hand a *composite account* contains properties of dissimilar character and useful lives; and a *classified account* has properties of homogeneous character without regard to useful life. In group accounting applications capital gains or losses are usually not permitted. Also, retirements are treated in a different manner, and allocation and depreciation charges are subject to mortality characteristics of the property group.[†]

PROBLEMS

8.1 Verify that equation (8.3), which gives the depreciation charge for year t, can be derived from the annual equivalent cost of capital recovery that provides for the recovery of capital plus a return on the unrecovered investment, when i is zero. That is,

$$A = (P - F)(A/P, i\%, N) + Fi$$

8.2 Verify equation (8.6).

8.3 Derive equation (8.19) from the following equation:

$$D_t = (P - F)(A/F, i\%, N)$$
$$+ i[(P - F)(A/F, i\%, N)(F/A, i\%, t - 1)]$$

8.4 An air compressor is purchased for \$34,000. It has a service life of 8 years and a salvage value of \$2,000. Using straight-line depreciation find (a) the annual depreciation charge, (b) the depreciation rate as a percentage of first cost, and (c) the book value after 5 years.

8.5 A lathe used in the manufacturing of precision machine parts costs \$52,400. The machine has a useful life of 10 years and a salvage value of \$5,000. Using the double-declining-balance method of depreciation, calculate (a) the declining balance rate, (b) the depreciation charge after the third year, and (c) the book value after 7 years.

8.6 A construction firm purchased a 5-year-old, 12-ton, pneumatic tired, self-propelled earth roller for \$7,950. The estimated life of the roller will be an additional 5 years, at which time it can be sold for \$1,000. The firm's accountants are going to use sum-of-years' digits depreciation. Make a table of annual depreciation costs and book values for the remaining life of the equipment.

[†]Those who are interested in the application of group properties should read Marston, Winfrey, and Hempstead [55], Winfrey [75, 76], Fitch, Wolf, and Bissinger [29], and Smith [66].

8.7 A warehouse has just been constructed for $125,000. It is anticipated that the warehouse will be used for 20 years and then sold for $5,000, neglecting the value of the land. Using the sinking-fund method calculate (a) the annual sinking-fund deposit, (b) the amount depreciated by the end of the 8th year, and (c) the book value after 15 years. Use an interest rate of 6%.

8.8 A metal-forming machine has been purchased for $45,000 and is expected to last 5 years; then it will be sold for $4,000. It is estimated that the machine is able to produce 125,000 units during its lifetime. Estimated annual production is 20,000 units the first year, 30,000 units the second, 30,000 units the third, 25,000 units the fourth, and 30,000 units the fifth year. Calculate the depreciation rate per unit of production and make a schedule showing the yearly depreciation allocation, the accrued depreciation, and the book value.

8.9 An asset is purchased by a company with a first cost of $17,500 and an estimated life of 10 years at which time it should be sold for $1,700. Plot, on the same set of coordinates, the book value of the asset for the first 3 years using:

(a) Straight-line method

(b) Sum-of-the-years' digit method

(c) Double-declining-balance method

(d) Sinking-fund method with 5% interest

8.10 Find a declining-balance rate that results in a book value of
(a) 25% and (b) 5% after 15 years.

8.11 Specialized machinery is being installed in a plastics plant. The installed cost is $125,000. The firm plans on keeping the machine for 10 years, but there is some disagreement as to its salvage value. One group feels salvage will be 15% of the first cost, and another thinks it will only be 5%. What difference will it make to percentage depreciation rate if the declining-balance rate is used?

8.12 A material-handling system with a first cost of $56,000 and an estimated life of 16 years has zero salvage value. The system will produce an excess of receipts over disbursements of $12,000 a year before taxes. Straight-line depreciation will be used. Estimate the rate of return by using the present worth of net cash flow equal to zero. Assume cash flow for taxes to be one-half the annual depreciation.

8.13 An automobile had been purchased for $3,200 five years ago. Since that time the owner has been offered the following amounts for the automobile:

Year	1	2	3	4	5
Offer	$2800	$2300	$2000	$1600	$1200

(a) On the basis of the offers, calculate the depreciated and undepreciated value of the automobile. (b) How does this compare with straight-line depreciation with zero salvage value after 10 years? Is the owner better off by accepting the offers? If so, which one?

8.14 A small office building costs $55,000 new. It has an estimated life of 20 years at which time it will have a salvage value of $6,000. What is the straight-line annual depreciation charge? What is the depreciation rate?

8.15 Given the data in Problem 8.14, (a) what is the declining-balance rate using the double-declining-balance method, (b) what is the 5th year depreciation charge, and (c) what is the book value after 10 years?

8.16 Using the same figures for the office building in Problem 8.15, and the sinking-fund depreciation method of 8%, (a) what is the annual sinking-fund deposit and (b) what will the book value be in 10 years?

8.17 Using the sum-of-the-years' digits method of depreciation, what would be (a) the depreciation charge in the first year, (b) the depreciation charge the 5th year, and (c) the book value at the end of 10 years for the office building in Problem 8.14.

8.18 A trenching machine has a first cost of $45,000 and an expected salvage value of $4,000 at the end of its 7-year life. How much depreciation can be charged off in 4 years using (a) the straight-line method and (b) the sum-of-the-years' digits method.

8.19 Assume that a building has a first cost of $30,000 and find the required declining-balance rate, if the book value after 5 years is $13,925. What is the salvage value after 15 years?

8.20 Using the double-declining-balance method, determine what the book value would be at the end of 12 years if the first cost of a rock crusher is $60,000. The estimated useful life is 20 years at which time there will be a $500 salvage value.

8.21 If the rock crusher in Problem 8.20 is bought at the end of 10 years at the book value using the double-declining-balance method, what will the book value be 5 years later using the sum-of-years' digits method? Assume that useful life and salvage value remain the same.

8.22 The first cost of a new piece of production equipment is $45,000. If the estimated useful life is 10 years and the salvage value is $1,750, what is the book value of the equipment at the end of 6 years using the 7% sinking-fund method?

8.23 If the depreciation method in Problem 8.22 had been changed to the straight-line method at the end of the 4th year, what would be the book value at the end of 6 years?

8.24 Assume that the LongLivecyclones Corporation has purchased office furniture and equipment on January 1, 1985, for one of its branches for $500,000. Determine its ACRS depreciation schedule.

8.25 Mr. Joe Theengineer has purchased a microcomputer on January 1, 1984, for his consulting engineering business for $10,000. Determine its ACRS depreciation schedule.

8.26 The Nogas & Nopower Public Utility Company has purchased a dump truck on January 1, 1985, with a useful life of 20 years, for $50,000. Determine its ACRS depreciation schedule for the first 5-year period.

8.27 Repeat Example 8.9 assuming that Mr. Smart has sold the property on January 1, 1985, for $180,000

8.28 Calculate the depletion allowance for the following assets assuming that the percentage depletion method has been used in the past.

Asset	Asset (Natural Resource) Type	Depletion Rate ($x\%$)	Amount Removed This year ($y\%$)	Cost Basis (CB)	Gross Income (GI)	Deductible Expenses (DE)
1	Uranium	22	10	$500,000	$200,000	$100,000
2	Oil	22	5	1,000,000	600,000	200,000
3	Dolomite	14	10	100,000	60,000	40,000
4	Coal	10	5	400,000	300,000	100,000
5	Sand	5	8	200,000	100,000	50,000

____9
INCOME TAX CONSIDERATIONS

Don't tax me, don't tax thee,
Tax that fellow behind the tree.
UNKNOWN AUTHOR

In this world nothing is certain but death and taxes.
BENJAMIN FRANKLIN, 1757

9.1 INTRODUCTION

It is interesting to note that the United States Constitution did not allow the federal government to tax incomes earned by individuals until the Sixteenth Amendment[†] was ratified in 1913. The federal income tax was followed by state income taxes in later years. Today, the Internal Revenue Service (IRS) collects taxes and publishes regulations that explain and carry out legislation passed by Congress. Also, each state (almost all of them with few exceptions), counties, and cities have similar entities to collect and/or regulate appropriate taxes. Of course, the tax laws of the United States have been revised many times since 1913 in an attempt to provide a perfect tax system. For various reasons there may never be a *perfect tax system*,[‡] that is, one

---

[†]However, taxes have been levied, at one time or another, on individuals throughout human history. For example, the Old Roman Empire taxed individual incomes, at 40% or more, approximately 2000 years ago. At that time a tax collector was called a *publican*, which also meant robber. Other examples include unjust taxation in England that resulted in the Magna Carta (the great charter of English political and civil liberties granted by King John at Runnymede on June 15, 1215) as well as, a few hundred years later, the Boston Tea Party (a protest staged by American colonists in Boston on December 16, 1773, against the excessive British tax on imported tea. The colonists, disguised as Indians, boarded British ships in Boston Harbor and threw chests of tea overboard). Of course, as it is well known, the Boston Tea Party contributed to the independence movement in the American colonies. It is also interesting to note that the word *tax* came from the Middle English *taxen*, which meant to assess, tax, from the Old French *taxer*, which in turn came from Medieval Latin *taxāre*.
[‡]As succinctly put by Edmund Burke in a speech, "On American Taxation," in 1774: *To tax and to please, no more than to love and be wise, is not given to men.*

237

which is considered to be (1) efficient, (2) fair and equal, (3) simple, (4) certain and predictable, and (5) neutral.

9.2 TYPES OF TAXES

There are various types of taxes in the United States. The following are some of the more common taxes:

1. *Income taxes* are assessed (or levied) against the *taxable income* of individuals and corporations. Such taxes are based on net "taxable" income, which is the difference between gross income and certain deductions permitted in the tax laws. The income tax due is generally determined as a percentage of the taxable income. Income taxes are assessed by the federal government as well as by most states and some municipal governments.
2. *Property taxes*, often called *ad valorem* taxes, are assessed as a function of the *value of property*,[†] that is, against the value of real estate, business, and personal property. They are commonly assessed by school districts, municipalities, counties, and states.
3. *Sales* or *use taxes* are levied on the *transfer* of property from one owner to another. The tax assessment is a function of the value of the property sold and is generally assessed by a state or city.
4. Excise taxes are *federal* taxes and are based on the value of a *unnecessity* commodity at a certain stage of manufacture or transfer. Examples of such unnecessity commodities include alcohol, tobacco, gasoline, automobiles, tires, telephone and teletypewriter services, civil aircrafts, air transportation, and firearms. Usually, the excise tax is paid by the supplier or manufacturer and is included in the price charged to the customer.
5. *Other taxes* may include *user's tax, value-added tax, unemployment tax,* and *social security contributions.*

In this book only income taxes will be taken into account. As mentioned before income taxes are assessed by the federal government as well as by most of the states.

[†]A given property is generally taxed on the basis of *millage*. Here, one *mill* is equal to one-tenth of one cent (i.e., 1 mill = 0.1 cent). Thus, the tax rate given in millage indicates the number of mills that will be paid on each dollar of assessed property value. For example, if the property is valued by the tax assessor (of the county) at $100,000 and the millage rate for that type of property is 20 mills, the resulting property tax owed is

$$\$100,000(20 \text{ mills}/\$1 \text{ valuation}) = 2,000,000 \text{ mills}$$

Since $1 = 1,000 mills, the proper tax bill is $2,000.

9.3 THE TAX REFORM ACT OF 1986

On October 22, 1986, President Ronald Reagan signed into law one of the most sweeping overhauls of the tax code in the history of the United States. This landmark tax overhaul is entitled the *Tax Reform Act of 1986*. It is also called the *Internal Revenue Code of 1986*. According to President Reagan: "This is a tax code designed to take us into a future of technological invention and economic achievement, one that will keep America competitive and growing into the twenty-first century."

As explained in Section 8.13, the Tax Reform Act of 1986 has modified the ACRS depreciation method by (1) revising the recovery periods and/or rates of recovery and (2) prescribing depreciation methods rather than statutorily prescribed rates. In general, under the modified ACRS system, assets are classified into six groups of personal property based generally on the assets' depreciation range (ADR) midpoint life, and into two classes of real property. Each class is assigned a recovery period and a depreciation method, as given in Table 8.14.

In the United States the federal government regulates the monetary and fiscal policies of the country to control the level of economic activity. For example, its *monetary policy* affects the cost and availability of credit, whereas its *fiscal policy* controls government revenues and expenditures. Therefore, taxation is the main factor in fiscal policy. The basic methods for changing government revenues, in the order of importance, include (1) altering the tax rate, (2) altering the depreciation rates, and (3) permitting tax credits and deductions.

9.4 INDIVIDUAL FEDERAL INCOME TAX

The amount of federal income taxes due is a function of taxable income and the income tax rates. *Taxable income* is defined as earned income minus adjustments and minus allowable deductions. Therefore, the term *adjusted gross income* means an individual's total net earned income as determined according to the provisions of federal income tax law. Therefore, for individual taxpayers

$$
\begin{aligned}
\text{Taxable income} = \ &\text{Adjusted gross income} \\
&- \text{Deductions for personal exemptions} \\
&- \text{Other permissible deductions} \qquad (9.1)
\end{aligned}
$$

Possibly the most dramatic feature of the new tax law is that beginning in 1988, it compresses those previously existing 15 tax brackets into just 2: 15 and 28%. The new tax rate structure for individuals starting in 1988 is given in Table 9.1. The act phases out the benefit of the 15% rate for taxpayers with high taxable income. Note that this provision in effect imposes a third

TABLE 9.1   The New Tax Rate Structure for Individuals Beginning in 1988

	Taxable Income		
	Joint Returns	Heads of Household	Single Individuals
15	Up to $29,750	Up to $23,900	Up to $17,850
28	Over 29,750	Over 23,900	Over 17,850

top rate of 33% for these taxpayers on a portion of their taxable income. This is accomplished by means of an additional tax of 5% on taxable income falling within certain ranges. In general, the additional 5% tax is applicable to taxable income levels between $71,900 and $149,250 for joint returns, $61,650 and $123,790 for heads of household, $43,150 and $89,560 for singles. Once taxable income is equal to or greater than the top of a high-income range, the benefit of the 15% tax bracket totally disappears for wealthier taxpayers because they will receive a 5% surcharge tax when taxable income falls within certain ranges. In addition the 5% surcharge will continue to be applicable until such taxpayers lose the benefits of claiming personal exemptions, children, and other dependents on their tax return. In effect, this surcharge neutralizes the incomes of more prosperous taxpayers so that they pay an average of 28% tax.

The Tax Reform Act of 1986 has increased the personal exemption amount to $1,950 in 1988 and $2,000 in 1989. Beginning in 1990, the $2,000 exemption will be indexed for inflation. Also, beginning in 1988, personal exemptions will be phased out for certain high-income taxpayers. This phase out of the $1,950 exemption starts for taxable income above the break-points. For example, $149,250 for joint returns, $123,790 for heads of household, and $89,560 for single individuals. (Beginning in 1989, these breakpoints will be indexed for inflation.) Similar to the phase out of the 15% tax rate, the personal exemption phase out is achieved by a 5% additional tax on taxable income surpassing the applicable breakpoint. For income above the breakpoint each personal exemption for 1988 would otherwise yield a tax savings of $546 (i.e., 28% of $1,950). Therefore, the maximum phase-out tax in 1988 is $546 per exemption.

Individuals who do not itemize their deductions can claim standard deductions. For example, beginning in 1988, the new standard deduction amounts for joint returns, heads of household, and single individuals are $5,000, $4,400, and $3,000, respectively. Starting in 1989, the standard deductions will also be indexed for inflation. Furthermore, there have been substantial changes made in individual deductible items. For example, the act does not change the range of items qualifying for the medical expense deduction. However, it raises the floor for deducting itemized medical expenses to 7.5% of adjusted gross income.

Also, under the act, the deduction for personal interest expense is phased out. Personal interest includes interest paid or incurred to purchase an asset for personal use and credit card charges for personal purchases. However, interest expense attributable to mortgages secured by the taxpayer's principal residence and one second residence (e.g., a vacation home) remains deductible.

Furthermore, the act repeals the capital-gain deduction for individuals, therefore taxing long-term (or short-term) capital gains at the same rates as ordinary income. Capital losses are fully deductible against capital gains at the same rates as ordinary income. Capital losses are fully deductible against capital gains but still may offset only $3,000 of ordinary income in any taxable year. However, every dollar of net capital loss can offset a dollar of ordinary income. Therefore, for purposes of the $3,000 limitation, the distinction between long-term and short-term losses incurred is no longer relevant. However, any capital loss exceeding the $3,000 limitation carries forward to the succeeding taxable year.

Example 9.1 Assume that Mr. and Mrs. Nonames have taxable income of $149,250 in 1988. Determine the following:

(a) Their total federal income tax for the year 1988.
(b) The applicable *effective tax rate.*

Solution

(a) Their total federal income tax for the year can be calculated in the following manner:

Tax Bracket	Tax Rate (5)	Income Tax
0 to $29,750	15	$4,462
29,750 to 71,900	28	11,802
71,900 to 149,250	33	25,526
		Total tax = $41,790

(b) The additional tax of 5% effectively eliminates the benefit of the 15% bracket. Therefore, the Nonames have an *effective tax rate* of 28%. Thus, their total tax is still $41,790. Since

$$\$149,250 \times 0.28 = \$41,790$$

Example 9.2 Assume that a family of four has a taxable income of $190,000 in 1988. Determine whether or not the family can benefit from the personal exemptions.

Solution Since the taxable income exceeds the breakpoint for the joint returns by

$$\$190,000 - \$149,250 = \$40,750$$

the additional tax is

$$\$40,750 \times 5\% = \$2,038$$

The tax benefit of the family's four exemptions is

$$(\$1,950 \times 4) \times 28\% = \$2,184$$

This means that the family's four exemptions have been almost completely phased out. Therefore, the net tax benefit of the four exemptions is

$$\$2,184 - \$2,038 = \$146$$

9.5 CORPORATION FEDERAL INCOME TAX

In general, the business expenditures of a corporation can be classified as *capital expenditures* and *operational expenditures* (which are also called necessary *cash operating costs*). In the accounting records of the corporation the capital expenditures are *capitalized* (i.e., they are distributed over the useful lives of the assets), whereas the operational expenditures are *expensed* (i.e., they are charged against the revenues) in the year that they occurred. The capital expenditures can be classified as *capital expenditures for depreciable assets* and *capital expenditures for nondepreciable assets*. The capital expenditures for depreciable assets occur when a corporation purchases facilities or productive equipment, with useful lives that are greater than one year, so that the investment can be recovered through annual depreciation charges; whereas the capital expenditures for nondepreciable assets take place when a corporation purchases land or other nondepreciable assets that cannot be used in a trade or business or for the production of revenue. On the other hand the operational expenditures include all operating costs (i.e., direct or indirect labor costs, direct material, productive equipment with useful lives of one year or less, and overhead costs).

The revenue (i.e., income) of a corporation[†] is called the *gross income*. From the gross income all operational expenditures except capital expenditures are subtracted; also subtracted are applicable depreciation and depletion charges. Therefore, for corporations

---

[†]Note that the term *corporation*, as employed in income tax law, is not restricted to the artificial entity generally known as a corporation but can also involve joint stock associations or companies, limited partnerships, and certain types of trusts.

Taxable income = Gross income
      − All expenditures except capital expenditures
      − Depreciation and depletion charges (9.2)

Figure 9.1 shows a representation of the taxable income concept. Note that the depreciation charge is not a cash flow because depreciation is simply

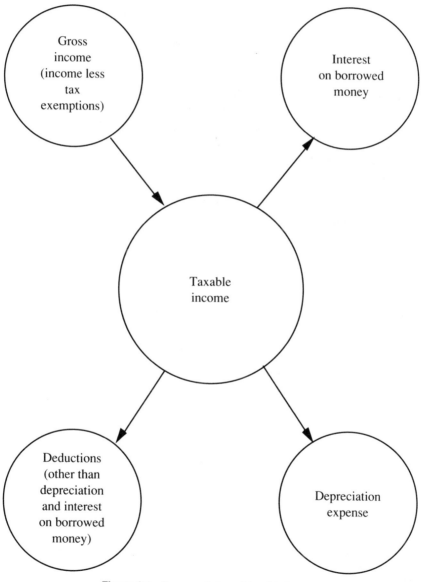

Figure 9.1 Representation of taxable income.

treated as an expense in computing taxable income. In a sense the taxable income of a corporation is practically the same as the *before-tax net profit*. It is also called *before-tax cash flow.*[†] Therefore, for corporations

$$\text{Income tax} = (\text{Tax rate})(\text{Taxable income}) \qquad (9.3)$$

where the taxable income includes return of the investment and return on the investment.

9.6 INCOME TAX RATES FOR CORPORATIONS

The Tax Reform Act of 1986 introduced major changes into the rates of tax on corporate taxable income. Table 9.2 gives the new tax rate structure for corporations beginning on or after July 1, 1987.

Note that the maximum corporate tax rate now exceeds the maximum individual tax rate[‡] (i.e., 34 versus 28%). Because of the rate differential, shareholders in a closely held corporation should consider electing S corpo-

TABLE 9.2 The New Tax Rate Structure for Corporations Beginning on July 1, 1987

Tax Rate (%)	Taxable Income
15	Not over $25,000
15	$25,001 through $50,000
25	$50,001 through $75000
34	$75,001 through $100,000
34[a]	Over $100,000

[a]An additional 5% tax up to $11,750 is imposed on corporate taxable income over $100,000, up to $335,000. Corporations with taxable income of at least $335,000 thus pay a flat rate of 34%.

[†]In this chapter (unless noted otherwise), it is assumed the debt ratio is zero; that is, financing is totally by equity capital, and the debt ratio is time invariant. For those readers interested in an in-depth review of the effects of the debt ratios in the engineering economy applications, Chapter 10 of Smith [66] is highly recommended.

[‡]Note that individual tax rate is applicable to sole proprietors and individual members of partnerships. A person engaging in business alone is a sole proprietor. A partnership must file a partnership income return, which is simply an information return. Each partner is taxed on his share of the partnership earning whether or not distributed to the individual. However, corporation income is commonly taxed to the corporation at corporation rates. Corporation earnings, if they are distributed to the shareholders, are taxed again as dividends or ordinary income at the appropriate individual tax rate. This is called the *double taxation* of the same income. However, earnings of a corporation structured under Subchapter S of the Internal Revenue Service code are taxed at individual income tax rates.

ration status in order to shift the tax burden on corporate earnings only to the shareholder level. Here, the S corporation (i.e., "Subchapter S" corporation) is a form of corporation whose shareholders elect under the tax laws to be taxed individually.

9.7 AFTER-TAX CASH FLOW

After income taxes are subtracted from the *before-tax cash flow*, the remainder is called the *after-tax cash flow*,[†] as shown in Figure 9.2. Similarly,

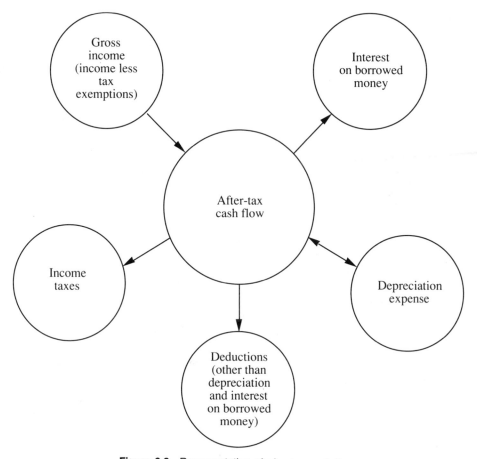

Figure 9.2 Representation of after-tax cash flow.

[†]Note that the two-way arrow in Figure 9.2 that connects the depreciation expense to after-tax cash flow reflects the fact that the resulting tax savings due to the depreciation charge becomes part of the after-tax cash flow after the determination of the accrued income tax for the gross income.

after income taxes are subtracted from the *before-tax net profit*, the remainder is often called the *after-tax net profit*. Therefore,

$$\text{After-tax cash flow} = \text{Before-tax cash flow} - \text{Income tax} \qquad (9.4)$$

or

$$\text{After-tax cash flow} = \text{Before-tax cash flow} - t \text{ (before-tax cash flow}$$
$$- \text{Interest on debt} - \text{Depreciation expense)}$$
$$(9.5)$$

Thus,

$$\text{Before-tax cash flow} = \frac{1}{1-t} \text{ After-tax cash flow} - \frac{t}{1-t} \text{ (Interest on debt}$$
$$+ \text{ Depreciation expense)} \qquad (9.6)$$

where t is the combined effective income tax rate.

Income taxes affect all business and industrial corporations except those owned by the government or tax-exempt entities, such as certain cooperatives and other nonprofit organizations (e.g., charitable organizations, churches, and hospitals). There are various reasons to make an after-tax economic study rather than a before-tax study. For example: (1) The effects of income tax considerations often are substantially different from one prospective investment project to another. Therefore, it generally is very important to compare the relative economics of investment project alternatives on an after-tax basis to have a valid economic analysis. (2) The before-tax approach does not take into account the rates of depreciation, depletion, or other types of write-offs. Thus, it does not provide any guidance for the selection of proper write-off method. (3) Since income taxes, both federal and state, if applicable, are major project costs (just as the costs of labor, material, etc.), it does not make any sense to ignore them. (4) In general, the before-tax approach provides a rate of return that is less than the actual rate of return of a project. Also, it overstates the revenue requirements for assets that are depreciable. (5) In a capital budgeting process, the ranking of projects may be different depending on the before-tax versus the after-tax approach. (6) The financial structure of a corporation (in terms of debt and equity) cannot be included in the before-tax approach. Therefore, unless there is a strong reason for neglecting income taxes, they should always be included in economic studies for the corporation.

Example 9.3 Assume that the taxable income of the ABC Company is averaging at $800,000 per year and the top management of the company is considering introducing a new product and has requested that its engineering manager make a financial feasibility analysis. The new product requires the purchase of a certain manufacturing equipment that has a 5-year useful life and costs $300,000 including its installation. The salvage value of the equipment at the end of its useful life is negligible. It is estimated that the new product will have operating revenues of $450,000 and cash operating costs of $100,000 per year. The new venture will require a debt capital of $100,000 at 8% interest. Use the modified ACRS and the half-year convention for the equipment and a combined effective income tax rate of 37.9% for the resulting additional taxable income. Determine the following for the first year:

(a) Before-tax cash flow.
(b) The depreciation expense.
(c) The interest on debt capital.
(d) The taxable income.
(e) The combined federal and state income taxes.
(f) The return on equity capital.
(g) The after-tax cash flow.

Solution

(a) Before-tax cash flow = Operating revenues − Cash operating cost
$$= \$450,000 - \$100,000 = \$350,000$$

(b) Based on the modified ACRS method, for the first and the last years, a half-year convention is used for personal property. Thus, under this convention property placed in service or disposed of during a taxable year is considered placed in service or disposed of at the midpoint of that year. Since from Table 8.14 it can be found that the property falls into the "5-year, 200%" category, therefore double-declining-balance depreciation can be used. Hence, the first year depreciation expense is

$$D_1 = \tfrac{1}{2} \times \tfrac{2}{5}(\$300,000 - 0) = \$60,000$$

(c) The interest on debt capital is

$$\$100,000 \times 0.08 = \$8,000$$

(d) From equation (9.2)

$$\text{Taxable income} = \text{Before-tax cash flow} - \text{Interest on debt}$$

$$- \text{Depreciation expense}$$

$$= \$350,000 - \$8,000 - \$60,000 = \$282,000$$

(e) From equation (9.3)

$$\text{Income tax} = \text{Tax rate} \times \text{Taxable income}$$
$$= (0.3796)(\$282,000) = \$107,047$$

(f) Return on equity = Taxable income − Income tax
$$= \$282,000 - \$107,047 = \$174,953$$

(g) After-tax cash flow = Return on debt and equity
$$+ \text{Depreciation expense}$$

where

$$\text{Return on debt and equity} = \text{Return on debt} + \text{Return on equity}$$
$$= \$8,000 + \$174,953 = \$182,953$$

Thus

$$\text{After-tax flow} = \$182,953 + \$60,000 = \$242,953$$

9.8   COMBINED FEDERAL AND STATE INCOME TAXES

In general, in addition to federal income taxes, most individuals and corporations also pay state income taxes. Therefore, it may be convenient to determine a *combined effective tax rate* that takes into account both the federal and state taxes. In general, the state income taxes are deductible for purposes of calculating federal income taxes; whereas, the federal income taxes are not generally deductible for calculating the state income taxes. Thus, the state income tax rate is applied to a *greater* taxable income than the federal income tax rate. Therefore, the combined effective income tax rate is not the sum of the two tax rates. Thus, at a given level of income, the total of state and federal income taxes can be expressed as

Total state and federal income taxes
$$= [\text{State tax rate} + \text{Federal tax rate} \times (1 - \text{State tax rate})]$$
$$\times \text{Taxable income} \tag{9.7}$$

Therefore, the combined effective income tax rate can be given as

Combined effective income tax rate = State tax rate + Federal tax rate
$$\times (1 - \text{State tax rate}) \tag{9.8}$$

Example 9.4 Assume that the International Zubits Corporation has a taxable income of $500,000 which puts the corporation in the 34% federal income tax bracket and at the 6% state tax rate. Determine the following:

(a) The combined effective income tax rate.
(b) The total state and federal income taxes.

Solution

(a) From equation (9.8)

Combined effective income tax rate

$$= \text{State tax rate} + \text{Federal tax rate} \times (1 - \text{State tax rate})$$

$$= 0.06 + 0.34(1 - 0.06)$$

$$= 0.3796 \text{ or } 37.96\%$$

(b) From equation (9.7)

Total state and federal income taxes

$$= [\text{State tax rate} + \text{Federal tax rate} \times (1 - \text{State tax rate})]$$

$$\times \text{Taxable income}$$

Example 9.5 Assume that Mr. and Mrs. Smart have a taxable income of $500,00, which puts them in the (flat) 28% federal income tax bracket and at the 6% state tax rate. Determine the following:

(a) The combined effective income tax rate.
(b) The total state and federal income taxes.

Solution

(a) From equation (9.8)

$$\text{Combined effective income tax rate} = 0.06 + 0.28(1 - 0.06)$$

$$= 0.3232 \text{ or } 32.32\%$$

(b) Thus, from equation (9.7)

$$\text{Total state and federal income taxes} = 0.3232 \times \$500,000$$

$$= \$161,600$$

Note that as individuals Mr. and Mrs. Smart pay $28,000 less income taxes than the corporation for the same amount of taxable income.

Example 9.6   Assume that a $400,000 investment made today will provide an after-tax cash flow of $150,000 at the end of each of the next 5 years. Assume that the salvage value is negligible at the end of the 5-year period and determine the after-tax rate of return of the investment.

Solution   Based on the net present worth method,

$$NPW = -\$400{,}000 + \$150{,}000(P/A, \, i\%, \, 5) = 0$$

or

$$\$400{,}000 = \$150{,}000(P/A, \, i\%, \, 5)$$

Try $i = 25\%$:

$$\$400{,}000 = \$150{,}000(2.689) = \$403{,}350$$

Thus, i is too low. Try $i = 30\%$:

$$\$400{,}000 = \$150{,}000(2.436) = \$365{,}400$$

Hence, i is too high. Therefore, the after-tax rate of return (ATROR) is

$$\text{ATROR} = 25\% + \frac{\$403{,}350 - \$400{,}000}{\$403{,}350 - \$365{,}400} \, 5\% = 25.44\%$$

Example 9.7   Assume that a $500,000 investment made today will provide a net before-tax cash flow of $200,000 at the end of each of the next 6 years. Assume that the salvage value is $50,000 at the end of the useful life and that the applicable combined effective income tax rate of the company is 37.96%. Use the straight-line depreciation method and determine the following:

(a) Straight-line depreciation charge for the year.
(b) Prepare a cash flow table.
(c) Before-tax rate of return.
(d) After-tax rate of return.

Solution

(a) Straight-line depreciation charge for the year is

$$D = \frac{P - F}{N} = \frac{\$500{,}000 - \$50{,}000}{6} = \$75{,}000$$

(b) The cash flow table is given in Table 9.3.

(c) For before-tax rate of return

$$NPW = -\$500,000 + \$200,000(P/A, i\%, 6) + \$50,000(P/F, i\%, 6)$$

or

$$\$500,000 = \$200,000(P/A, i\%, 6) + \$50,000(P/F, i\%, 6)$$

Try $i = 30\%$:

$$\$500,000 = \$200,000(2.643) + \$50,000(0.2072) = \$538,960$$

which means 30% is too low. Try $i = 40\%$:

$$\$500,000 = \$200,000(2.168) + \$50,000(0.1328) = \$440,240$$

which means 40% is too high. Therefore, the before-tax rate of return (BTROR) is

$$BTROR = 30\% + \frac{\$538,900 - \$500,000}{\$538,900 - \$440,240} 10\% = 33.94\%$$

(d) For the after-tax rate of return

$$NPW = -\$500,000 + \$152,550(P/A, i\%, 6) + \$500,000(P/A, i\%, 6)$$

or

TABLE 9.3 Cash Flow Table for Example 9.7

Year, A	Before-Tax Cash Flow, B	Depreciation Charge, C	Taxable Income (B–C), D	37.96% Income Taxes, E	After-Tax Cash Flow (D–E) + C, F
0	−$500,000				−$500,000
1	200,000	$75,000	$125,000	$47,450	152,220
2	200,000	75,000	125,000	47,450	152,550
3	200,000	75,000	125,000	47,450	152,550
4	200,000	75,000	125,000	47,450	152,550
5	200,000	75,000	125,000	47,450	152,550
6	{ 200,000 / 50,000	75,000	125,000	47,450	{ 152,550 / 50,000

$$\$500,000 = \$152,550(P/A, i\%, 6) + \$50,000(P/F, i\%, 6)$$

Try $i = 20\%$:

$$\$500,000 = \$152,550(3.326) + \$50,000(0.3349) = \$523,960$$

which means 20% is too low. Try $i = 25\%$:

$$\$500,000 = \$152,550(2.951) + \$50,000(0.2621) = \$463,133$$

Thus, the after-tax rate of return is

$$\text{ATROR} = 20\% + \frac{\$523,960 - \$500,000}{\$523,960 - \$463,133} 5\% = 21.97\%$$

PROBLEMS

9.1 Assume that a married couple with no dependents earned $200,000 in 1988. Take into account their personal exemptions and determine the following:

(a) Their total federal income tax for 1988.

(b) The applicable effective tax rate.

9.2 Solve Example 9.2 but assume that the family is a family of three.

9.3 Assume that taxable income in 1988 is $400,000 and that the state income tax rate is 10%. Determine the following:

(a) Combined effective income tax rate for a married couple filing a joint tax return.

(b) Combined effective income tax rate for a corporation.

9.4 Assume that you are married and earning $40,000 per year. You are in the 28% federal income tax bracket and at the 10% state income tax rate. You have an offer to do some consulting work to provide you with $10,000 extra income. Determine the following:

(a) Combined effective income tax rate.

(b) Total state and federal income taxes without the consulting work.

(c) Total state and federal income taxes with the consulting work.

(d) The net income from the consulting work after paying the associated taxes.

9.5 Consider Example 9.3 and determine the following for each of the remaining years:
(a) The before-tax cash flow.
(b) The depreciation expense.
(c) The taxable income.
(d) Income tax.
(e) After-tax cash flow.

9.6 Assume that a $500,000 investment made today will provide an after-tax cash flow of $200,000 at the end of each of the next 6 years. The salvage value is negligible. Find the after-tax rate of return.

9.7 Assume that a $1,000,000 investment made today will provide an after-tax cash flow of $200,000 at the end of each of the next 6 years. The salvage value is negligible. Find the after-tax rate of return.

9.8 Modernization of an assembly line will cost $80,000. It is estimated that the initial expenditure will reduce the annual operating expenses by $12,000 for 10 years. The machinery will be depreciated using the straight-line method. It will have a negligible salvage value at the end of its 10-year useful life because it is all specially designed for this singular implacement. The tax rate is 48%. What will be the prospective rates of return before and after taxes?

9.9 Because of the uniqueness of the assembly line and because the job is a government defense contract, the company in Problem 9.8 has been given a 6% investment tax credit. What is the after-tax rate of return now for Problem 9.8?

9.10 A wholesale produce building has a first cost of $100,000 with a useful life of 20 years and a salvage value of $15,000. The annual receipts are expected to be $30,000, and the annual disbursements for utilities and maintenance is projected to be $5,000. The building will be depreciated using the straight-line method and the tax rate is 48%. What is the after-taxes rate of return?

9.11 What would be the after-tax rate of return in Problem 9.10 if the sum-of-the-years' digits method was used for depreciation purposes?

9.12 A manufacturing firm invests $150,000 a year for research and development. The gross income is around $800,000 a year, and the operating expenses average about 60% of the gross income. State income tax is 6% and is deducted from the taxable income, which is taxed at 48%. What has been this company's after-tax rate of return on its R&D investment over the past 4 years?

9.13 Given the same situation as in Problems 9.8 and 9.9 but that the 6% tax credit cannot be applied until the end of year 4, what will be the after-tax rate of return?

9.14 A company purchases a machine for $110,000 that will have a salvage value of $30,000 in 15 years. The machine will provide an income of $35,000 for the first year, and this income will then diminish $1,500 annually for the remaining 14 years because of steadily increasing maintenance and operating costs. If the tax rate is 48% and depreciation is not considered, what is the after-tax rate of return?

9.15 Rework Problem 9.14 using the straight-line method of depreciation to determine the after-tax rate of return.

9.16 You have an opportunity to invest $5,000 in a new commodity investment group. You have set a minimum acceptable rate of return on your money of 7%. The investment group has guaranteed you a return of $500 a year for 3 years after which time you will get your original $5,000 back. Because of the nature of the commodity market, your annual return is considered short-term capital gain and is taxed at 48%. Does this investment meet your investment criterion after taxes?

9.17 An asset worth $90,000 has a salvage value of $21,000 at the end of 10 years. Income produced by the asset will be $20,000 more annually than the disbursements. Using a tax rate of 48% and the sum of the years method of depreciation, what is the after-tax rate of return?

9.18 An oyster cannery in Monterey is considering the purchase of a semiautomatic oyster shucker for $21,000. The owner thinks he will be able to eliminate some of the shuckers who are paid on a piece rate basis, thereby saving about $12,000 in labor costs a year. However, due to salt water and the wearing action of broken shells, maintenance costs are $2,000 a year and the machine has zero salvage after 5 years. Using straight-line depreciation, find the after-tax rate of return. Assume a 48% effective tax rate.

9.19 The oyster cannery in Problem 9.18 bought the semiautomatic oyster shucker. The owner depreciated the machine over 5 five years, but due to good maintenance and good fortune, the oyster shucker was found to function well enough to last an additional 5 years. Assuming the same data as in Problem 9.18, what is the after-tax rate of return at the end of the 10th year?

9.20 (a) Find the single effective tax rate, if federal tax is 48% and the state tax is 5%, when the state income tax *is* deductible from the federal income tax.

(b) Estimate the MARR, *before taxes*, for an individual subject to 36% federal income tax and 4% state income tax. Assume the federal income tax *is* deductible from the state income tax. MARR after taxes is 7%.

9.21 Compare the after-tax rate of return of two proposals that are identical except for their estimated lifes:

	Proposal A	Proposal B
First cost	$65,000	$65,000
Salvage	5,000	5,000
Life	5 years	10 years
Annual cash flow before tax	20,000	20,000

Assume an income tax rate of 48% and straight-line depreciation.

9.22 A processed food company is contemplating the installation of a carbon treater to improve the color characteristics of their product. Marketing people believe the product's price can be raised by $0.02/ lb with improved color. The firm is currently selling one million pounds a year. The first costs associated with the carbon treater are $85,000. It is estimated to have a 10-year life with zero salvage value. The finance department has determined the sum-of-years'-digits depreciation should be used, but the engineering department thinks that straight-line depreciation is more appropriate. Operating and mainte-nance costs for the carbon treater are estimated at $6,000 a year. Assuming a 48% effective tax rate, calculate the after-tax rate of return for both depreciation methods. Which method should be used in this case if the interest rate *i* is 8%?

9.23 A small businessman needs to expand his facilities. He is considering several models of temporary metal buildings. The various models all cost about the same, but due to design features on the roof, around windows and doors, and anchoring to the foundation, the estimated life of the buildings varies significantly. The Biltrite structure costs $15,000 and will last 10 years. The Durahouse building costs the same but will last 20 years. Assuming straight-line depreciation and zero salvage, would it be advantageous to the owner to buy Durahouse considering the allowable 20% "additional first year depreciation," which can be taken above regular depreciation?

___10
REPLACEMENT ANALYSIS

Who will change old lamps for new?
ANONYMOUS
The Arabian Nights, **1700**

10.1 INTRODUCTION

In general, a given property, in terms of equipment or some other type of asset (with the notable exception of land[†]), has various distinct "lives," illustrated in Figure 10.1. Such definitions of the life of a property include (1) actual useful life, (2) economic life, (3) ownership life, (4) physical life, (5) depreciation life, and (6) warranteed, guaranteed, or assured life.

1. *Actual useful life,* as the name implies, is the period over which the investment is actually used. However, it may or may not coincide with economic life or depreciation life.

2. *Economic life* is also called *service life.* For an equipment it is the duration of time spent between the time of installation and the time of retirement (either by demotion or disposal) from its *proposed* service. For other types of assets it is the time duration between the start of the use and the end of the use of the asset. The *economic life* can also be defined as the life (or period) for which the net annual worth (or cost) is minimum. The term *life* here is used to define the period of time that the property is used by one owner.

3. *Ownership life* is the time duration between the time of purchase and the time of disposal of a given property by a specific owner. Of course, a given property may have more than one service life (through a series of demotions) for a given owner, as clearly illustrated in Figure 10.1.

[†]As mentioned before, land is always assumed to have a life of infinity.

256

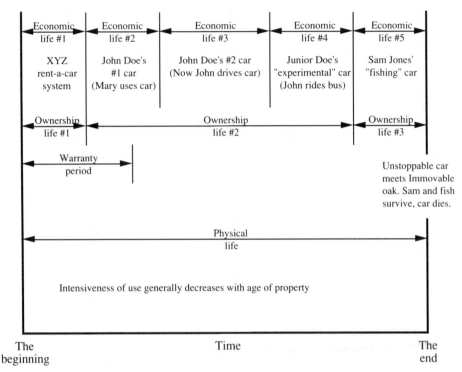

Figure 10.1 Various *lives* of a property. (Reprinted by permission from *Engineering Economy: Analysis of Capital Expenditures*, Fourth Edition, by Gerald Smith © 1987 by Iowa State University Press, Ames, Iowa.)

4. *Physical life* is the time duration between the time of purchase of a property by its first owner and the time of its disposal by its last owner. For example, in the car example given in Figure 10.1, it starts by its purchase by the XYZ Rent-a-Car System, and it continues until it has been put out of commission by the immovable oak tree.

5. *Depreciation life* is also called *accounting life*. It is the expected time duration over which the property is anticipated to be used and to be depreciated from its new installed cost to its net salvage value.

6. *Warranteed, guaranteed, or assured life* is the minimum period of service life that is guaranteed by the manufacturer of a product.

10.2 REASONS FOR REPLACEMENT

The reasons for considering replacement can be the result of a number of factors, including inadequacy, excessive maintenance, declining efficiency, obsolescense (in terms of both functional and economic life), rental or lease possibilities, and, of course, physical impairment. For example, increasing demands can cause an existing production asset (building, equipment, etc.) to be inadequate to meet such demand. This, in turn, may cause such an asset either to be supplemented or replaced. As illustrated in Figure 10.2, as an asset gets old, it shows a tendency to detiorate gradually and increasingly over time, which causes less efficient operation with consequent increasing operation costs and/or increasing costs of maintenance and repairs. This, in turn, may cause decreasing receipts for product or service and increased costs because of decreasing quality. A decrease or a cessation in demand may cause the associated asset to be functionally obsolete. For example, after the introduction of electronic pocket calculators, the machines used to produce slide rules become functionally obsolete. In general, new and improved designs can cause an existing asset to be obsolete economically. For example, the newer mainframe computers continuously make the older ones economically obsolete. As a result of this trend, many companies have bitterly learned to rent or lease such computers rather than to purchase them. Further, of course, an existing asset that is worn out extensively, as a result of its normal use or an accident, and therefore cannot provide its service, is a good candidate for replacement. In most situations, an asset is replaced for more than one reason. For example, an asset may start to need more maintenace because of increasing downtimes, and/or it may start to operate at a decreased level of efficiency. Furthermore, it may not always be capable of meeting the demands placed on it. The existence of a possible

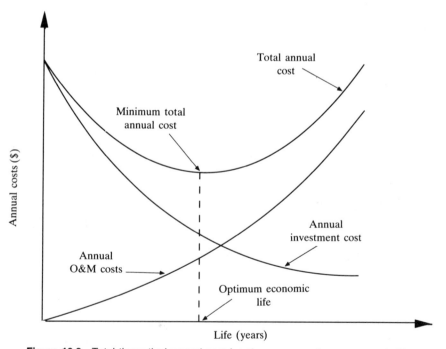

Figure 10.2 Total theoretical annual cost function versus optimum economic life.

replacement, even though it may have a higher investment cost but lower annual O&M costs, may require an *economic feasibility study* of replacing the existing asset.

10.3 OPTIMUM ECONOMIC LIFE

In theory, the replacement of an asset should take place when it is most economical rather than when the asset is worn out. As indicated in Figure 10.2, the optimum economic life of an asset is the point in time at which the total annual cost of the asset is minimum. Note that for any given year the total annual cost of the asset is the sum of the annual investment cost and the annual O&M costs. Also note that the annual O&M costs are increasing as the asset gets older. The *optimum economic life* (which is also called the *optimum service life*) can also be defined as

$$\text{Optimum economic life} = \text{Optimum retirement age}$$

$$- \text{Optimum acquisition age} \qquad (10.1)$$

Of course, the optimum economic life concept is equally applicable to both the defender and the challenger.

Usually, the criterion of annual equivalent cost (AEC) minimization is the preferable criterion to determine the optimum economic life,[†] the optimum retirement age, and the optimum acquisition age for a given asset. It has the distinct advantage of not requiring an estimate of the magnitude of annual revenues.

In general, the disposal of an asset by its owner is called *retirement*. Of course, as illustrated in Figure 10.1, a retired asset can still be useful for other owners at the same or different capacity, whereas a *replacement* takes place when a retired asset is used at a different (usually *inferior* use) capacity by demotion,[‡] the new asset can still be considered as a replacement.

[†]However, in practice, the optimum economic life is *not* necessarily an indication of the retirement date. The actual retirement of an asset should be fully evaluated so that such decision is based on the particular combination of economical and technological factors and considerations existing at that time.

[‡]The replacement of a piece of equipment does not necessarily mean that it is retired and disposed of. However, it is more possible that, on such replacement, the apparatus involved will be retained for service on a demoted (or degraded) task level somewhere within the company. Thus, equipment can be replaced a number of times, each in a different service, before its final retirement. For example, a turbogenerator (i.e, turbine generator) installed in a power plant is usually demoted several times before its final disposal. At the beginning, while its efficiency is the highest among the installed generators, it will be used to supply the *base load*. Later, it may be replaced by a more efficient generator and demoted to secondary duty with regard to the best units. However, later on, it may be replaced in this task and demoted to be a peak unit (i.e., being in use only during system's peak demand period) that operates only a few hours a day. Eventually, it may be further demoted to serve only as a standby unit to serve only in emergencies. Finally, in time, it may be displaced from its final task and retired and sold as scrap.

TABLE 10.1   Data for Example 10.2

Year (N)	Annual Maintenance Costs ($)	End of Year Salvage Value ($)
1	0	16,000
2	2,000	14,000
3	3,000	12,000
4	4,000	10,000
5	5,000	8,000
6	6,000	6,000

Example 10.1   Assume that Bluegrass Company has purchased a new piece of equipment for $15,000. It is estimated that its salvage value after 5 years will be $500 and that its O&M costs will be $2,500 at the end of year 1 and will be increased by $2,000 each year. Use a before-tax MARR of 25% and determine the annual equivalent cost of owning the equipment for 5 years.

Solution   The annual equivalent cost of the equipment is the sum of the annual equivalent of the investment costs and the annual equivalent of the O$M costs. Thus,

$$AEC = AEC_{O\&M} + P(A/P, \ i\%, \ N) - F(A/F, \ i\%, \ N)$$

$$= \$2,500 + \$2,000(A/G, \ 25\%, \ 5) + \$15,000(A/P, \ 25\%, \ 5)$$

$$- \$500(A/F, \ 25\%, \ 5) = \$11,143$$

Example 10.2   Assume that a custom sedan automobile has been purchased by the XYZ Rental Car Company for $20,000, and its expected annual maintenance costs and salvage values are as given in Table 10.1. Determine its optimum economic life, in integer years, if the MARR is 20%.

TABLE 10.2   Solution of Example 10.2

Year (N)	AEC of Investment Cost $20,000(A/P, 20%, N)	AEC of Maintenance Costs $2,000(A/G, 20%, N)	AEC Salvage Value F(A/F, 20%, N)	Total AEC for the Year
1	−$24,000	−$ 0	$16,000	−$8,000
2	− 13,091	− 910	6,364	− 7,637
3	− 9,495	− 1,758	3,297	− 7,956
4	− 7,726	− 2,548	1,863	− 8,411
5	− 6,688	− 3,282	1,075	− 8,895
6	− 6,014	− 3,958	604	− 9,368

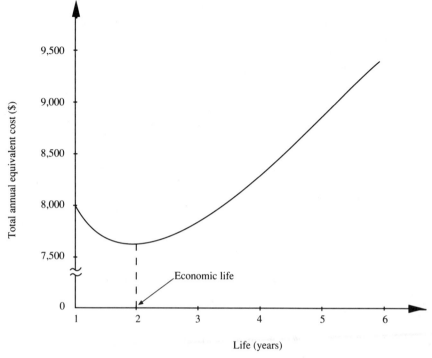

Figure 10.3   Total annual equivalent cost versus economic life.

Solution   The solution, given in Table 10.2, shows that the minimum AEC is $7,637, and therefore the optimum economic life of the automobile is 2 years. The plot, given in Figure 10.3, shows that the optimum economic life is 2 years.

10.4   THE CONCEPT OF DEFENDER VERSUS CHALLENGER

In general, a replacement analysis is performed to determine if and when an asset presently in use should be replaced by a proposed new and more economical alternative. In such studies it has been customary to define the existing (old) asset as the *defender* and the one or more alternative replacement (new) assets as the *challengers.*[†] Engineers and/or engineering managers have the responsibility to detect when an asset is no longer used efficiently, what replacement alternatives have to be taken into account, and

---

[†]The titles of *defender* and *challenger* were coined by George Terborgh of the Machinery and Allied Products Institute (MAPI), who is the author of several important books on replacement economy [69, 70].

when replacement is economically feasible. The replacement decision should be based on the performance economy of the asset rather than on physical deterioration. Usually, there is a reluctance on the part of engineering managers to replace a physically satisfactory piece of equipment even though there will be economic savings resulting from its replacement. Usually, the duration and the magnitude of cash flows for old existing assets (i.e., defenders) and new assets (i.e., challengers) are very different. New assets generally have high investment (i.e., first cost) and low operating and maintenance costs, whereas old assets generally have a low investment cost and high operating and maintenance costs. The current value of a defender is its present market value,[†] and therefore it should be used as the first cost of the defender. The first cost of the challenger must include all expenses necessary to make it operational. Also, the remaining life of a defender is characteristically short, and therefore the future of the asset can be estimated with relative certainty.

The essence of the replacement analysis is to find the answer for the following question: "Should the existing asset (i.e., defender) be replaced by the new one (i.e., challenger) now, or continued in service for one or more additional years?" Note that the question is not *if* the defender will be replaced, but it is rather *when* it will be replaced.[‡]

As mentioned in Section 10.3, the usual criterion to use, in such replacement studies, is the minimization of AEC. However, in some situations, the maximization of NPW criterion may possibly be an acceptable criterion to employ. Figure 10.4 illustrates the use of the minimization of AEC criterion[§] in such replacement analysis. Note that at the ideal replacement date the AECs of defender and challenger are equal to each other. The figure also shows the resulting cost of a one-year delay in replacement. It also illustrates the fact that if the defender is kept beyond the ideal replacement date, the costs of the defender usually grow increasingly more, which, in turn, makes its replacement a more pressing matter. However, it is possible that under certain circumstances, a *wait-and-see* policy may be acceptable. For example, if such delay is as a result of waiting for a better piece of equipment (or an improved asset), then it may be a sensible decision. Therefore, by keeping the defender for the present, it will be possible to replace it later by a better, or improved, challenger.

As succinctly put by White et al. [74, pp. 175–176][¶]:

[†] It is also called the *fair-market value.*

[‡] Of course, it is known (or expected) that the defender will eventually be replaced some time in the future.

[§] Note that if the service period is long enough so that it may have a series of replacement units, the criteria of the minimization of AEC, maximization of NAW, or maximization of NPW are identical. However, the criterion of the minimization of AEC is preferable to use since it does not need to have an estimation of revenues.

[¶] Reprinted from J. A. White, M. H. Agee, and K. E. Case, *Principles of Engineering Economy Analysis.* Copyright © 1977. Used by permission of John Wiley & Sons, Inc.

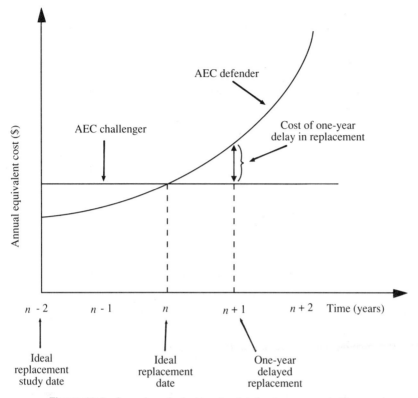

Figure 10.4 Annual equivalent costs of defender versus challenger.

some reasons for delaying the replacement of assets beyond the economic replacement are:

1. The firm is making a profit with its present equipment.
2. The present equipment is operational and is producing an acceptable quality product.
3. There is risk or uncertainty associated with predicting the expenses of a new machine, whereas one is relatively certain about the expenses of the current machine.
4. A decision to replace equipment is a stronger commitment for a period of time into the future than keeping the existing equipment.
5. Management tends to be conservative in decisions regarding the replacement of costly equipment.
6. There may be a limitation on funds available for purchasing new equipment, but no limitation on funds for maintaining existing equipment.
7. There may be considerable uncertainty concerning the future demand for the services of the equipment in question.

8. Sunk costs psychologically affect decisions to replace equipment.

9. An anticipation that technological improvements in the future might render obsolete equipment available currently; a wait-and-see attitude prevails.

10. Reluctance to be a pioneer in adopting new technology; instead of replacing now, wait for the competition to act.

10.5 SUNK COST

As mentioned in Chapter 2, unrecoverable past costs are *sunk costs* and are not to be taken into account in engineering economy applications that deal with the future. This principle is especially useful in replacement studies dealing with existing assets. In such cases only the future of the assets should be considered and *sunk costs[†] should be ignored*. Thus, the sunk cost is defined as

$$\text{Sunk cost} = \text{Present book value} - \text{Present market value} \qquad (10.2)$$

The present book value of an asset is the current worth of the asset in the accounting records; that is, it is the remaining value of an investment after deducting the total amount of accrued depreciation to date. In replacement studies *the only relevant value is the present market value*. The original cost, present book value, or replacement cost that can be obtainable from a comparable asset are all irrelevant. Therefore, for replacement analysis, the sunk costs should not be included in the economic comparison. However, of course, the sunk costs may affect income taxes if the present asset is sold. Some so-called experts try to *recover* the sunk cost of the defender by adding it to the first cost of the challenger. In reality, such cost should rather be charged to an account called *unrecovered capital* or something similar, and it should be finally reflected in the annual income statement of the company.

Similarly, the *trade-in value* is also not a correct value to use for the current value of an asset because the trade-in price is frequently and "artificially" overstated (along with the inflated price of the new asset) to make the exchange appear as an attractive deal to the buyer.[‡]

[†]Assume that a car buyer has just negotiated and purchased a car for $10,000 from a new-car dealer. After driving around for a couple of hours, the buyer has decided to give the car back to the car dealer and get the $10,000 back. Assume that the car dealer has agreed to accept the car back but will pay only $7,500. If the buyer has agreed to accept the new deal, then the difference of $2,500 is the *sunk cost* for the buyer.

[‡]This is a rather common practice in the new automobile sales industry and the "extra" amount of the trade-in allowance is known as the *overtrade*. In such situations one might be better off by first negotiating the price of the new car, without including the old car in the deal. After the negotiation for the price of the new car is completed, then the negotiation for the trade-in price of the old car should be started. This approach may provide a better idea about the actual value of the trade-in car.

Furthermore, it is also interesting to note that if, instead of purchasing the new asset, the old (or existing) asset is kept, one is giving up the opportunity to obtain the net realizable salvage value at that time. Therefore, this represents the *opportunity cost* (based on so-called *opportunity foregone principle*) of continuing to keep the defender.

10.6 OUTSIDER VIEWPOINT

As mentioned before, sunk costs must not be taken into account in evaluating expected future cost of one alternative versus another. To treat sunk costs and trade-in values correctly in a replacement analysis, the analysis should be based on the *outsider viewpoint*. With this outsider viewpoint it is assumed that a third party (i.e., the outsider) exists who owns neither the defender nor the challenger but needs the service that can be provided by one of these two assets. Since it is assumed that the outsider does not own the defender presently, if it is selected, then its present market value must be paid by the outsider. Otherwise, if the challenger is selected, then the installed investment cost of the challenger must be paid by the outsider.

10.7 REPLACEMENT BY LEASING

Leasing can be defined as a method of financing an asset through lease payments over the lease agreement period rather than actually purchasing it. Sometimes a building is built, then sold, and then leased back. The examples include office buildings, supermarkets, airplanes, cars, office machines, trucks, railroad cars, and so on. As mentioned in Section 10.3, the *lease or buy* question is often raised in companies that are subject to rapid growth. This, in turn, has caused the rapid growth of leasing companies. Today, it is possible to lease practically any type of equipment (or other physical facilities such as office or plant buildings and warehouses) that is not custom designed for a very specialized service. The reason for such an increase in leasing is that leasing presents various advantages. For example, by leasing one can avoid the responsibilities of ownership, including maintenance, obsolescence, deterioration, aging, replacement of equipment (or other asset), and protection against loss and destruction. All these, of course, by selecting the lease option, become someone else's problems. It may even be possible that the lessor may provide a better and more economic service in handling particularly specialized apparatus. If the equipment in question has a high investment cost and low utilization rate, it becomes a good candidate for the lease-or-buy consideration. For example, many contractors may consider it more economical to rent large construction equipment such as power shovels, bulldozers, cement mixers, steam rollers, rock drills, trucks, or other types of transportation equipment, air compressors, and others than to purchase them, especially for small contracts. Also, by leasing, a company can avoid large amounts of funds that would otherwise be allocated into such investments. Thus, assets that are leased will not be shown on the books as assets or as funded debt (if borrowing is involved to finance such purchase). Therefore, leasing rather than buying can also affect debt ratio (by improving it) as well as other balance sheet ratios of the company.

Example 10.3 Assume that a manufacturing company has equipment (i.e., defender) that was installed 6 years ago for $150,000 and has a present market value of $50,000 that is expected to decrease $5,000 per year. If the defender is kept one more year, its O&M costs will be $75,000 with increases of $20,000 per year thereafter. The engineering manager of the company is considering installing new equipment (i.e., challenger) at a cost of $200,000. The challenger will have an expected salvage value of $10,000 at the end of its useful life of 10 years. Its annual O&M costs will be $50,000. If MARR is 20%, determine when the defender should be replaced. Assume that the estimates of the installed first cost and salvage value of the challenger are going to remain constant.

Solution The annual equivalent cost of the challenger can be found, from equation (5.14) as

$$\text{AEC}_{\text{challenger}} = (\$200,000 - \$10,000)(A/P,\ 20\%,\ 10) + \$10,000(0.20)$$
$$+ \$50,000 = \$97,319$$

The annual equivalent cost of the defender can be found, based on the assumption that the defender will be retained for N years, as follows:
For N = 1 year

$$\text{AEC}_{\text{defender}} = (\$50,000 - \$45,000)(A/P,\ 20\%,\ 1) + \$45,000 \times 0.20$$
$$+ \$75,000 = \$90,000$$

where the $45,000 represents the market value of the defender a year from now (i.e., $50,000 - $5,000 = $45,000).
For N = 2 years

$$\text{AEC}_{\text{defender}} = (\$50,000 - \$40,000)(A/P,\ 20\%,\ 2) + \$40,000 \times 0.20$$
$$+ [\$75,000(P/F,\ 20\%,\ 1) + \$95,000(P/F,\ 20\%,\ 2)]$$
$$\times (A/P,\ 20\%,\ 2)$$
$$= \$98,633$$

Therefore, the defender should be kept for the first year but replaced for the second year.

Example 10.4 Assume that 5 years ago manufacturing equipment was installed in the plant of the Zubits International Corporation at a cost of $30,000. At the time of installation it was estimated that the equipment would have a useful life of 15 years. Today, due to the doubled demand for zubits, the production capacity has to be doubled. This can be achieved in two ways. The first alternative (i.e., the defender) is to install an identical second equipment, in addition to the first equipment (which is still in good condition to operate). It is assumed that the second unit will also have an installed cost of $30,000 and a salvage value of $3,000 as the first unit. Also the annual O&M costs of both units are the same and are $4,000. The second alternative (i.e., the challenger) is to install an equipment that has the required double capacity and scrap the existing equipment. The equipment with double capacity will have an installed cost of $45,000 and have a salvage value of $5,000 at the end of its useful life of 15 years. Its annual O&M costs are $6,000. Presently, the existing equipment has a fair-market value of $8,000, if it is sold. Use a MARR of 20% and a study period of 10 years and determine the following:

(a) The annual equivalent cost of the first alternative.
(b) The remaining so-called unused value of the second unit at the end of the 10-year study period.
(c) The annual equivalent cost of the second alternative.
(d) The remaining unused value of the equipment at the end of the 10-year study period.
(e) Select the preferred alternative and explain the reasoning involved in the selection.

Solution

(a) The first alternative (i.e., the defender) has two units, that is, the existing (old) one, and the new one. Thus,

$$\text{AEC}_{\text{old}} = (\$8,000 - \$3,000)(A/P, \ 20\%, \ 10) + \$3,000 \times 0.20$$
$$+ \$4,000 = \$5,793$$

and

$$\text{AEC}_{\text{new}} = (\$30,000 - \$3,000)(A/P, \ 20\%, \ 15) + \$3,000 \times 0.20$$
$$+ \$4,000 = \$10,375$$

Therefore, the total AEC of the defender is

$$\text{AEC}_{\text{defender}} = \text{AEC}_{\text{old}} + \text{AEC}_{\text{new}} = \$16,168$$

Note that the present value of the old unit is not $30,000, but it is simply equal to its present market value, that is, $8,000. The difference of $22,000 between $30,000 and $8,000 is simply a sunk cost and therefore cannot be used in the study.

(b) The remaining unused value (or the terminal value) of the second unit at the end of the 10-year study period is

$$\text{Unused value}_{\text{defender}} = [(\$30,000 - \$3,000)(A/P, \ 20\%, \ 15)$$
$$+ \$3,000 \times 0.20](P/A, \ 20\%, \ 5) = \$19,068$$

(c) The annual equivalent cost of the second alternative (i.e., the challenger) is

$$\text{AEC}_{\text{challenger}} = (\$45,000 - \$5,000)(A/P, \ 20\%, \ 15) + \$5,000 \times 0.20$$
$$+ \$6,000 = \$15,555$$

(d) The remaining unused value of the second alternative at the end of the 10-year study period is

$$\text{Unused value}_{\text{challenger}} = [(\$45,000 - \$5,000)(A/P, \ 20\%, \ 20)$$
$$+ \$5,000 \times 0.20](P/A, \ 20\%, 5) = \$28,580$$

(e) It is obvious that the challenger is a better alternative than the defender. This conclusion is primarily based on the calculated values of the AECs even though the calculated remaining unused values also indicate that the challenger is superior to the defender. However, the calculated amounts of unused values of the equipment involved are not totally dependable. This skeptical view is due to the fact that the concept of the unused value is not a concrete concept. For example, having calculated the unused value of $28,580 does not guarantee that the market value of the challenger is indeed going to have such a value 10 years from today. It simply indicates the relative superiority of the unused value of the challenger over the unused value of the defender 10 years from now, when they are sold as used equipment; but their actual values will be determined by their fair-market values.[†]

10.8 AFTER-TAX REPLACEMENT ANALYSIS

Assume that t represents the combined effective income tax rate for a given corporation. Therefore, a general expression for the after-tax AEC of a piece of equipment (or an asset) is

---

[†]Note that here it is assumed that the total financing is done by equity capital. For an excellent review of the situation when there is also a debt capital involvement, the interested readers should see Chapter 10 of Smith [66].

$$AEC = AEM + \frac{P(A/P,\ i\%,\ N) - F(A/F,\ i\%,\ N) - t(AED)}{1 - t}$$

(10.3)

where

AEM = annual equivalent of operating and maintenace costs,
P = installed first cost of the equipment,
F = salvage value of the equipment at the end of its useful life N,
AED = annual equivalent of depreciation expense.

Similarly, the after-tax PEC of a piece of equipment can be calculated as

$$PEC = AEC(P/A,\ i\%,\ N)$$

(10.4)

or

$$PEC = PEM + \frac{P - F(P/F,\ i\%,\ N) - t(PED)}{1 - t}$$

(10.5)

where

PEC = present equivalent cost of the equipment,
PEM = present equivalent of operating and maintenance costs,
PED = present equivalent of annual depreciation expenses.

Note that equation (10.3) can also be expressed as

$$AE(BTCFR) = \frac{P(A/P,\ i\%,\ N) - F(A/F,\ i\%,\ N) - t(AED)}{1 - t}$$

(10.6)

if the AEM is zero. The BTCFR is before-tax cash flow required.

If the combined effective tax rate t is zero, then the AEC becomes

$$AEC = AEM + P(A/P,\ i\%,\ N) - F(A/F,\ i\%,\ N)$$

(10.7)

Of course, the after-tax net present worth of a project, if the resulting present equivalent of the revenues are known, can be expressed as

$$NPW = (PER - PEC)(1 - t)$$

(10.8)

where PER is the present equivalent of revenues. Substituting equation (10.5) into equation (10.8), the after-tax net present worth of a project can be expressed as

$$\text{NPW} = (\text{PER} - \text{PEM})(1 - t) - P + F(P/F, \; i\%, \; N) + t(\text{PED}) \tag{10.9}$$

Similarly, the after-tax net annual worth of a project can be expressed as

$$\text{NAW} = (\text{AER} - \text{AEM})(1 - t) - P(A/P, \; i\%, \; N) + F(A/F, \; i\%, \; N)$$
$$+ \; t(\text{AED}) \tag{10.10}$$

where AER is the annual equivalent of revenues. Of course, if the NPW is already known, then

$$\text{NAW} = \text{NPW}(A/P, \; i\%, \; N) \tag{10.11}$$

Similarly, if the NAW is already known, then

$$\text{NPW} = \text{NAW}(P/A, \; i\%, \; N) \tag{10.12}$$

Further, if the PEC represents the sum of the present equivalent investment cost or the required operating revenues, then it can be expressed as

$$\text{PEC} = \sum_{j=1}^{N} C_j (P/F, \; i\%, \; N) \tag{10.13}$$

where C_j is the investment cost or required (operating) revenue for year j.

If the PEM represents the sum of the present equivalent of (cash) operating and maintenance (O&M) cost, then it can be expressed as

$$\text{PEM} = \sum_{j=1}^{N} M_j (P/F, \; i\%, \; N) \tag{10.14}$$

Furthermore, if the PED represents the sum of the present equivalent annual depreciation expenses, then it can also be expressed as

$$\text{PED} = \sum_{j=1}^{N} D_j (P/F, \; i\%, \; N) \tag{10.15}$$

where D_j is the annual depreciation expense for year j.

Example 10.5   Assume that the engineering manager of Blueskies Corporation is considering replacing an existing piece of equipment with a new model. The present equipment is fully depreciated. Its present net market value and present net book value are the same and are equal to $3,000. It is expected that the future net market value of the present equipment will also remain $3,000. The annual end-of-year O&M costs of the new and old equipment are given as \$6,000 and \$9,000, respectively. The new equipment will have a negligible salvage value at the end of its 8-year useful life, and it will be depreciated by using the straight-line method. Assume that the applicable federal and state income tax rates are 0.34 and 0.06, respectively, and that the state income taxes cannot be deducted for the purpose of calculating federal income taxes. Use a MARR of 20% and determine the following:

(a) The combined effective income tax rate.
(b) The maximum amount that can be justified for the new equipment.

Solution

(a) The combined effective income tax rate is

$$t = \text{State tax rate} + \text{Federal tax rate}$$

$$= 0.06 + 0.34 = 0.40$$

(b) Since at the breakeven point,

$$\text{AEC}_{\text{new}} = \text{AEC}_{\text{old}}$$

and using equation (10.3),

$$\$6,000 + \frac{P(A/P,\ 20\%,\ 8) - 0.40(P/8)}{1 - 0.40} = \$9,000$$

$$+ \frac{\$3,000(A/P,\ 20\%,\ N) - \$3,000(A/F,\ 20\%,\ N) + 0.40(0)}{1 - 0.40}$$

or

$$\$6,000 + \frac{P(0.26061) - 0.05P}{0.60} = \$9,000 + \frac{\$3,000(0.20)}{0.60}$$

where

$$(A/P,\ 20\%,\ N) - (A/F,\ 20\%,\ N) \overset{\Delta}{=} 0.20$$

Therefore, $P = \$11,396$. Thus, the maximum amount that can be justified for the new equipment is \$11,396.

Example 10.6 Assume that the engineering manager of Zubits International Corporation is considering retiring an existing and broken piece of equipment by a new model. It is estimated that the net salvage value of the existing equipment, after cost of removal, is negligible. The new equipment will have an installed cost of $50,000 and a net salvage value of $5,000 at the end of its 10-year useful life. Its end-of-year O&M costs will be $4,000 for the first year and will increase by $1,000 per year after the first year. Use the straight-line depreciation method and the combined effective income tax rate of 40%. Assume that its annual equivalent of revenues is enough to generate a pretax rate of return of 30% and determine the following:

(a) The straight-line depreciation charge per year.
(b) The before-tax annual equivalent of revenues in dollars.
(c) The prospective after-tax rate of return from the investment.

Solution

(a) The straight-line depreciation charge per year is

$$D = \frac{P - F}{N} = \frac{\$50,000 - \$5,000}{10} = \$4,500$$

(b) The before-tax annual equivalent of revenues sufficient to generate a before-tax rate of return of 30% is

$$\text{AER} = \$4,000 + \$1,000(A/G,\ 30\%,\ 10) + \$50,000(A/P,\ 30\%,\ 10)$$
$$- \$5,000(A/F,\ 30\%,\ 10) = \$22,607$$

(c) From equation (10.10) the prospective after-tax rate of return can be computed as

$$\text{NAW} = (\text{AER} - \text{AEM})(1 - t) - P(A/P,\ i\%,\ N) + F(A/F,\ i\%,\ N)$$
$$+ t(\text{AED}) = 0$$

thus,

$$\text{NAW} = [\$22,607 - \$4,000 - \$1,000(A/G,\ i\%,\ 10)](1 - 0.40)$$
$$- \$50,000(A/P,\ i\%,\ 10) + \$5,000(A/F,\ i\%,\ 10)$$
$$+ 0.40(\$4,500 = 0$$

At $i = 18\%$

$$\text{NAW} = \$135$$

At $i = 20\%$

$$NAW = -\$614$$

Therefore,

$$i = 18\% + \left(\frac{\$135}{\$749}\right)(2\%) = 18.4\%$$

Note that since the old equipment is retired and its net salvage value is zero, it cannot be considered as an alternative (i.e., the defender). Therefore, this problem is actually a retirement problem rather than a replacement problem.

10.9 RETIREMENT PATTERNS FOR GROUP PROPERTIES

As discussed in Section 8.15, a *group property* can be defined as a set of two or more similar units of property. The estimated service life of such group property then is the estimate of the average of the individual service lives. Since the service life of each unit (that makes up the group) is not the same, one can observe a *dispersion* of service lives. Therefore, for any group of equipment of the same type, one can establish a *frequency distribution* showing the percentage of the equipment that will be retired, or replaced, between any life intervals. Further, based on such data, a *survivorship* curve (also called *survivor curve*), shows the percentage of the units surviving to each level. In other words a survivor curve indicates the percentage of the group property (given in terms of physical units or dollars) that survives in service at ages from zero to maximum life. Figure 10.5 shows such survivor curve in addition to frequency curve and probable life curve that have been drawn based on the data given in Table 10.3. Note that a *probable-life curve* shows the probable average life of the survivors at any age from zero to maximum life.

There are basically two methods to determine actual service lives: (1) the original-group approach, and (2) the annual rate approach. The first one is based on the records of the retirements each year of all units of one type of asset that were placed in one year, whereas the second one is based on an analysis of the rate of retirement of the assets in each group that were in service during one or more given recent years.

In the event that the data at hand is incomplete, the plot of such data provides *incomplete survivorship curve* (also called the *stub survivor*, or *survivorship*, *curve*). Thus, such incomplete survivorship curve, by definition, does not extend to zero percent surviving because of a lack of retirement data. Therefore, such incomplete survivorship curves are extrapolated to zero to allow the calculation of the average or expected life. Of course, where the distribution of lives is approximately symmetric, the medial life (age at which 50% of the units are retired) will be close to the

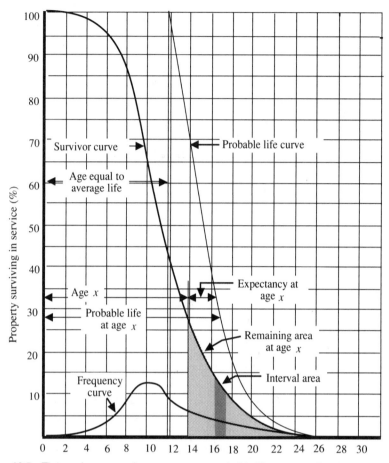

Figure 10.5 The survivor curve, frequency curve, probable life curve, and their nomenclature. (Reprinted by permission from *Engineering Valuation and Depreciation* by A. Marston, R. Winfrey, and J. C. Hempstead © 1953 by Iowa State University Press, Ames, Iowa.)

average. The extrapolation that is involved can be performed in numerous ways. For example:

1. By using visual means to obtain a smooth curve.
2. By using statistical method (e.g., a least-squares method) to fit a curve.
3. By using a suitable type of survivorship curve that has been previously developed, for example, the use of the comprehensive set of survivorship curves developed by the Iowa Engineering Experiment Station. Each type of survivorship curve is drawn on a transparent sheet of paper with curves for a wide range of average service lives. In the application of such *Iowa curves*, as shown in Figure 10.6, the Iowa

TABLE 10.3 Example Data for Survivor, Frequency, and Probable Life Curves.

Age Interval (years) (1)	Percent Surviving at Beginning of Age Interval[a] (2)	Percent Retired during the Age Interval (3)	Interval Area Under Survivor Curve (%-years) (4)	Remaining Area under Survivor Curve to Right of Beginning of Age Interval (%-years) (5)	Expectancy of Survivors at Beginning of Age Interval (years) (6)	Probable Average Service Life of Survivors at Beginning of Age Interval (years) (7)
$0-0\frac{1}{2}$	100.00	0.00	50.00	1,249.98	12.50	12.50
$0\frac{1}{2}-1\frac{1}{2}$	100.00	0.00	100.00	1,199.98	12.00	12.50
$1\frac{1}{2}-2\frac{1}{2}$	100.00	0.08	99.96	1,099.98	11.00	12.50
$2\frac{1}{2}-3\frac{1}{2}$	99.92	0.33	99.76	1,000.02	10.01	12.51
$3\frac{1}{2}-4\frac{1}{2}$	99.59	0.76	99.21	900.26	9.04	12.54
$4\frac{1}{2}-5\frac{1}{2}$	98.83	1.38	98.14	801.05	8.11	12.61
$5\frac{1}{2}-6\frac{1}{2}$	97.45	2.32	96.29	702.91	7.21	12.71
$6\frac{1}{2}-7\frac{1}{2}$	95.13	3.92	93.17	606.62	6.38	12.88
$7\frac{1}{2}-8\frac{1}{2}$	91.21	6.27	88.07	513.45	5.63	13.13
$8\frac{1}{2}-9\frac{1}{2}$	84.94	8.83	80.53	425.38	5.01	13.51
$9\frac{1}{2}-10\frac{1}{2}$	76.11	10.68	70.77	344.85	4.53	14.03
$10\frac{1}{2}-11\frac{1}{2}$	65.43	11.20	59.83	274.08	4.19	14.69
$11\frac{1}{2}-12\frac{1}{2}$	54.23	10.42	49.02	214.25	3.95	15.45
$12\frac{1}{2}-13\frac{1}{2}$	43.81	8.89	39.36	165.23	3.77	16.27
$13\frac{1}{2}-14\frac{1}{2}$	34.92	7.24	31.30	125.87	3.60	17.10
$14\frac{1}{2}-15\frac{1}{2}$	27.68	5.83	24.77	94.57	3.42	17.92
$15\frac{1}{2}-16\frac{1}{2}$	21.85	4.78	19.46	69.80	3.19	18.69
$16\frac{1}{2}-17\frac{1}{2}$	17.07	3.97	15.08	50.34	2.95	19.45
$17\frac{1}{2}-18\frac{1}{2}$	13.10	3.32	11.44	35.26	2.69	20.19
$18\frac{1}{2}-19\frac{1}{2}$	9.78	2.74	8.41	23.82	2.44	20.94
$19\frac{1}{2}-20\frac{1}{2}$	7.04	2.19	5.95	15.41	2.19	21.69
$20\frac{1}{2}-21\frac{1}{2}$	4.85	1.69	4.00	9.46	1.95	22.45
$21\frac{1}{2}-22\frac{1}{2}$	3.16	1.23	2.55	5.46	1.73	23.23
$22\frac{1}{2}-23\frac{1}{2}$	1.93	0.85	1.50	2.91	1.41	24.01
$23\frac{1}{2}-24\frac{1}{2}$	1.08	0.54	0.81	1.41	1.31	24.81
$24\frac{1}{2}-25\frac{1}{2}$	0.54	0.31	0.39	0.60	1.11	25.61
$25\frac{1}{2}-26\frac{1}{2}$	0.23	0.15	0.15	0.21	0.91	26.41
$26\frac{1}{2}-27\frac{1}{2}$	0.08	0.06	0.05	0.06	0.75	27.25
$27\frac{1}{2}-28\frac{1}{2}$	0.02	0.02	0.01	0.01	0.50	28.00
$28\frac{1}{2}-29\frac{1}{2}$	0.00	—	—	0.00	0.00	—
Total	1,349.98	100.00	1,249.98	—	—	—

[a]The percentages surviving in column (2) are assumed for purposes of this illustration of the basic curves.

Source: Reprinted by permission from *Engineering Valuation and Depreciation* by A. Marston, R. Winfrey, and J. C. Hempstead © 1953 by Iowa State University Press, Ames, Iowa.

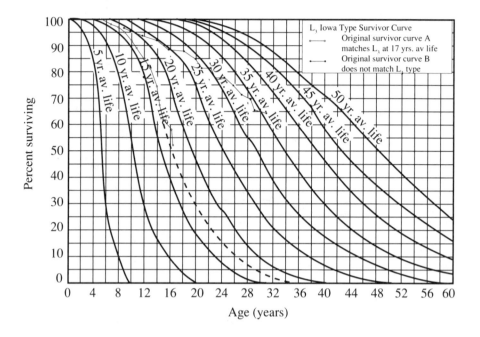

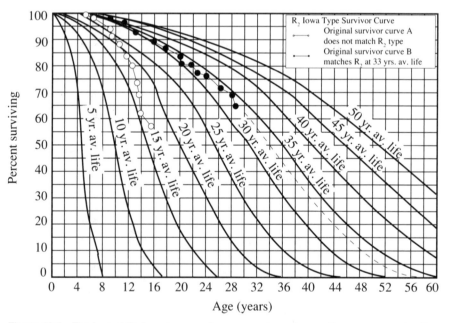

Figure 10.6 The L_3 and R_2 Iowa-type survivor curves drawn to specific average service lives to illustrate the matching method of smoothing and extending original survivor curves. (Reprinted by permission from *Engineering Valuation and Depreciation* by A. Marston, R. Winfrey, and J. C. Hempstead © 1953 by Iowa State University Press, Ames, Iowa.)

curves on the transparent sheet are matched to the original incomplete survivorship curve to get the best fit. Note that the L_3 type curves given in the top figure provide a reasonably good fit for survivorship curve A, but not for survivorship curve B; whereas the R_2 type curves of the bottom panel provide a reasonably good fit for survivorship curve B.

In general, for the electric utility applications in the United States, the generally accepted group dispersion retirement patterns are those generated by such research at the Iowa Engineering Experiment Station at the Iowa State University in the 1930s and earlier.[†] The resulting Iowa curves were developed from studies of various plant items and were standardized into 18 distinct patterns. The utility companies have, since then, increased the number of patterns to 28 by interpolation of the original curves. The utility companies have concluded that there are various reasons for using a group method, rather than dealing with individual units separately. They have discovered that only about 10% of the plant retirements are due to failures. The majority of retirements result from the more unpredictable processes of human decision and innovation, obsolescense, population movement, highway relocation, or system expansion. Furthermore, the developed reliable and predictive statistical models are based on group data and then applied to each item within the group.

When the distribution of asset retirements is plotted as a function of age, it forms the well-known *Iowa dispersion curve* (also called the *frequency curve*). Here, the word *dispersion* (or *frequency*) describes the pattern of asset (i.e., plant or equipment) retirements as a function of age. It is the shape of such a pattern that permits the utilities to accurately predict the average life expectations of a group of equipment and, more importantly, the probable life remaining to those who have attained any specific age. Note that each such curve is designated by a letter and a number. Here, the letter refers to the shape of the curve. As shown in Figure 10.7(a), the *Type S* curves are *symmetrical* about the average life, for example, the frequency of retirements occurring 2 years before the average life equals the frequency of retirements occurring 2 years after the average life. Note that the *Type L* curves, as shown in Figure 10.7(b), are *left moded*. Therefore, annual retirements are more frequent in the years before the average life but have some survivors that last a longer time; whereas, the *Type R* curves, as shown in Figure 10.7(c), are *right-moded*. Thus, annual retirements are less frequent in the years before the average life but are more frequent in the remaining years. There are also two special curve types, *Type SC* and *Type SQ*, shown in Figures 10.8(a) and 10.8(b), respectively. The type SC

[†]For further information, see Winfrey [75, 76] and Marston, Winfrey, and Hempstead [55].

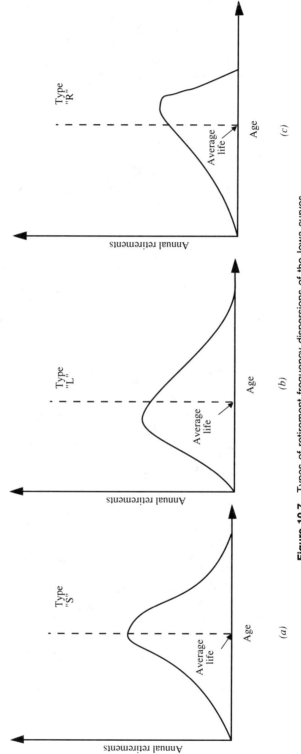

Figure 10.7 Types of retirement frequency dispersions of the Iowa curves.

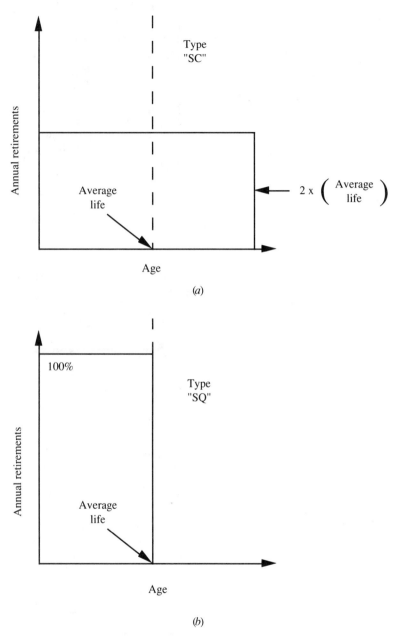

Figure 10.8 Types of retirement frequency dispersions of Type SC and Type SQ Iowa curves.

dispersion is used for those assets with uniform retirements that take place each year. The ultimate life for Type SC assets is twice the average, as shown in Figure 10.8(*a*); whereas, Type SQ dispersion is used for those assets that retire at the same time. Note that, for Type SQ assets, the average life, ultimate life, and the useful life are represented by the same value.

In the Iowa curves the numerical curve classifications range from 0 to 6. Thus, the larger the number, the more the annual retirements that take place near the average life. For example, it can be seen in Figure 10.9 that an S_2 curve has 12% retirements in the year of its average life, whereas an S_6 has 50%. Since the original development of the Iowa curves, 28 more curves have been developed by interpolation of the previously developed curves [36].

As shown in Figures 10.5 and 10.10, the survivor curve represents the percentage of an original group still surviving at a particular point in time. As illustrated in Figure 10.10, the average service life of the asset is reached at the 50% point on the Type S survivor curves. Note that survivor curves are developed by subtracting the retirements shown in the retirement dispersion curves from 100%. By using the survivor curves, one does not have to total up all the previous retirements to find the number of survivors at any given age for a particular retirement dispersion.

Figure 10.5 also shows the *probable-life curve*, also called the *remaining-life curve*. These curves are also very important since the depreciation rate

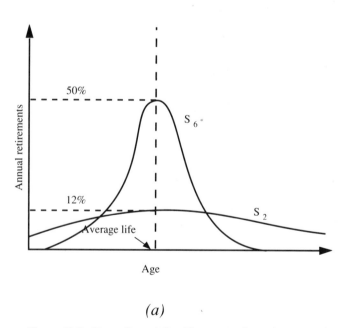

(a)

Figure 10.9   Types S_2 and S_6 of frequency dispersion curves.

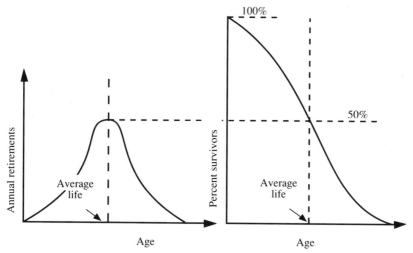

Figure 10.10 Illustration of the relationship between retirement and survivor curves.

applied to the plant in service is based on the remaining life. Note that the horizontal difference between the survivor curve and the probable-life curve represents the remaining life, as can be seen from Figure 10.5.

PROBLEMS

10.1 Assume that a construction company has just purchased a new truck for $80,000. It is estimated that its salvage value after 10 years will be $5,000 and the its O&M costs will be $4,000 at the end of year 1 and will be increased by $3,000 each year. Use a before-tax MARR of 20% and determine the annual equivalent cost of owning the truck for 10 years.

10.2 Assume that a compact automobile has been purchased by the XYZ Rental Car Company for $12,000, and its expected annual O&M costs and salvage values are given in Table P10.2. Determine its optimum economic life, in integer years, if the MARR is 30%.

TABLE P10.2

Year (N)	Annual O&M Costs ($)	End of Year Salvage Value ($)
1	$2,000	$9,000
2	3,000	8,000
3	4,000	7,000
4	5,000	6,000
5	6,000	5,000

10.3   Repeat Example 10.3 assuming that the O&M expenses of the defender will increase $10,000 per year after the first year (rather than $20,000 per year).

10.4   Repeat Example 10.4 assuming that the new unit of the defender will have an installed cost and a salvage value of $35,000 and $5,000, respectively. Use a MARR of 25%.

10.5   Assume that a piece of equipment was purchased 4 years ago for $15,000 with an estimated useful life of 10 years, salvage of $1,000, and annual operating cost of $2,500. The present book value of the equipment is $9,400. A challenger (equipment) is now offered for $10,000 and a trade-in value of $7,000 on the old equipment. It is estimated that the useful life, salvage value, and annual operating costs are 12 years, $1,500, and $2,000, respectively. The new estimates for the old equipment given for realizable salvage value, remaining life, and operating costs are $2,000, 4 years, and the same as before, respectively. Determine the present investment costs, useful lives, salvage values, and annual operating costs for the defender and the challenger. Also, find out whether or not there is any sunk cost involved and if so, how much?

10.6   Repeat Example 10.5. Assume that both the new and the old equipment are operating at 50% capacity, and therefore their annual end-of-year O&M costs are $4,000 and $6,000, respectively. Also assume that the state income taxes can be deducted for the purpose of calculating federal income taxes. Use a MARR of 20% and determine the following:

(a) The combined effective income tax rate, if federal and state income tax rates are 0.34 and 0.10, respectively.

(b) The maximum amount that can be justified for the new equipment.

10.7   Solve Problem 10.6 but assume that the state income taxes cannot be deducted for the purpose of calculating federal income taxes.

10.8   Repeat Example 10.6 but use the SYD depreciation method to calculate the annual depreciation expenses.

10.9   Repeat Example 10.6 but use the modified ACRS system to calculate the annual depreciation expenses.

10.10   Assume that a particular piece of equipment costs $10,000 today. Its O&M expenses are $2,000 for the first year and increases by $500 per year after the first year. Assume that its salvage value will be zero at the end of its 8-year useful life. If the before-tax ROR is 20%, determine the year-by-year salvage values that are required for the annual equivalent costs of the equipment to be independent of the retention period.

10.11 Assume that a 2-year-old asset has annual operating costs of $10,000, net salvage of $4,000, and a useful life of 6 more years. The selected challenger will cost $30,000, have a life of 10 years, salvage of $6,000, and annual operating costs of $5,000. Find the minimum trade-in deal that the owner can accept and still buy the new asset if this class asset has a 10% ROR.

___11
INFLATION AND DEFLATION

Nothing so weakens government as persistent inflation.
JOHN KENNETH GALBRAITH, *The Great Crash, 1929*, 1955

Money alone sets all the world in motion.
PUBLILIUS SYRUS, 1st Century B.C.

You cannot pay yourself more money unless you do more work;
You cannot print more money unless you produce more goods;
You cannot have more jobs unless you have more investment;
You cannot have more investment unless you have more savings;
You cannot have more savings unless you keep faith with the saver;
You cannot keep faith with the saver unless you have sound money;
You cannot have sound money if you spend beyond your means;
But you can't increase your means unless you increase your effort;
And that takes you right back to the beginning of the catechism.
AUTHOR UNKNOWN

11.1 INTRODUCTION

What is *inflation*? There may not be a perfect answer, but a definition can
nonetheless prove useful. Samuelson [63] defines "inflation as a time of
generally rising prices for goods and factors of production." If a rise in all
prices and incomes had little or no effect on the allocation of resources,
inflation would not be economically detrimental. One's real income would
be unchanged if one's absolute income increased at the same rate as prices.
However, inflation, in terms of increasing absolute prices, is frequently
detrimental, for two reasons: (1) Certain incomes, such as pensions and life
insurance, are fixed in dollar terms, and others, such as bonds and mortgages, have fixed interest rates. (2) The changes in prices and incomes do
not take place simultaneously. For example, if prices double, incomes will
probably double eventually, but not immediately. Further, even then,
incomes tend to not all increase at the same rate. People whose incomes rise
most rapidly have an economic advantage over those with slowly increasing
incomes, a situation that exists particularly in developing countries [38].

284

The two worst evils that can trouble an economy are unemployment and inflation. The cost of unemployment can be assessed in terms of man-hours of lost work, lost wages, or lost goods and services, i.e., the difference between actual and potential gross national product (GNP); whereas measuring the cost of inflation is more difficult. Inflation decreases purchasing power of consumers and the value of their savings. Companies pay higher prices for their equipment, land, and buildings. It is more difficult for an economy to prevent deficits in international balance of payments since foreign goods cost more to import. Consumers and investors ultimately must pay higher taxes since the cost of government services increases. However, it is rather difficult to measure just how much inflation affects these things. Inflation also results in an economic system that operates inefficiently. People tend to buy more inflation-proof assets rather than holding much cash or maintaining large checking accounts. Similarly, it is profitable during a time of inflation for investors to invest in real properties such as real estate, land, or gold since the monetary value of such things will increase in proportion to the rate of inflation. Of course, this type of investment is unproductive since the same money could be used to finance real additions to the capital stock of the economy.

Furthermore, once business planning and decision making are based on the assumption of continued inflation, the trend is difficult to reverse. If the expected inflation does not materialize, prior commitments based on this assumption are more difficult to fulfill. Also, if excessive spending is curtailed, and inflation therefore slowed, many prices do not immediately decrease to their equilibrium levels, which results in decreased production and employment. If spending continues to be limited, however, the rate of inflation will decrease, resulting in increased production.

Also, it is interesting to note that the expectation of inflation either can speed up or can delay plant and equipment replacement decisions in industry. For example, if inflation is perceived to affect first cost more than other costs, replacement decisions in industry are more likely to be delayed; whereas expected wage increases can cause labor-saving apparatus to appear more desirable and therefore can make their replacement and/or purchasing more urgent and/or more attractive.

11.2 INFLATION AND INTEREST RATES

While inflation rate averaged only 2% in the 1950s and 1960s, it has averaged 7–8% in the 1970s. Further, inflation rate has fluctuated widely, at times being *double digit*. For example, the inflation rates in 1979 and 1980 were 11.3 and 13.5%, respectively. Of course, this change in inflation has resulted in a paramount increase in interest rates from what prevailed in the previous periods. Consequently, prices of existing corporate bonds have decreased, and the cost of debt financing by companies has been sharply increased. With inflation, profits reported for accounting purposes are distorted. For example, the sale of previously purchased low-cost inventories causes higher reported earnings. Furthermore, depreciation charges on existing assets are less than the cost of replacing them. Consequently, reported profits and the taxes paid on these profits are greater than the true economic profits of corporations and the taxes that would be paid on such profits. Of course, capital investment and financing decisions are subject to a higher degree of risk and uncertainty than would take place in the times of stable and low inflation rates.

One of the prime factors affecting inflation in any given country is the fact that the government of that country is spending more money each year than the revenues, in terms of taxes, it receives. The result is a deficit in the budget. Therefore, in order to cover the resulting deficit budget spending, the government increases the money supply or extends more credit through its central banking system. Of course, the result of having more money in circulation to compete for goods and services is price increases, without an associating increase in productivity, that is, inflation.[†] Therefore, during inflationary times,[‡] the purchasing power (i.e., value) of money decreases. Thus, inflation makes future dollars less valuable than present dollars.

Deflation is just the opposite of inflation. During deflationary times, prices tend to decrease causing future dollars to have more purchasing power than present dollars. In the United States deflation has not occurred since 1932.[§]

11.3 INFLATION AND PRICE INDEXES

In general, there are two very different sides of price changes. The first is the change in the purchasing power of money, causing a change in the general level of prices. It results in a tendency for all prices in the economy to rise. The second is differential price change, causing some prices to change at a different rate than the change in the general price level. Note that the first is called *inflation* whereas the second one is called *escalation*.

Price trends for groups of items of special interest are frequently condensed into a price index format. Such a *price index* is a ratio of the price of some stipulated market basket of commodities (ordinarily both goods and services) at one date to the prices of the same market basket at some other

---

[†]Many economists, since Adam Smith, have considered inflation as a *concealed form of bankruptcy* since it facilitates governments repaying debts with considerably depreciated currencies. Because of this, one may assume that inflation is here to stay. Of course, its rate is hard to predict ahead of time.

[‡]Note that inflation is not a new phenomenon, it has been observed throughout much of the commercial history of the civilized world. For example, in A.D. 301 the Emperor Diocletian declared that inflation threatened to destroy the economy of the Roman Empire.

[§]With the exception of a very small amount of deflation that took place in 1954.

date. Such indexes are compiled by agencies of the U.S. government. The most often used are the *consumer price index* (CPI), the *wholesale price index* (WPI), and the *implicit price index* (IPI). The consumer price index is made up of the *weighted average of basket of goods* that includes 400 typical goods and services commonly purchased by a middle-income family. Prices for these goods are obtained monthly and averaged according to demographic distributions. The consumer price index[†] is one of the most closely followed indexes. The wholesale price index determines inflation at the wholesale level for both consumer and industrial goods but not services; whereas the implicit price index determines the effect of general price-level changes on the gross national product in terms of the total market value of all goods and services produced by the economy of a given nation. In the construction industry there are several indexes[‡] that are employed to determine cost trends. Of course, increases in these indexes indicate increases in prices and the associating decrease in the purchasing power of money.

Example 11.1 The consumer price indexes for the years 1978, 1979, 1980, and 1981 are 195.4, 217.4, 246.8, and 271.3, respectively. Determine the percent change in CPI (i.e., the inflation rates) for the years 1979, 1980, and 1981. Note that the given consumer price indexes are based on the CPI of 100 for the year 1967.

Solution The percent change in CPI for the year 1979 with respect to the previous year is

$$\Delta CPI_{1979} = \frac{CPI_{1979} - CPI_{1978}}{CPI_{1978}} \times 100 = \frac{217.4 - 195.4}{195.4} \times 100 = 11.3\%$$

That is, the inflation rate for year 1979 is 11.3%.
  Similarly, for 1980

$$\Delta CPI_{1980} = \frac{CPI_{1980} - CPI_{1979}}{CPI_{1979}} \times 100 = \frac{246.8 - 217.4}{217.4} \times 100 = 13.5\%$$

and for 1981

$$\Delta CPI_{1981} = \frac{CPI_{1981} - CPI_{1980}}{CPI_{1980}} \times 100 = \frac{271.3 - 246.8}{246.8} \times 100 = 9.9\%$$

[†]It is also called the *cost of living* index.
[‡]Among them, the *engineering news-record construction cost index* is the most often used. The electric power industry uses the annual cost indexes published by the *Electric World* trade magazine.

11.4 EFFECTS OF INFLATION ON DEBTORS AND CREDITORS

Whether or not debtors and creditors benefit during inflationary times depends on whether or not the inflation is expected because the rate of a loan will ordinarily include the expected inflation. In the event that inflation takes place over the period of a loan at the expected rate, the gain or less of the borrower will be nil in comparison to the inflation.

However, in the event that there is an *unanticipated increase* in inflation, the borrower might gain since the borrower previously has *locked in* financing at a lower rate than the one presently existing. In other words the company is able to pay off the debt with *cheaper money* than was previously anticipated. Of course, the opposite takes place for the financial assets of a company. If there is is an unanticipated inflation rate, that is, the actual rate of inflation is greater than the one that was originally expected, a creditor receives a real rate of return that is less than the expected one; whereas if there is an unexpected decrease in inflation, a creditor benefits and a debtor loses because the real rate of return is greater than the one previously expected. Therefore, the crucial point is the unexpected change in inflation rate rather than the inflation itself. In the event of an unexpected increase in inflation, there will be a transfer of real wealth from creditors to debtors. Of course, the opposite is true if there is an unexpected decrease in inflation.[†]

11.5 THE METHODS FOR TAKING INTO ACCOUNT INFLATION OR DEFLATION

Since the inflated dollars of the future will be worth less than today's dollars, the higher future costs will be paid for with dollars that are worth less. Therefore, it is obvious that the effects of inflation must be taken into account under such circumstances. There are two alternative methods of treating inflation or deflation in a financial analysis.

1. Convert all cash flows to constant-worth or real or today's dollar amounts (with *constant purchasing power*) to eliminate the effects of inflation. Then use the regular interest rate (i.e., the one without an inflation rate component) in the interest formulas. This method is most appropriate for before-tax analysis, when all cash flow components inflate at uniform rates.

2. Express the future cash flows in then-current (or future or "actual") dollars and use an interest rate that includes inflation that can be called an

---

[†]For example, people on fixed incomes, such as retired people, etc., with little or no debt obviously are hurt by (both expected and unexpected) inflation since the purchasing power of their income or capital decreases each year approximately proportional to the annual inflation rate.

TABLE 11.1 Data for Example 11.2

End of Year	Real Dollars (No Inflation)		5% Inflation	Actual Dollars (Inflation Cash Flow)
0	−$1,100			
1	500	×	$1.05 =$	$525
2	500	×	$(1.05)^2 =$	551
3	500	×	$(1.05)^3 =$	579

inflated interest rate or a *combined interest–inflation rate*. This method is usually easier to use and understand and is more adaptable than the constant-worth method.

Example 11.2 Assume that a project proposal has a first cost of $1,100 and is anticipated to generate net returns of $500 per year for the next 3 years in today's dollars. Also assume that the MARR has been increased from 15 to 20% to compensate for an expected 5% inflation in the next several years. Determine whether or not the project should be accepted.

Solution If the cash flow were given in today's dollars and the MARR were compensated for inflation, then

$$NPW = -\$1,000 + \$500(P/A, 20\%, 3) = -\$47$$

However, such calculation would unfairly penalize the project proposal since the MARR is determined from the future (or actual or then-current) dollar amounts of cash flow rather than today's dollar (or real or constant-worth) amounts. Therefore, since the result is negative, the proposal would be rejected; whereas the correct way to treat the proposal is first to convert the given cash flow in terms of real dollars to actual dollars by inflating them by 5%, as shown in Table 11.1.

Therefore, the inflated revenues can be discounted at the inflation-adjusted MARR as

$$NPW = -\$1,000 + \$525(P/F, 20\%, 1) + \$551(P/F, 20\%, 2)$$
$$+ \$579(P/F, 20\%, 3) = \$55$$

Thus, the proposed project is acceptable.

11.6 INFLATION AND COMBINED INTEREST–INFLATION RATE

Assume that an investor requires a real rate of return of i_r increase in purchasing power after inflation from an investment of P and that the rate of inflation is i_f; therefore, the future worth F of this investment, after N years can be expressed as

$$F = P(1 + i_r)^N(1 + i_f)^N \tag{11.1}$$

or

$$F = P(1 + i_c)^N$$

where

i_r = required annual rate of return after inflation, or real increase in purchasing power, measured by then-correct dolars. It is also simply called interest rate.

i_f = inflation rate.

i_c = combined interest–inflation rate. It represents both the minimum required rate of return and the inflation rate.

Therefore, the combined interest–inflation rate can be expressed as

$$i_c = (1 + i_r)(1 + i_f) - 1 \tag{11.3}$$

or

$$i_c = i_r + i_f + i_r i_f \tag{11.4}$$

If i_r and i_f are small, then the combined interest inflation rate can be approximately expressed as

$$i_c \cong i_r + i_f \tag{11.5}$$

The required annual rate of return after inflation can be given as

$$i_r = \frac{1 + i_c}{1 + i_f} - 1 \tag{11.6}$$

11.7 DEFLATION AND COMBINED INTEREST–DEFLATION RATE

The effects of deflation is opposite to the ones of inflation. It results in a *decrease* in the monetary price for goods and equipment (or services) and therefore causes an *increase* in the real value or purchasing power or money. Thus, equation (11.1) can be reexpressed as

$$F = P(1 + i_r)^N(1 - i_d)^N \tag{11.7}$$

or

$$F = P(1 + i_c)^N \tag{11.8}$$

where i_d is the deflation rate. Thus, the combined interest–deflation rate can be expressed as

$$i_c = (1 + i_r)(1 - i_d) - 1 \tag{11.9}$$

or

$$i_c = i_r - i_d - i_r - i_r i_d \tag{11.10}$$

If i_r and i_d are small, then the combined interest–deflation rate can approximately be expressed as

$$i_c \cong i_r - i_d \tag{11.11}$$

The required annual rate of return after deflation can be found as

$$i_r = \frac{1 + i_c}{1 - i_d} - 1 \tag{11.12}$$

Example 11.3   Assume that the interest rate is 8% per year and inflation rate is 6% per year. Determine the combined interest–inflation rate by using:

(a) Equation (11.4).
(b) Equation (11.5).

Solution

(a) Since $i_c = i_r + i_f + i_r i_f$

$$= 0.08 + 0.06 + 0.08(0.06) = 0.1448 \text{ or } 14.48\%$$

(b) Since $i_c \cong i_r + i_f = 0.08 + 0.06 = 0.14$ or 14%.

Example 11.4   Assume that the present amount and the future amount after 3 years are $2,000 and $6,000, respectively. If the inflation rate is given as 5%, determine:

(a) The combined interest–inflation rate.
(b) The real annual rate of return after inflation.
(c) The annual rate of return if inflation is not considered.

Solution

(a) Since $F/P = (1 + i_c)^N$ or $\$6,000/\$2,000 = (1 + i_c)^3$ thus

$$i_c = 3^{1/3} - 1 = 0.4422 \text{ or } 44.22\%$$

(b) the real ROR after inflation is

$$i_r = \frac{1 + i_c}{1 + i_f} - 1 = \frac{1 + 0.4422}{1 + 0.05} - 1 = 0.37.36 \text{ or } 37.36\%$$

(c) If inflation is not considered, the ROR is

$$i_r = i_c = 0.4422 \text{ or } 44.22\%$$

Example 11.5 Assume that a proposal that requires an investment of $2,000 today will provide a uniform series of net year-end receipts of $1,000 per year for the next 4 years. If the interest rate is 10% per year and the inflation rate is 6% per year, determine the following:

(a) The NPW of the project assuming that the receipts are given in terms of today's dollars.
(b) The combined interest–inflation rate.
(c) The NPW of the project assuming that the receipts are in terms of then-current dollars.
(d) Repeat part (c) but use the approximate value of the combined interest–inflation rate calculated from equation (11.5).
(e) Repeat part (c) but first convert the future cash flows into today's dollars and then find the NPW by using the regular interest rate.

Solution

(a) NPW $= -\$2,000 + \$1,000(P/A, 10\%, 4) = \$1,170.$
(b) $i_c = i_r + i_f + i_r i_f = 0.10 + 0.06 + 0.10(0.06) = 0.166$ or 16.6%.
(c) NPW $= -\$2,000 + \$1,000(P/A, 16.6\%, 4) = 764.$
(d) Since $i_c \cong i_r + i_f = 0.6$ or 16%

$$\text{NPW} = -\$2,000 + \$1,000(P/A, 16\%, 4) = \$800$$

(e) First converting the future cash flows into today's dollars,

$$F_1 = \$1,000(P/F, 6\%, 1) = \$943$$
$$F_2 = \$1,000(P/F, 6\%, 2) = \$890$$
$$F_3 = \$1,000(P/F, 6\%, 3) = \$840$$
$$F_4 = \$1,000(P/F, 6\%, 4) = \$792$$

then using the regular interest rate,

$$NPW = -\$2,000 + \$943(P/F, 10\%, 1) + \$890(P/F, 10\%, 2)$$
$$+ \$840(P/F, 10\%, 3) + \$792(P/F, 10\%, 4) = \$764$$

Note that the value of NPW is the same as the one found in part (c).

11.8 THE EFFECTS OF INFLATION ON AFTER-TAX CALCULATIONS

In the previous sections the effects of inflation on the after-tax cash flows have not been taken into account. However, the effects of taxes are important since deductions permitted for depreciation and loan interest are not associated with inflation since depreciation is determined only by the first cost of an asset rather than its inflated replacement cost. Further, the interest charges on the borrowed funds are limited by agreement in actual dollars without any possible correction for inflation. Therefore, the borrowed funds are obtained in real dollars and paid back in actual dollars. Thus, as mentioned before, during inflationary times, borrowers receive benefits from inflation if the lenders do not dictate an inflation-adjusted interest rate in the agreement.

Example 11.6   Assume that a $10,000 investment will provide a uniform annual net benefit before tax of $3,200 in terms of the base-year dollars over the next 5 years. Assume straight-line depreciation and a combined effective income tax rate of 37.96%. Use an after-tax MARR of 10% without including inflation. Determine the NPW of the investment under the following conditions:

(a) There will be no inflation during the next 5 years.
(b) There will be an annual inflation rate of 6%.

Solution

(a) The after-tax cash flows for the investment under no inflation is given in Table 11.2.
Thus,

$$NPW = -\$10,000 + \$2,744(P/A, 10\%, 5) = \$403$$

TABLE 11.2 After-Tax Cash Flows under No Inflation

Year t	Before-Tax Cash Flow A_t	Straight-Line Depreciation D_t	Taxable Income $A_t - D_t$	Income Tax T_t	After-Tax Cash Flow Y_t
0	−$10,000	—	—	—	−$10,000
1–5 (each)	3,200	$2,000	$1,200	$456	2,744

(b) To compute the after-tax cash flows for the investment under 6% inflation, the given before-tax cash flow A_t in terms of base-year dollars is first inflated at 6% to then-current dollars for the purpose of computing the taxable income and income taxes. The resulting after-tax flow Y_t' in terms of then-current dollars is converted back to base-year dollars Y_t, as given in Table 11.3. Note that in the table

$$A_t' = A_t(F/P, 6\%, N) \qquad (11.13)$$

$$T_t' = (A_t' - D_t)0.3796 \qquad (11.14)$$

$$Y_t' = A_t' - T_t'$$
$$= A_t' - (A_t' - D_t)0.3796 \qquad (11.15)$$

$$Y_t = Y_t'(P/F, 6\%, N) \qquad (11.16)$$

Therefore,

$$\text{NPW} = -\$10,000 + \$2,702(P/F, 10\%, 1) + \$2,662(P/F, 10\%, 2)$$
$$+ \$2,628(P/F, 10\%, 3) + \$2,585(P/F, 10\%, 4)$$
$$+ \$2,553(P/F, 10\%, 5)$$
$$= -\$19$$

Note that with 10% inflation, this investment is no longer attractive since higher income taxes are paid on the annual taxable incomes that are determined in terms of then-current dollars.

TABLE 11.3 After-Tax Cash Flows under 6% Inflation

t	A_t	A_t'	D_t	$A_t' - D_t$	T_t'	Y_t'	Y_t
0	−$10,000	—	—	—	—	−$10,000	−$10,000
1	3,200	$3,392	$2,000	$1,392	$528	2,864	2,702
2	3,200	3,597	2,000	1,597	606	2,991	2,662
3	3,200	3,811	2,000	1,811	687	3,130	2,628
4	3,200	4,038	2,000	2,038	774	3,264	2,585
5	3,200	4,282	2,000	2,282	866	3,416	2,553

11.9 PRESENT WORTH OF ESCALATING SERIES

In the event that there is a *price instability*, prices for goods and services do not vary proportionately over time. Thus, such price instability may influence the acceptance decision among alternatives. For example, assume that two alternative projects have identical cash flows in terms of today's dollars and are therefore equally attractive. However, further assume that the positive cash flows of one of the two proposals is due to energy savings that inflated 16% annually and that positive cash flows of the other alternative resulted from raw material cost savings that escalated 8% annually. Of course, the first alternative project would be selected.

In general, there are frequently one or more components of a cash flow stream that have *escalation rates* that are substantially different than the given *overall* (or general) inflation rate. The cash flow patterns of such components can be expressed in terms of actual dollar amounts or specific inflation rates that are different than the general inflation rate. Of course, specifying such changes of annual cash flows allows the decision maker to observe the annual changes in the rate of escalation among the years. On the other hand, employing a specific inflation rate confines the cash flow to a continuous growth pattern.

Assume that a given cash flow follows an *escalating series* type of cash flow pattern in which individual cash flows change by a constant *percentage* among the consecutive cash flows rather than by a constant *dollar* amount. Such cash flow patterns can be represented by the geometric cash flow series that takes place when the amount of a cash flow increases (or decreases) by a fixed percentage from one time period to the next. If j represents the percent change (or escalation rate) in the amount of a cash flow from one period to the next, the amount of the tth cash flow can be expressed as

$$A_t = A_{t-1}(1+j) \qquad t = 2, 3, \ldots, N \qquad (11.17)$$

or

$$A_t = A_1(1+j)^{t-1} \qquad t = 1, 2, 3, \ldots, N \qquad (11.18)$$

Of course, in a given geometric series, the growth is represented by positive j, whereas the decay is represented by negative j of costs and/or revenues as a result of inflation or recession. Thus, the present worth of the cash flows given by equation (11.18) is

$$PW = \sum_{t=1}^{N} A_1(1+j)^{t-1}(1+i)^{-t} \qquad (11.19)$$

or

$$PW = A_1(1+j)^{-1} \sum_{t=1}^{N} \left(\frac{1+j}{1+i}\right)^t \qquad (11.20)$$

Alternatively,

$$PW = A_1 \left[\frac{1-(1+j)^N(1+i)^{-N}}{i-j}\right] \qquad \text{for } i \neq j \qquad (11.21)$$

and

$$PW = \frac{NA_1}{1+i} \qquad \text{for } i = j \qquad (11.22)$$

Note that if the escalation rate $j \geq 0$ and the interest rate is not equal to escalation rate, i.e., $i \neq j$, then

$$PW = A_1 \left[\frac{1-(F/P, j\%, N)(P/F, i\%, N)}{i-j}\right] \qquad \text{for } i \neq j \text{ and } j \geq 0 \qquad (11.23)$$

Example 11.7 Assume that labor costs are given as \$40,000 for the next year and that they are expected to increase for the next 4 years at a rate of 6%. Find the amount of money that should be put into a reserve account today to cover the labor costs of the next 4 years if inflation is *not* to be considered.

 (a) If the interest rate is 9%.
 (b) If the interest rate is 6%.

Solution

 (a) By using equation (11.23),

$$PW = \$40,000 \left[\frac{1-(F/P, 6\%, 4)(P/F, 9\%, 4)}{0.09-0.06}\right]$$

$$= \$40,000 \left[\frac{1-(1.262)(0.7084)}{0.09-0.06}\right] = \$141,332$$

 (b) By using equation (11.22),

$$PW = \$40,000 \left(\frac{4}{1.06}\right) = \$150,943$$

Example 11.8 Consider Example 11.7 and assume that inflation rate is 8% and resolve only part (a).

Solution   By using equation (11.4),

$$i_c = i_r + i_f + i_r i_f = 0.09 + 0.08 + 0.09(0.08) = 0.1772 \text{ or } 17.72\%$$

Therefore, from equation (11.17)

$$PW = \$40{,}000 \left[\frac{1 - (F/P, 6\%, 4)(P/F, 17.72\%, 4)}{0.1772 - 0.06} \right]$$

$$= \$40{,}000 \left[\frac{1 - (1.262)(0.521)}{0.1772 - 0.06} \right] = \$116{,}882$$

11.10 SOME FURTHER NOTES ON INFLATION

There are several theories about inflation. However, none of them can explain every situation. As succinctly put by Shapiro [64, p. 13]: "The sources of inflation at any one time may differ in developed and under-developed countries, in countries with strong labor organizations and those with weak ones, and countries with a more competitive structure and relatively closed economies and economies that are heavily involved in trade with other countries." In general, economists categorized inflation into three distinctive types: (1) demand-pull inflation, (2) cost-push inflation, and (3) structural inflation.[†]

11.10.1 Demand-Pull Inflation

Demand-pull inflation is the most common of the three inflation types and is also called *excess demand inflation*. In general, it can be defined as *too much money chasing too few goods*. It describes the cause of inflation to be the supply of goods and services not meeting the demand, a situation most likely to take place during the times of full employment since then it would be hard to produce more goods and services to meet the demand. Prices are forced to increase by competition for relatively rare goods and services. Therefore, such excess demand or excess spending takes place in the event of consumers starting to spend their savings, consumer credit being too liberal, government deficits too big, or the money supply or other forms of purchasing power grow faster than the supply of goods and services.

11.10.2 Cost-Push Inflation

The primary cause of *cost-push inflation* is the *price inflation* resulting from increased costs instead of increased demand. Therefore, the cause of such inflation is generally believed to be cost, and particularly wage cost,

---

[†]For further information, see Gönen and Bekiroglu [32].

increases. When there is no excess demand for labor, strong labor unions, through collective bargaining, can frequently obtain wage increases that cannot be justified by corresponding increases in productivity. Of course, the increased costs of wages are passed on to the consumer in terms of higher prices. The resulting higher prices in turn decrease the purchasing power of wages and that causes demands for still greater wages, which again causes higher prices, and so on. This is called the *wage–price spiral*.

11.10.3 Structural Inflation

The basic cause *structural inflation* is the considerable shift in demand from one industry to another. Here, it is assumed that prices are flexible enough to increase but not sufficient to decrease due to administered pricing and labor union pressures. As an example, assume that demand considerably shifts from the products of industry A to the products of industry B. Under such circumstances industry B will try to increase production, and, in the process, will probably pay greater wage and material costs than normal, as a result of the immobility of labor and other resources, that will cause the prices to increase. Further, the increased demand for industry B's product will cause the prices to go up. Such increase, in turn, would cause the general prices to increase since it is not probable that industry A's prices will not decrease despite the fact that demand has declined. Of course, the increase in wages and prices in industry B can cause wage increases and eventually price increases in industry A because the employers of industry A may be forced to pay greater wages. Such greater wages may be required as a result of higher cost of living and to prevent experienced and skilled workers from leaving their individual companies, despite the fact that total production and employment have declined. In this sense structural inflation is a combination of demand-pull and cost-push inflation that can take place in fully or underemployed economy.

11.10.4 Possible Remedies

Among the solutions for all three types of inflation is increased productivity. In the event that productivity can be increased to meet the demand for additional goods and services, the cause of demand-pull inflation is eliminated. Furthermore, demand can be controlled by decreasing the money supply and/or spendable income of the nation. Of course, excessive growth in spendable income can be prevented if excessive wage increases are prevented. The all-time golden rule is that *wage increases should be justified by increased production* [32]. If such increase in production can be achieved, then wages and thus prices can be controlled, which in turn can decrease the tendency toward cost-push and structural inflation.

PROBLEMS

11.1 Consider Example 11.1 and determine the average inflation rate that has occurred over the last 3 years, that is, between 1979 through 1981.

11.2 Consider Example 11.1 and assume that the base of the consumer price index is required to be changed from 1967 to 1978 by setting the index for 1978 at 100. Determine the new CPIs for the years 1979, 1980, and 1981.

11.3 Solve Problem 11.1, using compound interest tables.

11.4 The cost of mailing first-class letters has increased from 6 cents in 1968 to 25 cents in 1988. Using these values, determine the inflation rate f in postage cost for the 20-year period.

11.5 The cost of mailing first-class letters has increased from 13 cents in 1978 to 25 cents in 1988. Using these values, determine the inflation rate f in postage cost for the 10-year period.

11.6 Assume that interest rate is 10% per year and inflation rate is 5% per year. Determine the combined interest–inflation rate by using:
(a) Equation (11.4).
(b) Equation (11.5).

11.7 Assume that the present worth and the future worth after 4 years is given as $1,500 and $5,500, respectively. If the inflation rate is 6%, determine:
(a) The combined interest–inflation rate.
(b) The required annual rate of return after inflation.

11.8 Verify equation (11.6).

11.9 Assume that the annual inflation rate in the next 2 years is anticipated to be 7% and that in the following 4 years it increases to 9%. If a cash flow stream for the next 6 years consists of a uniform annual amount of $2,000 given in terms of today's dollars, determine their value in terms of then-current dollars.

11.10 Assume that the present price of an automobile is $10,000. The rate of inflation is expected to be 7% for the next 5 years. For the next 5 years determine the following:
(a) Annual (year-end) cost increase due to inflation.
(b) Future cost in then-current dollars.
(c) Future cost in today's dollars.
(d) Present worth of the future costs calculated in part (c) discounted at 10%.

11.11   Assume that the present price of an automobile is $10,000. The rate of inflation is expected to be 7% for the next 5 years. Use an annual interest rate of 10% and determine the following for the next 5 years:

(a) Annual combined interest–inflation rate.

(b) Future (year-end) cost in then-current dollars.

(c) $(P/F, i_c\%, N)$ factor.

(d) Present worth of the future cost calculated in then-current dollars.

11.12   Assume that a proposal that requires an investment of $4,000 today will provide a uniform series of net year-end revenues of $2,000 per year for the next 5 years. If the interest rate is 10% per year and inflation rate is 8% per year, determine the following:

(a) The NPW of the project assuming that the revenues are given in terms of today's dollars.

(b) The combined interest–inflation rate.

(c) The NPW of the project assuming that the revenues are in terms of then-current dollars.

(d) Repeat part (c) but use the approximate value of the combined interest–inflation rate calculated from equation (11.5).

(e) Repeat part (c) but first convert the future cash flows into today's dollars and then find the NPW by using the regular interest rate.

11.13   Resolve Example 11.6 based on the assumption that the annual inflation rate is 5%.

11.14   Assume that a $15,000 investment will provide a uniform annual net benefit before tax of $5,000 in terms of the base-year dollars over the next 5 years with no salvage value at the end of 5 years. Assume straight-line depreciation and a combined effective income tax rate of 37.96%. Use an after-tax MARR of 9% without including inflation. Determine the NPW of the investment under the following conditions:

(a) There will be no inflation during the next 5 years.

(b) there will be an annual inflation rate of 7%.

11.15   Assume that equipment has an installed first cost of $10,000 and is expected to last 10 years, with a zero salvage value at the end of the 10th year. The annual O&M costs of the equipment is expected to be $2,000 the first year, increasing 12% per year thereafter. Do not take into account inflation and determine the present worth of the costs of the equipment for the next 10 years using an interest rate of 15%.

11.16   Solve Problem 11.15 but assume that inflation is 10% per year.

___12

ECONOMIC ANALYSIS OF PROJECTS IN THE PUBLIC SECTOR

Something deeply hidden had to be behind things.
ALBERT EINSTEIN

It takes all sorts of in and outdoor schooling
To get adapted to my kind of fooling.
ROBERT FROST, *It Takes All Sorts*, 1972

12.1 INTRODUCTION

In general, contrary to the notions of *big government* or *government is best which governs least*, there are certain activities and/or public projects that can be best authorized, financed, and/or operated by governmental agencies, by federal, state, county, or city organizations, whichever are more appropriate. In that sense such an organization may resemble a big corporation in which the elected officials and the citizens may be likened to a board of directors and stockholders, respectively. For example, at the federal level, the primary purpose of the U.S. government, as given in the Constitution, is the *national defense* and the *general welfare* of its citizens. The term *general welfare* covers a very large portion of activites that can include all kinds of government projects and agencies. For instance, such activities include all economic services for the public, public safety and protection, management of natural resources, and public education and cultural development. Many public projects are very large and complex and require large amounts of investment. One other interesting characteristic of the public project is the fact that public projects (and associated project investment) often benefit those who do not make the investments. For instance, the required money for the road repairs of a given town may be provided through taxes assessed on the properties of the townspeople even though most of the people who actually use the repaired roads may be coming from other nearby towns. For that matter, some taxpayers may not even drive or have automobiles. In general, public projects frequently create *public goods*, in terms of facilities and services, that may be readily utilized by all if they may be utilized by one. In the event that a public project may affect third parties that are not directly involved in the project (such as the people that use the roads and come from nearby towns, as is the case in the previous example), the resulting benefit (or cost) is called the *spillover benefit* (or *spillover cost*).

Evaluation of public projects are usually based on *benefit–cost* (also called *cost–benefit*) analyses, in addition to other economic evaluation techniques, for example, NPW or NAW. The concept that benefits of a project should be measured (in monetary terms) and that the benefits should be greater than the costs involved to justify the funding of the project was established in the United States by the Flood Control Act of June 22, 1936, which states "that the Federal Government should improve or participate . . . if the benefits to whomsoever they may accrue are in excess of the estimated costs" [73]. Therefore, the act officially established the principle of *benefit–cost analysis* for public projects. Later, the report to the Federal Inter-Agency River Basin Committee [60], prepared by the Subcommittee on Benefits and Costs in May 1950, defined *the ratio of benefits to costs* as the *criterion* to indicate the relative merits of different proposals. The report, which is often called the *green book*, provides a rational method for accepting public projects. Therefore, the method of economic evaluation that employs the benefit–cost ratio as a decision criterion is called the *benefit–cost ratio method*. The greater the ratio above unity (i.e., 1.0), the more favorably a public project is usually considered. Alternatively, the measure of acceptability of such public projects can be expressed as a positive net difference between benefit and cost.

Furthermore, the American Association of State Highway Officials also uses the benefit–cost ratio method as the only method of economic evaluation in its information report by the Committee on Planning and Design Policies on Road User Benefit Analyses for Highway Improvements [3]. The report is also known as the *red book*.

12.2   THE ROLE OF POINT OF VIEW IN PUBLIC PROJECTS

The selection of the *proper point of view* is one of the most important aspects in determination of the success of a given public project. In general, a proper point of view should take into account all of the significant results of the project that is being studied. Thus, a given public project may have a viewpoint that includes an individual (e.g., a city council member) or a company, town, city, a particular district of a given city, state, a number of states in a given region, nation, or international. A proper point of view should include those who pay the costs involved and those who benefit from the project. Of course, it is very hard to claim that a given point of view is economic or political in nature. Often, a public project has economic impact but is decided in a political manner. Such decisions may also be affected by the attitude or the belief (or even by the prejudice) of the decision maker(s). Therefore, the resulting study and/or decision may reflect the personal views rather than objective and unbiased points of view.

Also, even with the use of proper points of view, the objective of the benefit–cost method is to set the minimum threshold of acceptability of a public project rather than to rank such projects. Therefore, the benefit–cost method should be used as a rational guide to decision makers in the public sector, as suggested by the Subcommittee on Priorities and Economy in Government of the United States Congress [68, p. 17]:

> If benefit–cost analysis is to be implemented and used to its fullest potential, renewed efforts must be made by policy makers in both the executive and legislative branches of government. The economic profession has made significant advances in the level of sophistication of their analyses which should aid this task, but one thing is clear—benefit–cost analysis does not make decisions.
>
> Analysis can provide an important and helpful tool for making decisions, but it is no more than a tool. Problems involving social policy and value judgments must be considered and weighed in conjunction with the results of benefit–cost analysis and the final decision made by the human policy-maker.

12.3 FINANCING PUBLIC PROJECTS

Public projects are funded by various ways that include (1) taxation (e.g., income taxes, property taxes,[†] sales taxes, gasoline taxes, vehicle licensing fees, and special assessments); (2) internal funds through income-generating activities (e.g., by municipally owned or federal government owned power plants, such as the Tennessee Valley Authority, the Rural Electrification Administration, or the Bonneville Power Administrations, by the United States Postal System, by a city- or state-owned water systems, or by state-owned turnpikes (and toll bridges); and (3) borrowing (e.g., through the issuance of bonds, for either general use or particular projects, or by bills or notes, etc.). In general, gederal projects are financed by tax money and borrowing. Such projects may be funded through *direct payment*, that is, the 100% funding of the project. Examples for such funding include the projects of flood control, irrigation, and navigation (as in the case of various Army Corps of Engineers' projects) or military projects, or restoration of historic buildings, and so on. The direct payment financing may be 100%, that is, total financing, or partial (e.g., 90 or 50%, etc.). Usually, the federal government funds 90% of interstate highways, and the remaining 10% of the cost is shared by the states involved. Other examples of federal financing include a large number of subsidies and insured loans, such as the loans

---

[†]They are also called *ad valorem taxes*.

issued by the Federal Housing Administration (FHA), the low-interest loans to universities and college students.

12.4   THE INTEREST RATE SELECTION FOR PUBLIC PROJECTS

In the past, the interest rate,[†] discount rate, or MARR to be used in a given public project was a matter of judgment. In general, it was understood that it was supposed to be more than the rate paid for funds borrowed for the projects. In general, the interest rate used in public projects should reflect (1) the interest rate on borrowed funds, (2) the opportunity cost of funds to the government agency, and (3) the opportunity cost of funds to the taxpayers. In recent years due to a greater recognition of the importance of such interest rates, the MARR for public projects have been increased. For example, the Office of Management and Budget (OMB) dictates since 1972 that, with certain exceptions, federal agencies have to employ a discount rate of 10% in federal project evaluations [27]. Note that this 10% rate, without including inflation, is comparable to the opportunity cost of capital in the private sector.[‡] Since the 10% does not take into account the prevailing inflation rate, the *combined* interest rate has to be higher. Of course, any present risk and uncertainty should also be reflected in such interest rate, as it is the case in the private sector.

12.5   BENEFIT–COST RATIO ANALYSIS

In general, the *benefit–cost (B/C) ratio*[§] is defined as the ratio of the equivalent worth of benefits to the equivalent worth of costs. Of course, often the estimation of costs and benefits involves forecasting future events. Thus, the estimation of costs is easier than the benefits, especially in the case of public projects, since it is usually difficult to place monetary values on social benefits. The equivalent worths of benefits and costs are usually given either in present worths or in annual worths. Therefore, the *conventional B/C ratio* is defined as

$$\text{Conventional B/C} = \frac{\text{Net benefits to the public}}{\text{All costs to the government}} \qquad (12.1)$$

where the net benefits to the public are defined as the gross benefits to the public minus disbenefits (or disadvantages) to the public in terms of public

---

[†]It is also called the social discount rate.
[‡]In recent years the rate was increased to 12% for a period of time.
[§]Note that the B/C ratio is also referred to as the *savings–investment ratio* (SIR) by some government agencies and departments [24].

costs. Similarly, all costs to the government include the initial investment cost to the government plus the operating and maintenance (O&M) costs to the government; whereas the "modified" B/C ratio uses the same data, but the O&M costs to the government are considered as negative benefits rather than as costs. Therefore, the modified B/C ratio is expressed as

$$\text{Modified B/C} = \frac{\text{Net benefits to the public} - \text{Governmental O\&M costs}}{\text{Governmental investment cost}}$$

(12.2)

It is interesting to note that both methods give consistent results in terms of project attractiveness. A given project is desirable if the B/C ratio is greater than unity or, at least, is equal to unity. To be more specific, if the B/C ratio is greater than unity, accept the project. If it is less than the unity, reject the project; whereas if it is equal to unity, be indifferent to the project.

Alternatively, collecting terms as in the conventional B/C ratio, for a given public project

NPW = PW of net benefits to the public − AW of all costs to the government

(12.3)

or

NAW = AW of net benefits to the public − AW of all costs to the government

(12.4)

Similarly, grouping terms as in the modified B/C ratio,

NPW = PW of net benefits to the public

− (PW of governmental investment cost

+ PW of government O&M costs)

(12.5)

or

NAW = AW of net benefits to the public

− (AW of governmental investment cost

+ AW of governmental O&M costs)

(12.6)

Note that if any one of the equations (12.3) through (12.6) are used, a given project is desirable when the NPW or NAW is positive. If they are negative, the project is not desirable; whereas if they are equal to zero, be indifferent to the project.

Example 12.1   Assume that the Ghost City council has a public project that has first cost, annual benefits, and annual O&M costs of $25,000, $12,000, and $5,000, respectively. Its salvage value at the end of its useful life of 6 years is $2,000. If the applicable MARR is 7%, determine:

(a) The annual equivalent cost (AEC) of the project.
(b) The conventional B/C ratio.
(c) The modified B/C ratio.

Solution

(a) The net annual cost (i.e., the capital recovery cost) of the project, taking into account the salvage value but not the O&M costs, is

$$\text{AEC} = (\$25,000 - \$2,000)(A/P, 7\%, 6) + \$2,000(0.07) = \$4,966$$

(b) From equation (12.1)

$$\text{Conventional } \frac{B}{C} \text{ ratio} = \frac{\text{Net benefits to the public}}{\text{All costs to the government}}$$

$$= \frac{B}{\text{AEC} + \text{O\&M}} = \frac{\$12,000}{\$4,966 + \$5,000}$$

$$= 1.2 > 1.0$$

(c) From equation (12.2),

$$\text{Modified } \frac{B}{C} \text{ ratio} =$$

$$\frac{\text{Net benefits to the public} - \text{Governmental O\&M costs}}{\text{Governmental investment cost}}$$

$$= \frac{B - \text{O\&M}}{\text{AEC}} = \frac{\$12,000 - \$5,000}{\$4,966}$$

$$= 1.4 > 1.0$$

Example 12.2   Consider the results of Example 12.1 and determine the following:

(a) The NAW using equation (12.4).
(b) The NAW using equation (12.6).

Solution

(a) NAW = AW of net benefits to the public

$\quad\quad$ − AW of all costs to the government

$\quad\quad$ = $(B - \text{AEC}) + \text{O\&M} = (\$12,000 - \$4,966) + \$5,000$

$\quad\quad$ = \$2,034

(b) NAW = AW of net benefits to the public

$\quad\quad$ − (AW of governmental investment cost

$\quad\quad$ + AW of governmental O&M costs)

$\quad\quad$ = $B - (\text{AEC} + \text{O\&M}) = \$12,000 - (\$4,966 + \$5,000)$

$\quad\quad$ = \$2,034

12.6 B/C ANALYSIS FOR MULTIPLE ALTERNATIVES

The B/C analysis of multiple mutually exclusive alternatives is based on the incremental B/C ≥ 1.0 and dictates that the largest *justified* investment is chosen. The procedure is similar to the procedure used in the incremental rate of return analysis reviewed in Chapter 6. Those alternatives that have an overall B/C that is less than 1.0 can be eliminated right away without further considering them in the incremental analysis.

Assume that there are two mutually exclusive alternatives A and B, the associated incremental $\Delta B/\Delta C$ ratio is computed and the following decision rule is used:

$\quad$ If $(\Delta A/\Delta C)_{B-A} > 1.0$, accept alternative B.

$\quad$ If $(\Delta B/\Delta C)_{B-A} \leq 1.0$, reject alternative B and keep alternative A.

Example 12.3 Consider the mutually exclusive alternative public projects A, B, C, D, and E given in Table 12.1. Assume that the interest rate is 7% and useful life of each project is 20 years with negligible salvage values. Determine the best alternative assuming that the do-nothing alternative is not available.

Solution Since alternative E has a B/C ratio that is less than 1.0, it is eliminated immediately and need not be considered any further.

Using equation (12.4), for each of the remaining alternatives,

TABLE 12.1   Data for Example 12.3

Alternative	Annual Net Benefit to Public	Total Annual Costs to Government (AEC of Investment + Annual O&M Costs)	Conventional B/C Ratio
A	$500,000	$200,000	2.5
B	360,000	180,000	2.0
C	240,000	160,000	1.5
D	168,000	140,000	1.2
E	100.000	130,000	0.8

$$NAW_A = \$500{,}000 - \$200{,}000 = \$300{,}000$$

$$NAW_B = \$360{,}000 - \$180{,}000 = \$180{,}000$$

$$NAW_C = \$240{,}000 - \$160{,}000 = \$80{,}000$$

$$NAW_D = \$168{,}000 - \$140{,}000 = \$28{,}000$$

Based on the results, alternative A is selected because it maximizes NAW and therefore minimizes the combined annual cost to the public and governmental agency financing the project. Otherwise, all four projects provide a B/C ratio that is greater than 1.0.

Example 12.4   Consider the data given in Example 12.3 and determine the best alternative based on the incremental $\Delta B/\Delta C$ ratios. Assume that the do-nothing alternative is available.

Solution   Since the do-nothing alternative is to be taken into account, the cash flow of such an alternative is assumed to be zero. Alternative E is no longer present. Therefore, the alternative that requires the least amount of investment is alternative D, and thus it is compared to the do-nothing alternative that has zero benefit at zero cost. Thus, the incremental $\Delta B/\Delta C$ ratio is expressed as

$$(\Delta B/\Delta C)_{D-0} = \frac{\$168{,}000 - \$0}{\$140{,}000 - \$0} = 1.20$$

Hence, alternative D is better than the do-nothing alternative.

$$(\Delta B/\Delta C)_{C-D} = \frac{\$240{,}000 - \$168{,}000}{\$160{,}000 - \$140{,}000} = 3.6$$

So, alternative C is better than alternative D.

$$(\Delta B / \Delta C)_{B-C} = \frac{\$360,000 - \$240,000}{\$180,000 - \$160,000} = 6.0$$

Therefore, alternative B is better than alternative C.

$$(\Delta B / \Delta C)_{A-B} = \frac{\$500,000 - \$360,000}{\$200,000 - \$180,000} = 7.0$$

Thus, alternative A is better than alternative B. Hence, alternative A is the best alternative in the set.

12.7 SOME COMMENTS ON THE B/C RATIO ANALYSIS

A given B/C ratio takes into account the benefits and costs of a specific project but does not provide information of how valuable the benefits are with respect to other projects, or in relation to funds involved. For example, two projects may have the same B/C ratios even though one may have a cost of $10,000 whereas the other one may have a cost of $1,000,000. In general, the proponents of this method claim that this method facilitates the most efficient projects to be accepted first, regardless of investment dollar involved, to be followed by the less efficient projects. However, this claim is not true for ranking projects under constraint conditions. It cannot be used to rank projects. It provides only the minimum level of threshold for acceptability. However, if there are no constraints, it is a sufficient selection criterion, but it does not provide more information than NPW criterion. It is simply a useful tool to guide the decision maker in the evaluation of public projects, but the final decision has to be made by the human policymaker.

12.8 MULTIPURPOSE PUBLIC PROJECTS

Due to their nature, many public projects are multipurpose projects that may involve a large number of purposes and benefits. For example, a given water resource project may provide a large number of such functions, including flood control, irrigation, navigation, water quality control, water supply, drainage, hydroelectric power generation, recreation, land stabilization, and fish and wildlife preservation. However, it is possible that a multipurpose public project may have conflicting purposes that may induce difficulties into the justification of the project. Therefore, whenever it is possible, any specific benefit has to be separately considered with respect to its incremental cost.

12.9   A SYSTEMATIC PROCEDURE FOR COMPARISON OF MULTIPLE ALTERNATIVES

Oglesby, Bishop, and Willeke [59] have suggested a systematic procedure for selecting the best among multiple proposals for a location of an urban freeway, taking into account the fact that different locations have different expected effects on the community involved. It is common knowledge in highway design that different community effects favor different locations, and that the possible highway routes that seem to be best if only irreducibles are taken into account are not the same highway routes that appear to be best if only estimated benefits and costs are taken into account. Note that the *irreducibles* are defined as the expected results of a decision that is not possible to be given in actual monetary terms. They have pointed out a large number of possible community effects and have suggested one or more different possible units that might be applied to each type of effect. Figure 12.1 shows the flow diagram suggested by Oglesby, Bishop, and Willeke for a systematic procedure that can be used in paired comparisons of multiple alternatives.

12.10   COST-EFFECTIVENESSS ANALYSIS

In general, financial studies of the effectiveness of a number of alternative system project proposals with respect to their costs are often called *cost-effectiveness evaluations.*[†] According to Kazanowski [48], the following three conditions have to exist to be able to perform *cost-effectiveness analyses*: (1) common objectives or purposes that can be identifiable and attainable, (2) alternative means for obtaining such objectives, and (3) visible restrictions to define the problem. Further, Kazanowski [48] provides the following ten steps as a standardized approach to perform a cost-effectiveness evaluation:

Step 1: Define the goals, objectives, missions, or purposes that are to be achieved. Thus, cost-effectiveness analysis can indicate the best alternative to meet such goals.

Step 2: Find out the requirements necessary for achieving such goals.

Step 3: Develop two or more alternatives for accomplishing the defined goals.

Step 4: Establish evaluation criteria to associate capabilities of alternatives to the goal requirements. Typical criteria suggested by Kazanowski [49] include performance, availability, reliability, and maintainability.

[†]Also note that the *cost effectiveness* is sometimes called the *economic evaluation of engineered systems.*

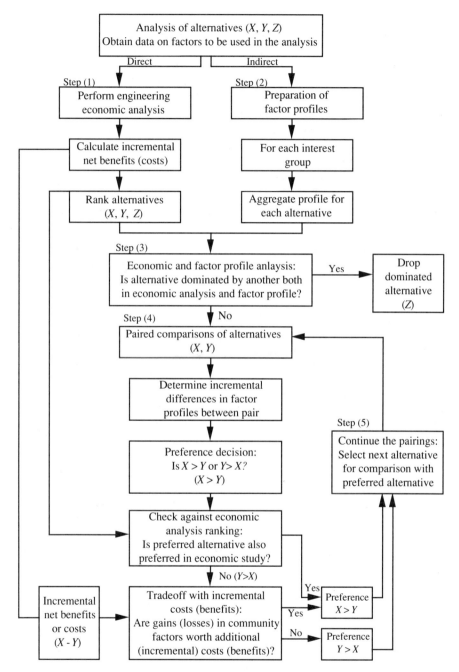

Figure 12.1   Flow diagram of a systematic procedure for evaluating alternative freeway routes [59].

Step 5: Choose the fixed-effectiveness or fixed-cost method. In the fixed-effectiveness method, the selection criterion is the cost incurred to achieve a given level of effectiveness. It is especially used when a number of alternatives that can provide the same service are compared based on their costs; whereas, in the fixed-cost method the criteria for selection is the cost incurred to achieve a given level of effectiveness. Here, the term *cost* usually represents a present worth of annual worth of *life-cycle costing* that is associated with R&D, engineering, construction, production or manufacturing, testing, operation, maintenance, salvage, and other costs that take place throughout the life cycle of the alternative.

Step 6: Determine the capabilities of the alternatives with respect to the evaluation criteria.

Step 7: Present the alternatives and their capabilities in a proper and revealing manner.

Step 8: Analyze the selected alternatives according to the effectiveness criteria and cost considerations. Discard the alternatives that are dominated by others from any further consideration.

Step 9: Apply sensitivity analysis to the selected alternative or alternatives to find out the assumptions and conditions that can cause reversals in the preferences of alternatives.

Step 10: Document all considerations, purposes, assumptions, methodolgy, and decisions from the preceding steps.

In general, public utilities by definition are *monopolies*; that is, they have the exclusive right to sell their product in a given *service area.*† In other words a public utility company operates in a domain where it is a monopoly as far as the services that it provides. The *domain* may be a geographic area or class of service given to it. In return, a given public utility company pays for such franchise in terms of being subject to regulation by public agencies as far as the rates it can charge for its adequately good quality services that it provides. Example of such public utility companies include electric and gas companies, telephone companies, cable TV companies, natural gas producing companies, public transportation companies, pipeline companies, and water companies. Most public utilities operating in the United States are *privately owned*. However, there are public utilities that are owned and operated by governmental bodies, often owned by towns and cities, or by states, or even by the federal government (for example, the TVA). If they are owned by the governmental bodies, they are essentially the same as other governmentally owned and operated entities. Therefore, the engineering economy studies involved are the same as the ones reviewed in the previous sections of this chapter.

---

†However, there are some public utilities that are not granted such exclusive service areas. Examples include those companies, such as trucking and bus lines, railroad and steamship lines, and airlines, that often have duplicate routes in the transportation industry.

If the public utility is privately owned, it pays for this *franchise* by being subject to regulation by public agencies as to the rates it can charge for its services and the quality of such services. *Intrastate* public utilities (i.e., the public utilities that operate only within one state) generally are regulated by the public utility commission or agency in that state; whereas *interstate* public utilities (i.e., the public utilities that operate within a region that includes two or more states) are regulated by federal agencies such as the Federal Power Commission, the Federal Communications Commission, or the Interstate Commerce Commission. Therefore, the rates for public utilities are regulated by the appropriate regulatory commissions that take into account both the general level of rates for all groups of utility customers and the relative rate level for different classes of customers. For example, most electric and gas utility companies apply rate structures that differentiate between three classes, commonly referred to as *residential*, *commercial*, and *industrial* customers.

The total revenue that a utility may be authorized to collect through the sales of its services should be equal to the company's total cost of service, which includes a fair return to the utility. Here, the concept of a *fair return* is commonly based on the rate of return required to satisfy the lenders of funded debt and to meet the expectations of the shareholders. Thus, the fair rate of return can be defined as a rate that includes a proper allowance for interest plus a proper provision for risks, uncertainties, and high managerial costs not otherwise rewarded. Therefore, such a fair return can be expressed as

$$\text{Fair return} = \text{Equitable rate or fair rate of return}$$
$$\times \text{Rate base or total investment} \qquad (12.7)$$

Note that the total investment is the net valuation of the company's investment. Thus, the revenue requirement can be expressed as

$$\text{Revenue requirement} = \text{Operating expenses} + \text{Depreciation expenses}$$
$$+ \text{Taxes} + \text{Rate base or net valuation}$$
$$\times \text{Fair rate of return} \qquad (12.8)$$

Of course, the determination of the revenue requirement is a matter of regulatory commission decision. Thus, designing schedules of rates that will produce the revenue requirement is a management responsibility subject to commission review. However, a regulatory commission cannot guarantee a specific rate of earnings; it can only declare that a public utility has been given the opportunity to try to earn it. In theory, a fair return should be sufficiently high to allow the public utility company to provide high-quality service to existing customers, to permit adequate funds to be raised at reasonable interest rates for expansion to meet demands of new customers, to allow the timely retirement or replacement of aging equipment, and to allow research and development for improvement of the quality of service at reduced costs. However, the rate schedules, by law, should avoid unjust and unreasonable discrimination, that is, customers using the utility's service under similar conditions should be billed at similar prices. Of course, it is a matter of necessity to categorize the customers into classes and subclasses, but all customers in a given class should be treated the same.

PROBLEMS

12.1 Assume that I is the PW of net capital invested by the government, O is the PW of net annual governmental O&M costs, and B is the PW of net benefits to the public. Assume that the B/C ratio is given as

$$\text{B/C} = \frac{B}{I + O} > 1$$

Verify that the expression of $B - (I + O) > 0$ is correct.

12.2 Consider Problem 12.1 and assume that the B/C ratio is given as

$$\text{B/C} = \frac{B - O}{I} > 1$$

Verify that the expression of $B - (I + O) > 0$ is correct.

12.3 Assume that two alternative routes to Ghost City are under consideration by the state highway department for location of a new highway. It is estimated that if route 1 is selected, it will cost $6,000,000 to construct and will provide annual benefits of $550,000 to local businesses; whereas if route 2 is selected, it will cost $5,000,000 to buid and will provide annual benefits of $450,000 to the local business community. Assume that the annual maintenance costs are $120,000 for route 1 and $100,000 for route 2, respectively. If the life of each highway is estimated to be 25 years and a MARR of 9% is employed, determine the following:

(a) The conventional B/C ratio for both routes.

(b) The modified B/C ratio for both routes.

(c) Select the best alternative route.

12.4 Solve Problem 12.3 but assume that the annual benefits of highway routes 1 and 2 are $800,000 and $700,000, respectively.

12.5 Assume that Ghost City is considering installing a new traffic pattern that has an installed cost of $300,000. It is estimated that the pattern will cost $6,000 per year to maintain, but it will save the traffic police department about $30,000 per year in man-hours. Also, the motorists will save time valued at $40,000 per year, but it will cost extra gasoline and car operating costs of $10,000 per year. Assume an interest rate of 8% and a useful life of 20 years with zero salvage value. Determine the following:

(a) Annual amount of net savings.

(b) Ratio of annual worth of savings to annual cost of capital recovery.

(c) Conventional B/C ratio.

(d) Modified B/C ratio.

(e) Rate of return of the project.

12.6 Consider the mutually exclusive alternative public projects A, B, C, and D given in Table P12.6. Determine the best alternative assuming that the do-nothing alternative is not available.

TABLE P12.6 Data for Problem 12.6

Alternative	Annual Net Benefit to the Public	Total Annual Costs to the Government (AEC of Investment + Annual O&M Costs)	Conventional B/C Ratio
A	$200,000	$ 50,000	4.0
B	250,000	70,000	3.6
C	275,000	90,000	3.1
D	300,000	110,000	2.7

12.7 Consider the data given in Table P12.6 and determine the best alternative based on the incremental $\Delta B/\Delta C$ ratios. Assume that the do-nothing alternative is available.

_____13

ECONOMIC DECISION MAKING UNDER RISK AND UNCERTAINTY

I shall never believe that God plays dice with the world.
                                          ALBERT EINSTEIN

Chance is perhaps the pseudonym of God when He did not want to sign.
                        ANATOLE FRANCE, *Le Jardin d'Epicure*, **1894**

Only one thing is certain—that is, nothing is certain.
If this statement is true, it is also false.
                                          ANCIENT PARADOX

13.1   INTRODUCTION

In industry and/or the business world, in terms of evaluating projects and making choices among investment alternatives, every engineering manager or manager is painfully aware that he or she cannot and will not always be right. In general, the *riskiness* of an investment proposal can be thought of as the variability of its possible returns. Thus, decision situations can be categorized as three types: *certainty*, *risk*, and *uncertainty*.[†] All investment decisions that have been reviewed so far, that is, in the previous chapters, were considered to be made under *certainty* conditions. In other words the probability of success was considered to be 1.0 for each project evaluated. In reality, however, there is rarely an example in which estimated quantities can be assumed to be certain. Therefore, the cash flow profile of an investment will be affected by future events, the outcomes of which are uncertain and cannot be controlled by the decision maker. Such future events can be international or national in scope or of an industrywide or

[†]Note that the study of risk and uncertainty requires a basic knowledge of statistical concepts that include variation, random variables, and probability theory, etc. Here, it is assumed that the reader has the adequate knowledge necessary in such tropics. Therefore, only a brief review of such topics is included.

local character. At the company level a change of its management, or management's attitudes, or a natural or man-made disaster can affect the capability of the company substantially. Of course, it is impossible to forecast in advance the outcome of any such event, let alone every event or assumed value that is associated with an investment decision. For example, the profitability of a given project cannot be known until it has been operated over its useful life. Only then, with some degree of certainty, can its profitability be determined.

On the other hand, the terms *risk* and *uncertainty* refer to the possibility that the profitability of a given project will be different than the one predicted at the time of decision. Of course, however, the engineering manager, and/or top management, will not be unhappy in the event that the results become better than expected as would happen if the results are worse than expected.

Usually, in the real world it is not necessary to differentiate between the meanings of the words *risk* and *uncertainty*, and therefore they can be employed interchangeably. However, when it is needed, the distinction between risk and uncertainty is that risk involves situations in which the probabilities of a particular event occurring are known; whereas with uncertainty these probabilities are not known.[†] As mentioned previously, a large number of factors may force the engineering manager to consider risk and uncertainty in capital investment projects. The economy in general, economic factors associated with investment, competition, labor conditions, changing consumer preferences, technological developments, and so on make it impossible to predict the future.[‡] Therefore, the investment cost, as well as future O&M costs, future revenues, and useful life of a project become less than certain.[§]

13.2 BRIEF REVIEW OF BASIC PROBABILITY THEORY

Probability can be defined as the relative frequency of events (either discrete or continuous) in the long run. An event is said to occur if any one of its outcomes occur. For example, the event of tossing heads with a coin is one of the two possible outcomes (the other being the event of tossing tails) and has a probability of 50%, that is, 0.5. A series of events is said to be random

---

[†]Alternatively, *uncertainty* represents the degree of lack of confidence that the estimated probability distribution is correct.

[‡]Of course, different investment projects have different degrees of risk. Accepting a large capital investment project or group of projects changes the business risk appearance of the company; thus investors and creditors may view the company differently in terms of its perceived risk. This, in turn, may affect the total valuation of the company.

[§]For those readers interested in more in-depth review of the subjects of risk and uncertainty analyses, seeing Canada and White [19], Bussey [17], White, Agee, and Case [74], and DeGarmo, Canada, and Sullivan [23] is highly recommended.

if one event has no predictable effect on the next. For example, having tossed a heads has no effect on the result of the second toss. The probability of an event E_i is a number between 0 and 1:

$$0 \leq P(E_i) \leq 1 \tag{13.1}$$

for all i. If the event cannot occur, its probability is 0. On the other hand, if it must occur (its occurrence is certain), its probability is 1. Otherwise, its probability is somewhere in between 0 and 1.

The sum of the probabilities of all possible *mutually exclusive outcomes* for a given event is equal to 1.0. Therefore,

$$P(A) + P(\bar{A}) = 1 \tag{13.2}$$

where

$P(A) =$ probability of event A occurring,
$P(\bar{A}) =$ probability of event A *not* occurring.

The probability of either of two mutually exclusive events occuring is equal to the sum of the probabilities of the two events. Thus,

$$P(A + B) = P(A) + P(B) \tag{13.3}$$

where $A + B$ is the event A or B, that is, the occurrence of one of them excludes the occurrence of the other.[†]

When events A and B are *independent* events, the probability of the two mutually exclusive events occurring simultaneously (i.e., together) is equal to the product of the probabilities of the two events. Hence,

$$P(AB) = P(A)P(B) \tag{13.4}$$

An example for the independent events is the rolling of two dice where the outcome of rolling one die is independent of the roll of the second one. For instance, assume that a fair die is tossed twice; since the two tosses are made independently of each other, the probability of getting a pair of 5s is

$P(\text{pair of 5s}) = P(\text{five spots on first toss}) P(\text{five spots on second toss})$

$$= \tfrac{1}{6} \times \tfrac{1}{6} = \tfrac{1}{36}$$

The *conditional probability* of an event B given another event A is denoted by $P(B|A)$ and is defined by

---

[†]That is to say that you cannot have the cake and eat it, too.

$$P(B|A) = \frac{P(A \text{ and } B)}{P(A)} \qquad \text{if } P(A) \neq 0 \qquad (13.5)$$

or

$$P(B|A) = \frac{P(AB)}{P(A)} \qquad \text{if } P(A) \neq 0 \qquad (13.6)$$

Substituting equation (13.4) into equation (13.6),

$$P(B|A) = \frac{P(A)P(B)}{P(A)} \qquad \text{if } P(A) \neq 0 \qquad (13.7)$$

A *random variable* is defined as a function that gives a value to each event that is part of the set of all possible events. For example, in the event of tossing a coin twice, a random variable that defines the number of tails taking place can have the values 0, 1, or 2. Since the associated random variable is discrete, the probability of the random variable being equal to a particular value x_j is defined by a *probability mass function* and is denoted by $P(x_j)$. Therefore, for a given random variable x_j

$$0 \leq P(x_j) \leq 1 \qquad (13.8)$$

and

$$\sum_{j=1}^{n} P(x_j) = 1 \qquad (13.9)$$

If a given random variable is continuous, a *probability density function* is employed to relate the probability of an event to a value or range of values for the random variable x. Therefore, the probability of an event taking place is defined by the area under the probability density function for those values of x_j included in the event. However, a probability density function must display the following characteristics:

$$0 \leq f(x) < \infty \qquad (13.10)$$

and

$$\int_{-\infty}^{\infty} f(x)\, dx = 1 \qquad (13.11)$$

Thus, the probability of an event that takes place in the range a to b is

$$P(a \leq x \leq b) = \int_{a}^{b} f(x)\, dx \qquad (13.12)$$

13.3 EXPECTED VALUE AND VARIANCE

Assume that $x_1, x_2, \ldots, x_n$ are the mutually exclusive possible *discrete* outcomes (i.e., random variables) of an event, and that $p_1, p_2, \ldots, p_n$ are the probabilities of their occurrence, respectively, such that

$$p_1 + p_2 + \cdots + p_n = 1$$

The *expected value* (also called the *mean* value) of an outcome is

$$E[x] = \sum_{j=1}^{n} x_j p_j \tag{13.13}$$

Such expected (or mean) value of a probability distribution is used as a measure of central tendency or concentration of mass for the distribution and is denoted by

$$E[x] = \mu$$

Note that equation (13.13) can also be expressed as

$$E[x] = \sum_{j=1}^{n} x_j P(x_j) \tag{13.14}$$

If the outcome function (that represents a continuous random variable) is continuous, the expected value is expressed as

$$E[x] = \int_{-\infty}^{\infty} x f(x) \, dx \tag{13.15}$$

or

$$E[x] = \int_{-\infty}^{\infty} x p(x) \, dx \tag{13.16}$$

The measure of the spread (or dispersion) of the probability distribution is called the *variance* and is denoted by σ^2, or $V[x]$, and is expressed as

$$\sigma^2 = \sum_{j=1}^{n} p_j x_j^2 - \mu^2 \tag{13.17}$$

If the outcome function is *discrete*, the variance of a random variable x can be expressed as

$$V[x] = \sum_{j=1}^{n} (x_n - E[x])^2 P(x_j) \tag{13.18}$$

or

$$V[x] = \sum_{j=1}^{n} x_j^2 P(x_j) - (E[x])^2 \qquad (13.19)$$

or

$$V[x] = E[x^2] - (E[x])^2 \qquad (13.20)$$

where

$$E[x^2] = \sum_{j=1}^{n} x_j^2 P(x_j) \qquad (13.21)$$

$$(E[x])^2 = \left\{ \sum_{j=1}^{n} x_j P(x_j) \right\}^2 \qquad (13.22)$$

However, if the outcome function is *continuous*, the variance can still be found from equation (13.20) but $E[x^2]$ and $(E[x])^2$ are computed from

$$E[x^2] = \int_{-\infty}^{\infty} x^2 f(x)\, dx \qquad (13.23)$$

and

$$(E[x])^2 = \left\{ \int_{-\infty}^{\infty} x f(x)\, dx \right\}^2 \qquad (13.24)$$

It is important to note that the variance is a useful measure of the dispersion of the outcomes but by no means the only measure of all the characteristics of risk. For example, the quantity σ is called the *standard deviation* and has the same unit as μ. Therefore, it may be a more convenient measure of the dispersion and is expressed as

$$\sigma = \left(\sum_{j=1}^{n} p_j x_j^2 - \mu^2 \right)^{1/2} \qquad (13.25)$$

that is, it is the square root of the variance. Also, another quantity that can be used to measure the dispersion is called the *coefficient of variation*, which is defined as

$$C = \frac{\sigma}{\mu} \qquad (13.26)$$

It provides a measure of the variability of event x in dimensionless form and indicates the dispersion relative to the expected value.

Example 13.1   Assume that the Zubits International Corporation is considering an investment project that has the probabilistic outcomes given in Table 13.1.

TABLE 13.1   Data for Example 13.1

Outcome x_j	Probability of Occurrence $P(x_j)$
-$110,000	0.80
530,000	0.20

Determine the following:

(a) Expected value of the project.
(b) Variance of the project.
(c) Standard deviation of the project.
(d) Range of the outcomes.

Solution

(a) From equation (13.14)

$$E[x] = x_1 P(x_1) + x_2 P(x_2)$$
$$= -\$110{,}000(0.80) + \$530{,}000(0.20) = \$18{,}000$$

(b) From equation (13.18)

$$V[x] = (x_1 - E[x])^2 P(x_1) + (x_2 - E[x])^2 P(x_2)$$
$$= (-\$110{,}000 - \$18{,}000)^2(0.80) + (\$530{,}000 - \$18{,}000)^2(0.20)$$
$$= \$6{,}5536 \times 10^{10}$$

(c) The standard deviation is

$$\sigma = (V[x])^{1/2} = (\$6.5536 \times 10^6)^{1/2} = \$256{,}000$$

(d) The range of the outcomes of the project is

$$R[x] = \$530{,}000 - (-\$110{,}000) = \$640{,}000$$

Example 13.2   Assume that the NP & NL Utility Company has decided to replace a small portion of its protection system by one of the three alternatives given in Table 13.2. The table gives the installed investment cost and the probability of failure for each alternative. In the event of a failure of the selected (out of any one of the three) protection system alternatives, it is

TABLE 13.2   Data for Example 13.2

Alternative	Installed Investment Cost	Probability of Failure in Any Given Year
1	$350,000	0.10
2	400,000	0.05
3	600,000	0.009

estimated that the cost of such failure will be $600,000 with probability of 0.30, and $900,000 with probability of 0.70. Assume that the probabilities of such failure occurring in any given year are independent of the probabilities of a failure, if it does take place. Assume that the annual fixed charge rate of each alternative is 25% of its investment cost. Determine the best alternative with respect to the expected total annual costs.

Solution   If it takes place, the expected cost of a failure is

$$E[\text{failure cost}] = \$600,000(0.30) + \$900,000(0.70) = \$810,000$$

Thus, the total expected annual cost for each alternative can be found as shown in Table 13.3. Therefore, alternative 2 is the best alternative with respect to total expected annual cost. However, selection of alternative 3 would provide better customer satisfaction in terms of improved service reliability as well as decrease the probability of a loss of $600,000 and $900,000 in any given year.

Example 13.3   Assume that the probabilities (i.e., the relative frequencies) of the useful life of equipment lasting 0, 1, 2, 3, 4, and 5 years are estimated as 0.0, 0.1, 0.2, 0.4, 0.2, and 0.1, respectively. Determine the following:

(a) Plot the probability density function of the given probability distribution.

TABLE 13.3   Results for Example 13.2

Alternative	Annual Fixed Charges on Investment	Expected Annual Cost of Failure	Total Expected Annual Cost
1	$350,000(25%) = $87,500	$810,000(0.10) = $81,000	$168,500
2	400,000(25%) = 100,000	810,000(0.05) = 40,500	140,500
3	600,000(25%) = 150,000	810,000(0.09) = 7,290	157,290

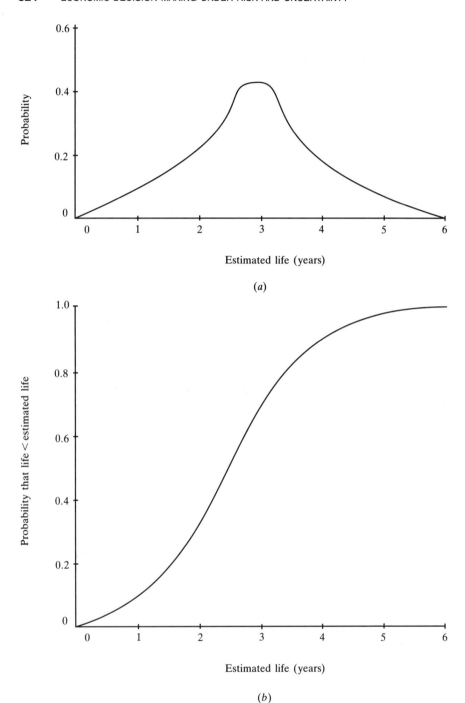

Figure 13.1   For Example 13.3: (*a*) probability density function and (*b*) cumulative probability distribution.

TABLE 13.4 Useful Life Estimates Given in Cumulative Probability Form

Useful Life N (years)	P(Useful life ≤ N)
1	0.0
2	0.1
3	0.3
4	0.7
5	0.9
6	1.0

(b) Find the corresponding cumulative probabilities that the useful life of the equipment will be equal or less than the given useful life of 0, 1, 2, 3, 4, and 5 years, respectively.

(c) Plot the cumulative probability distribution of the given data.

Solution

(a) The plot of the probability density function of the given probability distribution is shown in Figure 13.1(*a*).

(b) The corresponding cumulative probabilities are given in Table 13.4

(c) The plot of the cumulative probability distribution found in part (b) is shown in Figure 13.1(*b*).

13.4 BRIEF REVIEW OF PROBABILITY DISTRIBUTIONS

As mentioned previously, one of the techniques used to assess outcomes, in terms of subjective probabilities, is to fit a smooth curve to the historical relative frequency plotted against the random variable. Of course, the fitted curve must have a reasonable shape, and the sum of the relative frequencies under the curve must be equal to one. Example 13.3 illustrates such technique. Figure 13.1(*a*) shows the plot of the conversion of the given estimates into the more commonly represented probability density form, assuming a continuous distribution. Figure 13.1(*b*) shows the plot of the cumulative probability distribution of the given data. Note that the probability density function (height of the curve) for a continuous distribution equals the slope of the cumulative probability distribution function over the entire range of the element estimated.

As mentioned before, the purpose of a risk analysis is to consider the imprecision in predicting the input data that is necessary in performing economic evaluations. Such imprecision is shown in terms of a probability distribution. It has been determined that some of the commonly known theoretical probability distributions, especially the beta distribution and the normal distributions (with a lesser degree, the binomial distribution and the Poisson distribution) are often appropriate and convenient for describing the variability of estimated outcomes. If the subjective probability distribution cannot be represented accurately using a well-known theoretical distribution, one has to estimate directly the probability distribution for the random variable.

13.4.1 Beta Distribution

To obtain the estimates of the mean and variance for each random variable easily, the properties of the beta distribution can be used. Such distribution can be used to define a large range of left-skew and right-skew (as well as a host of many other) conditions of differing variances.[†] This method dictates making an optimistic estimate, a *pessimistic* estimate, and a *most likely* estimate for the random variable involved. These three estimates are assumed to correspond to the upper bound, the lower bound, and the mode, respectively, of the beta distribution. This method emphasizes the unlikely situations where all parameters prove to be very favorable or very unfavorable, and where neither is likely to happen. Instead, there is likely to be a blend of results with the parameters assuming values near to the most likely estimate, but with due consideration for the possible range of values. Therefore, a typical beta distribution defined in this manner will resemble a normal distribution, as shown in Figure 13.2, but having the following differences: (1) it may be skewed left or right, contrary to the normal distribution, which is symmetrical, and (2) its density function is truncated in the tails, rather than continuing indefinitely as does the normal distribution. Of course, such beta density function will be skewed whenever its mode, that is, its most likely value, is not midway between the extreme bounds (which are the optimistic and the pessimistic values). Such beta distribution represents probability density function with six standard deviations between the bounds. Its mean and the variance, respectively, can be approximately expressed as

$$E[Y] \cong \frac{P + 4M + O}{6} \qquad (13.27)$$

and

[†]The beta distribution is used extensively in the PERT network planning and scheduling technique. Note that, in reality, the beta distribution has two very distinctive classes of distributions, namely the beta I and the beta II distributions. The beta I (usually called just beta) distribution can be used to represent random variables that range between zero and one; whereas the beta II distribution can be used for variables ranging over any set of outcomes, including a wide range of left-skew and right-skew conditions of differing variances that have been mentioned in this chapter. However, regardless of the specific type involved, it will simply be referred to as the beta distribution in this book.

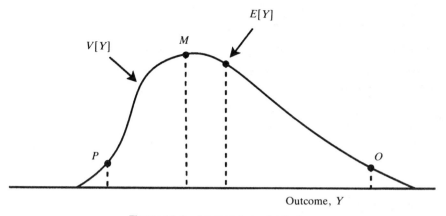

Figure 13.2 A typical beta distribution.

$$V[Y] \cong \left(\frac{O - P}{6}\right)^{2} \qquad (13.28)$$

where

$E[Y]$ = expected (or mean) value of the estimated values,
$V[Y]$ = variance of the estimated values,
P = pessimistic estimate,
O = optimistic estimate,
M = most likely estimate.

It is interesting to note that equations (13.27) and (13.28) represent an approximation of the beta distribution due to the weighting factors used. However, the difference between the approximate expected values as computed by using equation (13.27) and the exact formula is usually very small, whereas the difference between the approximate variance as computed by using equation (13.28) and the exact formula can be very large. Usually, the approximate variance is less than its exact value.

Example 13.4 Assume that the XYZ Company is considering an investment proposal. The optimistic, most likely, and pessimistic estimates for its various parameters are given in Table 13.5.
Determine the following:

(a) Expected value of the first cost.
(b) Expected value of the net annual revenue.
(c) Expected value of the useful life.
(d) Expected value of the salvage.
(e) Expected value of the rate of return from the investment.

TABLE 13.5 Data for Example 13.4

Parameter	Optimistic (O) Estimate	Most Likely (M) Estimate	Pessimistic (P) Estimate
First cost	$100,000	$100,000	$150,000
Net annual revenue	$25,000	$20,000	$15,000
Useful life	10 years	10 years	8 years
Salvage value	$10,000	$5,000	0

Solution

(a) From equation (13.27)

$$E[\text{First cost}] = \frac{P + 4M + O}{6}$$

$$= \frac{\$100,000 + 4(\$100,000) + \$150,000}{6} = \$108,333$$

(b) $E[\text{Net annual revenue}] = \dfrac{\$25,000 + 4(\$20,000) + \$15,000}{6} = \$20,000$

(c) $E[\text{Useful life}] = \dfrac{10 + 4(10) + 8}{6} = 9.7$

(d) $E[\text{Salvage value}] = \dfrac{\$10,000 + 4(\$5,000) + 0}{6} = \$5,000$

(e) The expected value of the rate of return from the investment is found from

$$\text{NPW} = -\$108,333 + \$20,000(P/A, i\%, 9.7) + \$5,000(P/F, i\%, 9.7)$$

Thus, from compound interest tables

$$E[\text{ROR}] \cong 13\%$$

13.4.2 Normal Distribution

The normal distribution is one of the best-known distributions. It is characterized by a bell-shaped curve that is symmetrical with respect to its mean μ and has points of inflection at $x = \mu \pm \sigma$. The normal distribution is defined mathematically by

$$Y = y(x) = \frac{1}{\sigma\sqrt{2\pi}} \exp\left[-\frac{1}{2}\left(\frac{x-\mu}{\sigma}\right)^2\right] \qquad (13.29)$$

where

$Y = y(x) =$ height of the curve at point x,

$x =$ any point along the x axis,

$\mu =$ mean of the distribution,

$\sigma =$ standard deviation.

Note that exp is an exponential function of the natural base e of the logarithm, and x covers the range from $-\infty$ to $+\infty$. The probabilities of occurrence at intervals of σ are represented by the respective areas under the curve for such intervals, as shown in Figure 13.3. Therefore, the probabilities that a normally distributed random variable x will have a value with σ, 2σ, or 3σ on either side of the expected value are approximately 68.28, 95.45, and 99.73%, respectively.[†] The expected value and the stan-

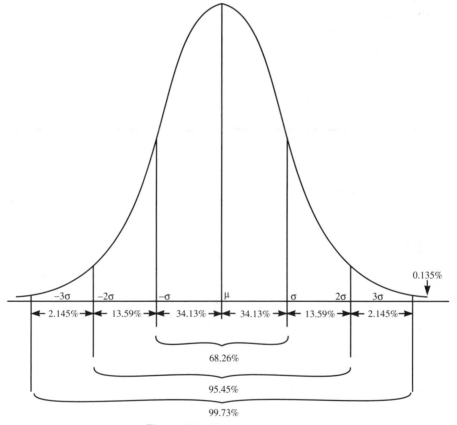

Figure 13.3 Normal distribution.

[†]Since equation (13.29), which defines the normal distribution, is difficult to use, the required data is usually found from a table of the distribution with a mean value of $\mu = 0$ and a standard deviation of $\sigma = 1$. Thus, for continuous probability distributions, the area under the curve is equal to the probability. Since the sum of the probabilities for all possible outcomes is equal to one, the total area under such normal curve is also equal to one.

dard deviation are the two fundamental parameters describing the central tendency and the dispersion of a probability distribution, respectively.

Of course, with the knowledge of risk a company cannot be impartial between two investment project proposals that have the same NPWs or RORs as was the case in the previous chapters. Such measures of profitability are based only on the expected values of the possible cash flows in various future periods. For example, assume that there are two investment proposals, each requiring $12,000 at the present time and providing expected net cash flows (net revenues) of $6,000 at the end of each of the next 3 years, after which no cash flows or salvage values are expected. Based on the information given in the previous chapters, one would rank them equally; whereas assume that the probability distributions of the annual net cash inflows are given as shown in Figure 13.4. As one can see from the figure, the values of the two project proposals are not the same since the dispersion of the probability distribution of possible cash flows for proposal B is greater than that for proposal A. Of course, if risk is related to the deviation of actual outcome from that which is expected, proposal B is the riskier investment.

In statistics one often makes observations on a small sample of outcomes of a random variable and makes statistical inferences about its probability distribution as if it were possible to observe all possible outcomes. Here, the possible implications of such statistical sampling will not be considered. Therefore, equations (13.14) and (13.18) will be employed for calculating

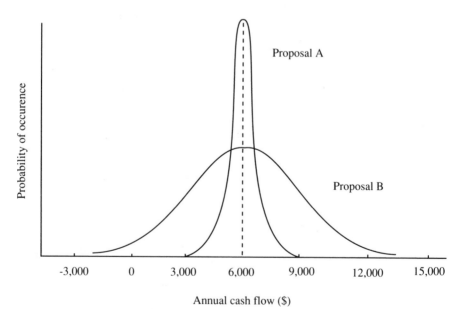

Figure 13.4 Comparison of probability distribution.

the mean and the standard deviation in spite of the number of observations. Hence, the coefficient of variation can also be calculated from equation (13.26).

The expected value and the standard deviation of the probability distribution of possible NPWs provide sufficient information to evaluate the risk involved in a given project proposal. In the event that the probability distribution is approximately normal, one can compute the probability of a prospective project's yielding a NPW of less or more than a particular amount. Of course, such probability is determined by finding the area under the curve to the left or to the right of a specified point of interest. For example, to find the probability that the NPW will be zero or less, it is necessary first to compute the difference between zero and the expected value of NPW for the project. Then, this difference is standardized[†] by dividing it by the standard deviation of possible NPW as

$$z = \frac{x - \mu}{\sigma} \tag{13.30}$$

or

$$z = \frac{x - E[\text{NPW}]}{\sigma} \tag{13.31}$$

Of course, if the x distribution is normal in form, then the distribution of the z as given will also have a normal distribution but with a mean equal to zero and a variance (and a standard deviation) equal to one. This new distribution is known as the *standard normal distribution*. Any given z is called a *standard normal deviate* because it signifies the amount any given value (of NPW) deviates from the mean of its distribution in terms of the units of the standard normal distribution. The advantage of transforming the value x into standard values is that the infinite number of normal distributions with different means and variances all can be related to a single theoretical relative frequency distribution by the transformation given by equation (13.30). Alternatively, from equation (13.30)

$$x = \mu + z\sigma \tag{13.32}$$

gives the deviation of any value of x from the mean of the distribution. Thus, any point x on a specific distribution that has σ and μ, has an equivalent point z on the standardized normal distribution. This relationship, in turn, permits the relationship of the standardized normal distribution to any other normal distribution. Therefore, if a random sample is

[†]This process is similar to having just any distribution that undergoes a change of the scale of measurement by converting values to standard value form. Similarly, the scale underlying a normal distribution can be changed by converting the measures into standard values.

taken from the standardized normal distribution, one can relate this to an equivalent random sample for any normal distribution. A given point on such standardized normal distributions is totally defined by giving the number of standard deviations the point to the left (negative) or to the right (positive) of the mean.

According to the *central limit theorem* of the probability theory, the sum of independently distributed random variables tends to be normally distributed as the number of terms in the summation increases.[†] Thus, as N increases, the NPW tends to be normally distributed with an expected value of $E[NPW]$ and variance of $V[NPW]$.

Example 13.5   Assume that there are two investment project proposals under consideration. Their discrete probability distributions of expected cash flows in each of the next 3 years are given in Table 13.6. Determine the following:

(a) Expected value of net cash flows for project A.
(b) Expected value of net cash flows for project B.
(c) Standard deviation of project A.
(d) Standard deviation of project B.
(e) Coefficient of variation for each project.
(f) Based on the risk involved, select one of the projects.

Solution

(a) The expected value of net cash flows in each of the next 3 years for project A is

$$E[\text{Net cash flows}] = 0.10(\$20,000) + 0.25(\$30,000) + 0.30(\$40,000)$$
$$+ .25(\$50,000) + 0.10(\$60,000) = \$40,000$$

TABLE 13.6   Data for Example 13.5

Project Proposal A		Project Proposal B	
Probability	Net Cash Flows	Probability	Net Cash Flows
0.10	$20,000	0.10	$30,000
0.25	30,000	0.20	35,000
0.30	40,000	0.40	40,000
0.25	50,000	0.20	45,000
0.10	60,000	0.10	50,000

[†]There is also an additional condition that the random variables have finite moments. However, this condition is usually met in risk analysis.

(b) For the project B

$$E[\text{Net cash flows}] = 0.10(\$30,000) + 0.20(\$35,000) + 0.40(\$40,000)$$
$$+ 0.20(\$45,000) + 0.10(\$50,000) = \$40,000$$

(c) The standard deviation for project A is

$$\sigma_A = [0.10(\$20,000 - \$40,000)^2 + 0.25(\$30,000 - \$40,000)^2$$
$$+ 0.30(\$40,000 - \$40,000)^2 + 0.25(\$50,000 - \$40,000)^2$$
$$+ 0.10(\$60,000 - \$40,000)^2]^{1/2} = \$11,400$$

(d) For project B

$$\sigma_B = [0.10(\$30,000 - \$40,000)^2 + 0.20(\$35,000 - \$40,000)^2$$
$$+ 0.40(\$40,000 - \$40,000)^2 + 0.20(\$45,000 - \$40,000)^2$$
$$+ 0.10(\$50,000 - \$40,000)^2]^{1/2} = \$5,480$$

(e) The coefficient of variation for projection A is

$$C_A = \frac{\sigma_A}{\mu_A} = \frac{\$11,400}{\$40,000} = 0.285$$

For project B

$$C_B = \frac{\sigma_B}{\mu_B} = \frac{\$5,480}{\$40,000} = 0.137$$

(f) Since C_A is greater than C_B, the risk is greater for project A. Therefore, select project B assuming that everything else is comparable.

Example 13.6 Assume that the Zubits International Corporation is considering an investment project that requires an investment of $100,000 now. The expected values of net cash flows from the investment at the end of years 1, 2, and 3 are $50,000, $40,000, and $30,000, respectively. The associated probabilities are given in Table 13.7.
  Determine the following:

(a) Standard deviation of net cash flows for each of the 3 years.
(b) The expected NPW of the project assuming a MARR of 10%.
(c) Assume that the net cash flows of the next 3 years are independent of each other and therefore their variances for the 3 years are additive. Find the variance and the standard deviation of the expected NPW.

TABLE 13.7 Data for Example 13.6

Year 1		Year 2		Year 3	
Probability	Expected Net Cash Flow	Probability	Expected Net Cash Flow	Probability	Expected Net Cash Flow
0.10	$30,000	0.10	$20,000	0.10	$10,000
0.25	40,000	0.25	30,000	0.25	20,000
0.30	50,000	0.30	40,000	0.30	30,000
0.25	60,000	0.25	50,000	0.25	40,000
0.10	70,000	0.10	60,000	0.10	50,000

Solution

(a) Standard deviation of net cash flows for year 1 is

$$\sigma_1 = [0.10(\$30,000 - \$50,000)^2 + 0.25(\$40,000 - \$50,000)^2$$
$$+ 0.30(\$50,000 - \$50,000)^2 + 0.25(\$60,000 - \$50,000)^2$$
$$+ 0.10(\$70,000 - \$50,000)^2]^{1/2} = \$11,400$$

Note that since the probability distributions for years 2 and 3 have the same dispersion about their expected values as that for year 1, the standard deviations are the same.

$$\sigma_1 = \sigma_2 = \sigma_3 = \$11,400$$

(b)
$$E[\text{NPW}] = \sum_{t=0}^{N} \frac{E[Y_t]}{(1+i)^t} \qquad (13.33)$$

$$= -\$100,000 + \$50,000(P/F, 10\%, 1)$$
$$+ \$40,000(P/F, 10\%, 2)$$
$$+ \$30,000(P/F, 10\%, 3) = \$1,050$$

(c) Under the assumption of mutual independence of cash flows over time, the variances for the N periods are additive. Therefore, the variance is

$$V[\text{NPW}] = \sum_{t=0}^{N} \frac{\sigma_t^2}{(1+i)^{2t}} \qquad (13.34)$$

where σ_t^2 is the variance of the tth net cash flow. Thus

$$V[\text{NPW}] = \frac{\$11,400^2}{1.10^2} + \frac{\$11,400^2}{1.10^4} + \frac{\$11,400^2}{1.10^6} = \$256,796,687$$

and

$$\sigma = \$16,025$$

Example 13.7 Assume that the useful life of a specific piece of equipment is normally distributed with a mean life of 20 years and a standard deviation of 3.2 years. Determine the following:

(a) The useful life's one standard deviation below and above the mean life, respectively.
(b) The useful life's two standard deviations below and above the mean life, respectively.
(c) The useful life's three standard deviations below and above the mean life, respectively.

Solution

(a) From equation (13.32) the useful life's one standard deviation below and above the mean life, respectively, are

$$N_1 = \mu - z\sigma = 20 - 1(3.2) = 16.8 \text{ years}$$

and

$$N_2 = \mu + z\sigma = 20 + 1(3.2) = 23.2 \text{ years}$$

(b) Similarly, for the two standard deviations

$$N_3 = 20 - 2(3.2) = 13.6 \text{ years}$$

and

$$N_4 = 20 + 2(3.2) = 26.4 \text{ years}$$

(c) Also, for the two standard deviations

$$N_5 = 20 - 3(3.2) = 10.4 \text{ years}$$

and

$$N_6 = 20 + 3(3.2) = 29.6 \text{ years}$$

Example 13.8   Assume that on a specific section of the major highway near Ghost City a large number of speed violations has been observed. Based on the collected data, it is believed that the speed of cars is normally distributed with mean and standard deviation of 65 and 6 miles per hour, respectively. Assume a random sample of 10 cars traveling on the highway and determine their speeds by using the random normal deviates given in Table D.2 in Appendix D.

Solution   Randomly select 10 random normal deviates (or numbers) from Table D.2 and assume that they (the zs) are 1.102, 0.148, 2.372, −0.145, 0.104, 1.419, 0.069, 0.797, −0.393, and −0.874. Using the selected first value, the speed of the first car can be determined using equation (13.32) as

$$x_1 = \mu + z\sigma = 65 + (1.102)6 \cong 71.6 \text{ miles}$$

Similarly,

$$x_2 = 65 + (0.148)6 \cong 65.9 \text{ miles}$$

$$x_3 = 65 + (2.372)6 \cong 79.2 \text{ miles}$$

$$x_4 = 65 + (-0.145)6 \cong 64.1 \text{ miles}$$

$$x_5 = 65 + (0.104)6 \cong 65.6 \text{ miles}$$

$$x_6 = 65 + (1.419)6 \cong 73.5 \text{ miles}$$

$$x_7 = 65 + (0.069)6 \cong 65.4 \text{ miles}$$

$$x_8 = 65 + (0.797)6 \cong 69.8 \text{ miles}$$

$$x_9 = 65 + (-0.393)6 \cong 62.6 \text{ miles}$$

$$x_{10} = 65 + (-0.874)6 \cong 59.8 \text{ miles}$$

Example 13.9   Assume that a company has a MARR of 10% and it is considering an investment project proposal. The investment requirement of the project is given with expected value and variance of $240,000 and 2×10^6, respectively. The net annual cash flows at the end of each year, for the next 10 years, are given with expected value and variance as $40,000 and 3×10^4, respectively. Determine the following:

(a) Expected value of the NPW of the project.
(b) Variance of the NPW of the project.
(c) Probability of a negative NPW.

Solution

(a) Expected value of the NPW of the project is

$$E[\text{NPW}] = -\$240,000 + \sum_{j=1}^{10} \$40,000(1.10)^{-j}$$

or

$$E[\text{NPW}] = -\$240,000 + \$40,000(P/A, 10\%, 10) = \$5,800$$

(b) Variance of the NPW of the project is

$$V[\text{NPW}] = 2 \times 10^6 + (3 \times 10^4) \sum_{j=1}^{10} (1.10)^{-2j}$$

or alternatively[†]

$$V[\text{NPW}] = 2 \times 10^6 + (3 \times 10^4)(P/A, 10\%, 20)/2.10 = 212.1629 \times 10^4$$

(c) The probability of a NPW ≤ 0 can be found as

$$P(\text{NPW} \leq 0) = P\left(z \leq \frac{0 - E[\text{NPW}]}{V[\text{NPW}]^{1/2}}\right)$$

$$= P\left(z \leq -\frac{\$5,800}{\$1,456.6}\right)$$

$$= P(z \leq -3.9819) \cong 0.00003$$

Note that the probability of a negative NPW is almost zero and it is found from Table D.3.

13.5 SENSITIVITY ANALYSIS UNDER THE CONDITIONS OF UNCERTAINTY

Sensitivity analysis has already been reviewed in Chapter 7. Such sensitivity analysis can be used as a means to evaluate the effects of uncertainty on investment by determining how an investment alternative's profitability changes as one or more parameters are varied that affect economic evaluation results. In other words a sensitivity analysis can be used as a means to gather information about the behavior of the measure of economic effective-

---

[†]Use the relation of $\sum_{j=1}^{N} (1 + i)^{-2j} = P/A, i\%, 2N)/(2 + i)$.

ness due to errors in estimating various values of the parameters and the potential for reversals in the preferences for economic investment alternatives. Some of the typical investment parameters that often permit a variance for sensitivity analysis are initial investment cost, selling price, project life, annual O&M costs, and salvage value. Sensitivity analysis can be performed by using (1) one-at-a-time sensitivity analysis procedures that take into account the measure of effectiveness as a result of changes in a single parameter, (2) multiparameter sensitivity analysis procedures that consider the possibility of interaction among parameters and investigate the sensitivity of the measure of effectiveness to multiple parameters,[†] and (3) probabilistic sensitivity analysis procedures that take into account the probabilities of occurrence that are associated with the various levels of each investment parameter, as suggested in Section 13.4.

13.6   MONTE CARLO SIMULATION

Simulation can be defined as the repetitive analysis of a mathematical model. The *Monte Carlo simulation*[‡] is the name given to a class of simulation techniques to decision making in which probability distributions are used to obtain investment parameters. The use of the Monte Carlo simulation to evaluate risky investments was first suggested by Hess and Quigley [43]. Hertz [40] proposed the use of a simulation model to obtain the expected return and dispersion about this expected return for an investment proposal.[§]

The Monte Carlo simulation technique can be used in decision situations that can be represented by empirical or theoretical probability distributions. In this technique these distributions are used to generate random outcomes for each parameter that is considered to be important and has a probabilistic value. Note that the random outcomes can be assumed to have normal, binomial, or Poisson distribution, and so on or some empirical probability distribution, as mentioned before. The assignment of such probability distributions to each of the selected parameters is based on the management's assessment of the probable outcomes. Therefore, the possible outcomes are charted for each factor according to their probability of occurrence. In the next step these random outcomes are then used in computations to determine the answer in terms of the measure of merit (or decision criterion) such as NPW, NAW, or ROR.

It is important to note that the outcomes of all parameters involved must be *randomly* selected from the distributions representing them. The best

---

[†]It is also called the sensitivity surface approach.
[‡]It is also called the method of statistical trials.
[§]For further information on the application of the Monte Carlo technique to financial models, see Hertz [39], Hillier [45], and Bussey and Stevens [18].

way to achieve this is to use a digital computer employing one of the simulation languages such as the GPSS[†] or SIMPSCRIPT. However, if the number of trials and the number of parameters involved are not large, the random selection can be done by using random number tables and associating these numbers to the distributions of the variables. One of the important questions in the Monte Carlo simulation is the number of trials (or runs, in the case of computerized process) necessary to get satisfactory answers. The answer is that the trials of a simulation must continue long enough until steady-state conditions in the measure of merit is reached. Here, the *steady-state condition* is defined as the situation in which the answers resulting from the consecutive trials become very close to each other. Among the advantages of using the Monte Carlo simulation are the following: (1) it can be used for situations for which analytic methods of solving have not yet been found, (2) it can be used for situations involving mathematical models that are either too complex or too tedious to use, (3) it can be used without disturbing the operations of a company, (4) it can be used for situations for which it is very hard or dangerous to create the same operating conditions for each experiment, (5) it facilitates continued experimentation with numerous types of alternatives that could not be achieved in real life, and (6) it is used for situations that would be very expensive and/or take much greater length of time to get the same sample size that is used.

Of course, both mathematical (i.e., analytic) and Monte Carlo models have the same problem: that is, the validity of the model used with respect to the real world. However, in Monte Carlo simulations the sample size must be large enough to decrease sampling variation to an acceptably small amount. The probabilities of events must be based on the best judgments of peope involved with the project, and then the analysis must be based on these estimates even though they are subjective in nature. Since any evaluation model is only as good as the estimates of the input parameters, the Monte Carlo simulation technique must be employed together with sound engineering logic and managerial judgment.

Example 13.10 Assume that a company is considering installing new equipment that will reduce the annual operation expenses by $5,000. The salvage value of the equipment is zero at the end of its useful life. The installed cost of the equipment is assumed to be normally distributed with a mean of $25,000 and a standard deviation of $2,500. The useful life of the equipment is assumed to have a frequency distribution given in Table 13.8. Use the Monte Carlo simulation technique for 10 random samples and determine the following:

[†]For a practical application of the Monte Carlo simulation using the GPSS, see Gönen and Bekiroglu [31].

TABLE 13.8   Frequency Distribution for Useful Life of Equipment

Useful Life N (years)	P(N)
8	0.10
10	0.25
12	0.35
14	0.20
16	0.10

(a) Rate of return for each outcome.

(b) Frequency distribution of the rates of return and the associated probabilities for the sample.

(c) The mean and variance for the computed rates of return of the sample.

Solution

(a) Assign random numbers to each outcome (i.e., useful life) in proportion to the probability of each outcome given in Table 13.8. Since two-digits probabilities are given in Table 13.8., sets of only two random digits are needed, as shown in Table 13.9.

The next step is to generate useful life outcomes by *randomly* picking random numbers and finding the useful life that associates with each with respect to the list given in Table 13.9. Table 13.10 gives 10 two-digit random numbers taken arbitrarily (i.e., randomly selecting the direction of movement within the table in terms of up, down, to the left, etc.) from a table of random numbers given in Table D.1 in Appendix D. Here, also note that it is predetermined to select the first two digits of the five-digit numbers appearing in Table D.1, together with the associating useful lives, taken from Table 10.9.

TABLE 13.9   Assignment of Random Numbers for Useful Life

Useful Life N (years)	Random Numbers
8	00–09
10	10–34
12	35–69
14	70–89
16	90–99

TABLE 13.10   Random Generation of Useful Lives

Random Number	Useful Life N (years)
48	12
86	14
25	10
89	14
40	12
16	10
20	10
15	10
34	10
33	10

Next, to sample from a normal distribution, 10 random normal deviates are *randomly* picked from Table D.2 and are given in Table 13.11. Then, to obtain the installed cost of the equipment use equation (13.32). For example, the first installed cost, using the corresponding (to the first) random normal deviate, is computed as

$$N = \mu + z\sigma$$
$$= \$25,000 + (0.951)\$2,500 = \$27,378$$

Having these values computed, the net cash flow for year 0 is $27,378 and the net cash flow (of course, in terms of annual savings) for each of the next 12 years is $5,000. Therefore, the prospective rate of return is computed as

TABLE 13.11   Results of 10 Random Samples for Example 13.10

Random Number	Useful Life	Random Normal Deviate	First Cost	Computed Rate of Return (%)
48	12	0.951	$27,378	15
86	14	1.065	27,663	15
25	10	0.742	26,855	15
89	14	0.579	26,448	15
40	12	−0.844	22,890	21
16	10	2.323	30,808	12
20	10	−0.800	23,000	19
15	10	0.485	26,213	16
34	10	0.396	25,990	16
33	10	1.925	29,813	13

$$NPW = -\$27{,}378 + \$5{,}000(P/A, i\%, 12) = 0$$

or

$$i = ROR \cong 15\%$$

Table 13.11 shows the results when this process is repeated 10 times to get the corresponding RORs.

(b) The frequency distribution of the rates of return and the associated probabilities for the samples are given in Table 13.12.

(c) From equation (13.14) the mean is computed as

$$E[x] = x_1 P(x_1) + x_2 P(x_2) + x_3 P(x_3) + x_4 P(x_4) + x_5 P(x_5) + x_6 P(x_6)$$
$$= (12\%)0.10 + (13\%)0.10 + (15\%)0.40 + (16\%)0.20$$
$$+ (19\%)(0.10) + (21\%)0.10 = 15.7\%$$

From equation (13.18) the variance is computed as

$$V[x] = \sum_{j=1}^{6} (x_j - E[x])^2 P(x_j)$$
$$= (12 - 15.7)^2 0.10 + (13 - 15.7)^2 0.10 + (15 - 15.7)^2 0.40$$
$$+ (16 - 15.7)^2 0.20 + (19 - 15.7)^2 0.10$$
$$+ (21 - 15.7)^2 0.10$$
$$= 6.21\%$$

TABLE 13.12 Frequency Distribution and Associated Probabilities

Computed Rate of Return	Frequency in Ten Trials	Probability
12	1	0.10
13	1	0.10
15	4	0.40
16	2	0.20
19	1	0.10
21	1	0.10
	10	1.00

13.7 DECISION TREE ANALYSIS

In capital budgeting some investment opportunities may involve a sequence of decisions over time. Thus, future decisions may be affected by actions that are taken at the present. Often decisions made without taking into account their long-term effects result in nonoptimum solutions. In such problems an analytical technique, called a *decision tree* (or *decision* diagram or decision flow diagram), can be used to take into account sequences of decisions and known probabilities of future events. The name *decision tree* describes the graphical appearance of a time diagram used to illustrate variable outcomes and sequencial decisions over time.

Since when many different outcomes are possible over a period of time, such a time diagram ends up having many branches and the diagram often ends up looking very much like a drawing of a tree. It shows branches for each possible alternative for a given decision and branches for each possible outcome (i.e., event) that can result from each alternative. A given decision tree drawing starts at the left and moves to the right until it reaches the end of the project life. It is drawn in the same order as the actual sequence in which the decision choices and possible outcomes occur in practice. The nodes of the tree from which the branches of the tree emanate are either called *decision nodes* and represented by a square figure or are called *chance nodes* and represented by a circle. The occurrence of a chance event can be thought to be a random variable over which the decision maker has no control. The sum of the probabilities of occurrence of different branches that emanate from a decision node is 1.0. Obviously, such decision trees can reduce abstract thinking to a logical visual representation of cause and effect. It is customary to show the costs and revenues (or in terms of NPW or NAW, etc.) related to each of the decision alternatives and the possible chance outcomes (i.e., the probabilities) on the associated branches of the tree.[†]

Example 13.11 Assume that a company is considering an investment proposal. If the project is accepted, the first cost of the project will be either $100,000 with a probability of 0.4 or $150,000 with a probability of 0.6. The resulting annual after-tax cash flow[‡] will be either $25,000 with a probability of 0.6 or $30,000 with a probability of 0.4 for the next 10 years. Assume that the after-tax MARR of the company is 10%, and that the salvage value will be zero at the end of useful life of the project. Use the decision tree approach and determine the following:

[†]For more information see Raiffa [61], Magee [53–54], Hespos and Strassman [42], and Canada and White [19].
[‡]Of course, the after-tax cash flow (ATCF) is equal to operating revenues minus operating costs minus income taxes.

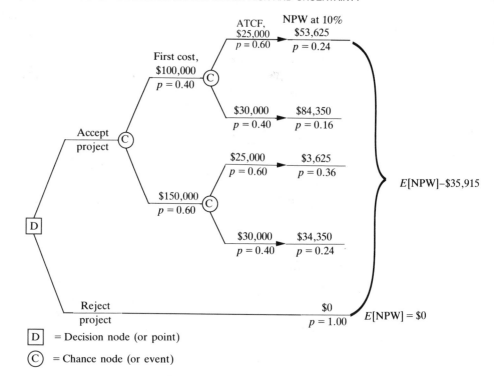

Figure 13.5   Decision-tree diagram for Example 13.11.

(a) Illustrate the problem by drawing its decision tree diagram.
(b) Net present worth of the project with all possible chance outcomes.
(c) Expected net present worth of the project.
(d) Whether or not to accept the project.

Solution

(a) The associated decision tree diagram is shown in Figure 13.5.
(b) Since NPW $= -P + (\text{ATCF})(P/A, 10\%, 10)$, the resulting NPWs,
     with the associated probabilities, are given in Table 13.13.

TABLE 13.13   Data for Example 13.11

(ATCF)(P/A, 10%, 10)	−First Cost	= NPW	Associated Probability
$25,000(6.145)	$100,000	$53,625	0.4(0.6) = 0.24
30,000(6.145)	100,000	84,350	0.4(0.4) = 0.16
25,000(6.145)	150,000	3,625	0.6(0.6) = 0.36
30,000(6.145)	150,000	34,350	0.6(0.4) = 0.24

(c) Expected net present worth of the project is

$$E[\text{NPW}] = \$53{,}625(0.24) + \$84{,}350(0.16) + \$3{,}625(0.36)$$
$$+ \$34{,}350(0.24) = \$35{,}915$$

(d) Based on the expected net present worth, the project should be accepted.

13.8 DECISION MAKING UNDER COMPLETE UNCERTAINTY

If the outcomes are known for different future states but the associated probabilities for the states are unknown (i.e., not even a vague approximation), such situation is called *decision making under complete uncertainty*. At first, decisions under risk and uncertainty are entertained in the same manner; that is, possible future states are recognized, and their outcomes are estimated under the presumption that each state will actually take place. However, under complete uncertainty, since the associated probabilities cannot be determined, some other criteria have to be used to choose the preferred alternative.

13.8.1 Payoff Matrix

The *payoff matrix* is simply a matrix showing the interaction of decision alternatives (i.e., *courses of action*) and a number of possible outcomes (i.e., *states of nature*). Note that in such a matrix the *result* (i.e., effect) of each alternative on each possible outcome is known but the probabilities of occurrence of each possible outcome is not known, as shown in Table 13.14. Note that the states of nature or possible outcomes have been indicated by S_i (i.e., S_1, S_2, and S_3), and the alternatives have been indicated by A, B, C, and D. Even though the individual outcomes (i.e., payoff values) in the payoff matrix shown in Table 13.14 are in millions of dollars, in general, such payoff values can also be qualitative in nature, for example, in utilities. However, it is crucial that they all are given in the same measure of merit such as in NPW or NAW, and so on.

TABLE 13.14   Payoff Matrix in Millions of Dollars of NPW

	States of Nature		
Alternatives	S_1	S_2	S_3
A	1	2	3
B	2	1	4
C	3	2	3
D	−1	1	2

13.8.2   Dominance Criterion

Before applying any decision rules to the payoff matrix, it must be checked for dominance in order to minimize the work involved and at the same time simplify the selection process. In the event that out of two alternatives one would *always* be chosen over the other regardless of which state takes place, this chosen alternative is said to *dominate* the other. Therefore, the dominated alternative can be discarded from any further consideration. For example, alternative D in Table 13.14 can be deleted from any further consideration since it is dominated by other alternatives in each state. The resulting payoff matrix[†] is shown in Table 13.15.

13.8.3   The Laplace Rule or Principle

Consider Table 13.15 and assume that a decision maker (an engineer or engineering manager) were willing to specify probabilities to the states of nature, then such a problem would be considered as decision making involving risk rather than under uncertainty. However, if the decision maker is unwilling to assign probabilities to the states of nature, then one might assume that all possible outcomes are equally likely because there is no particular reason for one state of nature to be more, or less, likely than the others. Therefore, according to the Laplace rule, since all possible outcomes are considered to be equally likely, one can select simply on the basis of expected outcomes as determined using equal probabilities for all outcomes.

Example 13.12   Use the payoff matrix given in Table 13.15 and determine the best alternative using the Laplace principle.

Solution   The expected outcomes can be calculated for each alternative using equal probabilities

TABLE 13.15   Reduced Payoff Matrix in Millions of Dollars of NPW

	States of Nature		
Alternatives	S_1	S_2	S_3
A	1	2	3
B	2	1	4
C	3	2	3

[†]Note that if *all* payoffs for one alternative are better than those of a second alternative, it is called *strict dominance*. Otherwise, if some payoffs are *equal to* and others are *greater than* the corresponding payoffs of the other alternative, it is still called *dominance*.

$$E[A] = \$1 \times 10^6 (\tfrac{1}{3}) + \$2 \times 10^6 (\tfrac{1}{3}) + \$3 \times 10^6 (\tfrac{1}{3}) = \$2 \times 10^6$$

$$E[B] = \$2 \times 10^6 (\tfrac{1}{3}) + \$1 \times 10^6 (\tfrac{1}{3}) + \$4 \times 10^6 (\tfrac{1}{3}) = \$2,333,333$$

$$E[C] = \$3 \times 10^6 (\tfrac{1}{3}) + \$2 \times 10^6 (\tfrac{1}{3}) + \$3 \times 10^6 (\tfrac{1}{3}) = \$2,666,667$$

Note that the probability of occurrence of each outcome is the same and is equal to ($\tfrac{1}{3}$). Thus, based on the expected values, select alternative C.

13.8.4 Maximin and Minimax Rules or Principles

The *maximin* rule is based on an extremely pessimistic (or conservative) view of the outcome of nature. Its application selects an alternative that assures the best of the worst possible outcomes. In other words the decision maker first selects the minimum payoff (profit) that is related to each alternative and then chooses the alternative that maximizes the minimum payoff.

The *minimax* rule is similarly used in the case of costs (or losses) and is also pessimistic in nature. Its application selects an alternative that assures the least of the worst possible outcomes. In other words the decision maker first selects the maximum cost that is related to each alternative and then chooses the alternative that minimizes the maximum cost.

Example 13.13   Use the payoff matrix given in Table 13.15 and determine the following:

(a) Alternative that would maximize the minimum possible profit.
(b) Assume that Table 13.15 gives the cost matrix, find the alternative that would minimize the maximum possible cost.

Solution

(a) The minimum payoffs for alternatives A, B, and C are 1, 1, and 2, respectively. Therefore, select alternative C.
(b) The maximum costs for alternatives A, B, and C are 3, 4, and 3. Thus, it appears that one can select either alternatives A or C. However, at a closer look, one can see that alternative A is better than alternative C.

13.8.5 Maximax and Minimin Rules or Principles

Contrarily to the rules given in Section 13.8.4, both the maximax and minimum rules are based on an extremely optimistic (or nonconservative) view of the outcome of nature. According to the *maximax* rule, the decision maker first selects the maximum payoff (profit) that is related to each alternative and then chooses the alternative that maximizes the maximum payoff.

The *minimin* rule is similarly used in the case of costs (or losses). Accordingly, the decision maker first selects the minimum cost that is related to each alternative and then chooses the alternative that minimizes the minimum cost.

Example 13.14 Use the payoff matrix given in Table 13.15 and determine the following:

(a) Alternative that would maximize the maximum possible profit.
(b) Assume that Table 13.15 gives the cost matrix, find the alternative that would minimize the minimum possible cost.

Solution

(a) The maximum payoffs for alternatives A, B, and C are 3, 4, and 3, respectively. Thus, select alternative B.
(b) The minimum costs for alternatives A, B, and C are 1, 1, 2, respectively. Therefore, it appears that one can select either alternatives A or B. However, at a closer look, one can see that alternative A is better than alternative B.

13.8.6 Hurwicz Rule or Principle

The Hurwicz rule can be used for those situations in which the decision maker feels neither extremely optimistic nor extremely pessimistic. The degree of optimism is established by using a coefficient α, which is called an index of optimism, such that $0 \le \alpha \le 1$. Thus, $\alpha = 0$ is used when the decision maker is pessimistic about the outcome of nature (as in maximin rule), and $\alpha = 1$ is used when the decision maker is optimistic about the outcome of nature (as in maximax rule). Therefore, according to the Hurwicz rule, after choosing an index of optimism α, calculate the weighted outcome: α(value of profit or cost if most pessimistic outcome takes place) $+ (1 - \alpha)$(value of profit or cost if most pessimistic outcome takes place). Hence, based on the results, select the alternative that optimizes the weighted outcome. However, the Hurwicz rule can be criticized due to the difficulty of assigning a particular value to α.

Example 13.15 Consider the payoff matrix given in Table 13.15 and assume that $\alpha = 0.40$. Determine the best alternative based on the Hurwicz rule.

Solution The expected outcome for each alternative is

$$E_A = [0.40(3) + (1 - 0.40)(1)] \times 10^6 = \$1.8 \times 10^6$$
$$E_B = [0.40(4) + (1 - 0.40)(1)] \times 10^6 = \$2.2 \times 10^6$$
$$E_C = [0.40(3) + (1 - 0.40)(2)] \times 10^6 = \$2.4 \times 10^6$$

Therefore, based on the expected payoffs, select alternative C.

13.8.7 Minimax Regret Rule or Savage Principle[†]

In the event that a decision maker chooses an alternative and a state of nature takes place in such a manner that it would have done better by choosing some other alternative, the decision maker *regrets* the original choice. It is similar to the minimax and maximin rules. Here, the *regret* is defined as the difference between the maximum payoff that could have been received and the payoff that was actually obtained from the alternative selected. Therefore, the minimax regret rule is based on the assumption that a decision maker wants to avoid any regret or at least to minimize the maximum regret about a choice. To use the rule, first a *regret matrix* is developed by finding out the maximum payoff for each state (i.e., column). Second, each payoff in the column is subtracted from the maximum payoff that has been recognized, and this process is reiterated for each column. Finally, the alternative that minimizes the maximum regret is then selected.

Example 13.16 Consider the payoff matrix given in Table 13.15 and develop a regret matrix to obtain a solution. Determine the best alternative based on the minimum regret rule.

Solution In Table 13.15 the maximum payoffs for S_1, S_2, and S_3 are 3, 2, and 4, respectively. Therefore, the regrets for S_1, applicable to alternatives A, B, and C, are $(\$3 - \$1) \times 10^6 = \$2 \times 10^6$, $(\$3 - \$2) \times 10^6 = \$1 \times 10^6$, and $(\$3 - \$3) \times 10^6 = \$0$, respectively. Similarly, performing the same process for states S_2 and S_3 produces the regret matrix given in Table 13.16. One can

TABLE 13.16 Regret Matrix in Millions of Dollars of NPW for Example 13.16

Alternative	States of Nature			Maximum of States
	S_1	S_2	S_3	
A	$2	$0	$1	$2
B	1	1	0	1
C	0	0	1	1 (min. of all max.)

[†]It was proposed by L. J. Savage.

see that the highest (or worst) regret is for alternative A, and the lowest regret is for both alternatives B and C. Thus, alternative C is chosen since it provides the minimum of these maximum regrets.[†]

13.9 SOLUTION METHODS FOR MULTIPLE OBJECTIVES AND CRITERIA

There are a large number of quantitative and nonquantitative methods that can be used for the selection of an alternative with multiple attributes, that is, objectives or factors. Some of them are (1) *ordinal scaling*, that is, ranking attributes in order of decreasing importance; (2) *weighting factors*, that is, quantifying the relative importance of attributes on a dimensionless scale from, for example, 0 to 1 or from 0 to 100; (3) *weighted evaluation of alternatives*, that is, first quantifying how well each alternative meets each attribute on a dimensionless scale and then adding the product of the *evaluations* and the respective *weightings* for each alternative; (4) *alternatives–objectives score card*, that is, displaying a matrix of alternatives versus attributes together with numbers and/or other symbols used to show how well each alternative meets each of the objectives; and (5) *multicriteria utility models*, that is, determination of utility functions for individual criteria.[‡]

PROBLEMS

13.1   The variance of an uncertain event x is defined as the expected value of the function $(x - \mu)^2$ that has possible outcomes of $(x_1 - \mu)^2$, $(x_2 - \mu)^2, \ldots,$ and $(x_n - \mu)^2$ with probabilities of occurrence $p_1, p_2, \ldots, p_n$, respectively. If so, verify equation (13.17).

13.2   Assume that the Zubits International Corporation is considering an investment project that has the probabilistic outcomes given in Table P13.2.
Determine the following:
(a) Expected value of the project.
(b) Variance of the project.
(c) Standard deviation of the project.
(d) Range of the outcomes.

[†]Note that alternative C is chosen over alternative B since it provides minimum regrets under both states of S_1 and S_2.

[‡]Note that detailed presentations of these methods are beyond the scope of this book; interested readers should see Canada and White [19]; White, Agee, and Case [74]; Gönen and Foote [35]; DeGarmo, Canada, and Sullivan [23]; Riggs [62]; and Ackoff and Sasieni [1].

TABLE P13.2   Data for Problem 13.2

Outcome x_j	Probability of Occurrence $P(x_j)$
−$100,000	0.25
350,000	0.50
500,000	0.25

13.3 Assume that the XYZ Company is considering an investment project that has the probabilistic outcomes given in Table P13.3. Determine the following:

(a) Expected value of the project.

(b) Variance of the project.

(c) Standard deviation of the project.

(d) Range of the outcomes.

TABLE P13.3   Data for Problem 13.3

Outcome x_j	Probability of Occurrence $P(x_j)$
−$100,000	0.40
150,000	0.20
200,000	0.30
250,000	0.10

13.4 Assume that the NP & NL Utility Company is required to serve a newly developed residential area. There are two possible routes for the construction of the necessary power line. Route A goes around a lake and will be built as an overhead line; route B is an underwater line that goes across the lake using submarine power cables. Table P13.4 gives the installed investment cost and the probability of failure for each alternative. If a loss does occur in alternative A, it will cost $100,000 per year to repair with a probability of 0.60 and $150,000 per year with a probability of 0.40; whereas if a loss does occur in alternative B, it will cost $200,000 per year to repair with a probability of 0.50 and $250,000 per year with a probability of 0.50. Assume that the probabilities of a failure, if it does take place. Assume that the NL & NP Company uses an annual fixed charge rate that includes the cost of depreciation, interest on investment, and O&M expenses, and it is based on 15% of any investment. Determine the best alternative with respect to expected total annual cost.

TABLE P13.4   Data for Problem 13.4

Alternative	Installed Investment Cost	Probability of Failure in any Given Year
A	$1,000,000	0.15
B	2,000,000	0.001

13.5 Assume that an engineering manager is considering an investment project. The optimistic, most likely, and pessimistic estimates for its various parameters are given in Table P13.5. Determine the following:

(a) Expected value of the first cost.

(b) Expected value of the net annual revenue.

(c) Expected value of the useful life.

(d) Expected value of the salvage.

(e) Expected value of the rate of return from the investment project.

TABLE P13.5   Data for Problem 13.5

Parameter	Optimistic (O) Estimate	Most Likely (M) Estimate	Pessimistic (P) Estimate
First cost	$50,000	$60,000	$40,000
Net annual revenue	$10,000	$8,000	$5,000
Useful life	10 years	10 years	10 years
Salvage value	$2,000	$1,000	0

13.6 Assume that there are two prospective investment projects of 1-year duration likely to generate net revenues at the end of 1 year under different conditions of the economy as given in Table P13.6. Assume that the chance of having each of these conditions is equally the same. Determine the following:

(a) Expected value of project A.

(b) Standard deviation of project A.

(c) Expected value of project B.

(d) Standard deviation of project B.

(e) Coefficient of variation for each project.

(f) Based on the risk involved, select one of the projects.

TABLE P13.6   Data for Problem 13.6

Condition of Economy	Net Revenues	
	Project A	Project B
Expansion	$20,500	$12,000
Stable	10,000	10,000
Recession	−500	8,000

13.7 Assume that an engineering manager wants to develop the probability distribution for the future salvage value of a piece of equipment at the end of 6 years. The estimate of salvage value has a range from $0 to $5,000 with the most likely value being $2,000 with a probability of 21%. It is estimated that there is a 17% chance of salvage value being $1,500. Since it is expected that the extreme values of $0 and $5,000 are not likely to take place, an S-shaped curve is chosen to represent the cumulative distribution function. Determine the following:

(a) Draw the cumulative probability distribution function by using the curve-fitting technique to the extremely sparse data.

(b) Transform the cumulative probability distribution function drawn in part (a) into the probability mass distribution function (in terms of frequency histogram) by using intervals of $500.

(c) Prepare a table that presents the midpoints of intervals and the associated probabilities that provide the probability mass distribution function.

13.8 Consider the solutions of Example 13.7 and determine the corresponding equivalent points on the standardized normal distribution.

13.9 Repeat Example 13.8 but assume that the sample size is six and that the cars speeding with mean and standard deviation of 60 and 5 miles per hour, respectively.

13.10 Assume that the Blue Grass Investment Corporation has a MARR of 15% and is considering a project proposal. The investment requirement of the project is given with the expected value and variance of $24,000 and 3×10^6, respectively. The net annual cash flows at the end of each year, for the next 8 years, are given with expected value and variance as $3,000 and 3×10^4, respectively. Determine the following:

(a) Expected value of the NPW of the project.

(b) Variance of the NPW of the project.

(c) Probability of a positive NPW.

13.11 Consider Example 13.9 and determine the probability of a positive NPW.

13.12 Repeat Example 13.10 but assume that the useful life of the equipment is uniformly distributed and ranges from 8 to 16 years. (Note that the probability of each given useful life is the same and is equal to 0.20.)

13.13 Repeat Example 13.11 but assume that the first cost of the project will be either $80,000 with a probability of 0.6 or $120,000 with a probability of 0.4. The resulting annual after-tax cash flow will be either $15,000 with a probability of 0.25 or $18,000 with a probability of 0.75. Use a useful life of 8 years and after-tax MARR of 12%.

13.14 Use the payoff matrix given in Table P13.14 and repeat Example 13.12.

TABLE P13.14 Payoff Matrix in Millions of Dollars of NPW

	States of Nature		
Alternatives	S_1	S_2	S_3
A	2	1	4
B	3	2	1
C	1	5	2

13.15 Use the payoff matrix given in Table P13.14 and repeat Example 13.13.

13.16 Use the payoff matrix given in Table P13.14 and repeat Example 13.14.

13.17 Use the payoff matrix given in Table P13.14 and repeat Example 13.15.

13.18 Use the payoff matrix given in Table P13.14 and repeat Example 13.16.

_____14
CAPITAL BUDGETING CONSIDERATIONS

An "engineer" is one who can do with a dollar what any bungler can do with two.

ARTHUR WELLINGTON, 1887

14.1 INTRODUCTION

Capital budgeting is one of the most important aspects of management decision making because the conception, continuing existence, and growth of a successful company totally depend on the selection and implementation of sound investments. In general, a company may continuously have a number of investment opportunities. However, in most cases, the amount of available capital is limited, or additional amounts can only be raised at increasingly large incremental costs. Therefore, such a company has a problem of *budgeting* (or *allocating* or *rationing*) the available capital among competing projects. Thus, *capital budgeting* can be defined as the collection of decisions by the company as to where the money for *capital expenditures* will come from and how it will be allocated among the various competing projects. Hence, such capital rationing occurs anytime there is a budget ceiling, or constraint, on the amount of funds that can be invested during a particular period of time, such as a year. Such budgetary constraints exist especially in those companies that have a policy of financing all capital expenditures internally. It is possible that in a large company each division, or department, is permitted to decide on capital expenditures[†] only up to a specified budget ceiling, over which the division, or department, has no control. With such capital rationing constraints, the company attempts to select the combination of investment proposals that will provide the greatest profitability in terms of rate of returns. Note that the possible sources of investment capital has already been reviewed briefly in Chapter 5.

[†]For an excellent treatment of the subject, see Smith [66].

14.2 TYPES OF INVESTMENT PROJECTS

For the purpose of capital budgeting, investment projects (i.e., capital expenditure alternatives) can be categorized as follows:

Independent Projects Two projects are defined to be economically independent if the acceptance or rejection of one does not measurably alter the cash flow stream generated by one project or does not affect the acceptance or rejection of the other; for example, a manufacturing company's prospective investment in special-purpose manufacturing robots and its prospective investment in trucks.

Mutually Exclusive Projects Two projects are defined to be mutually exclusive (or substitute) if the acceptance of one completely (technically or economically) prevents the acceptance of the other. In other words, mutually exclusive projects are *substitutes* for each other. For example, assume that a vacant land site can be used for building a gas station or supermarket on it but not both. Thus, a building decision of one excludes the other.

Dependent Projects Two projects are defined to be dependent if the expected cash flows of one are affected by (i.e., *contingent upon*) the acceptance or rejection of the other. Therefore, one is the *prerequisite* for the other. For example, the project of building a gas station depends on the decision of whether or not purchasing a particular vacant lot.

Complementary Projects Two projects are defined as complementary if the acceptance of both will increase the expected cash flows of each over what these flows would have been if only one of them were accepted. For example, a project of building a new road to a lake area and a project of building a resort area at the lake shore are complementary projects. Since development of the resort area may enhance the benefits of the road project greater than if the resort area were not developed and the construction of the road may make the benefits of the resort area greater than if the road were not constructed.

Imperfect Mutually Exclusive Projects Two projects are defined to be imperfect mutually exclusive if the acceptance of one of the projects discourages the acceptance of the other. Such projects are also called *imperfect substitute*. For example, purchasing a motorcycle versus purchasing a car.

Imperfect Dependent Projects Two projects are defined to be imperfect dependent projects if the acceptance of one of them encourages the acceptance of the other. For example, possession of a car encourages possession of a garage and vice versa, but neither is a prerequisite of the other.

Mandatory Projects The projects are defined to be mandatory projects if the acceptance of the projects are compulsory; for example, safety, or OSHA, related projects. None of these expenditures produce income by themselves, but all are necessary expenditures required for the continued operation of some important function.

14.3 CAPITAL RATIONING

As said before, *rationing* of capital takes place whenever the capital available for investment is not enough to allow the company to accept all otherwise acceptable prospective projects. In general, restrictions on funds for investment take place because of limitations dictated either by management (i.e., internal to the company) or by the capital market (i.e., external to the company). Usually, the internal capital rationing takes place (1) as a result of management decision to limit the total amount of capital available for capital expenditures to a fixed amount in a given time period or (2) as a result of management decision to set a cutoff rate for capital investments that is greater than the cost of capital to the company (in other words when MARR is higher than the cost of capital to the company). As a result of such capital rationing, some projects are rejected even though they would otherwise be acceptable from a profitability point of view if enough investment capital were available, as it is illustrated in Figure 14.1. On the other hand external capital rationing takes place when the company cannot obtain sufficient funds at an acceptable cost of capital. As shown in Figure 14.2, the cost of capital increases after a certain amount. Note that the intersection of the *incremental* rate of return curve with the *marginal* cost of capital curve dictates the amount to be raised and the amount of capital to be invested for the period.

Of course, in general, it is not possible that the total capital requirements of the entire set of alternative projects match exactly the investment funds at hand. Therefore, it is forseeable that even though a large number of smaller prospective projects individually will need only a small proportion of the investment capital available, some large prospective projects may need the use of a large proportion of the investment capital available. Therefore, it is possible to have a trade-off in the project selection process between, for example, a single large prospective project and several smaller prospective projects.

The cost to the company of a budget ceiling might be regarded as the *opportunity foregone* on the next profitable investment after the cutoff. The MARR sets a lower limit, that is, the project proposals yielding less than this required rate will not be accepted even if the budget were not exhausted. However, capital rationing usually results in an investment policy that is less than optimal. In some periods the company accepts prospective projects down to its MARR; in others it may reject prospective projects that would provide returns substantially in excess of the required rate.

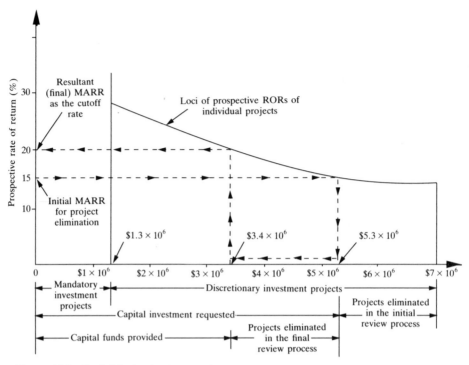

Figure 14.1 Capital budgeting process involving both mutually exclusive and independent investment project alternatives.

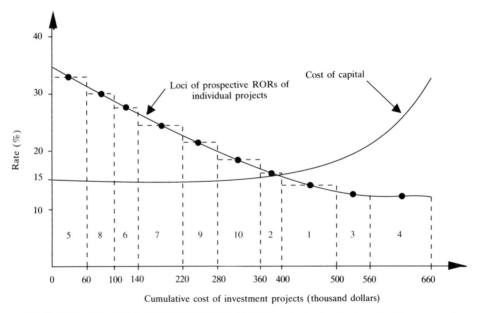

Figure 14.2 Cumulative cost of investment projects versus rate of return and the marginal cost of capital.

358

Figure 14.1 illustrates the capital budgeting process involving both mutually exclusive and independent investment project alternatives. Note that the investment projects are classified in terms of mandatory investment projects and discretionary investment projects and that first the mandatory investment projects of $1,300,000 are funded regardless of their prospective rates of return, if any. After the mandatory investment projects the rate of return for each of the discretionary investment projects are calculated, and then the associated projects are ranked in order of decreasing rate of return. Figure 14.1 shows the resulting loci of prospective rate of returns of individual projects and the projects eliminated in the initial review process. After the initial reduction, based on an initial MARR of 15%, a capital investment of $5,300,000 has been requested. However, after the second and final review process, only capital funds of $3,400,000 have been provided that, in turn, has caused the resultant (or final) MARR to increase to 20% as the cutoff rate of return. Note that for any set of ranked projects of any capital budget, the rate of return at which the budget is used up totally is called the *cutoff rate of return* [46]. Furthermore, also note that this cutoff rate of return is the *opportunity cost*, that is, the rate of return on the opportunity or project foregone, and also is the MARR.

In general, in order to take into account the after-tax effects of each prospective investment project, it is recommended to use the after-tax rate of return rather than the before-tax rate of return of each project in ranking them for the capital budgeting purposes. Furthermore, such after-tax rates of return should be adjusted based on the risks invoved.

Example 14.1 Assume that ABC Company is considering 10 independent projects given in Table 14.1 for investment. The table gives the required amount of investment, uniform annual after-tax cash flow at the end of each of the next 5 years, and computed rate of return for each project. Assume

TABLE 14.1 Data for Example 14.1

Project	Investment	Uniform Annual After-Tax Cash Flow (ATCF)	Computed Rate of Return (ROR)(%)
1	$100,000	$29,832	15
2	40,000	15,702	17
3	60,000	17,477	14
4	100,000	29,128	14
5	60,000	26,069	33
6	40,000	15,802	28
7	80,000	29,748	25
8	40,000	16,423	30
9	60,000	20,953	22
10	80,000	26,164	19

that the cost of capital is constant, at 15%, up to an amount of $310,000. Note that after $310,000, the cost of capital substantially increases. For example, it is 16.5, 26, and 32% for $400,000, $600,000, and $660,000, respectively. Also assume that the risk of each project is the same and that the salvage value of each project is zero.

Determine the following:

(a) Rank the investment projects based on their prospective rates of return and plot the results. Draw the loci of prospective RORs of individual projects.

(b) Plot the resultant marginal cost of capital curve, based on the given values, by superimposing it on the plot of part (a).

(c) Based on the results of parts (a) and (b), which projects should be selected and how much capital should be raised?

(d) If a capital budget of $280,000 is available, what is the cutoff rate of return (or opportunity cost of capital foregone)?

Solution

(a) The given investment projects, based on their prospective rates of return, has been ranked, and the results have been plotted, as shown in Figure 14.2. Note the way that the loci of prospective RORs of individual projects has been drawn.

(b) The resulting marginal cost of capital curve, based on the given values, has been superimposed on the plot of part (a), as shown in Figure 14.2.

(c) The intersection of the *incremental* rate of return curve (or the loci of prospective RORs of individual projects) with the marginal cost of capital curve determines the amount of capital to be raised and the amount of funds to be invested. Therefore, the amount of capital to be raised and invested is $400,000. Thus, the selected projects are projects 5, 8, 6, 7, 9, 10, and 2.

(d) If the available capital budget is $280,000, the projects that should be selected are projects 5, 8, 6, 7, and 9. Therefore, the cutoff rate of return (or the opportunity cost of capital foregone) is between 19 and 22%.

14.4   EFFECTS OF CAPITAL BUDGETING

Succinctly put, capital budgeting is the process in which independent investment opportunities compete for available (and usually limited) funds. According to Smith [66], such capital budgeting process can assist management to (1) prevent financial overcommitment, (2) prevent overlapping or conflicting projects, (3) establish project priorities based on a comparative and objective approach, (4) plan the long-run future of the organization, (5) stabilize the long-run capital expenditure pattern, and (6) put emphasis on the requirement for continuing search to discover new investment opportunities.

Example 14.2 Assume that Green Green Grass of Home Investment Company is considering various capital expenditure opportunities and that each prospective project is expected to produce a uniform after-tax cash flow (ATCF) at the end of each of the next 6 years, as shown in Table 14.2. The salvage value of each project at the end of its useful life is negligible and the risk associated with each project is the same. Also assume that alternative projects with the same prefix number represent mutually exclusive (i.e., substitute) alternatives. For example, 1A versus 1B or 2A versus 2C are mutually exclusive with respect to each other, respectively; whereas those projects with different prefix numbers represent independent projects. For example, 1A versus 2A or 2B versus 3C are independent projects with respect to each other, respectively. Also take into account the do-nothing alternatives and determine the following:

(a) The rate of return for each alternative investment.
(b) The incremental rate of return for each incremental investment. Present the results in a table.
(c) Use the rates of return found in parts (a) and (b) and Smith's [66] network diagrams to rank the associated incremental investment projects and give the results in a table.

Solution

(a) Since each investment will produce an ATCF over the next 6 years, use capital the capital recovery factor of $(A/P, i\%, 6)$ to determine

TABLE 14.2 Data for Example 14.2

Project	Investment	ATCF
1A	$20,000	$5,400
1B	30,000	9,800
1C	50,000	15,000
2A	20,000	6,000
2B	30,000	12,000
2C	40,000	18,000
3A	20,000	7,500
3B	40,000	16,500
3C	60,000	21,000

the rate of return for each project. For example, for investment project 1A, the capital recovery factor is

$$(A/P, i\%, 6) = \$5,400/\$20,000 = 0.27000$$

Since from Table A.4, $(A/P, 15\%, 6) = 0.26424$ and $(A/P, 18\%, 6) = 0.28591$, the rate of return on the project 1A is

$$i = 15\% + 3\%(576/1591) = 16.0861\% \cong 16.1\%$$

Similarly, each ROR of the remaining prospective investments can be found. The resulting RORs are given in Table 14.3 under column 0, where the 0 represents the ROR of the zero amount of incremental (i.e., no additional amount of investment above the given amount of investment).

(b) The incremental rate of return for each incremental investment is found similarly. For example, for incremental investment of (1B–1A), the additional investment of $\$30,000 - \$20,000 = \$10,000$ will produce incremental ATCF of $\$9,800 - \$5,400 = \$4,400$. Thus, the resulting capital recovery factor is

$$(A/P, i\%, 6) = \$4,400/\$10,000 = 0.44000$$

Since from Table A.4, $(A/P, 30\%, 6) = 0.37839$ and $(A/P, 40\%, 6) = 0.46126$, the incremental rate of return on the incremental investment of (1B–1A) is $i = 30\% + 10\%(6,161/8,287) \cong 37.4\%$. Similarly, each ROR of the remaining incremental investments can be found. The resulting ROR values are given in Table 14.3.

TABLE 14.3   Results of Parts (a) and (b) of Example 14.2

Project	Investment	ATCF	Alternative 0 (%)	Alternative A (%)	Alternative B (%)
				IROR on Incremental Investment with Respect to	
1A	$20,000	$5,400	16.1		
1B	30,000	9,800	23.4	37.4	
1C	50,000	15,000	19.9	22.5	42.2
2A	20,000	6,000	19.9		
2B	30,000	12,000	32.6	55.8	
2C	40,000	17,000	38.6	50.2	44.5
3A	20,000	7,500	29.6		
3B	40,000	16,500	34.1	38.6	
3C	60,000	21,000	26.4	24.8	9.3

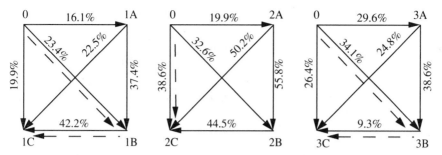

Figure 14.3 Smith's network diagrams for Example 14.2.

(c) Based on the results presented in Table 14.3, the resulting Smith network diagrams are shown in Figure 14.3. The associated incremental investment projects, based on the resulting decision paths that have been indicated on the Smith network diagrams, are given in Table 14.4.

EXAMPLE 14.3 Consider the results found in part (c) of Example 14.2 and determine the following:

(a) Tabulate the results in descending order of incremental rates of return.

(b) Plot the IRORs found in part (a) and draw the loci of prospective IRORs of the projects.

(c) Use the plot drawn in part (b) and determine the cutoff IRORs and the acceptable projects when available investment capital is (1) zero, (2) $130,000, and (3) $150,000. Tabulate the results.

(d) Assume that internally available investment capital is $100,000, but the top management of the company has decided to invest into projects that provide rates of return equal or greater than the present MARR of 20%. Find the amount of externally raised investment capital that is necessary and the projects that are to be funded.

TABLE 14.4 Incremental Investment Projects Based on Smith's Network Diagram Method

Project	Incremental Investment	IROR (%)
1B	$30,000	23.4
1C–1B	20,000	42.2
2C	40,000	38.6
3B	40,000	34.1
3C–3B	20,000	9.3

TABLE 14.5 Incremental Investment Projects Tabulated in Descending Order of IRORs

Project	Incremental Investment	IROR (%)
1C–1B	$20,000	42.2
2C	40,000	38.6
3B	40,000	34.1
1B	30,000	23.4
3C–3B	20,000	9.3

Solution

(a) The results found in part (c) of Example 14.2 have been tabulated in descending order of incremental rates of return and the results are given in Table 14.5.

(b) The IRORs found in part (a) have been plotted in Figure 14.4.

(c) The cutoff IRORs and the associated projects based on the available investment capital amounts are given in Table 14.6. For example, if the investment capital available is $130,000, the sum acceptable projects are (1C–1B) + (2C) + (3B) + (1B) or 1C + 2C + 3B. This is due to the fact that −1B and +1B would cancel each other.

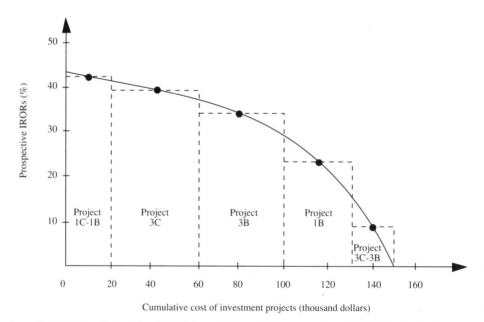

Figure 14.4 Cumulative cost of investment projects versus incremental rate of return.

TABLE 14.6 Investment Capital Available versus Associated IRORs

Investment Capital Available	Investment Projects Accepted	Cutoff IROR (%)
$0	None	Over 42.2
$130,000	1C, 2C, 3B	Between 9.3 and 23.4
$150,000	1C, 2C, 3C	Less than 9.3

(d) If top management has decided to invest into projects that provide rates of return equal or greater than 23.4%, projects 1C, 2C, and 3B will be accepted at a total investment capital requirement of $130,000. Since only $100,000 capital is available internally, the company has to raise $30,000 externally. Otherwise, if the company cannot raise the $30,000, the opportunity cost of funds will be the rate of return foregone, that is, 23.4%. Note that this is also equal to the cutoff rate and the MARR for investment purposes.

14.5 FACTORS AFFECTING CAPITAL BUDGETING

In addition to the factors mentioned in the previous sections, there are other factors that influence the overall level and particular combination of capital expenditures for a given period. These include (1) the financial policy of the company; (2) financial policies of the state or federal governments in terms of tax rates, investment credit, depreciation methods and associated property lives, changes in tax treatment of capital gains or losses, and other financial incentives; (3) balanced growth of the company in terms of its operational scope; (4) forecasted scales demand in the future; (5) managerial attitudes in terms of acting rapidly, effectively, and decisively in searching, formulation, beginning, and finishing investment projects; and (6) coordination among physical and financial plans of the company. Also, under certain circumstances holding back the resources of the company for ambiguously estimated future investment projects with unreliably estimated returns may be necessary. Thus, holding back the investment ability and reserving it for future projects may be justifiable. Therefore, when mutually exclusive investment opportunities (including the do-nothing alternative for each project) exist, the relative attractiveness of each of such projects must be judged based on the amount of the incremental rate of return on the incremental investments.

Furthermore, at times, it is almost inevitable to avoid personal biases in terms of psychological and personal interests, to play an important role in the decision-making process. For example, often a manager's salary and bonuses are subject to the annual performance of his or her department or division as measured by the accounting "profit" reported. Often a project will have a long economic life (e.g., manufacturing a product that is at the R&D stage or at the initial market-capturing stage) and may not provide any measurable gain in profits for several years, whereas the projects with short lives may show profit improvements right away. Therefore, managers often prefer projects with short lives over the ones with long lives despite the fact that the latter ones may provide much greater rates of return. As a result, often larger companies are not as innovative as young and small companies because a young company is often managed by an *enterpreneur* who will not be judged only on a profit picture based on a short time period. Therefore, an enterpreneur can take the *risk* of not showing a profit for several years.

14.6 CAPITAL BUDGETING UNDER RISK AND UNCERTAINTY

The concept of economic decision making under risk and uncertainty has been reviewed in Chapter 13. Risk considerations can be specifically included in the analysis of investments under capital rationing using the methods given in Chapter 13 when selection among competing prospective investment projects must be made. Further, it is possible to have two or more MARR figures according to risk levels. For example, a company may use a MARR of 45% for high-risk projects, a MARR of 30% for moderate-risk projects, and a MARR of 15% for low-risk projects. The method of determining such MARR values is the same as illustrated in Figure 14.1. Therefore, the company can rank prospective investment projects in each risk group based on their rates of return and investment requirements. After temporarily deciding the amount of investment capital that should be allocated to each risk group, the company can then decide the MARR values for each risk group using the method illustrated in Figure 14.1 for a single group. Furthermore, the company can, if necessary, reallocate its investment capital based on the alternatives available in each risk group and, therefore, can affect the MARR for each group. Of course, the higher the risk, the higher the return that the company has to take.

However, in general, the simplest way to take into account risk and uncertainty with respect to various elements (e.g., life, future cash flows, and/or rate of return) of a given project is to perform a sensitivity analysis. It is always recommended to see how much the estimates can change, in both directions, without changing the indicated decision. Such a sensitivity analysis always provides an insight into the degree of uncertainty that is tolerable in the decision process. Of course, the more sensitive an economy study result is to a given estimate and the greater the importance of the study to the company, the greater the effort is justified for that estimate.

Furthermore, it is possible to have inflation and deflation over a long period of time. However, if the investment alternatives that are under consideration are not different in nature, the effects of the inflation or deescalation will relatively be the same. Therefore, the differences among the alternatives will relatively be the same as if the effects of inflation and deflation had been taken into account in the computed results. However, if there are substantial differences in the nature of the investment alternatives, it is recommended to take inflation and deflation into account in the calculations.

PROBLEMS

14.1 Assume that Blue Grass Investment Company has a number of investment alternatives, as shown in Table P14.1. Note that additional information on ATCF, salvage values, useful lives, and so forth are provided for the calculation but not shown in the table. The table shows only the investment capital requirements and the calculated IRORs of the projects. Assume that alternative projects with the same prefix number represent mutually exclusive alternatives, whereas those projects with different prefix numbers represent independent projects. Also, take into account the do-nothing alternatives and determine the following:

(**a**) Use the IRORs given and rank the investment alternatives using Smith's network diagram method.

(**b**) Present the results of part (a) in a table.

TABLE P14.1   Data for Problem 14.1

| Project | Investment | IROR on Incremental Investment with Respect to | | |
		Alternative 0 (%)	Alternative A (%)	Alternative B (%)
1A	$100,000	25		
1B	200,000	20	22	
1C	300,000	15	16	8
2A	100,000	30		
2B	200,000	28	18	
2C	300,000	21	12	10
3A	100,000	19		
3B	200,000	14	17	
3C	300,000	10	13	11
4A	100,000	15		

14.2 Consider the results found in part (b) of Problem 14.1 and do the following:

(a) Tabulate the results in descending order of incremental rates of return.

(b) Plot the IRORs found in part (a) and draw the loci of prospective IRORs of the projects.

(c) Use the plot drawn in part (b) and determine the cutoff IRORs and acceptable projects when available investment capital is (1) $400,000, (2) $700,000, and (3) $1,000,000.

(d) Assume that internally available capital is $600,000, but the top management of the company has decided to invest into projects that provide rates of return that are equal or greater than the present MARR of 15%. Determine the amount of externally raised investment capital that is necessary and the projects that are to be funded.

14.3 Assume that Ghost City Company has a number of investment alternatives as are shown in Table P14.3. Note that additional information on ATCF, salvage values, useful lives, and so forth are provided for the calculation but not shown in the table. The table shows only the investment capital requirements and the calculated IRORs of the projects. Assume that alternative projects with the same prefix number represent mutually exclusive alternatives, whereas those projects with different prefix numbers represent independent projects. Also take into account the do-nothing alternatives and determine the following:

(a) Use the given IRORs and rank the investment alternatives using Smith's network diagram method.

(b) Present the results of part (a) in a table.

TABLE P14.3   Data for Problem 14.3

| | | IROR on Incremental Investment with Respect to | | |
| | | Alternative 0 | Alternative A | Alternative B |
Project	Investment	(%)	(%)	(%)
1A	$10,000	20		
1B	20,000	18	19	
1C	30,000	15	16	14
2A	10,000	25		
2B	20,000	22	17	
2C	30,000	20	14	12
3A	10,000	18		
3B	20,000	16	15	
3C	30,000	13	12	10

14.4 Consider the results found in part (a) of Problem 14.3 and do the following:

   (a) Tabulate the results in descending order of incremental rates of return.

   (b) Plot the IRORs found in part (a) and draw the loci of perspective IRORs of the projects.

   (c) Use the plot drawn in part (b) and determine the cutoff IRORs and acceptable projects when available investment capital is (1) $40,000, (2) $60,000, and (3) $90,000.

   (d) Find the opportunity cost if the available investment capital is $80,000.

   (e) Find the acceptable projects if the MARR is 15%.

14.5 Assume that Okie Company has a number of prospective projects as are shown in Table P14.5. Assume that alternative projects with the same prefix number represent mutually exclusive alternatives, whereas those projects with different prefix numbers represent independent projects. Also, take into account the do-nothing alternatives and determine the following:

   (a) Use the given IRORs and rank the investment alternatives using Smith's network diagram method.

   (b) Present the results of part (a) in a table.

   (c) Tabulate the results in descending order of incremental rates of return.

TABLE P14.5 Data for Problem 14.5

| | | IROR on Incremental Investment with Respect to | | |
| | | Alternative 0 | Alternative A | Alternative B |
Project	Investment	(%)	(%)	(%)
1A	$10,000	18		
1B	30,000	15	12	
2A	10,000	20		
2B	20,000	14	13	
2C	30,000	10	11	9
3A	10,000	16		

APPENDIX A
INTEREST TABLES

TABLE A.1 $i = \frac{1}{2}\%$ **Interest Factors for Discrete Compounding Periods**

	Single Payment		Uniform Payment Series				Gradient Series		
	Compound Amount Factor	Present Worth Factor	Present Worth Factor	Capital Recovery Factor	Compound Amount Factor	Sinking-Fund Factor	Gradient Uniform Series	Gradient Present Worth	Gradient Future Worth
	Find F Given P	Find P Given F	Find P Given A	Find A Given P	Find F Given A	Find A Given F	Find A Given G	Find P Given G	Find F Given G
N	F/P	P/F	P/A	A/P	F/A	A/F	A/G	P/G	F/G
1	1.005	0.9950	0.995	1.0050	1.000	1.0000	0.000	0.000	0.00
2	1.010	0.9901	1.985	0.5038	2.005	0.4998	0.499	0.990	1.00
3	1.015	0.9851	2.970	0.3367	3.015	0.3317	0.997	2.960	3.00
4	1.020	0.9802	3.950	0.2531	4.030	0.2481	1.494	5.901	6.00
5	1.025	0.9754	4.926	0.2030	5.050	0.1980	1.990	9.803	10.00
6	1.030	0.9705	5.896	0.1696	6.076	0.1646	2.485	14.655	15.20
7	1.036	0.9657	6.862	0.1457	7.106	0.1407	2.980	20.449	21.20
8	1.041	0.9609	7.823	0.1278	8.141	0.1228	3.474	27.176	28.20
9	1.046	0.9561	8.779	0.1139	9.182	0.1089	3.967	34.824	36.40
10	1.051	0.9513	9.730	0.1028	10.228	0.0978	4.459	43.386	45.60
11	1.056	0.9466	10.677	0.0937	11.279	0.0887	4.950	52.853	55.80
12	1.062	0.9419	11.619	0.0861	12.336	0.0811	5.441	63.214	67.20
13	1.067	0.9372	12.556	0.0796	13.397	0.0746	5.930	74.460	79.40
14	1.072	0.9326	13.489	0.0741	14.464	0.0691	6.419	86.583	92.80
15	1.078	0.9279	14.417	0.0694	15.537	0.0644	6.907	99.574	107.40
16	1.083	0.9233	15.340	0.0652	16.614	0.0602	7.394	113.424	122.80
17	1.088	0.9187	16.259	0.0615	17.697	0.0565	7.880	128.123	139.40
18	1.094	0.9141	17.173	0.0582	18.786	0.0532	8.366	143.663	157.20
19	1.099	0.9096	18.082	0.0553	19.880	0.0503	8.850	160.036	176.00
20	1.105	0.9051	18.987	0.0527	20.979	0.0477	9.334	177.232	195.80

21	1.110	0.9006	19.888	0.0503	22.084	0.0453	9.817	195.243	216.80
22	1.116	0.8961	20.784	0.0481	23.194	0.0431	10.299	214.061	283.80
23	1.122	0.8916	21.676	0.0461	24.310	0.0411	10.781	233.677	262.00
24	1.127	0.8872	22.563	0.0443	25.432	0.0393	11.261	254.082	286.40
25	1.133	0.8828	23.446	0.0427	26.559	0.0377	11.741	275.269	311.80
26	1.138	0.8784	24.324	0.0411	27.692	0.0361	12.220	297.228	338.40
27	1.144	0.8740	25.198	0.0397	28.830	0.0347	12.698	319.952	366.00
28	1.150	0.8697	26.068	0.0384	29.975	0.0334	13.175	343.433	395.00
29	1.156	0.8653	26.933	0.0371	31.124	0.0321	13.651	367.663	424.80
30	1.161	0.8610	27.794	0.0360	32.280	0.0310	14.126	392.632	456.00
31	1.167	0.8567	28.6508	0.0349	33.441	0.0299	14.6012	418.355	488.20
32	1.173	0.8525	29.5033	0.0339	34.609	0.0289	15.0750	444.762	521.80
33	1.179	0.8482	30.3515	0.0329	35.782	0.0279	15.5480	471.906	556.40
34	1.185	0.8440	31.1955	0.0321	36.961	0.0271	16.0202	499.758	592.20
35	1.191	0.8398	32.0354	0.0312	38.145	0.0262	16.4915	528.312	629.00
40	1.2208	0.8191	36.1721	0.0276	44.1587	0.0226	18.836	681.335	831.74
45	1.2516	0.7990	40.2071	0.0249	50.3240	0.0199	21.160	850.420	1064.80
50	1.2832	0.7793	44.1427	0.0227	56.6450	0.0177	23.462	1035.697	1329.00
55	1.3156	0.7601	47.9813	0.0208	63.1256	0.0158	25.745	1235.160	1625.00
60	1.3488	0.7414	51.7254	0.0193	69.7698	0.0143	28.006	1448.646	1953.96
65	1.3829	0.7231	55.3773	0.0181	76.5818	0.0131	30.247	1675.160	2316.36
70	1.4178	0.7053	58.9393	0.0170	83.5658	0.0120	32.468	1913.643	2713.16
75	1.4536	0.6879	62.4135	0.0160	90.7262	0.0110	34.668	2164.200	3145.24
80	1.4903	0.6710	65.8022	0.0152	98.0674	0.0102	36.847	2424.646	3613.48
85	1.5280	0.6545	69.107	0.0145	105.594	0.0095	39.006	2694.900	4118.80
90	1.5666	0.6383	72.331	0.0138	113.311	0.0088	41.145	2976.077	4662.20
95	1.6061	0.6226	75.475	0.0132	121.22	0.0082	43.263	3265.600	5244.00
100	1.6467	0.6073	78.542	0.0127	129.33	0.0077	45.361	3562.793	5866.00
∞	∞	0.0000	200.000	0.0050	∞	0.0000	200.000	40000.000	∞

TABLE A.2 $i = 1\%$ **Interest Factors for Discrete Compounding Periods**

	Single Payment		Uniform Payment Series				Gradient Series		
	Compound Amount Factor	Present Worth Factor	Present Worth Factor	Capital Recovery Factor	Compound Amount Factor	Sinking-Fund Factor	Gradient Uniform Series	Gradient Present Worth	Gradient Future Worth
	Find F Given P	Find P Given F	Find P Given A	Find A Given P	Find F Given A	Find A Given F	Find A Given G	Find P Given G	Find F Given G
N	F/P	P/F	P/A	A/P	F/A	A/F	A/G	P/G	F/G
1	1.010	0.9901	0.990	1.01000	1.000	1.00000	0.000	0.000	0.00
2	1.020	0.9803	1.970	0.50751	2.010	0.49751	0.498	0.980	1.00
3	1.030	0.9706	2.941	0.34002	3.030	0.33002	0.993	2.921	3.01
4	1.041	0.9610	3.902	0.25628	4.060	0.24628	1.488	5.804	6.04
5	1.051	0.9515	4.853	0.20604	5.101	0.19604	1.980	9.610	10.10
6	1.062	0.9420	5.795	0.17255	6.152	0.16255	2.471	14.321	15.20
7	1.072	0.9327	6.728	0.14863	7.214	0.13863	2.960	19.917	21.35
8	1.083	0.9235	7.652	0.13069	8.286	0.12069	3.448	26.381	28.57
9	1.094	0.9143	8.566	0.11674	9.369	0.10674	3.934	33.696	36.85
10	1.105	0.9053	9.471	0.10558	10.462	0.09558	4.418	41.844	46.22
11	1.116	0.8963	10.368	0.09645	11.567	0.08645	4.901	50.807	56.68
12	1.127	0.8874	11.255	0.08885	12.683	0.07885	5.381	60.569	68.25
13	1.138	0.8787	12.134	0.08241	13.809	0.07241	5.861	71.113	80.93
14	1.149	0.8700	13.004	0.07690	14.947	0.06690	6.338	82.422	94.74
15	1.611	0.8613	13.865	0.07212	16.097	0.06212	6.814	94.481	109.69
16	1.173	0.8528	14.718	0.06794	17.258	0.05794	7.289	107.273	125.79
17	1.184	0.8444	15.562	0.06426	18.430	0.05426	7.761	120.783	143.04
18	1.196	0.8360	16.398	0.06098	19.615	0.05098	8.232	134.996	161.47
19	1.208	0.8277	17.226	0.05805	20.811	0.04805	8.702	149.895	181.09
20	1.220	0.8195	18.046	0.05542	22.019	0.04542	9.169	165.466	201.90

21	1.232	0.8114	18.857	0.05303	23.239	0.04303	9.635	181.695	223.92
22	1.245	0.8034	19.660	0.05086	24.472	0.04086	10.100	198.566	247.16
23	1.257	0.7954	20.456	0.04889	25.716	0.03889	10.563	216.066	271.63
24	1.270	0.7876	21.243	0.04707	26.973	0.03707	11.024	234.180	297.35
25	1.282	0.7798	22.023	0.04541	28.243	0.03541	11.483	252.894	324.32
26	1.295	0.7720	22.795	0.04387	29.526	0.03387	11.941	272.196	352.56
27	1.308	0.7644	23.560	0.04245	30.821	0.03245	12.397	292.070	382.09
28	1.321	0.7568	24.316	0.04112	32.129	0.03112	12.852	312.505	412.91
29	1.335	0.7493	25.066	0.03990	33.450	0.02990	13.304	333.486	445.04
30	1.348	0.7419	25.808	0.03875	34.785	0.02875	13.756	355.002	478.49
31	1.361	0.7346	26.542	0.03768	36.133	0.02768	14.205	377.039	513.27
32	1.375	0.7273	27.270	0.03667	37.494	0.02667	14.653	399.586	549.41
33	1.389	0.7201	27.990	0.03573	38.869	0.02573	15.099	422.629	586.90
34	1.403	0.7130	28.703	0.03484	40.258	0.02484	15.544	446.157	625.77
35	1.417	0.7059	29.409	0.03400	41.660	0.02400	15.987	470.158	666.03
40	1.489	0.6717	32.835	0.03046	48.886	0.02046	18.178	596.856	888.64
45	1.565	0.6391	36.095	0.02771	56.481	0.01771	20.327	733.704	1148.11
50	1.645	0.6080	39.196	0.02551	64.463	0.01551	22.436	879.418	1446.32
55	1.729	0.5785	42.147	0.02373	72.852	0.01373	24.505	1032.815	1785.25
60	1.817	0.5504	44.955	0.02224	81.670	0.01224	26.533	1192.806	2166.97
65	1.909	0.5237	47.627	0.02100	90.937	0.01100	28.522	1358.390	2593.66
70	2.007	0.4983	50.169	0.01993	100.676	0.00993	30.470	1528.647	3067.63
75	2.109	0.4741	52.587	0.01902	110.913	0.00902	32.379	1702.734	3591.28
80	2.2167	0.4511	54.888	0.01822	121.672	0.00822	34.249	1879.877	8334.40
85	2.3298	0.4292	57.078	0.01752	132.979	0.00752	36.080	4119.200	9595.80
90	2.4486	0.4084	59.161	0.01690	144.863	0.00690	37.872	2240.567	10972.60
95	2.5735	0.3886	61.143	0.01636	157.354	0.00636	39.626	4845.200	12470.80
100	2.7048	0.3697	63.029	0.01587	170.481	0.00587	41.342	2605.776	14096.20
∞	∞	0.0000	100.000	0.01000	∞	0.00000	100.000	10000.00	∞

TABLE A.3 $i = 2\%$ Interest Factors for Discrete Compounding Periods

	Single Payment		Uniform Payment Series				Gradient Series		
	Compound Amount Factor	Present Worth Factor	Present Worth Factor	Capital Recovery Factor	Compound Amount Factor	Sinking-Fund Factor	Gradient Uniform Series	Gradient Present Worth	Gradient Future Worth
	Find F Given P	Find P Given F	Find P Given A	Find A Given P	Find F Given A	Find A Given F	Find A Given G	Find P Given G	Find F Given G
N	F/P	P/F	P/A	A/P	F/A	A/F	A/G	P/G	F/G
1	1.020	0.9804	0.980	1.02000	1.000	1.00000	0.000	0.000	0.00
2	1.040	0.9612	1.942	0.51505	2.020	0.49505	0.495	0.961	1.00
3	1.061	0.9423	2.884	0.34675	3.060	0.32675	0.987	2.846	3.02
4	1.082	0.9238	3.808	0.26262	4.122	0.24262	1.475	5.617	6.08
5	1.104	0.9057	4.713	0.21216	5.204	0.19216	1.960	9.240	10.20
6	1.126	0.8880	5.601	0.17853	6.308	0.15853	2.442	13.680	15.41
7	1.149	0.8706	6.472	0.15451	7.434	0.13451	2.921	18.903	21.71
8	1.172	0.8535	7.325	0.13651	8.583	0.11651	3.396	24.878	29.15
9	1.195	0.8368	8.162	0.12252	9.755	0.10252	3.868	31.572	37.73
10	1.219	0.8203	8.983	0.11133	10.950	0.09133	4.337	38.955	47.49
11	1.243	0.8043	9.787	0.10218	12.169	0.08218	4.802	46.998	58.44
12	1.268	0.7885	10.575	0.09456	13.412	0.07456	5.264	55.671	70.60
13	1.294	0.7730	11.348	0.08812	14.680	0.06812	5.723	64.948	84.02
14	1.319	0.7579	12.106	0.08260	15.974	0.06260	6.179	74.800	98.70
15	1.346	0.7430	12.849	0.07783	17.293	0.05783	6.631	85.202	114.67
16	1.373	0.7284	13.578	0.07365	18.639	0.05365	7.080	96.129	131.96
17	1.400	0.7142	14.292	0.06997	20.012	0.04997	7.526	107.555	150.60
18	1.428	0.7002	14.992	0.06670	21.412	0.04670	7.968	119.548	170.62
19	1.457	0.6864	15.678	0.06378	22.841	0.04378	8.407	131.814	192.03
20	1.486	0.6730	16.351	0.06116	24.297	0.04116	8.843	144.600	214.87

21	1.516	0.6598	17.011	0.05878	25.783	0.03878	9.276	157.796	239.17
22	1.546	0.6468	17.658	0.05663	27.299	0.03663	9.705	171.379	264.95
23	1.577	0.6342	18.292	0.05467	28.845	0.03467	10.132	185.331	292.25
24	1.608	0.6217	18.914	0.05287	30.422	0.03287	10.555	199.630	321.09
25	1.641	0.6095	19.523	0.05122	32.030	0.03122	10.974	214.259	351.51
26	1.673	0.5976	20.121	0.04970	33.671	0.02970	11.391	229.199	383.55
27	1.707	0.5859	20.707	0.04829	35.344	0.02829	11.804	244.431	417.22
28	1.741	0.5744	21.281	0.04699	37.051	0.02699	12.214	259.939	452.56
29	1.776	0.5631	21.844	0.04578	38.792	0.02578	12.621	275.706	489.61
30	1.811	0.5521	22.396	0.04465	40.568	0.02465	13.025	291.716	528.40
31	1.848	0.5412	22.938	0.04360	42.379	0.02360	13.426	307.954	568.97
32	1.885	0.5306	23.468	0.04261	44.227	0.02261	13.823	324.403	611.35
33	1.922	0.5202	23.989	0.04169	46.112	0.02169	14.217	341.051	655.58
34	1.961	0.5100	24.499	0.04082	48.034	0.02082	14.608	357.882	701.69
35	2.000	0.5000	24.999	0.04000	49.994	0.02000	14.996	374.883	749.72
40	2.208	0.4529	27.355	0.03656	60.402	0.01656	16.889	461.993	1020.10
45	2.438	0.4102	29.490	0.03391	71.893	0.01391	18.703	551.565	1344.64
50	2.692	0.3715	31.424	0.03182	84.579	0.01182	20.442	642.361	1728.97
55	2.972	0.3365	33.175	0.03014	98.587	0.01014	22.106	733.353	2179.33
60	3.281	0.3048	34.761	0.02877	114.052	0.00877	23.696	823.698	2702.58
65	3.623	0.2761	36.197	0.02763	131.126	0.00763	25.215	912.709	3306.31
70	4.000	0.2500	37.499	0.02667	149.978	0.00667	26.663	999.834	3998.90
75	4.416	0.2265	38.677	0.02586	170.792	0.00586	28.043	1084.639	4789.59
80	4.875	0.2051	39.745	0.0252	193.772	0.0052	29.357	1166.787	5688.60
85	5.383	0.1858	40.7113	0.0246	219.144	0.0046	30.606	1246.00	6707.20
90	5.943	0.1683	41.587	0.0240	247.157	0.0040	31.793	1322.170	7857.85
95	6.562	0.1524	42.380	0.0236	278.080	0.0036	32.919	1395.10	9154.00
100	7.245	0.1380	43.098	0.0232	312.232	0.0032	33.986	1464.753	10611.60
∞	∞	0.0000	50.000	0.0200	∞	0.0000	50.000	2500.00	∞

TABLE A.4 $i = 3\%$ **Interest Factors for Discrete Compounding Periods**

	Single Payment		Uniform Payment Series					Gradient Series		
	Compound Amount Factor	Present Worth Factor	Present Worth Factor	Capital Recovery Factor	Compound Amount Factor	Sinking-Fund Factor	Gradient Uniform Series	Gradient Present Worth	Gradient Future Worth
	Find F Given P	Find P Given F	Find P Given A	Find A Given P	Find F Given A	Find A Given F	Find A Given G	Find P Given G	Find F Given G
N	F/P	P/F	P/A	A/P	F/A	A/F	A/G	P/G	F/G
1	1.030	0.9709	0.971	1.03000	1.000	1.00000	0.000	0.000	0.00
2	1.061	0.9426	1.913	0.52261	2.030	0.49261	0.493	0.943	1.00
3	1.093	0.9151	2.829	0.35353	3.091	0.32353	0.980	2.773	3.03
4	1.126	0.8885	3.717	0.26903	4.184	0.23903	1.463	5.438	6.12
5	1.159	0.8626	4.580	0.21835	5.309	0.18835	1.941	8.889	10.30
6	1.194	0.8375	5.417	0.18460	6.468	0.15460	2.414	13.076	15.61
7	1.230	0.8131	6.230	0.16051	7.662	0.13051	2.882	17.995	22.08
8	1.267	0.7894	7.020	0.14246	8.892	0.11246	3.345	23.481	29.74
9	1.305	0.7664	7.786	0.12843	10.159	0.09843	3.803	29.612	38.64
10	1.344	0.7441	8.530	0.11723	11.464	0.08723	4.256	36.309	48.80
11	1.384	0.7224	9.253	0.10808	12.808	0.07808	4.705	43.533	60.26
12	1.426	0.7014	9.954	0.10046	14.192	0.07046	5.148	51.248	73.07
13	1.469	0.6810	10.635	0.09403	15.618	0.06403	5.587	59.420	87.26
14	1.513	0.6611	11.296	0.08853	17.086	0.05853	6.021	68.014	102.88
15	1.558	0.6419	11.938	0.08377	18.599	0.05377	6.450	77.000	119.96
16	1.605	0.6232	12.561	0.07961	20.157	0.04961	6.874	86.348	138.56
17	1.653	0.6050	13.166	0.07595	21.762	0.04595	7.294	96.028	158.72
18	1.702	0.5874	13.754	0.07271	23.414	0.04271	7.708	106.014	180.48
19	1.754	0.5703	14.324	0.06981	25.117	0.03981	8.118	116.279	203.90
20	1.806	0.5537	14.877	0.06722	26.870	0.03722	8.523	126.799	229.01

21	1.860	0.5375	15.415	0.06487	28.676	0.03487	8.923	137.550	255.88
22	1.916	0.5219	15.937	0.06275	30.537	0.03275	9.319	148.509	284.56
23	1.974	0.5067	16.444	0.06081	32.453	0.03081	9.709	159.657	315.10
24	2.033	0.4919	16.936	0.05905	34.426	0.02905	10.095	170.971	347.55
25	2.094	0.4776	17.413	0.05743	36.459	0.02743	10.477	182.434	381.98
26	2.157	0.4637	17.877	0.05594	38.553	0.02594	10.853	194.026	418.43
27	2.221	0.4502	18.327	0.05456	40.710	0.02456	11.226	205.731	456.99
28	2.288	0.4371	18.764	0.05329	42.931	0.02329	11.593	217.532	497.70
29	2.357	0.4243	19.188	0.05211	45.219	0.02211	11.956	229.414	540.63
30	2.427	0.4120	19.600	0.05102	47.575	0.02102	12.314	241.361	585.85
31	2.500	0.4000	20.000	0.05000	50.003	0.02000	12.668	253.361	633.42
32	2.575	0.3883	20.389	0.04905	52.503	0.01905	13.107	265.399	683.43
33	2.652	0.3770	20.766	0.04816	55.078	0.01816	13.362	277.464	735.93
34	2.732	0.3660	21.132	0.04732	57.730	0.01732	13.702	289.544	791.01
35	2.814	0.3554	21.487	0.04654	60.462	0.01654	14.037	301.627	848.74
40	3.262	0.3066	23.115	0.04326	75.401	0.01326	15.650	361.750	1180.04
45	3.782	0.2644	24.519	0.04079	92.720	0.01079	17.156	420.632	1590.66
50	4.384	0.2281	25.730	0.03887	112.797	0.00887	18.558	477.480	2093.23
55	5.082	0.1968	26.774	0.03735	136.072	0.00735	19.860	531.741	2702.39
60	5.892	0.1697	27.676	0.03613	163.053	0.00613	21.067	583.053	3435.11
65	6.830	0.1464	28.453	0.03515	194.333	0.00515	22.184	631.201	4311.09
70	7.918	0.1263	29.123	0.03434	230.594	0.00434	23.215	676.087	5353.14
75	9.179	0.1089	29.702	0.03367	272.631	0.00367	24.163	717.698	6587.70
80	10.641	0.0940	30.201	0.0331	321.363	0.0031	25.035	756.087	8045.43
85	12.336	0.0811	30.631	0.0326	377.857	0.0026	25.835	791.353	9761.90
90	14.300	0.0699	31.002	0.0323	443.349	0.0023	26.567	823.630	11778.30
95	16.578	0.0603	31.323	0.0319	519.272	0.0019	27.235	853.074	14142.40
100	19.219	0.0520	31.599	0.0316	607.288	0.0016	27.844	879.854	16909.60
∞	∞	0.0000	33.333	0.0300	∞	0.0000	33.333	1111.11	∞

TABLE A.5 *i* = 4% Interest Factors for Discrete Compounding Periods

	Single Payment		Uniform Payment Series				Gradient Series		
	Compound Amount Factor	Present Worth Factor	Present Worth Factor	Capital Recovery Factor	Compound Amount Factor	Sinking-Fund Factor	Gradient Uniform Series	Gradient Present Worth	Gradient Future Worth
	Find *F* Given *P*	Find *P* Given *F*	Find *P* Given *A*	Find *A* Given *P*	Find *F* Given *A*	Find *A* Given *F*	Find *A* Given *G*	Find *P* Given *G*	Find *F* Given *G*
N	*F/P*	*P/F*	*P/A*	*A/P*	*F/A*	*A/F*	*A/G*	*P/G*	*F/G*
1	1.040	0.9615	0.962	1.04000	1.000	1.00000	0.000	0.000	0.00
2	1.082	0.9246	1.886	0.53020	2.040	0.49020	0.490	0.925	1.00
3	1.125	0.8890	2.775	0.36035	3.122	0.32035	0.974	2.703	3.04
4	1.170	0.8548	3.630	0.27549	4.246	0.23549	1.451	5.267	6.16
5	1.217	0.8219	4.452	0.22463	5.416	0.18463	1.922	8.555	10.41
6	1.265	0.7903	5.242	0.19076	6.633	0.15076	2.386	12.506	15.82
7	1.316	0.7599	6.002	0.16661	7.898	0.12661	2.843	17.066	22.46
8	1.369	0.7307	6.733	0.14853	9.214	0.10853	3.294	22.181	30.86
9	1.423	0.7026	7.435	0.13449	10.583	0.09449	3.739	27.801	39.57
10	1.480	0.6756	8.111	0.12329	12.006	0.08329	4.177	33.881	50.15
11	1.539	0.6496	8.760	0.11415	13.486	0.07415	4.609	40.377	62.16
12	1.601	0.6246	9.385	0.10655	15.026	0.06655	5.034	47.248	75.65
13	1.665	0.6006	9.986	0.10014	16.627	0.06014	5.453	54.455	90.67
14	1.732	0.5775	10.563	0.09467	18.292	0.05467	5.866	61.962	107.30
15	1.801	0.5553	11.118	0.08994	20.024	0.04994	6.272	69.735	125.59
16	1.873	0.5339	11.652	0.08582	21.825	0.04582	6.672	77.744	145.61
17	1.948	0.5134	12.166	0.08220	23.698	0.04220	7.066	85.958	167.44
18	2.026	0.4936	12.659	0.07899	25.645	0.03899	7.453	94.350	191.14
19	2.107	0.4746	13.134	0.07614	27.671	0.03614	7.834	102.893	216.78
20	2.191	0.4564	13.590	0.07358	29.778	0.03358	8.209	111.565	244.45

21	2.279	0.4388	14.029	0.07128	31.969	0.03128	8.578	120.341	274.23
22	2.370	0.4220	14.451	0.06920	34.248	0.02920	8.941	129.202	306.20
23	2.465	0.4057	14.857	0.06731	36.618	0.02731	9.297	138.128	340.45
24	2.563	0.3901	15.247	0.06559	39.083	0.02559	9.648	147.101	377.07
25	2.666	0.3751	15.622	0.06401	41.646	0.02401	9.993	156.104	416.15
26	2.772	0.3607	15.983	0.06257	44.312	0.02257	10.331	165.121	457.79
27	2.883	0.3468	16.330	0.06124	47.084	0.02124	10.664	174.138	502.11
28	2.999	0.3335	16.663	0.06001	49.968	0.02001	10.991	183.142	549.11
29	3.119	0.3207	16.984	0.05888	52.966	0.01888	11.312	192.121	599.16
30	3.243	0.3083	17.292	0.05783	56.085	0.10783	11.627	201.062	652.12
31	3.373	0.2965	17.588	0.05686	59.328	0.01686	11.937	209.956	708.21
32	3.508	0.2851	17.874	0.05595	62.701	0.01595	12.241	218.792	767.54
33	3.648	0.2741	18.148	0.05510	66.210	0.01510	12.540	227.563	830.24
34	3.794	0.2636	18.411	0.05431	69.858	0.01431	12.832	236.261	896.45
35	3.946	0.2534	18.665	0.05358	73.652	0.01358	13.120	244.877	966.31
40	4.801	0.2083	19.793	0.05052	95.026	0.01052	14.477	286.530	1375.64
45	5.841	0.1712	20.720	0.04826	121.029	0.00826	15.705	325.403	1900.73
50	7.107	0.1407	21.482	0.04655	152.667	0.00655	16.812	361.164	2566.68
55	8.646	0.1157	22.109	0.04523	191.159	0.00523	17.807	393.689	3403.98
60	10.520	0.0951	22.623	0.04420	237.991	0.00420	18.697	422.997	4449.77
65	12.799	0.0781	23.047	0.04339	294.968	0.00339	19.491	449.201	5749.21
70	15.572	0.0642	23.395	0.04275	364.290	0.00275	20.196	472.479	7357.26
75	18.945	0.0528	23.680	0.04223	448.631	0.00223	20.821	493.041	9340.78
80	23.050	0.0434	23.915	0.0418	551.245	0.0018	21.372	511.116	11781.13
85	28.044	0.0357	24.109	0.0415	676.090	0.0015	21.857	526.938	14777.25
90	34.119	0.0293	24.267	0.0412	827.983	0.0012	22.283	540.737	18449.58
95	41.511	0.0241	24.398	0.0410	1012.785	0.0010	22.655	552.731	22944.63
100	50.505	0.0198	24.505	0.0408	1237.624	0.0008	22.980	563.125	28440.60
∞	∞	0.0000	25.000	0.0400	∞	0.0000	25.000	625.000	∞

TABLE A.6 $i = 5\%$ **Interest Factors for Discrete Compounding Periods**

	Single Payment		Uniform Payment Series				Gradient Series		
	Compound Amount Factor	Present Worth Factor	Present Worth Factor	Capital Recovery Factor	Compound Amount Factor	Sinking-Fund Factor	Gradient Uniform Series	Gradient Present Worth	Gradient Future Worth
	Find F Given P	Find P Given F	Find P Given A	Find A Given P	Find F Given A	Find A Given F	Find A Given G	Find P Given G	Find F Given G
N	F/P	P/F	P/A	A/P	F/A	A/F	A/G	P/G	F/G
1	1.050	0.9524	0.952	1.05000	1.000	1.00000	0.000	0.000	0.00
2	1.103	0.9070	1.859	0.53780	2.050	0.48780	0.488	0.907	1.00
3	1.158	0.8638	2.723	0.36721	3.153	0.31721	0.967	2.635	3.05
4	1.216	0.8227	3.546	0.28201	4.310	0.23201	1.439	5.103	6.20
5	1.276	0.7835	4.329	0.23097	5.526	0.18097	1.903	8.237	10.51
6	1.340	0.7462	5.076	0.19702	6.802	0.14702	2.358	11.968	16.04
7	1.407	0.7107	5.786	0.17282	8.142	0.12282	2.805	16.232	22.84
8	1.477	0.6768	6.463	0.15472	9.549	0.10472	3.245	20.970	30.98
9	1.551	0.6446	7.108	0.14069	11.027	0.09069	3.676	26.127	40.53
10	1.629	0.6139	7.722	0.12950	12.578	0.07950	4.099	31.652	51.56
11	1.710	0.5847	8.306	0.12039	14.207	0.07039	4.514	37.499	64.14
12	1.796	0.5568	8.863	0.11283	15.917	0.06283	4.922	43.624	78.34
13	1.886	0.5303	9.394	0.10646	17.713	0.05646	5.322	49.988	94.26
14	1.980	0.5051	9.899	0.10102	19.599	0.05102	5.713	56.554	111.97
15	2.079	0.4810	10.380	0.09634	21.579	0.04634	6.097	63.288	131.57
16	2.183	0.4581	10.838	0.09227	23.657	0.04227	6.474	70.160	153.15
17	2.292	0.4363	11.274	0.08870	25.840	0.03870	6.842	77.140	176.81
18	2.407	0.4155	11.690	0.08555	28.132	0.03555	7.203	84.204	202.65
19	2.527	0.3957	12.085	0.08275	30.539	0.03275	7.557	91.328	230.78
20	2.653	0.3769	12.462	0.08024	33.066	0.03024	7.903	98.488	261.32

21	2.786	0.3589	12.821	0.07800	35.719	0.02800	8.242	105.667	294.39
22	2.925	0.3418	13.163	0.07597	38.505	0.02597	8.573	112.846	330.10
23	3.072	0.3256	13.489	0.07414	41.430	0.02414	8.897	120.009	368.61
24	3.225	0.3101	13.799	0.07247	44.502	0.02247	9.214	127.140	410.04
25	3.386	0.2953	14.094	0.07095	47.727	0.02095	9.524	134.228	454.54
26	3.556	0.2812	14.375	0.06956	51.113	0.01956	9.827	141.259	502.27
27	3.733	0.2678	14.643	0.06829	54.669	0.01829	10.122	148.223	553.38
28	3.920	0.2551	14.898	0.16712	58.403	0.01712	10.411	155.110	608.05
29	4.116	0.2429	15.141	0.06605	62.323	0.01605	10.694	161.913	666.45
30	4.322	0.2314	15.372	0.06505	66.439	0.01505	10.969	168.623	728.78
31	4.538	0.2204	15.593	0.06413	70.761	0.01413	11.238	175.233	795.22
32	4.765	0.2099	15.803	0.06328	75.299	0.01328	11.501	181.739	865.98
33	5.003	0.1999	16.003	0.06249	80.064	0.01249	11.757	188.135	941.28
34	5.253	0.1904	16.193	0.06176	85.067	0.01176	12.006	194.417	1021.34
35	5.516	0.1813	16.374	0.06107	90.320	0.01107	12.250	200.581	1106.41
40	7.040	0.1420	17.159	0.05828	120.800	0.00828	13.377	229.545	1616.00
45	8.985	0.1113	17.774	0.05626	159.700	0.00626	14.364	255.315	2294.00
50	11.467	0.0872	18.256	0.05478	209.348	0.00478	15.223	277.915	3186.96
55	14.636	0.0683	18.633	0.05367	272.713	0.00367	15.966	297.510	4354.25
60	18.679	0.0535	18.929	0.05283	353.584	0.00283	16.606	314.343	5871.67
65	23.840	0.0419	19.161	0.05219	456.798	0.00219	17.154	328.691	7835.96
70	30.426	0.0329	19.343	0.05170	588.529	0.00170	17.621	340.841	10370.57
75	38.833	0.0258	19.485	0.05132	756.654	0.00132	18.018	351.072	13633.07
80	49.561	0.0202	19.596	0.0510	971.229	0.0010	18.353	359.646	17824.58
85	63.254	0.0158	19.684	0.0508	1245.087	0.0008	18.635	366.801	23201.74
90	80.730	0.0124	19.752	0.0506	1594.607	0.0006	18.871	372.749	30092.14
95	103.035	0.0097	19.806	0.0505	2040.694	0.0005	19.069	377.677	38913.88
100	131.501	0.0076	19.848	0.0504	2610.025	0.0004	19.234	381.749	50200.50
∞	∞	0.0000	20.000	0.0500	∞	0.0000	20.000	400.00	∞

TABLE A.7 $i = 6\%$ Interest Factors for Discrete Compounding Periods

	Single Payment		Uniform Payment Series				Gradient Series		
	Compound Amount Factor	Present Worth Factor	Present Worth Factor	Capital Recovery Factor	Compound Amount Factor	Sinking-Fund Factor	Gradient Uniform Series	Gradient Present Worth	Gradient Future Worth
	Find F Given P	Find P Given F	Find P Given A	Find A Given P	Find F Given A	Find A Given F	Find A Given G	Find P Given G	Find F Given G
N	F/P	P/F	P/A	A/P	F/A	A/F	A/G	P/G	F/G
1	1.060	0.9434	0.943	1.06000	1.000	1.00000	0.000	0.000	0.00
2	1.124	0.8900	1.833	0.54544	2.060	0.48544	0.485	0.890	1.00
3	1.191	0.8396	2.673	0.37411	3.184	0.31411	0.961	2.569	3.06
4	1.262	0.7921	3.465	0.28859	4.375	0.22859	1.427	4.946	6.24
5	1.338	0.7473	4.212	0.23740	5.637	0.17740	1.884	7.935	10.62
6	1.419	0.7050	4.917	0.20336	6.975	0.14336	2.330	11.459	16.26
7	1.504	0.6651	5.582	0.17914	8.394	0.11914	2.768	15.450	23.23
8	1.594	0.6274	6.210	0.16104	9.897	0.10104	3.195	19.842	31.62
9	1.689	0.5919	6.802	0.14702	11.491	0.08702	3.613	24.577	41.52
10	1.791	0.5584	7.360	0.13587	13.181	0.07587	4.022	29.602	53.01
11	1.898	0.5268	7.887	0.12679	14.972	0.06679	4.421	34.870	66.19
12	2.012	0.4970	8.384	0.11928	16.870	0.05928	4.811	40.337	81.17
13	2.133	0.4688	8.853	0.11296	18.882	0.05296	5.192	45.963	98.04
14	2.261	0.4423	9.295	0.10758	21.015	0.04758	5.564	51.713	116.92
15	2.397	0.4173	9.712	0.10296	23.276	0.04296	5.926	57.555	137.93
16	2.540	0.3936	10.106	0.09895	25.673	0.03895	6.279	63.459	161.21
17	2.693	0.3714	10.477	0.09544	28.213	0.03544	6.624	69.401	186.88
18	2.854	0.3503	10.828	0.09236	30.906	0.03236	6.960	75.357	215.09
19	3.026	0.3305	11.158	0.08962	33.760	0.02962	7.287	81.306	246.00
20	3.207	0.3118	11.470	0.08718	36.786	0.02718	7.605	87.230	279.76

21	3.400	0.2942	11.764	0.08500	39.993	0.02500	7.915	93.114	316.55
22	3.604	0.2775	12.042	0.08305	43.392	0.02305	8.217	98.941	356.54
23	3.820	0.2618	12.303	0.08128	46.996	0.02128	8.510	104.701	399.93
24	4.049	0.2470	12.550	0.07968	50.816	0.01968	8.795	110.381	446.93
25	4.292	0.2330	12.783	0.07823	54.865	0.01823	9.072	115.973	497.74
26	4.549	0.2198	13.003	0.07690	59.156	0.01690	9.341	121.468	552.61
27	4.822	0.2074	13.211	0.07570	63.706	0.01570	9.603	126.860	611.76
28	5.112	0.1956	13.406	0.07459	68.528	0.01459	9.857	132.142	675.47
29	5.418	0.1846	13.591	0.07358	73.640	0.01358	10.103	137.310	744.00
30	5.743	0.1741	13.765	0.07265	79.058	0.01265	10.342	142.359	817.64
31	6.088	0.1643	13.929	0.07179	84.802	0.01179	10.574	147.286	896.69
32	6.453	0.1550	14.084	0.07100	90.890	0.01100	10.799	152.090	981.50
33	6.841	0.1462	14.230	0.07027	97.343	0.01027	11.017	156.768	1072.39
34	7.251	0.1379	14.368	0.06960	104.184	0.00960	11.228	161.319	1169.73
35	7.686	0.1301	14.498	0.06897	111.435	0.00897	11.432	165.743	1273.91
40	10.286	0.0972	15.046	0.06646	154.762	0.00646	12.359	185.957	1912.70
45	13.765	0.0727	15.456	0.06470	212.744	0.00470	13.141	203.110	2795.73
50	18.420	0.0543	15.762	0.06344	290.336	0.00344	13.796	217.457	4005.60
55	24.650	0.0406	15.991	0.06254	394.172	0.00254	14.341	229.322	5652.87
60	32.988	0.0303	16.161	0.06188	533.128	0.00188	14.791	239.043	7885.47
65	44.145	0.0227	16.289	0.06139	719.083	0.00139	15.160	246.945	10901.38
70	59.076	0.0169	16.385	0.06103	967.932	0.00103	15.461	253.327	14965.54
75	79.057	0.0126	16.456	0.06077	1300.949	0.00077	15.706	258.453	20432.48
80	105.798	0.0095	16.509	0.0606	1746.600	0.0006	15.903	262.549	27776.67
85	141.579	0.0071	16.549	0.0604	2342.982	0.0004	16.062	265.810	37633.03
90	189.465	0.0053	16.579	0.0603	3141.075	0.0003	16.189	268.395	50851.25
95	253.546	0.0039	16.601	0.0602	4209.104	0.0002	16.290	270.437	68568.40
100	339.302	0.0029	16.618	0.0602	5638.368	0.0002	16.371	272.047	92306.13
∞	∞	0.0000	18.182	0.0600	∞	0.0000	16.667	277.778	∞

TABLE A.8 $i = 7\%$ Interest Factors for Discrete Compounding Periods

	Single Payment		Uniform Payment Series				Gradient Series			
	Compound Amount Factor	Present Worth Factor	Present Worth Factor	Capital Recovery Factor	Compound Amount Factor	Sinking-Fund Factor	Gradient Uniform Series	Gradient Present Worth	Gradient Future Worth	
	Find F Given P	Find P Given F	Find P Given A	Find A Given P	Find F Given A	Find A Given F	Find A Given G	Find P Given G	Find F Given G	
N	F/P	P/F	P/A	A/P	F/A	A/F	A/G	P/G	F/G	
1	1.070	0.9346	0.935	1.07000	1.000	1.00000	0.000	0.000	0.00	
2	1.145	0.8734	1.808	0.55309	2.070	0.48309	0.483	0.873	1.00	
3	1.225	0.8163	2.624	0.38105	3.215	0.31105	0.955	2.506	3.07	
4	1.311	0.7629	3.387	0.29523	4.440	0.22523	1.416	4.795	6.28	
5	1.403	0.7130	4.100	0.24389	5.751	0.17389	1.865	7.647	10.72	
6	1.501	0.6663	4.767	0.20980	7.153	0.13980	2.303	10.978	16.48	
7	1.606	0.6227	5.389	0.18555	8.654	0.11555	2.730	14.715	23.63	
8	1.718	0.5820	5.971	0.16747	10.260	0.09747	3.147	18.789	32.28	
9	1.838	0.5439	6.515	0.15349	11.978	0.08349	3.552	23.140	42.54	
10	1.967	0.5083	7.024	0.14238	13.816	0.07238	3.946	27.716	54.52	
11	2.105	0.4751	7.499	0.13336	15.784	0.06336	4.330	32.466	68.34	
12	2.252	0.4440	7.943	0.12590	17.888	0.05590	4.703	37.351	84.12	
13	2.410	0.4150	8.358	0.11965	20.141	0.04965	5.065	42.330	102.01	
14	2.579	0.3878	8.745	0.11434	22.550	0.04434	5.417	47.372	122.15	
15	2.759	0.3624	9.108	0.10979	25.129	0.03979	5.758	52.446	144.70	
16	2.952	0.3387	9.447	0.10586	27.888	0.03586	6.090	57.527	169.83	
17	3.159	0.3166	9.763	0.10243	30.840	0.03243	6.411	62.592	197.92	
18	3.380	0.2959	10.059	0.09941	33.999	0.02941	6.722	67.622	228.56	
19	3.617	0.2765	10.336	0.09675	37.379	0.02675	7.024	72.599	262.56	
20	3.870	0.2584	10.594	0.09439	40.995	0.02439	7.316	77.509	299.94	

21	4.141	0.2415	10.836	0.09229	44.865	0.02229	7.599	82.339	340.93
22	4.430	0.2257	11.061	0.09041	49.006	0.02041	7.872	87.079	385.80
23	4.741	0.2109	11.272	0.08871	53.436	0.01871	8.137	91.720	434.80
24	5.072	0.1971	11.469	0.08719	58.177	0.01719	8.392	96.255	488.24
25	5.427	0.1842	11.654	0.08581	63.249	0.01581	8.639	100.676	546.41
26	5.807	0.1722	11.826	0.08456	68.676	0.01456	8.877	104.981	609.66
27	6.214	0.1609	11.987	0.08343	74.484	0.01343	9.107	109.166	678.34
28	6.649	0.1504	12.137	0.08239	80.698	0.01239	9.329	113.226	752.82
29	7.114	0.1406	12.278	0.08145	87.347	0.01145	9.543	117.162	833.52
30	7.612	0.1314	12.409	0.08059	94.461	0.01059	9.749	120.972	920.87
31	8.145	0.1228	12.532	0.07980	102.073	0.00980	9.947	124.655	1015.33
32	8.715	0.1147	12.647	0.07907	110.218	0.00907	10.138	128.212	1117.40
33	9.325	0.1072	12.754	0.07841	118.933	0.00841	10.322	131.643	1227.62
34	9.978	0.1002	12.854	0.07780	128.259	0.00780	10.499	134.951	1346.55
35	10.677	0.0937	12.948	0.07723	138.237	0.00723	10.669	138.135	1474.81
40	14.974	0.0668	13.332	0.07501	199.635	0.00501	11.423	152.293	2280.50
45	21.002	0.0476	13.606	0.07350	285.749	0.00350	12.036	163.756	3439.28
50	29.457	0.0339	13.801	0.07246	406.529	0.00246	12.529	172.905	5093.27
55	41.315	0.0242	13.940	0.07174	575.929	0.00174	12.921	180.124	7441.84
60	57.946	0.0173	14.039	0.07123	813.520	0.00123	13.232	185.768	10764.58
65	81.273	0.0123	14.110	0.07087	1146.755	0.00087	13.476	190.145	15453.65
70	113.989	0.0088	14.160	0.07062	1614.134	0.00062	13.666	193.519	22059.06
75	159.876	0.0063	14.196	0.07044	2269.657	0.00044	13.814	196.104	31352.25
80	224.234	0.0045	14.222	0.0703	3189.063	0.0003	13.927	198.075	44415.19
85	314.500	0.0032	14.240	0.0702	4478.576	0.0002	14.015	199.572	62765.37
90	441.103	0.0023	14.253	0.0702	6287.185	0.0002	14.081	200.704	88531.21
95	618.670	0.0016	14.263	0.0701	8823.854	0.0001	14.132	201.558	124697.91
100	867.716	0.0012	14.269	0.0701	12381.662	0.0001	14.170	202.200	175452.3
∞	∞	0.0000	14.286	0.0700	∞	0.0000	14.286	204.082	∞

TABLE A.9 $i = 8\%$ Interest Factors for Discrete Compounding Periods

	Single Payment		Uniform Payment Series				Gradient Series		
	Compound Amount Factor	Present Worth Factor	Present Worth Factor	Capital Recovery Factor	Compound Amount Factor	Sinking-Fund Factor	Gradient Uniform Series	Gradient Present Worth	Gradient Future Worth
	Find F Given P	Find P Given F	Find P Given A	Find A Given P	Find F Given A	Find A Given F	Find A Given G	Find P Given G	Find F Given G
N	F/P	P/F	P/A	A/P	F/A	A/F	A/G	P/G	F/G
1	1.080	0.9259	0.926	1.08000	1.000	1.00000	0.000	0.000	0.00
2	1.166	0.8573	1.783	0.56077	2.080	0.48077	0.481	0.857	1.00
3	1.260	0.7938	2.577	0.38803	3.246	0.30803	0.949	2.445	3.08
4	1.360	0.7350	3.312	0.30192	4.506	0.22192	1.404	4.650	6.33
5	1.469	0.6806	3.993	0.25046	5.867	0.17046	1.846	7.372	10.83
6	1.587	0.6302	4.623	0.21632	7.336	0.13632	2.276	10.523	16.70
7	1.714	0.5835	5.206	0.19207	8.923	0.11207	2.694	14.024	24.04
8	1.851	0.5403	5.747	0.17401	10.637	0.09401	3.099	17.806	32.96
9	1.999	0.5002	6.247	0.16008	12.488	0.08008	3.491	21.808	43.59
10	2.159	0.4632	6.710	0.14903	14.487	0.06903	3.871	25.977	56.08
11	2.332	0.4289	7.139	0.14008	16.645	0.06008	4.240	30.266	70.57
12	2.518	0.3971	7.536	0.13270	18.977	0.05270	4.596	34.634	87.21
13	2.720	0.3677	7.904	0.12652	21.495	0.04652	4.940	39.046	106.19
14	2.937	0.3405	8.244	0.12130	24.215	0.04130	5.273	43.472	127.69
15	3.172	0.3152	8.559	0.11683	27.152	0.03683	5.594	47.886	151.90
16	3.426	0.2919	8.851	0.11298	30.324	0.03298	5.905	52.264	179.05
17	3.700	0.2703	9.122	0.10963	33.750	0.02963	6.204	56.588	209.38
18	3.996	0.2502	9.372	0.10670	37.450	0.02670	6.492	60.843	243.13
19	4.316	0.2317	9.604	0.10413	41.446	0.02413	6.770	65.013	280.58
20	4.661	0.2145	9.818	0.10185	45.762	0.02185	7.037	69.090	322.02

21	5.034	0.1987	10.017	0.09983	50.423	0.01983	7.294	73.063	367.79
22	5.437	0.1839	10.201	0.09803	55.457	0.01803	7.541	76.926	418.21
23	5.871	0.1703	10.371	0.09642	60.893	0.01642	7.779	80.673	473.67
24	6.341	0.1577	10.529	0.09498	66.765	0.01498	8.007	84.300	534.56
25	6.848	0.1460	10.675	0.09368	73.106	0.01368	8.225	87.804	601.32
26	7.396	0.1352	10.810	0.09251	79.954	0.01251	8.435	91.184	674.43
27	7.988	0.1252	10.935	0.09145	87.351	0.01145	8.636	94.439	754.38
28	8.627	0.1159	11.051	0.09049	95.339	0.01049	8.829	97.569	841.74
29	9.317	0.1073	11.158	0.08962	103.966	0.00962	9.013	100.574	937.07
30	10.063	0.0994	11.258	0.08883	113.283	0.00883	9.190	103.456	1041.04
31	10.868	0.0920	11.350	0.08811	123.346	0.00811	9.358	106.216	1154.52
32	11.737	0.0852	11.435	0.08745	134.214	0.00745	9.520	108.857	1277.67
33	12.676	0.0789	11.514	0.08685	145.951	0.00685	9.674	111.382	1411.88
34	13.960	0.0730	11.587	0.08630	158.627	0.00630	9.821	113.792	1557.83
35	14.785	0.0676	11.655	0.08580	172.317	0.00580	9.961	116.092	1716.46
40	21.725	0.0460	11.925	0.08386	259.057	0.00386	10.570	126.042	2738.21
45	31.920	0.0313	12.108	0.08259	386.506	0.00259	11.045	133.733	4268.82
50	46.902	0.0213	12.233	0.08174	573.770	0.00174	11.411	139.593	6547.13
55	68.914	0.0145	12.319	0.08118	848.923	0.00118	11.690	144.006	9924.04
60	101.257	0.0099	12.377	0.08080	1253.213	0.00080	11.902	147.300	14915.17
65	148.780	0.0067	12.416	0.08054	1847.248	0.00054	12.060	149.739	22278.10
70	218.606	0.0046	12.443	0.08037	2720.080	0.00037	12.178	151.533	33126.00
75	321.205	0.0031	12.461	0.08025	4002.557	0.00025	12.266	152.845	49094.46
80	471.955	0.0021	12.474	0.0802	5886.935	0.0002	12.330	153.800	72586.69
85	693.456	0.0014	12.482	0.0801	8655.706	0.0001	12.377	154.492	107133.8
90	1018.915	0.0010	12.488	0.0301	12723.939	0.0001	12.412	154.993	157924.2
95	1497.121	0.0007	12.492	0.0801	18701.507	0.0001	12.437	155.352	232581.3
100	2199.761	0.0005	12.494	0.0800	27484.516	0.0001	12.455	155.611	331056.5
∞	∞	0.0000	12.500	0.0800	∞	0.0001	12.500	156.250	∞

TABLE A.10 $i = 9\%$ Interest Factors for Discrete Compounding Periods

	Single Payment		Uniform Payment Series				Gradient Series		
	Compound Amount Factor	Present Worth Factor	Present Worth Factor	Capital Recovery Factor	Compound Amount Factor	Sinking-Fund Factor	Gradient Uniform Series	Gradient Present Worth	Gradient Future Worth
	Find F Given P	Find P Given F	Find P Given A	Find A Given P	Find F Given A	Find A Given F	Find A Given G	Find P Given G	Find F Given G
N	F/P	P/F	P/A	A/P	F/A	A/F	A/G	P/G	F/G
1	1.090	0.9174	0.917	1.09000	1.000	1.00000	0.000	0.000	0.00
2	1.188	0.8417	1.759	0.56847	2.090	0.47847	0.478	0.842	1.00
3	1.295	0.7722	2.531	0.39505	3.278	0.30505	0.943	2.386	3.09
4	1.412	0.7084	3.240	0.30867	4.573	0.21867	1.393	4.511	6.37
5	1.539	0.6499	3.890	0.25709	5.985	0.16709	1.828	7.111	10.94
6	1.677	0.5963	4.486	0.22292	7.523	0.13292	2.250	10.092	16.93
7	1.828	0.5470	5.033	0.19869	9.200	0.10869	2.657	13.375	24.45
8	1.993	0.5019	5.535	0.18067	11.028	0.09067	3.051	16.888	33.65
9	2.172	0.4604	5.995	0.16680	13.021	0.07680	3.431	20.571	44.68
10	2.367	0.4224	6.418	0.15582	15.193	0.06582	3.798	24.373	57.70
11	2.580	0.3875	6.805	0.14695	17.560	0.05695	4.151	28.248	72.89
12	2.813	0.3555	7.161	0.13965	20.141	0.04965	4.491	32.159	90.45
13	3.066	0.3262	7.487	0.13357	22.953	0.04357	4.818	36.073	110.59
14	3.342	0.2992	7.786	0.12843	26.019	0.03843	5.133	39.963	133.55
15	3.642	0.2745	8.061	0.12406	29.361	0.03406	5.435	43.807	159.57
16	3.970	0.2519	8.313	0.12030	33.003	0.03030	5.724	47.585	188.93
17	4.328	0.2311	8.544	0.11705	36.974	0.02705	6.002	51.282	221.93
18	4.717	0.2120	8.756	0.11421	41.301	0.02421	6.269	54.886	258.90
19	5.142	0.1945	8.950	0.11173	46.018	0.02173	6.524	58.387	300.21
20	5.604	0.1784	9.129	0.10955	51.160	0.01955	6.767	61.777	346.22

21	6.109	0.1637	9.292	0.10762	56.765	0.01762	7.001	65.051	397.38
22	6.659	0.1502	9.442	0.10590	62.873	0.01590	7.223	68.205	454.15
23	7.258	0.1378	9.580	0.01438	69.532	0.01438	7.436	71.236	517.02
24	7.911	0.1264	9.707	0.10302	76.790	0.01302	7.638	74.143	586.55
25	8.623	0.1160	9.823	0.10181	84.701	0.01181	7.832	76.926	663.34
26	9.339	0.1064	9.929	0.10072	93.324	0.01072	8.016	79.586	748.04
27	10.245	0.0976	10.027	0.09973	102.723	0.00973	8.191	82.124	841.37
28	11.167	0.0895	10.116	0.09885	112.968	0.00885	8.357	84.542	944.09
29	12.172	0.0822	10.198	0.09806	124.135	0.00806	8.515	86.842	1057.06
30	13.268	0.0754	10.274	0.09734	136.308	0.00734	8.666	89.028	1181.19
31	14.462	0.0691	10.343	0.09669	149.575	0.00669	8.808	91.102	1317.50
32	15.763	0.0634	10.406	0.09610	164.037	0.00610	8.944	93.069	1467.08
33	17.182	0.0582	10.464	0.09556	179.800	0.00556	9.072	94.931	1631.11
34	18.728	0.0534	10.518	0.09508	196.982	0.00508	9.193	96.693	1810.91
35	20.414	0.0490	10.567	0.09464	215.711	0.00464	9.308	98.359	2007.90
40	31.409	0.0318	10.757	0.09296	337.882	0.00296	9.796	105.376	3309.80
45	48.327	0.0207	10.881	0.09190	525.859	0.00190	10.160	110.556	5342.87
50	74.358	0.0134	10.962	0.09123	815.084	0.00123	10.430	114.325	8500.93
55	114.408	0.0087	11.014	0.09079	1260.092	0.00079	10.626	117.036	13389.91
60	176.031	0.0057	11.048	0.09051	1944.792	0.00051	10.768	118.968	20942.13
65	270.846	0.0037	11.070	0.09033	2998.288	0.00033	10.870	120.334	32592.09
70	416.730	0.0024	11.084	0.09022	4619.223	0.00022	10.943	121.294	50546.92
75	641.191	0.0016	11.094	0.09014	7113.232	0.00014	10.994	121.965	78202.58
80	986.552	0.0010	11.100	0.0901	10950.574	0.0001	11.030	122.431	—
85	1517.932	0.0007	11.104	0.0901	16854.800	0.0001	11.055	122.753	—
90	2335.527	0.0004	11.106	0.0900	25939.184		11.073	122.976	—
95	3593.497	0.0003	11.108	0.0900	39916.635		11.085	123.129	—
100	5529.041	0.0002	11.109	0.0900	61422.675		11.093	123.234	—
∞	∞	0.0000	11.111	0.0900	∞	0.0000	11.111	123.45	∞

TABLE A.11 $i = 10\%$ Interest Factors for Discrete Compounding Periods

	Single Payment		Uniform Payment Series				Gradient Series		
	Compound Amount Factor	Present Worth Factor	Present Worth Factor	Capital Recovery Factor	Compound Amount Factor	Sinking-Fund Factor	Gradient Uniform Series	Gradient Present Worth	Gradient Future Worth
	Find F Given P	Find P Given F	Find P Given A	Find A Given P	Find F Given A	Find A Given F	Find A Given G	Find P Given G	Find F Given G
N	F/P	P/F	P/A	A/P	F/A	A/F	A/G	P/G	F/G
1	1.100	0.9091	0.909	1.10000	1.000	1.00000	0.000	0.000	0.00
2	1.210	0.8264	1.736	0.57619	2.100	0.47619	0.476	0.826	1.00
3	1.331	0.7513	2.487	0.40211	3.310	0.30211	0.937	2.329	3.10
4	1.464	0.6830	3.170	0.31547	4.641	0.21547	1.381	4.378	6.41
5	1.611	0.6209	3.791	0.26380	6.105	0.16380	1.810	6.862	11.05
6	1.772	0.5645	4.355	0.22961	7.716	0.12961	2.224	9.684	17.16
7	1.949	0.5132	4.868	0.20541	9.487	0.10541	2.622	12.763	24.87
8	2.144	0.4665	5.335	0.18734	11.436	0.08744	3.004	16.029	34.36
9	2.358	0.4241	5.759	0.17364	13.579	0.07364	3.372	19.421	45.79
10	2.594	0.3855	6.145	0.16275	15.937	0.06275	3.725	22.891	59.37
11	2.853	0.3505	6.495	0.15396	18.531	0.05396	4.064	26.396	75.31
12	3.138	0.3186	6.814	0.14676	21.384	0.04676	4.388	29.901	93.84
13	3.452	0.2897	7.103	0.14078	24.523	0.04078	4.699	33.377	115.23
14	3.797	0.2633	7.367	0.13575	27.975	0.03575	4.996	36.800	139.75
15	4.177	0.2394	7.606	0.13147	31.772	0.03147	5.279	40.152	167.72
16	4.595	0.2176	7.824	0.12782	35.950	0.02782	5.549	43.416	199.50
17	5.054	0.1978	8.022	0.12466	40.545	0.02466	5.807	46.582	235.45
18	5.560	0.1799	8.201	0.12193	45.599	0.02193	6.053	49.640	275.99
19	6.116	0.1635	8.365	0.11955	51.159	0.01955	6.286	52.583	321.59
20	6.727	0.1486	8.514	0.11746	57.275	0.01746	6.508	55.407	372.75

21	7.400	0.1351	8.649	0.11562	64.002	0.01562	6.719	58.110	430.02
22	8.140	0.1228	8.772	0.11401	71.403	0.01401	6.919	60.689	494.03
23	8.954	0.1117	8.883	0.11257	79.543	0.01257	7.108	63.146	565.43
24	9.850	0.1015	8.985	0.11130	88.497	0.01130	7.288	65.481	644.97
25	10.835	0.0923	9.077	0.11017	98.347	0.01017	7.458	67.696	733.47
26	11.918	0.0839	9.161	0.10916	109.182	0.00916	7.619	69.794	831.82
27	13.110	0.0763	9.237	0.10826	121.100	0.00826	7.770	71.777	941.00
28	14.421	0.0693	9.307	0.10745	134.210	0.00745	7.914	73.650	1062.10
29	15.863	0.0630	9.370	0.10673	148.631	0.00673	8.049	75.415	1196.31
30	17.449	0.0573	9.427	0.10608	164.494	0.00608	8.176	77.077	1344.94
31	19.194	0.0521	9.479	0.10550	181.943	0.00550	8.296	78.640	1509.43
32	21.114	0.0474	9.526	0.10497	201.138	0.00497	8.409	80.108	1691.38
33	23.225	0.0431	9.569	0.10450	222.252	0.00450	8.515	81.486	1892.52
34	25.548	0.0391	9.609	0.10407	245.477	0.00407	8.615	82.777	2114.77
35	28.102	0.0356	9.644	0.10369	271.024	0.00369	8.709	83.987	2360.24
40	45.259	0.0221	9.779	0.10226	442.593	0.00226	9.096	88.953	4025.93
45	72.890	0.0137	9.863	0.10139	718.905	0.00139	9.374	92.454	6739.05
50	117.391	0.0085	9.915	0.10086	1163.909	0.00086	9.570	94.889	11139.09
55	189.059	0.0053	9.947	0.10053	1880.591	0.00053	9.708	95.562	18255.91
60	304.482	0.0033	9.967	0.10033	3034.816	0.00033	9.802	97.701	29748.16
65	490.371	0.0020	9.980	0.10020	4893.707	0.00020	9.867	98.471	48287.07
70	789.747	0.0013	9.987	0.10013	7887.469	0.00013	9.911	98.987	78174.69
75	1271.895	0.0008	9.992	0.10008	12708.953	0.00008	9.941	99.322	126339.54
80	2048.400	0.0005	9.995	0.1000	20474.002		9.961	99.561	—
85	3298.969	0.0003	9.997	0.1000	32979.690		9.974	99.712	—
90	5313.023	0.0002	9.998	0.1000	53120.226		9.983	99.812	—
95	8556.676	0.0001	9.999	0.1000	85556.761		9.989	99.877	—
100	13780.612	0.0001	9.999	0.1000	137796.123		9.993	99.920	—
∞	∞	0.0000	10.000	0.1000	∞	0.00000	10.000	100.000	∞

TABLE A.12 $i = 12\%$ **Interest Factors for Discrete Compounding Periods**

	Single Payment		Uniform Payment Series				Gradient Series			
	Compound Amount Factor	Present Worth Factor	Present Worth Factor	Capital Recovery Factor	Compound Amount Factor	Sinking-Fund Factor	Gradient Uniform Series	Gradient Present Worth	Gradient Future Worth	
	Find F Given P	Find P Given F	Find P Given A	Find A Given P	Find F Given A	Find A Given F	Find A Given G	Find P Given G	Find F Given G	
N	F/P	P/F	P/A	A/P	F/A	A/F	A/G	P/G	F/G	
1	1.120	0.8929	0.893	1.12000	1.000	1.00000	0.000	0.000	0.00	
2	1.254	0.7972	1.690	0.59170	2.120	0.47170	0.472	0.797	1.00	
3	1.405	0.7118	2.402	0.41635	3.374	0.29635	0.925	2.221	3.12	
4	1.574	0.6355	3.037	0.32923	4.779	0.20923	1.359	4.127	6.49	
5	1.762	0.5674	3.605	0.27741	6.353	0.15741	1.775	6.397	11.27	
6	1.974	0.5066	4.111	0.24323	8.115	0.12323	2.172	8.930	17.63	
7	2.211	0.4523	4.564	0.21912	10.089	0.09912	2.551	11.644	25.74	
8	2.476	0.4039	4.968	0.20130	12.300	0.08130	2.913	14.471	35.83	
9	2.773	0.3606	5.328	0.18768	14.776	0.06768	3.257	17.356	48.13	
10	3.106	0.3220	5.650	0.17698	17.549	0.05698	3.585	20.254	62.91	
11	3.479	0.2875	5.938	0.16842	20.655	0.04842	3.895	23.129	80.45	
12	3.896	0.2567	6.194	0.16144	24.133	0.04144	4.190	25.952	101.11	
13	4.363	0.2292	6.424	0.15568	28.029	0.03568	4.468	28.702	125.24	
14	4.887	0.2046	6.628	0.15087	32.393	0.03087	4.732	31.362	153.27	
15	5.474	0.1827	6.811	0.14682	37.280	0.02682	4.980	33.920	185.66	
16	6.130	0.1631	6.974	0.14339	42.753	0.02339	5.215	36.367	222.94	
17	6.866	0.1456	7.120	0.14046	48.884	0.02046	5.435	38.697	265.70	
18	7.690	0.1300	7.250	0.13794	55.750	0.01794	5.643	40.908	314.58	
19	8.613	0.1161	7.366	0.13576	63.440	0.01576	5.838	42.998	370.33	
20	9.646	0.1037	7.469	0.13388	72.052	0.01388	6.020	44.968	433.77	

21	10.804	0.0926	7.562	0.13224	81.699	0.01224	6.191	46.819	505.82
22	12.100	0.0826	7.645	0.13081	92.503	0.01081	6.351	48.554	587.52
23	13.552	0.0738	7.718	0.12956	104.603	0.00956	6.501	50.178	680.02
24	15.179	0.0659	7.784	0.12846	118.155	0.00846	6.641	51.693	784.63
25	17.000	0.0588	7.843	0.12750	133.334	0.00750	6.771	53.105	902.78
26	19.040	0.0525	7.896	0.12665	150.334	0.00665	6.892	54.418	1036.12
27	21.325	0.0469	7.943	0.12590	169.374	0.00590	7.005	55.637	1186.45
28	23.884	0.0419	7.984	0.12524	190.699	0.00524	7.110	56.767	1355.82
29	26.750	0.0374	8.022	0.12466	214.583	0.00466	7.207	57.814	1546.52
30	29.960	0.0334	8.055	0.12414	241.333	0.00414	7.297	58.872	1761.11
31	33.555	0.0298	8.085	0.12369	271.293	0.00369	7.381	59.676	2002.44
32	37.582	0.0266	8.112	0.12328	304.848	0.00328	7.459	60.501	2273.73
33	42.092	0.0238	8.135	0.12292	342.429	0.00292	7.530	61.261	2578.58
34	47.143	0.0212	8.157	0.12260	384.521	0.00260	7.596	61.961	2921.01
35	52.800	0.0189	8.176	0.12232	431.664	0.00232	7.658	62.605	3305.53
40	93.051	0.0107	8.244	0.12130	767.091	0.00130	7.899	65.116	6059.10
45	163.988	0.0061	8.283	0.12074	1358.230	0.00074	8.057	66.734	10943.58
50	289.002	0.0035	8.304	0.12042	2400.018	0.00042	8.160	67.762	19583.49
55	509.321	0.0020	8.317	0.12024	4236.005	0.00024	8.225	68.408	34841.71
60	897.597	0.0011	8.324	0.12013	7471.641	0.00013	8.266	68.810	61763.68
65	1581.873	0.0006	8.328	0.12008	13173.938	0.00008	8.292	69.058	109241.15
70	2787.800	0.0004	8.330	0.12004	23223.332	0.00004	8.308	69.210	192944.44
75	4913.056	0.0002	8.332	0.12002	40933.799	0.00002	8.318	69.303	340489.99
80	8658.483	0.0001	8.332	0.1200	72145.692		8.324	69.359	—
85	15259.206	0.0001	8.333	0.1200	127151.714		8.328	69.393	—
90	26891.934		8.333	0.1200	224091.118		8.330	69.414	—
95	47392.777		8.333	0.1200	394931.471		8.331	69.426	—
100	83522.266		8.333	0.1200	696010.547		8.332	69.434	—
∞	∞	0.00000	8.333	0.1200	∞	0.00000	8.333	69.444	∞

TABLE A.13 $i = 15\%$ Interest Factors for Discrete Compounding Periods

	Single Payment		Uniform Payment Series				Gradient Series			
	Compound Amount Factor	Present Worth Factor	Present Worth Factor	Capital Recovery Factor	Compound Amount Factor	Sinking-Fund Factor	Gradient Uniform Series	Gradient Present Worth	Gradient Future Worth	
	Find F Given P	Find P Given F	Find P Given A	Find A Given P	Find F Given A	Find A Given F	Find A Given G	Find P Given G	Find F Given G	
N	F/P	P/F	P/A	A/P	F/A	A/F	A/G	P/G	F/G	
1	1.150	0.8696	0.870	1.15000	1.000	1.00000	0.000	0.000	0.00	
2	1.323	0.7561	1.626	0.61512	2.150	0.46512	0.465	0.756	1.00	
3	1.521	0.6575	2.283	0.43798	3.473	0.28798	0.907	2.071	3.15	
4	1.749	0.5718	2.855	0.35027	4.993	0.20027	1.326	3.786	6.62	
5	2.011	0.4972	3.352	0.29832	6.742	0.14832	1.723	5.775	11.62	
6	2.313	0.4323	3.784	0.26424	8.754	0.11424	2.097	7.937	18.36	
7	2.660	0.3759	4.160	0.24036	11.067	0.09036	2.450	10.192	27.11	
8	3.059	0.3269	4.487	0.22285	13.727	0.07285	2.781	12.481	38.18	
9	3.518	0.2843	4.772	0.20957	16.786	0.05957	3.092	14.755	51.91	
10	4.046	0.2472	5.019	0.19925	20.304	0.04925	3.383	16.979	68.69	
11	4.652	0.2149	5.234	0.19107	24.349	0.04107	3.655	19.129	89.00	
12	5.350	0.1869	5.421	0.18448	29.002	0.03448	3.908	21.185	113.34	
13	6.153	0.1625	5.583	0.17911	34.352	0.02911	4.144	23.135	142.35	
14	7.076	0.1413	5.724	0.17469	40.505	0.02469	4.362	24.972	176.70	
15	8.137	0.1229	5.847	0.17102	47.580	0.02102	4.565	26.693	217.20	
16	9.358	0.1069	5.954	0.16795	55.717	0.01795	4.752	28.296	264.78	
17	10.761	0.0929	6.047	0.16537	65.075	0.01537	4.925	29.783	320.50	
18	12.375	0.0808	6.128	0.16319	75.836	0.01319	5.084	31.156	385.58	
19	14.232	0.0703	6.198	0.16134	88.212	0.01134	5.231	32.421	461.41	
20	16.367	0.0611	6.259	0.15976	102.444	0.00976	5.365	33.582	549.62	

21	18.822	0.0531	6.312	0.15842	118.810	0.00842	5.488	34.645	652.07
22	21.645	0.0462	6.359	0.15727	137.632	0.00727	5.601	35.615	770.88
23	24.891	0.0402	6.399	0.15628	159.276	0.00628	5.704	36.499	908.51
24	28.625	0.0349	6.343	0.15543	184.168	0.00543	5.798	37.302	1067.79
25	32.919	0.0304	6.464	0.15470	212.793	0.00470	5.883	38.031	1251.95
26	37.857	0.0264	6.491	0.15407	245.712	0.00407	5.961	38.692	1464.75
27	43.535	0.0230	6.514	0.15353	283.569	0.00353	6.032	39.289	1710.46
28	50.066	0.0200	6.534	0.15306	327.104	0.00306	6.096	39.828	1994.03
29	57.575	0.0174	6.551	0.15265	377.170	0.00265	6.154	40.315	2321.13
30	66.212	0.0151	6.566	0.15230	434.745	0.00230	6.207	40.753	2698.30
31	76.144	0.0131	6.579	0.15200	500.957	0.00200	6.254	41.147	3133.05
32	87.565	0.0114	6.591	0.15173	577.100	0.00173	6.297	41.501	3634.00
33	100.700	0.0099	6.600	0.15150	664.666	0.00150	6.336	41.818	4211.10
34	115.805	0.0086	6.609	0.15131	765.365	0.00131	6.371	42.103	4875.77
35	133.176	0.0075	6.617	0.15113	881.170	0.00113	6.402	42.359	5641.13
40	267.864	0.0037	6.642	0.15056	1779.090	0.00056	6.517	43.283	11593.94
45	538.769	0.0019	6.654	0.15028	3585.129	0.00028	6.583	43.805	23600.86
50	1083.657	0.0009	6.661	0.15014	7217.716	0.00014	6.620	44.096	47784.78
55	2179.622	0.0005	6.664	0.15007	14524.148	0.00007	6.641	44.256	96460.99
60	4383.999	0.0002	6.665	0.15003	29219.992	0.00003	6.653	44.343	194399.95
65	8817.788	0.0001	6.666	0.15002	58778.584	0.00002	6.659	44.390	391423.89
70	17735.721	0.0001	6.666	0.15001	118231.470	0.00001	6.663	44.416	787743.13
75	35672.869	0.0000	6.666	0.15000	237812.461	0.00000	6.665	44.429	1584916.41
80	71750.879		6.667	0.15000	478332.529		6.666	44.436	—
85	144316.647		6.667	0.1500	962104.313		6.666	44.440	—
90	290272.325		6.667	0.1500	1935142.168		6.666	44.442	—
95	583841.328		6.667	0.1500	3892268.851		6.667	44.443	—
100	1174313.451		6.667	0.1500	7828749.671		6.667	44.444	—
∞	∞	0.0000	6.667	0.1500	∞	0.00000	6.667	44.444	∞

TABLE A.14 $i = 18\%$ Interest Factors for Discrete Compounding Periods

	Single Payment		Uniform Payment Series					Gradient Series			
	Compound Amount Factor	Present Worth Factor	Present Worth Factor	Capital Recovery Factor	Compound Amount Factor	Sinking-Fund Factor		Gradient Uniform Series	Gradient Present Worth	Gradient Future Worth	
	Find F Given P	Find P Given F	Find P Given A	Find A Given P	Find F Given A	Find A Given F		Find A Given G	Find P Given G	Find F Given G	
N	F/P	P/F	P/A	A/P	F/A	A/F		A/G	P/G	F/G	
1	1.180	0.8475	0.847	1.18000	1.000	1.00000		0.000	0.000	0.00	
2	1.392	0.7182	1.566	0.63872	2.180	0.45872		0.459	0.718	1.00	
3	1.643	0.6086	2.174	0.45992	3.572	0.27992		0.890	1.935	3.18	
4	1.939	0.5158	2.690	0.37174	5.215	0.19174		1.295	3.483	6.75	
5	2.288	0.4371	3.127	0.31978	7.154	0.13978		1.673	5.231	11.97	
6	2.700	0.3704	3.498	0.28591	9.442	0.10591		2.025	7.083	19.12	
7	3.185	0.3139	3.812	0.26236	12.142	0.08236		2.353	8.967	28.56	
8	3.759	0.2660	4.078	0.24524	15.327	0.06524		2.656	10.829	40.71	
9	4.435	0.2255	4.303	0.23239	19.086	0.05239		2.936	12.633	56.03	
10	5.234	0.1911	4.494	0.22251	23.521	0.04251		3.194	14.352	75.12	
11	6.176	0.1619	4.656	0.21478	28.755	0.03478		3.430	15.972	98.64	
12	7.288	0.1372	4.793	0.20863	34.931	0.02863		3.647	17.481	127.39	
13	8.599	0.1163	4.910	0.20369	42.219	0.02369		3.845	18.877	162.33	
14	10.147	0.0985	5.008	0.19968	50.818	0.01968		4.025	20.158	204.54	
15	11.974	0.0835	5.092	0.19640	60.965	0.01640		4.189	21.327	255.36	
16	14.129	0.0708	5.162	0.19371	72.939	0.01371		4.337	22.389	316.33	
17	16.672	0.0600	5.222	0.19149	87.068	0.01149		4.471	23.348	389.27	
18	19.673	0.0508	5.273	0.18964	103.740	0.00964		4.592	24.212	476.33	
19	23.214	0.0431	5.316	0.18810	123.414	0.00810		4.700	24.988	580.08	
20	27.393	0.0365	5.353	0.18682	146.628	0.00682		4.798	25.681	703.49	

21	32.324	0.0309	5.384	0.18575	174.021	0.00575	4.885	26.300	850.12
22	38.142	0.0262	5.410	0.18485	206.345	0.00485	4.963	26.851	1024.14
23	45.008	0.0222	5.432	0.18409	244.487	0.00409	5.033	27.339	1230.48
24	53.109	0.0188	5.451	0.18345	289.494	0.00345	5.095	27.772	1474.97
25	62.669	0.0160	5.467	0.18292	342.603	0.00292	5.150	28.155	1764.46
26	73.949	0.0135	5.480	0.18247	405.272	0.00247	5.199	28.494	2107.07
27	87.260	0.0115	5.492	0.18209	479.221	0.00209	5.243	28.791	2512.34
28	102.967	0.0097	5.502	0.18177	566.481	0.00177	5.281	29.054	2991.56
29	121.501	0.0082	5.510	0.18149	669.447	0.00149	5.315	29.284	3558.04
30	143.371	0.0070	5.517	0.18126	790.948	0.00126	5.345	29.486	4227.49
31	169.177	0.0059	5.523	0.18107	934.319	0.00107	5.371	29.664	5018.44
32	199.629	0.0050	5.528	0.18091	1103.496	0.00091	5.394	29.819	5952.76
33	235.563	0.0042	5.532	0.18077	1303.125	0.00077	5.415	29.955	7056.25
34	277.964	0.0036	5.536	0.18065	1538.688	0.00065	5.433	30.074	8359.38
35	327.997	0.0030	5.539	0.18055	1816.652	0.00055	5.449	30.177	9898.06
40	750.378	0.0013	5.548	0.18024	4163.213	0.00024	5.502	30.527	22906.74
45	1716.684	0.0006	5.552	0.18010	9531.577	0.00010	5.529	30.701	52703.21
50	3927.357	0.0003	5.554	0.18005	21813.093	0.00005	5.543	30.786	120906.08
55	8484.841	0.0001	5.555	0.18002	49910.228	0.00002	5.549	30.827	276973.49
60	20555.140	0.0000	5.555	0.18001	114189.666	0.00001	5.553	30.846	634053.70
65	47025.180	0.0000	5.555	0.18000	261245.446	0.00000	5.554	30.856	1451002.48
70	107582.221	0.0000	5.556	0.18000	587673.452	0.00000	5.555	30.860	3320019.19
75	246122.059	0.0000	5.556	0.18000	1367339.232	0.00000	5.555	30.862	7595912.44
∞	∞	0.0000	5.556	0.1800	∞	0.00000	5.555	30.864	∞

TABLE A.15 $i = 20\%$ Interest Factors for Discrete Compounding Periods

	Single Payment		Uniform Payment Series				Gradient Series			
	Compound Amount Factor	Present Worth Factor	Present Worth Factor	Capital Recovery Factor	Compound Amount Factor	Sinking-Fund Factor	Gradient Uniform Series	Gradient Present Worth	Gradient Future Worth	
	Find F Given P	Find P Given F	Find P Given A	Find A Given P	Find F Given A	Find A Given F	Find A Given G	Find P Given G	Find F Given G	
N	F/P	P/F	P/A	A/P	F/A	A/F	A/G	P/G	F/G	
1	1.200	0.8333	0.833	1.20000	1.000	1.00000	0.000	0.000	0.00	
2	1.440	0.6944	1.528	0.65455	2.200	0.45455	0.455	0.694	1.00	
3	1.728	0.5787	2.106	0.47473	3.640	0.27473	0.879	1.852	3.20	
4	2.074	0.4823	2.589	0.38629	5.368	0.18629	1.274	3.299	6.84	
5	2.488	0.4019	2.991	0.33438	7.442	0.13438	1.641	4.906	12.21	
6	2.986	0.3349	3.326	0.30071	9.930	0.10071	1.979	6.581	19.65	
7	3.583	0.2791	3.605	0.27742	12.916	0.07742	2.290	8.255	29.58	
8	4.300	0.2326	3.837	0.26061	16.499	0.06061	2.576	9.883	42.50	
9	5.160	0.1938	4.031	0.24808	20.799	0.04808	2.836	11.434	58.99	
10	6.192	0.1615	4.192	0.23852	25.959	0.03852	3.074	12.887	79.79	
11	7.430	0.1346	4.327	0.23110	32.150	0.03110	3.289	14.233	105.75	
12	8.916	0.1122	4.439	0.22526	39.581	0.02526	3.484	15.467	137.90	
13	10.699	0.0935	4.533	0.22062	48.497	0.02062	3.660	16.588	177.48	
14	12.839	0.0779	4.611	0.21689	59.196	0.01689	3.817	17.601	225.98	
15	15.407	0.0649	4.675	0.21388	72.035	0.01388	3.959	18.509	285.18	
16	18.488	0.0541	4.730	0.21144	87.442	0.01144	4.085	19.321	357.21	
17	22.186	0.0451	4.775	0.20944	105.931	0.00944	4.198	20.042	444.65	
18	26.623	0.0376	4.812	0.20781	128.117	0.00781	4.298	20.680	550.58	
19	31.948	0.0313	4.843	0.20646	154.740	0.00646	4.386	21.244	678.70	
20	38.338	0.0261	4.870	0.20536	186.688	0.00536	4.464	21.739	833.44	

21	46.005	0.0217	4.891	0.20444	225.026	0.00444	4.533	22.174	1020.13
22	55.206	0.0181	4.909	0.20369	271.031	0.00369	4.594	22.555	1245.15
23	66.247	0.0151	4.925	0.20307	326.237	0.00307	4.647	22.887	1516.18
24	79.497	0.0126	4.937	0.20255	392.484	0.00255	4.694	23.176	1842.42
25	95.396	0.0105	4.948	0.20212	471.981	0.00212	4.735	23.428	2234.91
26	114.475	0.0087	4.956	0.20176	567.377	0.00176	4.771	23.646	2706.89
27	137.371	0.0073	4.964	0.20147	681.853	0.00147	4.802	23.835	3274.26
28	164.845	0.0061	4.970	0.20122	819.223	0.00122	4.829	23.999	3956.12
29	197.814	0.0051	4.975	0.20102	984.068	0.00102	4.853	24.141	4775.34
30	237.376	0.0042	4.979	0.20085	1181.882	0.00085	4.873	24.263	5759.41
31	284.852	0.0035	4.982	0.20070	1419.258	0.00070	4.891	24.368	6941.29
32	341.822	0.0029	4.985	0.20059	1704.109	0.00059	4.906	24.459	8360.55
33	410.186	0.0024	4.988	0.20049	2045.931	0.00049	4.919	24.537	10064.66
34	492.224	0.0020	4.990	0.20041	2456.118	0.00041	4.931	24.604	12110.59
35	590.668	0.0017	4.992	0.20034	2948.341	0.00034	4.941	24.661	14566.71
40	1469.772	0.0007	4.997	0.20014	7343.89	0.00014	4.973	24.847	36519.29
45	3657.262	0.0003	4.999	0.20005	18281.31	0.00005	4.988	24.932	91181.55
50	9100.438	0.0001	4.999	0.20002	45497.19	0.00002	4.995	24.970	227235.95
55	22644.802	0.0000	5.000	0.20001	113219.01	0.00001	4.998	24.987	565820.05
60	36347.513	0.0000	5.000	0.20000	281732.56	0.00000	4.999	24.994	1408362.83
65	40210.643	0.0000	5.000	0.20000	701048.21	0.00000	5.000	24.998	3504916.06
70	48888.946	0.0000	5.000	0.20000	1744439.73	0.00000	5.000	24.999	8721848.75
∞	∞	0.0000	5.000	0.20000	∞	0.00000	5.000	25.000	∞

TABLE A.16 $i = 25\%$ Interest Factors for Discrete Compounding Periods

	Single Payment		Uniform Payment Series				Gradient Series		
	Compound Amount Factor	Present Worth Factor	Compound Amount Factor	Present Worth Factor	Capital Recovery Factor	Sinking-Fund Factor	Gradient Uniform Series	Gradient Present Worth	Gradient Future Worth
	Find F Given P F/P	Find P Given F P/F	Find F Given A F/A	Find P Given A P/A	Find A Given P A/P	Find A Given F A/F	Find A Given G A/G	Find P Given G P/G	Find F Given G F/G
N									
1	1.250	0.8000	1.000	0.800	1.25000	1.00000	0.000	0.000	0.00
2	1.562	0.6400	2.250	1.440	0.69444	0.44444	0.444	0.640	1.00
3	1.953	0.5120	3.812	1.952	0.51230	0.26230	0.852	1.664	3.25
4	2.441	0.4096	5.766	2.362	0.42344	0.17344	1.225	2.893	7.06
5	3.052	0.3277	8.207	2.689	0.37185	0.12185	1.563	4.204	12.83
6	3.815	0.2621	11.259	2.951	0.33882	0.08882	1.868	5.514	21.04
7	4.768	0.2097	15.073	3.161	0.31634	0.06634	2.142	6.773	32.29
8	5.960	0.1678	19.842	3.329	0.30040	0.05040	2.387	7.947	47.37
9	7.451	0.1342	25.802	3.463	0.28876	0.03876	2.605	9.021	67.21
10	9.313	0.1074	33.253	3.571	0.28007	0.03007	2.797	9.987	93.01
11	11.642	0.0859	42.566	3.656	0.27349	0.02349	2.966	10.846	126.26
12	14.552	0.0687	54.208	3.725	0.26845	0.01845	3.115	11.602	168.83
13	18.190	0.0550	68.760	3.780	0.26454	0.01454	3.244	12.262	223.04
14	22.737	0.0440	86.949	3.824	0.26150	0.01150	3.356	12.833	291.80
15	28.422	0.0352	109.687	3.859	0.25912	0.00912	3.453	13.326	378.75
16	35.527	0.0281	138.109	3.887	0.25724	0.00724	3.537	13.748	488.43
17	44.409	0.0225	173.636	3.910	0.25576	0.00576	3.608	14.108	626.54
18	55.511	0.0180	218.045	3.928	0.25459	0.00459	3.670	14.415	800.18
19	69.389	0.0144	273.556	3.942	0.25366	0.00366	3.722	14.674	1018.22
20	86.736	0.0115	342.945	3.954	0.25292	0.00292	3.767	14.893	1291.78
21	108.420	0.0092	429.681	3.963	0.25233	0.00233	3.805	15.078	1634.72
22	135.525	0.0074	538.101	3.970	0.25186	0.00186	3.836	15.233	2064.40
23	169.407	0.0059	673.626	3.976	0.25148	0.00148	3.863	15.362	2602.51
24	211.758	0.0047	843.033	3.981	0.25119	0.00119	3.886	15.471	3276.13
25	264.698	0.0038	1054.791	3.985	0.25095	0.00095	3.905	15.562	4119.16
26	330.872	0.0030	1319.489	3.988	0.25076	0.00076	3.921	15.637	5173.96
27	413.590	0.0024	1650.361	3.990	0.25061	0.00061	3.935	15.700	6493.44
28	516.988	0.0019	2063.952	3.992	0.25048	0.00048	3.946	15.752	8143.81
29	646.235	0.0015	2580.939	3.994	0.25039	0.00039	3.955	15.796	10207.76
30	807.794	0.0012	3227.174	3.995	0.25031	0.00031	3.963	15.832	12788.70
∞	∞	0.0000	∞	4.000	0.25000	0.00000	4.000	16.000	∞

TABLE A.17 $i = 30\%$ Interest Factors for Discrete Compounding Periods

	Single Payment		Uniform Payment Series				Gradient Series		
	Compound Amount Factor	Present Worth Factor	Present Worth Factor	Capital Recovery Factor	Compound Amount Factor	Sinking-Fund Factor	Gradient Uniform Series	Gradient Present Worth	Gradient Future Worth
	Find F Given P	Find P Given F	Find P Given A	Find A Given P	Find F Given A	Find A Given F	Find A Given G	Find P Given G	Find F Given G
N	F/P	P/F	P/A	A/P	F/A	A/F	A/G	P/G	F/G
1	1.300	0.7692	0.769	1.30000	1.000	1.00000	0.000	0.000	0.00
2	1.690	0.5917	1.361	0.73478	2.300	0.43478	0.435	0.592	1.00
3	2.197	0.4552	1.816	0.55063	3.990	0.25063	0.827	1.502	3.30
4	2.856	0.3501	2.166	0.46163	6.187	0.16163	1.178	2.552	7.29
5	3.713	0.2693	2.436	0.41058	9.043	0.11058	1.490	3.630	13.48
6	4.827	0.2072	2.643	0.37839	12.756	0.07839	1.765	4.666	22.52
7	6.275	0.1594	2.802	0.35687	17.583	0.05687	2.006	5.622	35.28
8	8.157	0.1226	2.925	0.34192	23.858	0.04192	2.216	6.480	52.86
9	10.604	0.0943	3.019	0.33124	32.015	0.03124	2.396	7.234	76.72
10	13.786	0.0725	3.092	0.32346	42.619	0.02346	2.551	7.887	108.73
11	17.922	0.0558	3.147	0.31773	56.405	0.01773	2.683	8.445	151.35
12	23.298	0.0429	3.190	0.31345	74.327	0.01345	2.795	8.917	207.76
13	30.288	0.0330	3.223	0.31024	97.625	0.01024	2.889	9.314	282.08
14	39.374	0.0254	3.249	0.30782	127.913	0.00782	2.969	9.644	379.71
15	51.186	0.0195	3.268	0.30598	167.286	0.00598	3.034	9.917	507.62
16	66.542	0.0150	3.283	0.30458	218.472	0.00458	3.089	10.143	674.91
17	86.504	0.0116	3.295	0.30351	285.014	0.00351	3.135	10.328	893.38
18	112.455	0.0089	3.304	0.30269	371.518	0.00269	3.172	10.479	1178.39
19	146.192	0.0068	3.311	0.30207	483.973	0.00207	3.202	10.602	1549.91
20	190.050	0.0053	3.316	0.30159	630.165	0.00159	3.228	10.702	2033.88
21	247.065	0.0040	3.320	0.30122	820.215	0.00122	3.248	10.783	2664.05
22	321.184	0.0031	3.323	0.30094	1067.280	0.00094	3.265	10.848	3484.27
23	417.539	0.0024	3.325	0.30072	1388.464	0.00072	3.278	10.901	4551.55
24	542.801	0.0018	3.327	0.30055	1806.003	0.00055	3.289	10.943	5940.01
25	705.641	0.0014	3.329	0.30043	2348.803	0.00043	3.298	10.977	7746.01
26	917.333	0.0011	3.330	0.30033	3054.444	0.00033	3.305	11.005	10094.81
27	1192.533	0.0008	3.331	0.30025	3971.778	0.00025	3.311	11.026	13149.26
28	1550.293	0.0006	3.331	0.30019	5164.311	0.00019	3.315	11.044	17121.04
29	2015.381	0.0005	3.332	0.30015	6714.604	0.00015	3.319	11.058	22285.35
30	2619.996	0.0004	3.332	0.30011	8729.985	0.00011	3.322	11.069	28999.95
∞	∞	0.0000	3.333	0.30000	∞	0.00000	3.333	11.111	∞

TABLE A.18 $i = 40\%$ Interest Factors for Discrete Compounding Periods

	Single Payment		Uniform Payment Series				Gradient Series		
	Compound Amount Factor	Present Worth Factor	Present Worth Factor	Capital Recovery Factor	Compound Amount Factor	Sinking-Fund Factor	Gradient Uniform Series	Gradient Present Worth	Gradient Future Worth
	Find F Given P	Find P Given F	Find P Given A	Find A Given P	Find F Given A	Find A Given F	Find A Given G	Find P Given G	Find F Given G
N	F/P	P/F	P/A	A/P	F/A	A/F	A/G	P/G	F/G
1	1.400	0.7143	0.714	1.40000	1.000	1.00000	0.000	0.000	0.00
2	1.960	0.5102	1.224	0.81667	2.400	0.41667	0.417	0.510	1.00
3	2.744	0.3644	1.589	0.62936	4.360	0.22936	0.780	1.239	3.40
4	3.842	0.2603	1.849	0.54077	7.104	0.14077	1.092	2.020	7.76
5	5.378	0.1859	2.035	0.49136	10.946	0.09136	1.358	2.764	14.86
6	7.350	0.1328	2.168	0.46126	16.324	0.06126	1.581	3.428	25.81
7	10.541	0.0949	2.263	0.44192	23.853	0.04192	1.766	3.997	42.13
8	14.758	0.0678	2.331	0.42907	34.395	0.02907	1.919	4.471	65.99
9	20.661	0.0484	2.379	0.42034	49.153	0.02034	2.042	4.858	100.38
10	28.925	0.0346	2.414	0.41432	69.814	0.01432	2.142	5.170	149.53
11	40.496	0.0247	2.438	0.41013	98.739	0.01013	2.221	5.417	219.35
12	56.694	0.0176	2.456	0.40718	139.235	0.00718	2.285	5.611	318.09
13	79.371	0.0126	2.469	0.40510	195.929	0.00510	2.334	5.762	457.32
14	111.120	0.0090	2.478	0.40363	275.300	0.00363	2.373	5.879	653.25
15	155.568	0.0064	2.484	0.40259	386.420	0.00259	2.403	5.969	928.55
16	217.795	0.0046	2.489	0.40185	541.988	0.00185	2.426	6.038	1314.97
17	304.913	0.0033	2.492	0.40132	759.784	0.00132	2.444	6.090	1856.96
18	426.879	0.0023	2.494	0.40094	1064.697	0.00094	2.458	6.130	2616.74
19	597.630	0.0017	2.496	0.40067	1491.576	0.00067	2.468	6.160	3681.44
20	836.683	0.0012	2.497	0.40048	2089.206	0.00048	2.476	6.183	5173.02
21	1171.356	0.0009	2.498	0.4003	2925.889	0.0003	2.482	6.200	7262.22
22	1639.898	0.0006	2.498	0.4002	4097.245	0.0002	2.487	6.213	10188.11
23	2295.857	0.0004	2.499	0.4002	5737.142	0.0002	2.490	6.222	14282.86
24	3214.200	0.0003	2.499	0.4001	8032.999	0.0001	2.493	6.229	20022.50
25	4499.880	0.0002	2.499	0.4001	11247.199	0.0001	2.494	6.235	28055.50
26	6299.831	0.0002	2.500	0.4001	15747.079	0.0001	2.496	6.239	39302.70
27	8819.764	0.0001	2.500	0.4000	22046.910		2.497	6.242	55049.78
28	12347.670	0.0001	2.500	0.4000	30866.674		2.498	6.244	77099.19
29	17286.737	0.0001	2.500	0.4000	43214.344		2.498	6.245	—
30	24201.432	0.0001	2.500	0.4000	60501.081		2.499	6.247	—
∞	∞	0.0000	2.500	0.4000	∞	0.0000	2.500	6.250	∞

TABLE A.19 $i = 50\%$ Interest Factors for Discrete Compounding Periods

	Single Payment		Uniform Payment Series				Gradient Series		
	Compound Amount Factor	Present Worth Factor	Present Worth Factor	Capital Recovery Factor	Compound Amount Factor	Sinking-Fund Factor	Gradient Uniform Series	Gradient Present Worth	Gradient Future Worth
	Find F Given P	Find P Given F	Find P Given A	Find A Given P	Find F Given A	Find A Given F	Find A Given G	Find P Given G	Find F Given G
N	F/P	P/F	P/A	A/P	F/A	A/F	A/G	P/G	F/G
1	1.500	0.6667	0.667	1.50000	1.000	1.00000	0.000	0.000	0.00
2	2.250	0.4444	1.111	0.90000	2.500	0.40000	0.400	0.444	1.00
3	3.375	0.2963	1.407	0.71053	4.750	0.21053	0.737	1.037	3.50
4	5.063	0.1975	1.605	0.62308	8.125	0.12308	1.015	1.630	8.25
5	7.594	0.1317	1.737	0.57583	13.187	0.07583	1.242	2.156	16.37
6	11.391	0.0878	1.824	0.54812	20.781	0.04812	1.423	2.595	29.56
7	17.086	0.0585	1.883	0.53108	32.172	0.03108	1.565	2.947	50.34
8	25.629	0.0390	1.922	0.52030	49.258	0.02030	1.675	3.220	82.52
9	38.443	0.0260	1.948	0.51335	74.887	0.01335	1.760	3.428	131.77
10	57.665	0.0173	1.965	0.50882	113.330	0.00882	1.824	3.584	206.66
11	86.498	0.0116	1.977	0.50585	170.995	0.00585	1.871	3.699	319.99
12	129.746	0.0077	1.985	0.50388	257.493	0.00388	1.907	3.784	490.99
13	194.620	0.0051	1.990	0.50258	387.239	0.00258	1.933	3.846	748.48
14	291.929	0.0034	1.993	0.50172	581.859	0.00172	1.952	3.890	1135.72
15	437.894	0.0023	1.995	0.50114	873.788	0.00114	1.966	3.922	1717.58
16	656.841	0.0015	1.997	0.50076	1311.682	0.00076	1.976	3.945	2591.36
17	985.261	0.0010	1.998	0.50051	1968.523	0.00051	1.983	3.961	3903.05
18	1477.892	0.0007	1.999	0.50034	2953.784	0.00034	1.988	3.973	5871.57
19	2216.838	0.0005	1.999	0.50023	4431.676	0.00023	1.991	3.981	8825.35
20	3325.257	0.0003	1.999	0.50015	6648.513	0.00015	1.994	3.987	13257.03
21	4987.885	0.0002	2.000	0.5001	9973.770	0.0001	1.996	3.991	19905.54
22	7481.828	0.0001	2.000	0.5001	14961.655	0.0001	1.997	3.994	29879.31
23	11222.741	0.0001	2.000	0.5000	22443.483		1.998	3.996	44840.97
24	16834.112	0.0001	2.000	0.5000	33666.224		1.999	3.997	67284.45
25	25251.168		2.000	0.5000	50500.337		1.999	3.998	—
26	37876.752		2.000	0.5000	75751.505		1.999	3.999	—
27	56815.129		2.000	0.5000	113628.257		2.000	3.999	—
28	85222.693		2.000	0.5000	170443.386		2.000	3.999	—
29	127834.039		2.000	0.5000	255666.079		2.000	4.000	—
30	191751.059		2.000	0.5000	383500.118		2.000	4.000	—
∞	∞	0.0000	2.000	0.5000	∞	0.0000	2.000	4.000	∞

TABLE A.20 $i = 60\%$ Interest Factors for Discrete Compounding Periods

	Single Payment		Uniform Payment Series				Gradient Series		
	Compound Amount Factor	Present Worth Factor	Present Worth Factor	Capital Recovery Factor	Compound Amount Factor	Sinking-Fund Factor	Gradient Uniform Series	Gradient Present Worth	Gradient Future Worth
	Find F Given P	Find P Given F	Find P Given A	Find A Given P	Find F Given A	Find A Given F	Find A Given G	Find P Given G	Find F Given G
N	F/P	P/F	P/A	A/P	F/A	A/F	A/G	P/G	F/G
1	1.600	0.6250	0.625	1.6000	1.000	1.0000	0.000	0.000	0.00
2	2.560	0.3906	1.016	0.9846	2.600	0.3846	0.385	0.391	1.00
3	4.096	0.2441	1.260	0.7938	5.160	0.1938	0.698	0.879	3.60
4	6.554	0.1526	1.412	0.7080	9.256	0.1080	0.946	1.337	4.50
5	10.486	0.0954	1.508	0.6633	15.810	0.0633	1.140	1.718	18.02
6	16.777	0.0596	1.567	0.6380	26.295	0.0380	1.286	2.016	33.83
7	26.844	0.0373	1.605	0.6232	43.073	0.0232	1.396	2.240	60.12
8	42.950	0.0233	1.628	0.6143	69.916	0.0143	1.476	2.403	103.19
9	68.719	0.0146	1.642	0.6089	112.866	0.0089	1.534	2.519	173.11
10	109.951	0.0091	1.652	0.6055	181.585	0.0055	1.575	2.601	285.98
11	175.922	0.0057	1.657	0.6034	291.536	0.0034	1.604	2.658	467.56
12	281.475	0.0036	1.661	0.6021	467.458	0.0021	1.624	2.697	759.10
13	450.360	0.0022	1.663	0.6013	748.933	0.0013	1.638	2.724	1226.56
14	720.576	0.0014	1.664	0.6008	1199.293	0.0008	1.647	2.742	1975.49
15	1152.922	0.0009	1.665	0.6005	1919.869	0.0005	1.654	2.754	3174.78
16	1844.674	0.0005	1.666	0.6003	3072.791	0.0003	1.658	2.762	5094.65
17	2951.479	0.0003	1.666	0.6002	4917.465	0.0002	1.661	2.767	8167.44
18	4722.366	0.0002	1.666	0.6001	7868.944	0.0001	1.663	2.771	13084.91
19	7555.786	0.0001	1.666	0.6001	12591.311	0.0001	1.664	2.773	20952.19
20	12089.258	0.0001	1.667	0.6000	20147.097		1.665	2.775	33545.16
21	19342.813	0.0001	1.667	0.6000	32236.355		1.666	2.776	53692.26
22	30948.501		1.667	0.6000	51579.168		1.666	2.777	85928.61
23	49517.602		1.667	0.6000	82527.669		1.666	2.777	137507.78
24	79228.163		1.667	0.6000	132045.271		1.666	2.777	—
25	126765.060		1.667	0.6000	211273.433		1.666	2.777	—
26	202824.096		1.667	0.6000	338038.493		1.667	2.778	—
27	324518.554		1.667	0.6000	540862.589		1.667	2.778	—
28	519229.686		1.667	0.6000	865381.143		1.667	2.778	—
29	830767.497		1.667	0.6000	1384610.829		1.667	2.778	—
30	1329227.996		1.667	0.6000	2215378.326		1.667	2.778	—
∞	∞	0.0000	1.667	0.6000	∞	0.0000	1.667	2.778	∞

TABLE A.21 $i = 70\%$ Interest Factors for Discrete Compounding Series

	Single Payment		Uniform Payment Series				Gradient Series			
	Compound Amount Factor	Present Worth Factor	Present Worth Factor	Capital Recovery Factor	Compound Amount Factor	Sinking-Fund Factor	Gradient Uniform Series	Gradient Present Worth	Gradient Future Worth
	Find F Given P	Find P Given F	Find P Given A	Find A Given P	Find F Given A	Find A Given F	Find A Given G	Find P Given G	Find F Given G
N	F/P	P/F	P/A	A/P	F/A	A/F	A/G	P/G	F/G
1	1.700	0.5882	0.5882	1.7000	1.000	1.0000	0.0000	0.0000	0.00
2	2.890	0.3460	0.9343	1.0704	2.700	0.3704	0.3703	0.3460	1.00
3	4.913	0.2035	1.1378	0.8789	5.590	0.1789	0.6619	0.7531	3.70
4	8.352	0.1197	1.2575	0.7952	10.503	0.0952	0.8845	1.1123	9.29
5	14.199	0.0704	1.3280	0.7530	18.855	0.0530	1.0497	1.3940	19.79
6	24.138	0.0414	1.3694	0.7302	33.054	0.0302	1.1693	1.6012	38.65
7	41.034	0.0244	1.3938	0.7175	57.191	0.0175	1.2537	1.7474	71.70
8	69.758	0.0143	1.4081	0.7102	98.225	0.0102	1.3122	1.8477	128.89
9	118.590	0.0084	1.4165	0.7060	167.980	0.0060	1.3520	1.9152	227.11
10	201.600	0.0050	1.4215	0.7035	286.570	0.0035	1.3787	1.9598	395.10
11	342.720	0.0029	1.4244	0.7020	488.170	0.0020	1.3964	1.9890	681.67
12	582.620	0.0017	1.4261	0.7012	830.890	0.0012	1.4079	2.0079	1026.99
13	990.460	0.0010	1.4271	0.7007	1413.000	0.0007	1.4154	2.0200	2000.00
14	1684.000	0.0006	1.4277	0.7004	2404.000	0.0004	1.4203	2.0277	3414.29
15	2862.000	0.0003	1.4281	0.7002	4087.000	0.0002	1.4233	2.0326	5817.14
∞	∞	0.0000	1.4286	0.7000	∞	0.0000	1.4286	2.0408	∞

TABLE A.22 $i = 90\%$ Interest Factors for Discrete Compounding Series

	Single Payment		Uniform Payment Series				Gradient Series			
	Compound Amount Factor	Present Worth Factor	Present Worth Factor	Capital Recovery Factor	Compound Amount Factor	Sinking-Fund Factor	Gradient Uniform Series	Gradient Present Worth	Gradient Future Worth	
	Find F Given P	Find P Given F	Find P Given A	Find A Given P	Find F Given A	Find A Given F	Find A Given G	Find P Given G	Find F Given G	
N	F/P	P/F	P/A	A/P	F/A	A/F	A/G	P/G	F/G	
1	1.900	0.5263	0.5263	1.9000	1.000	1.0000	0.0000	0.0000	0.00	
2	3.610	0.2770	0.8033	1.2448	2.900	0.3448	0.3448	0.2770	1.00	
3	6.859	0.1458	0.9491	1.0536	6.510	0.1536	0.5991	0.5686	3.90	
4	13.032	0.0767	1.0259	0.9748	13.369	0.0748	0.7787	0.7988	10.41	
5	24.761	0.0404	1.0662	0.9379	26.401	0.0379	0.9007	0.9603	23.78	
6	47.046	0.0213	1.0875	0.9195	51.162	0.0195	0.9808	1.0666	50.18	
7	89.387	0.0112	1.0987	0.9102	98.208	0.0102	1.0319	1.1337	101.34	
8	169.84	0.0059	1.1046	0.9053	187.60	0.0053	1.0637	1.1750	199.56	
9	322.69	0.0031	1.1077	0.9028	357.43	0.0028	1.0831	1.1998	387.14	
10	613.11	0.0016	1.1093	0.9015	680.12	0.0015	1.0948	1.2144	744.58	
11	1165.00	0.0009	1.1102	0.9008	1293.00	0.0008	1.1017	1.2230	1424.44	
12	2213.00	0.0004	1.1106	0.9004	2458.00	0.0004	1.1057	1.2280	2717.78	
13	4205.00	0.0002	1.1108	0.9002	4671.00	0.0002	1.1080	1.2808	5175.55	
14	7990.00	0.0001	1.1110	0.9001	8877.00	0.0001	1.1094	1.2325	9847.78	
15	15181.00	0.0001	1.1110	0.9001	16867.00	0.0001	1.1101	1.2334	18724.44	
∞	∞	0.0000	1.1111	0.9000	∞	0.0000	1.1111	1.2346	∞	

TABLE A.23 $i = 110\%$ Interest Factors for Discrete Compounding Series

	Single Payment		Uniform Payment Series				Gradient Series		
	Compound Amount Factor	Present Worth Factor	Present Worth Factor	Capital Recovery Factor	Compound Amount Factor	Sinking-Fund Factor	Gradient Uniform Series	Gradient Present Worth	Gradient Future Worth
	Find F Given P	Find P Given F	Find P Given A	Find A Given P	Find F Given A	Find A Given F	Find A Given G	Find P Given G	Find F Given G
N	F/P	P/F	P/A	A/P	F/A	A/F	A/G	P/G	F/G
1	2.100	0.4762	0.4762	2.100	1.000	1.0000	0.0000	0.0000	0.00
2	4.410	0.2268	0.7029	1.423	3.100	0.3226	0.3326	0.2268	1.00
3	9.261	0.1080	0.8109	1.233	7.510	0.1332	0.5459	0.4427	4.10
4	19.448	0.0514	0.8623	1.160	16.771	0.0596	0.6923	0.5970	11.61
5	40.841	0.0245	0.8868	1.128	36.219	0.0276	0.7836	0.6949	28.38
6	85.766	0.0117	0.8985	1.113	77.060	0.0130	0.8383	0.7532	64.60
7	180.11	0.0055	0.9040	1.106	162.83	0.0061	0.8700	0.7865	141.66
8	378.23	0.0026	0.9067	1.103	342.93	0.0029	0.8879	0.8050	304.48
9	794.28	0.0013	0.9079	1.101	721.16	0.0014	0.8978	0.8151	647.42
10	1668.00	0.0006	0.9085	1.101	1515.00	0.0007	0.9031	0.8205	1368.18
11	3503.00	0.0003	0.9088	1.100	3183.00	0.0003	0.9059	0.8234	2883.64
12	7356.00	0.0001	0.9090	1.100	6686.00	0.0001	0.9075	0.8249	6067.27
∞	∞	0.0000	0.9090	1.000	∞	0.0000	0.9090	0.8265	∞

TABLE A.24 $i = 130\%$ Interest Factors for Discrete Compounding Periods

	Single Payment		Uniform Payment Series				Gradient Series		
	Compound Amount Factor	Present Worth Factor	Present Worth Factor	Capital Recovery Factor	Compound Amount Factor	Sinking-Fund Factor	Gradient Uniform Series	Gradient Present Worth	Gradient Future Worth
	Find F Given P	Find P Given F	Find P Given A	Find A Given P	Find F Given A	Find A Given F	Find A Given G	Find P Given G	Find F Given G
N	F/P	P/F	P/A	A/P	F/A	A/F	A/G	P/G	F/G
1	2.300	0.4348	0.4348	2.300	1.000	1.0000	0.0000	0.0000	0.00
2	5.290	0.1890	0.6239	1.603	3.300	0.3030	0.3030	0.1890	1.00
3	12.167	0.0822	0.7060	1.416	8.590	0.1164	0.5006	0.3534	4.30
4	27.984	0.0357	0.7417	1.348	20.757	0.0482	0.6210	0.4606	12.89
5	64.363	0.0155	0.7573	1.320	48.741	0.0205	0.6903	0.5228	33.65
6	148.04	0.0068	0.7640	1.309	113.10	0.0088	0.7284	0.5565	82.38
7	340.48	0.0029	0.7670	1.304	261.14	0.0038	0.7486	0.5742	195.49
8	783.11	0.0013	0.7682	1.302	601.62	0.0017	0.7590	0.5831	456.63
9	1801.00	0.0006	0.7688	1.301	1385.00	0.0007	0.7642	0.5875	1058.46
10	4143.00	0.0002	0.7690	1.300	3186.00	0.0003	0.7668	0.5897	2443.08
11	9528.00	0.0001	0.7691	1.300	7328.00	0.0001	0.7681	0.5908	5628.46
12	21915.00	0.0001	0.7692	1.300	16857.00	0.0001	0.7687	0.5913	12957.69
∞	∞	0.0000	0.7692	1.300	∞	0.0000	0.7692	0.5917	∞

TABLE A.25 $i = 150\%$ **Interest Factors for Discrete Compounding Periods**

	Single Payment		Uniform Payment Series					Gradient Series		
	Compound Amount Factor	Present Worth Factor	Present Worth Factor	Capital Recovery Factor	Compound Amount Factor	Sinking-Fund Factor	Gradient Uniform Series	Gradient Present Worth	Gradient Future Worth
	Find F Given P	Find P Given F	Find P Given A	Find A Given P	Find F Given A	Find A Given F	Find A Given G	Find P Given G	Find F Given G
N	F/P	P/F	P/A	A/P	F/A	A/F	A/G	P/G	F/G
1	2.500	0.4000	0.4000	2.500	1.000	1.0000	0.0000	0.0000	0.00
2	6.250	0.1600	0.5600	1.785	3.500	0.2857	0.2857	0.1600	1.00
3	15.625	0.0640	0.6240	1.602	9.750	0.1026	0.4615	0.2880	4.50
4	39.062	0.0256	0.6496	1.539	25.375	0.0394	0.5616	0.3648	14.25
5	97.656	0.0102	0.6598	1.515	64.437	0.0155	0.6149	0.4058	39.62
6	244.14	0.0041	0.6639	1.506	162.09	0.0062	0.6420	0.4262	104.06
7	610.35	0.0016	0.6656	1.502	406.23	0.0025	0.6552	0.4361	266.15
8	1526.00	0.0007	0.6662	1.501	1017.00	0.0010	0.6614	0.4401	672.67
9	3815.00	0.0003	0.6665	1.500	2542.00	0.0004	0.6643	0.4428	1688.00
10	9537.00	0.0001	0.6666	1.500	6357.00	0.0002	0.6656	0.4437	4231.33
11	23842.00	0.0000	0.6666	1.500	15894.00	0.0001	0.6662	0.4441	10588.67
12	59604.00	0.0000	0.6667	1.500	39736.00	0.0000	0.6665	0.4443	26482.67
∞	∞	0.0000	0.6667	1.500	∞	0.0000	0.6667	0.4444	∞

TABLE A.26 $i = 200\%$ **Interest Factors for Discrete Compounding Periods**

	Single Payment		Uniform Payment Series				Gradient Series		
	Compound Amount Factor	Present Worth Factor	Present Worth Factor	Capital Recovery Factor	Compound Amount Factor	Sinking-Fund Factor	Gradient Uniform Series	Gradient Present Worth	Gradient Future Worth
	Find F Given P	Find P Given F	Find P Given A	Find A Given P	Find F Given A	Find A Given F	Find A Given G	Find P Given G	Find F Given G
N	F/P	P/F	P/A	A/P	F/A	A/F	A/G	P/G	F/G
1	3.000	0.33333	0.3333	3.000	1.000	1.000	0.0000	0.0000	0.00
2	9.000	0.11111	0.4444	2.250	4.000	0.25000	0.2500	0.1111	1.00
3	27.000	0.03074	0.4815	2.077	13.000	0.07692	0.3846	0.1852	5.00
4	81.000	0.01235	0.4938	2.025	40.000	0.02500	0.4500	0.2222	18.00
5	243.000	0.00412	0.4979	2.008	121.000	0.00826	0.4793	0.2387	58.00
6	729.000	0.00137	0.4993	2.003	364.000	0.00275	0.4917	0.2455	179.00
7	2187.000	0.00046	0.4998	2.001	1093.000	0.00092	0.4968	0.2483	543.00
8	6561.000	0.00015	0.4999	2.000	3280.000	0.00030	0.4987	0.2493	1636.00
9	19683.000	0.00005	0.5000	2.000	9841.000	0.00010	0.4995	0.2498	4916.00
10	59049.000	0.00002	0.5000	2.000	29524.000	0.00003	0.4998	0.2499	14757.00
∞	∞	0.00000	0.5000	2.000	∞	0.00000	0.5000	0.2500	∞

APPENDIX B

COMPUTER-AIDED CAPITAL EXPENDITURE ANALYSES

B.1 INTRODUCTION

In today's planning and decision-making environment, the key factor is *change*. Thus, *planning*, by definition, is the *management of such change* in terms of a formal and systematic process that is designed to ensure the direction and control of the firm. Of course, careful and efficient planning is crucial in the often complex, uncertain, and quickly changing economic and financial environment of today. Since both the opportunities and risks are greater today than in the past, planning for the future is one of the most important and challenging assignments for an engineering manager. One of the primary prerequisites for effective planning and decision making is the ability and/or capacity to deal with a large number of alternatives and being able to answer "What if...?" type of questions quickly and effectively. Obviously, such tasks would dictate the use of computers in an interactive manner. Today, there are a large number of such financial planning tools available on the market. One of the best of such tools is known as the *Interactive Financial Planning System* (IFPS) and has been developed by the EXECUCOM Systems Corporation.[†] The major advantages of using IFPS include the following:[‡]

[†]The Interactive Financial Planning System (IFPS) computer programming package can be obtainable from the EXECUCOM Systems Corporation. The address of its corporate headquarters is P.O. Box 9758, Austin, Texas 78766. Its telephone number is (512) 346-4980.
[‡]For further information, see *IFPS User's Manual* [25].

1. The necessary computations can be performed much faster and more conveniently.

2. The model is a concise statement of the problem — easily understandable to anyone involved — thus facilitating communication between decision makers.

3. The decision maker can write his own models and do his own analyses without having to obtain the services of and communicate with a computer specialist.

4. The sensitivity analysis capabilities built into IFPS allow the user to determine which are the "important" decision variables and their relative effect on future results.

Once a financial analysis has been performed using IFPS, it takes only seconds to reformulate the analysis with "what if" type questions. Thus, the uncertainty of future conditions and the risks associated with alternative courses of action can be clearly understood with a minimal expenditure of time and effort. The following is a summary of the significant features and capabilities of IFPS:

- IFPS is not a canned program, i.e., interrelationships are defined in terms of the user's needs, not someone else's interpretation of those needs.
- The problem to be solved is formulated in English-like statements.
- A flexible report writer allows the user to tailor reports to his own specifications.
- The user has the choice of obtaining either complete reports or just the values for selected items.
- A consolidation feature useful in budgeting applications is available.
- Risk analysis is performed as easily as spread-sheet ("best guess") analysis.
- Powerful logic capabilities are provided in the IF expression.
- A special "what if" capability for testing alternatives and sensitivity analysis is available.
- Built-in financial analysis capabilities include present value, internal rate of return, depreciation, and amortization.
- Editing of reports and models is performed within IFPS.
- The user can define his own FORTRAN functions and subroutines for use in IFPS model." [25]

Recently, the IFPS has been extensively developed by the EXECUCOM Systems Corporation. Its new version is called IFPS/Plus, and a brief summary of its capabilities and organization has been given in the next section. Examples of computer applications using the IFPS system are given in Appendix C.

B.2 ORGANIZATION OF IFPS/PLUS†

FPS/Plus is a computer language with English-like terminology that you can easily use to develop customized applications. It is a multi purpose system offering the following capabilities:

- A *modeling language* with which you can describe business relationships and perform financial/quantitative computations and projections.
- A *reporting language* with which you can easily organize information into any desired, presentation-quality format.
- A *data-manipulation language* that allows you to conveniently organize data separately from the model (in a database or a data file), to make changes or updates easily, to generate reports directly from the data, and to internally create or consolidate new data files from existing information, and to interactively query the data in a database relation.
- A *command language* with which you can designate a sequence of IFPS/Plus commands, directives, and/or options (allowing conditional branching and user choice as appropriate). Processing can be then initiated on subsequent occasions with a single command.

The highest level of control in IFPS/Plus is called the *Executive level*. The Executive level is activated with you first enter IFPS/Plus, as indicated when you receive the prompt:

READY FOR EXECUTIVE COMMAND
?

A whole group of commands known as "Executive commands" process at the Executive level.

Below the Executive level are a number of *subsystems*. You may issue an Executive level command which transfers execution control to any appropriate subsystem, in order to perform the corresponding activities of that subsystem. That is, subsystems set a context in which certain commands (such as SOLVE) can manipulate or use the particular entity associated with that subsystem, whereas other commands are recognized and execute everywhere. Most execution of IFPS/Plus takes place within these subsystems.

Table B.1 depicts the levels of IFPS/Plus execution (Executive level and subsystems) and indicates the primary functions of each. However, there is no hierarchy among the subsystems themselves; each may be considered one level directly below the Executive level.

---

†This section has been taken from the *IFPS/Plus User's Manual* [26]. It has been included here with the permission of the EXECUCOM Systems Corporation. Copyright © 1987 by EXECUCOM Systems Corporation, Austin, Texas, 78759.

TABLE B.1 IFPS/Plus Organization and Functions

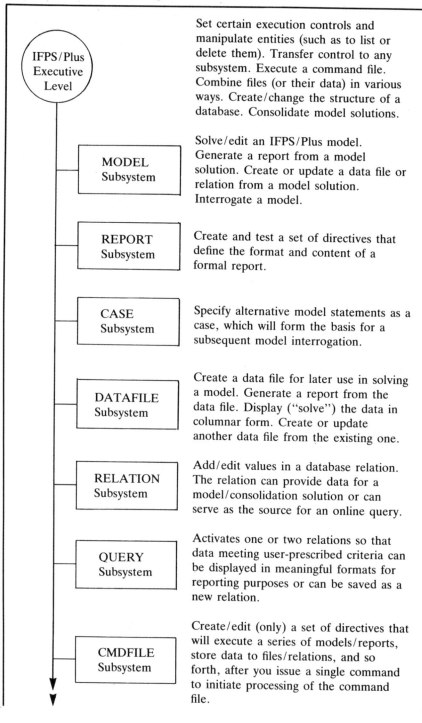

IFPS/Plus Executive Level	Set certain execution controls and manipulate entities (such as to list or delete them). Transfer control to any subsystem. Execute a command file. Combine files (or their data) in various ways. Create/change the structure of a database. Consolidate model solutions.
MODEL Subsystem	Solve/edit an IFPS/Plus model. Generate a report from a model solution. Create or update a data file or relation from a model solution. Interrogate a model.
REPORT Subsystem	Create and test a set of directives that define the format and content of a formal report.
CASE Subsystem	Specify alternative model statements as a case, which will form the basis for a subsequent model interrogation.
DATAFILE Subsystem	Create a data file for later use in solving a model. Generate a report from the data file. Display ("solve") the data in columnar form. Create or update another data file from the existing one.
RELATION Subsystem	Add/edit values in a database relation. The relation can provide data for a model/consolidation solution or can serve as the source for an online query.
QUERY Subsystem	Activates one or two relations so that data meeting user-prescribed criteria can be displayed in meaningful formats for reporting purposes or can be saved as a new relation.
CMDFILE Subsystem	Create/edit (only) a set of directives that will execute a series of models/reports, store data to files/relations, and so forth, after you issue a single command to initiate processing of the command file.

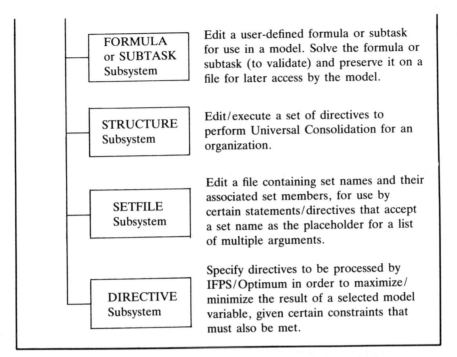

FORMULA or **SUBTASK** Subsystem	Edit a user-defined formula or subtask for use in a model. Solve the formula or subtask (to validate) and preserve it on a file for later access by the model.
STRUCTURE Subsystem	Edit/execute a set of directives to perform Universal Consolidation for an organization.
SETFILE Subsystem	Edit a file containing set names and their associated set members, for use by certain statements/directives that accept a set name as the placeholder for a list of multiple arguments.
DIRECTIVE Subsystem	Specify directives to be processed by IFPS/Optimum in order to maximize/ minimize the result of a selected model variable, given certain constraints that must also be met.

APPENDIX C
EXAMPLES OF COMPUTER APPLICATIONS

In this appendix a number of examples have been given to illustrate the applications of Interactive Financial Planning System (IFPS) that could be used in a range of engineering economy problems.

Example C.1   Solve Example 3.20 by using the IFPS computer program.

Solution

```
MODEL A VERSION OF 01/30/88  11:36 SOLUTION OF EXAMPLE C.1
10 *
20 *
30 *
40 UNIFORM SERIES VALUE=4000
50 *
60 GRADIENT SERIES VALUE=500
70 *
80 INTEREST RATE=.12
90 LIFE=5
100 *
110 X=1/L80
120 *
130 Z=1+L80
140 M=XPOWERY(L130,L90)
150 PAYDA=L140-1
160 Y=L90/L150
170 *
180 A OVER G = L110-L160
190 *
200 EQ UNI ANNUAL WORTH=L40-L60*L180
END OF MODEL
INPUT: SOLVE
MODEL A  VERSION OF 01/30/88 11:36 --1 COLUMNS 11 VARIABLES
ENTER SOLVE OPTIONS
INPUT: ALL
```

1
SOLUTION OF EXAMPLE C.1

UNIFORM SERIES VALUE	4000
GRADIENT SERIES VALUE	500
INTEREST RATE	.1200
LIFE	5
X	8.333
Z	1.120
M	1.762
PAYDA	.7623
Y	6.559
A OVER G	1.775
EQ UNI ANNUAL WORTH	3113

```
ENTER SOLVE OPTIONS
INPUT; QUIT,NO
```

Example C.2 Solve Example 3.12 by using the IFPS computer program.

Solution

```
MODEL B VERSION OF 01/30/88 11:34 SOLUTION OF EXAMPLE C.2
10 *
20 *
30 *
40 PRESENT VALUE=542048
50 INTEREST RATE=.10
60 LIFE=20
70 *
80 AMORT(L40,0,L50,L60,1,1,ANNUITY)
END OF MODEL
INPUT: SOLVE
MODEL B VERSION OF 01/30/88 11:34 -- 1 COLUMNS 4 VARIABLES
ENTER SOLVE OPTIONS
INPUT: ALL
```

```
                              1

                 SOLUTION OF EXAMPLE C.2

PRESENT VALUE               542048
INTEREST RATE                .1000
LIFE                            20

ANNUITY                      63669

ENTER SOLVE OPTIONS
INPUT: QUIT,NO
```

Example C.3 Solve Example 3.7 by using the IFPS computer program.

Solution

```
MODEL C  VERSION OF 01/30/88 15:01 SOLUTION OF EXAMPLE C.3
10 *
20 *
30 *
40 YEARLY PREMIUM = 2000
50 INTEREST RATE=.10
60 LIFE=35
70 INVESTMENT=0
80 *
90 X=1+L50
100 F OVER P=XPOWERY(L90,L60)
110 *
120 *
130 PRESENT VALUE=NPV(L40,L50,L60,L70)
140 *
150 TOTAL SAVINGS=PRESENT VALUE * F OVER P
END OF MODEL
INPUT: SOLVE
MODEL C  VERSION OF 01/30/88 15:01 -- 1 COLUMNS 8 VARIABLES
INPUT:  ALL
```

SOLUTION OF EXAMPLE C.3

YEARLY PREMIUM	2000
INTEREST RATE	.1000
LIFE	35
INVESTMENT	0
X	1.100
F OVER P	28.10
PRESENT VALUE	19288
TOTAL SAVINGS	542049

ENTER SOLVE OPTIONS
INPUT: QUIT,NO

Example C.4   Solve Example 3.8 by using the IFPS computer program.

Solution

```
MODEL D   VERSION OF 01/30/88 15:01 SOLUTION OF EXAMPLE C.4
10 *
20 *
30 *
40 YEARLY PREMIUM=2000
50 FIRST INTEREST RATE=.10
60 SECOND INTEREST RATE=.15
70 FIRST LIFE=20
80 SECOND LIFE=15
90 INVESTMENT=0
100 *
110 X=1+L50
120 Y=1+L60
130 *
140 *
150 FIRST F OVER P=XPOWERY(L110,L70)
160 SECOND F OVER P=XPOWERY (L120,L80)
170 *
180 *
190 FIRST PRESENT VALUE=NPV(L40,L50,L70,L90)
200 *
210 FIRST STEP FUTURE VALUE=L190*L150
220 SECOND STEP FUTURE VALUE=L210*L160
230 *
240 SECOND PART PRESENT VALUE=NPV(L40,L60,L80,L90)
250 SECOND PART FUTURE VALUE=L240*L160
260 *
270 *
280 TOTAL SAVINGS=L220+L250
END OF MODEL
INPUT: SOLVE
MODEL D   VERSION OF 01/30/88 15:01 -- 1 COLUMNS 16 VARIABLE
INPUT ALL
```

1
SOLUTION OF EXAMPLE C.4

YEARLY PREMIUM	2000
FIRST INTEREST RATE	.1000
SECOND INTEREST RATE	.1500
FIRST LIFE	20
SECOND LIFE	15
INVESTMENT	0
X	1.100
Y	1.150
FIRST F OVER P	6.727
SECOND F OVER P	8.137
FIRST PRESENT VALUE	17027
FIRST STEP FUTURE VALUE	114550
SECOND STEP FUTURE VALUE	932100
SECOND PART PRESENT VALUE	11695
SECOND PART FUTURE VALUE	95161
TOTAL SAVINGS	1027261

ENTER SOLVE OPTIONS
INPUT: QUIT,NO

Example C.5 Solve Example 3.22 by using the IFPS computer program.

Solution The solution is presented in two different versions.

```
MODEL E  VERSION OF 01/30/88 11:35  SOLUTION OF EXAMPLE C.5
10 *
20 *
30 *
40 ANN MAINTENANCE COST=5000
50 INTEREST RATE=.10
60 INCREASE AT INT RATE=.15
70 LIFE=10
80 *
90 X=1+L60
100 Y=1+L50
110 Z=L90/L100
120 *
130 EFF INTEREST RATE=L110-1
140 *
150 XY=1+L130
160 XZ=XPOWERY(L150,L70)
170 PAY=L160-1
180 FACTOR=L170/L130
190 *
200 XYZ=L40/L100
210 *
```

```
220 PRE W OF MAINT COST=L200*L180
END OF MODEL
INPUT: SOLVE
MODEL E VERSION OF 01/30/88 11:35 -- 1 COLUMNS 14 VARIABLES
ENTER SOLVE OPTIONS
INPUT: ALL
```

                              1
                  SOLUTION OF EXAMPLE C.5

ANN MAINTENANCE COST	5000
INTEREST RATE	.1000
INCREASE AT INT RATE	.1500
LIFE	10
X	1.150
Y	1.100
Z	1.045
EFF INTEREST RATE	.0455
XY	1.045
XZ	1.560
PAY	.5597
FACTOR	12.31
XYZ	4545
PW OF MAINTENANCE COST	55974

```
ENTER SOLVE OPTIONS
INPUT: QUIT,NO
```

Example C.6 Solve Example 3.21 by using the IFPS computer program.

Solution

```
MODEL F VERSION OF 01/30/88 11:39  SOLUTION OF EXAMPLE C.6

10 *
20 *
30 *
40 PAYMENT=4000
50 *
60 INTEREST RATE=.12
70 PERIOD LENGTH=5
80 AMORT(L40,0,L60,L70,1,1,ANNUITY)
90 P OVER A=1/L60
100 *
110 *
120 TOTAL PRESENT WORTH=L80*L90
END OF MODEL
INPUT: SOLVE
MODEL F VERSION OF 01/30/88 11:39 -- 1 COLUMNS 6 VARIABLES
ENTER SOLVE OPTIONS
INPUT:  ALL
```

```
                                  1
                     SOLUTION OF EXAMPLE C.6

PAYMENT                          4000

INTEREST RATE                    .1200
PERIOD LENGTH                        5
ANNUITY                           1110
P OVER A                         8.333

TOTAL PRESENT WORTH              9247
ENTER SOLVE OPTION
INPUT: QUIT,NO
```

Alternatively, Example C.6 can also be solved as given below.

```
MODEL G VERSION OF 01/30/88 11:39 SOLUTION OF EXAMPLE C.6
10 *
20 *
30 *
40 PAYMENT=4000
50 *
60 INTEREST RATE=.12
70 PERIOD LENGTH=5
80 *
90 X=1+L60
100 y=XPOWERY(L90,L70)
110 PAY=L60*L100
120 PAYDA=L100-1
130 A OVER P=L110/L120
140 *
150 P OVER A=1/L60
160 *
170 TOTAL PRESENT WORTH=L40*L130*L150
END OF MODEL
INPUT: SOLVE
MODEL G VERSION OF 01/30/88 11:39 -- 1 COLUMNS 10 VARIABLES
ENTER SOLVE OPTIONS
INPUT: ALL
                                  1
                     SOLUTION OF EXAMPLE C.6

PAYMENT                          4000

INTEREST RATE                    .1200
PERIOD LENGTH                        5

X                                1.120
y                                1.762
PAY                              .2115
PAYDA                            .7623
A OVER P                         .2774

P OVER A                         8.333

TOTAL PRESENT WORTH              9247

ENTER SOLVE OPTIONS
INPUT:  QUIT, NO
ENTER SOLVE OPTIONS
```

Example C.7   Solve Example 4.6 by using the IFPS computer program.

Solution

MODEL H VERSION OF 01/31/88 00:10 SOLUTION OF EXAMPLE C.7

```
10 *
20 *
30 *
40 ANNUITY=5000
50 INTEREST RATE=.12
60 LIFE=7
70 UST=L50*L60
80 STATEMENT=NATEXP(L70)
90 PAY=L80-1
100 PAYDA=L50*L80
110 *
120 FACTOR=L90/L100
130 *
140 EQ PRE WORTH=L40*L120
150 *
160 *          SOLUTION OF EXAMPLE C.7(PART B)
170 *
180 EQ FUTURE WORTH=L140&L80
END OF MODEL
INPUT: SOLVE
MODEL H VERSION OF 01/31/88 00:10 -- 1 COLUMNS 10 VARIABLES
ENTER SOLVE OPTIONS
INPUT: ALL
                      1
```

SOLUTION OF EXAMPLE C.7 (PART A)

ANNUITY	5000
INTEREST RATE	.1200
LIFE	7
UST	.8400
STATEMENT	2.316
PAY	1.316
PAYDA	.2780
FACTOR	4.736
PRESENT WORTH	23679

SOLUTION OF EXAMPLE C.7 (PART B)

FUTURE WORTH	54849

```
ENTER SOLVE OPTIONS
INPUT:  QUIT,NO.
```

PROBLEMS

C.1 Solve Example 5.10 by using the IFPS computer program.

C.2 Solve Example 5.11 by using the IFPS computer program.

C.3 Assume that two alternative pieces of production equipment are being considered. Equipment A costs $35,000 and will save $0.42 of labor per time unit produced. Equipment B costs $82,000 and will save $0.73 of labor time per unit produced. MARR is 20%. Assume that ad valorem (property) taxes are 3% of the first cost. Both pieces of equipment have zero salvage value at the end of their 10-year useful lives. Use the IFPS computer package and determine:

(a) Annual production rate that is necessary for equipment B to repay its costs, including return.

(b) Annual production rate that is necessary for equipment A to be selected.

C.4 The Zubits International Corporation is considering purchasing a particular truck at a price of $50,000. The salvage value of the truck will be $10,000 at the end of its useful life of 7 years. The cost of its license and insurance is $4,500 per year. The cost of operation and maintenance of the truck is $250 per day of operation. On the other hand the corporation can also rent the truck and hire its operator. The cost of renting the truck and hiring its operator is $370 per day. Treat the daily cash flows as if they take place at the end of each year. MARR is 25%. Use the IFPS computer package and determine the minimum number of days per year for which the services of the truck is necessary to justify the purchase of the truck.

C.5 A company is considering purchasing a small mainframe computer for $17,000. It has a salvage value of $2,000 at the end of its useful life of 4 years. Maintenance expenses are given as $3,000 per year, whereas the operating expenses are $60 per day. The same computer can be rented at an average cost of $150 per day. Use a MARR of 20% and the IFPS computer package. How many days per year must the computer be used to justify its purchase?

C.6 Assume that machine A costs $2,500 and has a zero salvage value at the end of 8 years, whereas machine B costs $5,200 and has a $950 salvage value at the end of 8 years. The labor costs per unit of product produced employing machines A and B are $2.15 and $0.93, respectively. Use the IFPS computer package and a MARR of 15%. Determine the annual rate of production that will make the two machines break even in annual equivalent costs.

C.7 Assume that the following data has been given for a depreciable asset. Its first cost is $200,000 and its salvage value is $20,000 at the end of its 25-year useful life. Use the IFPS computer package and determine the depreciation allocation for each year, that is, prepare a depreciation schedule, if the depreciation method used is

(a) Straight-line method.

(b) Sum-of-years' digits method.

(c) Double-declining-balance method.

(d) Sinking-fund method; use $i = 12\%$.

(e) Five-year write-off.

(f) Unit of production method. Assume that total production of 525,000 units of production is estimated to be produced at the rate of 20,000 units per year for the first 5 years, 25,000 units per year for the next 15 years, and 10,000 units per year for the last 5 years.

C.8 Assume that a piece of equipment has a first cost of $100,000 and a salvage value of $5,000 at the end of its 10-year useful life. Use the IFPS computer package and determine the depreciation schedule for the equipment using:

(a) Straight-line method.

(b) Sum-of-years' digits method.

(c) Double-declining-balance method.

(d) Sinking-fund method; use $i = 10\%$.

C.9 Five years ago Sevil Manufacturing Corporation bought an asset for $150,000; at that time the estimated useful life of the asset was 15 years with a zero salvage value. Today the corporation sold the asset for $65,000. Use the IFPS computer package and determine the capital gain or loss on the transaction, if the depreciation method used was

(a) Straight-line method.

(b) Sum-of-years' digits method.

(c) Double-declining-balance method.

C.10 Assume that a utility company is providing electric energy to a group of rural customers using an overhead feeder. Due to severe weather conditions, the feeder requires repair at an average cost of $2,000 per repair. The company is considering installing an underground cable replacing the overhead feeder. Assume that the study period is 25 years, no salvage, interest rate is 25%, and that its operating costs are constant. Use the IFPS computer package and determine the maximum amount that the company can spend, and justify it, for the underground feeder, if it uses the data that has been given in Table C.10.

TABLE C.10   Data for Problem C.10

Number of Repairs per Year (x)	Probability of Repairs, i.e., Prob(x)	
	For Overhead Feeder	For Underground Feeder
0	0.1	0.95
1	0.2	0.05
2	0.3	0.00
3	0.3	0.00
4	0.1	0.00

C.11 Assume that the Green Ozark Manufacturing Company is contemplating installing a 100-horsepower, three-phase electric induction motor. There are two possible alternatives; the installed cost of motor A is $3,000, and it has an efficiency of 97%, whereas the installed cost of motor B is $2,500, and it has an efficiency of 92%. Assume negligible salvage values for both motors at the end of their useful lives of 10 years. Also, assume that the interest rate is 15% and that the cost of electrical energy is 5 cents/kWh. (Note that 1 horsepower is 0.746 kW.) Assume that the annual usage of the selected motor is probabilistic and statistically independent as given in Table C.11. Use the IFPS computer package and find the probability that motor A is favorable to motor B.

TABLE C.11   Data for Problem C.11

Annual Motor Usage (hours)	Probability of Such Usage
4,000	0.05
5,000	0.10
6,000	0.40
7,000	0.30
8,000	0.15

C.12 Assume that a project has a first cost of $100,000 and uniform revenues of $20,000 per year and that its salvage value is negligible. Use the IFPS computer package and determine the probability that the project is acceptable (i.e., it is profitable) if its MARR is 15% and the probability distribution of its project life is as given in Table C.12.

TABLE C.12   Data for Problem C.12

Project Life (N)	Probability of Such Project Life Prob(N)
7 years	0.05
8	0.15
9	0.25
10	0.40
11	0.10
12	0.05

C.13 Assume that the first cost of the project that is given in Problem C.12 has a probability distribution as given in Table C.13. Use the IFPS computer package and determine the probability that the project is acceptable, that is, profitable.

TABLE C.13   Data for Problem C.13

First Cost (P)	Probability of Such First Cost Prob(P)
$80,000	0.10
$90,000	0.25
$100,000	0.30
$110,000	0.25
$120,000	0.10

C.14 Resolve Problem C.12 but assume that the interest rate (i.e., MARR) has a probability distribution as given in Table C.14. Use the IFPS computer package.

TABLE C.14   Data for Problem C.14

Interest Rate, i (%)	Probability of Such Interest Rate Prob(i%)
10	0.10
15	0.25
20	0.30
25	0.25
30	0.10

C.15 Resolve Problem C.12 but assume that there is a salvage value, of the project, that depends on the life of the project as given in Table C.15. Use the IFPS computer package.

TABLE C.15   Data for Problem C.15

Project Life (N)	Salvage Value (F)
7 years	$15,000
8	13,000
9	11,000
10	9,000
11	7,000
12	5,000

C.16 Assume that there are three independent investment alternatives as given in Table C.16. Ignore any tax considerations since they are not applicable. Use the IFPS computer package and determine the following:

(a) Use a MARR of 12% and find the conventional B/C ratio for each alternative.

(b) Repeat part (a) by using modified B/C ratios.

(c) Compare the three alternatives using the rate of return method.

TABLE C.16   Data for Problem C.16

Alternative	Investment Cost	Annual User Benefits	Annual O&M Savings	Life (years)
1	$150,000	$25,000	−$10,000	25
2	150,000	10,000	6,000	25
3	150,000	3,000	5,000	25

C.17 Assume that if a specific road is repaired, the annual maintenance cost will decrease to $500 per mile from $1,000 per mile. Annual traffic on the road is 200,000 vehicles. Total annual costs of the road user is $8,500 per mile. This cost will be reduced to $3,000 per mile if the road is repaired. The repair cost is $15,000 per mile and it will last about 15 years. Use the IFPS computer package and a MARR of 10% and determine the following:

(a) Conventional B/C ratio.

(b) Modified B/C ratio.

(c) Rate of return.

(d) Net benefits.

(e) NPW of benefits.

C.18 Consider the three mutually exclusive alternatives given in Table C.18. Use the IFPS computer package and determine:

(a) Conventional B/C ratio for each alternative, if the MARR is 12%.

(b) The RORs of each alternative based on the NAW of savings.

TABLE C.18   Data for Problem C.18

Alternative	Investment Cost	Annual User Benefits	Annual O&M Savings	Life (years)
A	$50,000	$6,000	$5,000	20
B	75,000	9,000	10,000	20
C	120,000	15,000	15,000	20

C.19 Assume that the first cost of a project is $150,000 with a salvage value of $25,000 at the end of its useful life of 12 years. Annual operating revenues are $42,000. Its annual O&M costs are $10,000. Use an effective combined state and federal tax rate of 50% and the straight-line depreciation method. Employ the IFPS computer package and determine the prospective after-tax rate of return of the project.

C.20 Solve Problem C.19 using the following depreciation methods:

(a) Sum-of-years' digits method.

(b) Double-declining-balance method.

(c) Accelerated Cost Recovery System (ACRS) of 1981.

C.21 Use the IFPS computer package and assume that the following data is given for an investment project. Its first cost is $209,000 and its salvage value is $20,000 at the end of its life of 15 years. Assume that its O&M costs are $15,000 for the first year, then increasing by $1,000 per year. Its annual revenues are $49,000 and applicable effective combined state and federal income tax rate is 50%. Use the straight-line depreciation method.

(a) Prepare a cash flow table for the investment on a year-by-year basis.

(b) Find the prospective after-tax ROR.

C.22 Solve Problem C.21 using the following depreciation methods:

(a) Sum-of-years' digits method.

(b) Double-declining-balance method.

(c) Sinking-fund method; use $i = 10\%$.

(d) Accelerated Cost Recovery System (ACRS) of 1981.

TABLE C.24 Data for Problem C.24

Year	Estimated Cash Flow for Alternative A			Estimated Cash Flow for Alternative B			Estimated Cash Flow for Alternative C		
	Pessimistic $P_A = 0.3$	Most Likely $P_A = 0.6$	Optimistic $P_A = 0.1$	Pessimistic $P_B = 0.2$	Most Likely $P_B = 0.5$	Optimistic $P_B = 0.3$	Pessimistic $P_C = 0.3$	Most Likely $P_C = 0.4$	Optimistic $P_C = 0.3$
0	-$200,000	-$200,000	-$200,000	-$200,000	-$200,000	-$200,000	-$200,000	-$200,000	-$200,000
1	7,000	10,000	15,000	-15,000	-10,000	-5,000	18,000	20,000	25,000
2	8,000	12,000	20,000	-15,000	-10,000	-5,000	17,000	20,000	25,000
3	9,000	14,000	25,000	8,000	10,000	15,000	25,000	30,000	35,000
4	10,000	16,000	25,000	13,000	15,000	17,000	25,000	35,000	35,000
5	10,000	18,000	30,000	13,000	15,000	20,000	20,000	25,000	30,000
6	10,000	20,000	30,000	15,000	20,000	25,000	30,000	40,000	45,000
7	11,000	22,000	30,000	20,000	30,000	30,000	25,000	30,000	35,000
8	12,000	24,000	25,000	30,000	40,000	45,000	-15,000	-5,000	0
9	13,000	26,000	25,000	30,000	40,000	45,000	10,000	15,000	19,000
10	14,000	28,000	20,000	35,000	50,000	55,000	15,000	20,000	25,000

C23 Assume that a solar system can be installed at a total cost of $30,000. The estimated savings in annual heating cost is $4,500 per year. The useful life of the solar system is uncertain and is given in terms of a pessimistic estimate of 14 years, most likely 17 years, and an optimistic 20 years. Determine the expected BTROR by using the Beta II approximation formula. Use the IFPS computer package.

C.24 Assume that there are three alternative investment projects under consideration and that all three have the same investment requirements and project lives. Also assume that the cash flows of each alternative are estimated with certain probabilities for pessimistic, most likely, and optimistic outcomes. Use a useful life of 10 years, a salvage value of zero at that time, and MARR of 15%. The data is given in Table C.24. Use the IFPS computer package and determine the following:
  (a) NPW for each alternative when pessimistic, most likely, and optimistic values are used.
  (b) Expected value of the NPW for each alternative.
  (c) Develop a decision tree and indicate $E(NPW)$ for each case.

C.25 Solve Problem C.24 but assume that the investment (i.e., first cost) requirements for alternatives A, B, and C are given as $250,000, $300,000, and $225,000, respectively.

C.26 Table C.26 gives the estimates for an investment opportunity. Use the IFPS computer package and determine:
  (a) The NPW for each of the three possible data sets.
  (b) The NAW for each of the three possible data sets.

TABLE C.26   Data for Problem C.26

Parameters	Optimistic	Most Likely	Pessimistic
First cost	$150,000	$175,000	$200,000
Salvage value	$5,000	0	−$5,000
Useful life	23 years	20 years	17 years
Net annual revenue	$45,000	$40,000	$35,000
MARR	15%	15%	15%

C.27 Assume that the salvage value of an investment project is a random variable and it depends on the useful life of the project as given in Table C.27. Assume that the project life is uniformly distributed, that is, the probability of each project life is the same. Use a first cost of $100,000 and a MARR of 20% and find the AEC distribution of the project by generating 10 outcomes (i.e., trials) using the Monte Carlo simulation technique. Use the IFPS computer package.

TABLE C.27 Data for Problem C.27

Life	Prob (salvage value)				
(years)	$20,000	$24,000	$28,000	$32,000	$36,000
5	0.10	0.10	0.15	0.50	0.15
7	0.13	0.15	0.45	0.25	0.12
9	0.10	0.30	0.30	0.20	0.10
11	0.30	0.50	0.20	0	0
13	0.40	0.40	0.15	0.05	0

C.28 Assume that an investment opportunity has a first cost of $200,000 and a project life that is given by a uniform distribution with a minimum value of 10 years and a maximum value of 20 years. It is estimated that the salvage value will be $30,000 if the project life is less than 13 years, $20,000 if the project life is 13 to 17 years, and $10,000 if the project life is 18 or more years. Use a MARR of 20%, and round the project lives to the nearest whole year, and use the Monte Carlo simulation technique. Employ the IFPS computer package.

(a) The AEC distribution by generating 20 outcomes (i.e., trials).

(b) Expected value of the AEC found in part (a).

(c) Variance of the AEC found in part (a).

(d) The PEC distribution by generating 20 outcomes.

APPENDIX D
STATISTICAL TABLES

TABLE D.1   Random Numbers.

48867	33971	29678	13151	56644	49193	93469	43252	14006	47173
32267	69746	00113	51336	36551	56310	85793	53453	09744	64346
27345	03196	33877	35032	98054	48358	21788	98862	67491	42221
55753	05256	51557	90419	40716	64589	90398	37070	78318	02918
93124	50675	04507	44001	06365	77897	84566	99600	67985	49133
98658	86583	97433	10733	80495	62709	61357	66903	76730	79355
68216	94830	41248	50712	46878	87317	80545	31484	03195	14755
17901	30815	78360	78260	67866	42304	07293	61290	61301	04815
88124	21868	14942	25893	72695	56231	18918	72534	86737	77792
83464	36749	22336	50443	83576	19238	91730	39507	22717	94719
91310	99003	25704	55581	00729	22024	61319	66162	20933	67713
32739	38352	91256	77744	75080	01492	90984	63090	53087	41301
07751	66724	03290	56386	06070	67105	64219	48192	70478	84722
55228	64156	90480	97774	08055	04435	26999	42039	16589	06757
89013	51781	81116	24383	95569	97247	44437	36293	29967	16088
51828	81819	81038	89146	39192	89470	76331	56420	14527	34828
59783	85454	93327	06078	64924	07271	77563	92710	42183	12380
80267	47103	90556	16128	41490	07996	78454	47929	81586	67024
82919	44210	61607	93001	26314	26865	26714	43793	94937	28439
77019	77417	19466	14967	75521	49967	74065	09746	27881	01070
66225	61832	06242	40093	40800	76849	29929	18988	10888	40344
98534	12777	84601	56336	00034	85939	32438	09549	01855	40550
63175	70789	51345	43723	06995	11186	38615	56646	54320	39632
92362	73011	09115	78303	38901	58107	95366	17226	74626	78208
61831	44794	65079	97130	94289	73502	04857	68855	47045	06309
42502	01646	88493	48207	01283	16474	08864	68322	92454	19287
89733	86230	04903	55015	11811	98185	32014	84761	80926	14509
01336	66633	26015	66768	24846	00321	73118	15802	13549	41335
72623	56083	65799	88934	87274	19417	84897	90877	76472	52145
74004	68388	04090	35239	49379	04456	07642	68642	01026	43810
09388	54633	27684	47117	67583	42496	20703	68579	65883	10729
51771	92019	39791	60400	08585	60680	28841	09921	00520	73135
69796	30304	79836	20631	10743	00246	24979	35707	75283	39211
98417	33403	63448	90462	91645	24919	73609	26663	09380	30515
56150	18324	43011	02660	86574	86097	49399	21249	90380	94375
76199	75692	09063	72999	94672	69128	39046	15379	98450	09159
74978	98693	21433	34676	97603	48534	59205	66265	03561	83075
85769	92530	04407	53725	96963	19395	16193	51018	70333	12094
63819	65669	38960	74631	39650	39419	93707	61365	46302	26134
18892	43143	19619	43200	49613	50904	73502	19519	11667	53294
32855	17190	61587	80411	22827	38852	51952	47785	34952	93574
29435	96277	53583	92804	05027	19736	54918	66396	96547	00351
36211	67263	82064	41624	49826	17566	02476	79368	28831	02805
73514	00176	41638	01420	31850	41380	11643	06787	09011	88924
90895	93099	27850	29423	98693	71762	39928	35268	59359	20674
69719	90656	62186	50435	77015	29661	94698	56057	04388	33381
94982	81453	87162	28248	37921	21143	62673	81224	38972	92988
84136	04221	72790	04719	34914	95609	88695	60180	58790	12802
58515	80581	88442	65727	72121	40481	06001	13159	55324	93591
20681	59164	75797	08928	68381	12616	97487	84803	92457	88847

Reproduced with permission from the Rand Corporation, *A Million Random Numbers*. (New York: The Free Press, 1955).

TABLE D.2 Random Normal Deviates (z)

1.102	− .944	.401	.226	1.396	−1.030	−1.723	− .368	2.170	.393
.148	−1.140	.492	−1.210	− .998	.573	.893	− .855	−2.209	− .267
2.372	1.353	− .900	− .554	− .343	.470	−1.033	−1.026	2.172	.195
− .145	.466	.854	− .282	−1.504	.431	− .060	.952	− .343	.735
.104	.732	.604	− .016	− .266	1.372	− .925	−1.594	−2.004	1.925
1.419	−1.853	− .347	.155	−1.078	.623	− .024	.498	.466	.049
.069	− .411	− .661	− .037	.703	.532	− .177	.395	− .278˙	.240
.797	.488	−1.070	− .721	−1.412	− .976	−1.953	− .206	1.848	.632
− .393	− .351	.222	.557	−1.094	1.403	.173	− .113	.806	.939
− .874	−1.336	.523	.848	.304	− .202	−1.279	.501	.396	.859
.125	−1.170	− .192	1.387	2.291	− .959	.090	1.031	.180	−1.389
−1.091	− .649	− .514	− .232	−1.198	.822	.240	.951	−1.736	.270
2.304	.481	− .987	−1.222	.549	−1.056	.277	− .919	.148	1.517
− .961	2.057	− .546	− .896	.165	− .343	.696	.628	− .929	− .965
− .783	.854	− .139	1.087	.515	− .876	− .448	.485	.589	− .804
.487	.557	.327	1.280	−1.731	− .339	.295	− .724	.720	.331
− .299	.979	− .924	− .649	.574	1.407	− .292	− .775	− .511	.026
1.831	− .937	−1.321	−1.734	1.677	−1.393	−1.187	− .079	− .181	− .844
.243	.466	−1.330	1.078	−1.102	1.123	− .421	− .674	2.951	− .743
−2.181˙	−1.854	−1.059	− .478	−1.119	.272	− .800	.841	− .061	2.261
.154	− .333	1.011	−1.565	1.261	.776	1.130	1.552	− .563	.558
−1.065	1.610	.463	.062	− .086	.021	1.633	1.788	.480	2.824
1.083	− .760	− .012	.183	.155	.676	−1.315	.067	.213	2.380
.615	− .594	− .028	− .506	− .054	3.173	.817	.210	1.699	1.950
.178	− .500	1.100	1.613	1.048	2.323	− .174	− .033	2.220	− .661
− .507	−1.273	.596	.690	−1.724	−1.689	.163	− .199	− .450	.244
.362	− .588	−1.386	.072	.778	− .591	.365	.465	2.472	1.049
.775	1.546	.217	−1.012	.778	.246	1.055	1.071	.447	− .585
.818	.561	−1.024	2.105	− .868	.060	− .385	1.089	.017	− .873
.014	.240	− .632	− .225	− .844	.448	1.651	1.423	.425	.252
−1.236	−1.045	−1.628	.687	.983	− .840	−1.835	−1.864	1.327	− .408
− .567	−1.161	.010	− .853	.111	1.145	1.015	.056	.141	1.471
.278	−1.783	.170	− .358	.705	− .054	1.098	.707	− .585	− .305
− .959	− .497	.688	− .268	−1.431	− .791	− .727	.958	.237	.092
1.249	.037	.497	.579	− .227	.860	.349	2.355	2.184	−1.744
− .915	− .164	−1.166	1.529	.008	.636	−1.080	− .688	2.444	−1.316
.132	2.809	−1.918	−1.083	− .642	− .179	.339	.637	.063	− .079
− .156	−1.664	1.140	.295	1.086	−2.546	− .002	− .672	.205	− .039
.538	−1.143	− .390	.165	− .160	.457	−1.307	.273	− .670	− .988
.027	− .057	.742	− .149	− .801	1.702	− .346	− .053	.892	−1.181
.023	.423	1.051	− .831	− .325	− .795	−1.129	− .287	.172	− .793
− .196	−1.457	1.060	.557	− .190	− .891	− .768	.282	−1.432	− .447
.133	.577	− .332	−1.932	.220	.189	−1.521	.896	− .781	− .899
.020	− .217	− .856	.605	.072	.520	1.222	− .181	− .266	−1.222
1.405	1.065	1.350	1.353	−2.289	−1.003	.375	1.621	−1.126	.937
.178	−1.237	− .520	− .603	−1.615	− .358	.605	− .407	−2.579	−1.811
−1.438	.104	−1.821	− .390	− .630	1.294	1.470	.991	− .355	−1.285
1.768	− .175	− .450	.915	− .221	− .019	1.864	.038	.058	1.212
.099	1.076	2.348	−1.550	.458	.147	−1.223	.994	−1.657	1.264
.951	.252	−1.261	− .963	.221	− .036	− .395	− .252	−1.379	1.885

TABLE D.3 The Areas under the Standardized Normal Distribution Function

z	0 z	0 z	z	0 z	0 z	z	0 z	0 z
0.00	.0000	.5000	0.55	.2088	.2912	1.10	.3643	.1357
0.01	.0040	.4960	0.56	.2123	.2877	1.11	.3665	.1335
0.02	.0080	.4920	0.57	.2157	.2843	1.12	.3686	.1314
0.03	.0120	.4880	0.58	.2190	.2810	1.13	.3708	.1292
0.04	.0160	.4840	0.59	.2224	.2776	1.14	.3729	.1271
0.05	.0199	.4801	0.60	.2257	.2743	1.15	.3749	.1251
0.06	.0239	.4761	0.61	.2291	.2709	1.16	.3770	.1230
0.07	.0279	.4721	0.62	.2324	.2676	1.17	.3790	.1210
0.08	.0319	.4681	0.63	.2357	.2643	1.18	.3810	.1190
0.09	.0359	.4641	0.64	.2389	.2611	1.19	.3830	.1170
0.10	.0398	.4602	0.65	.2422	.2578	1.20	.3849	.1151
0.11	.0438	.4562	0.66	.2454	.2546	1.21	.3869	.1131
0.12	.0478	.4522	0.67	.2486	.2514	1.22	.3888	.1112
0.13	.0517	.4483	0.68	.2517	.2483	1.23	.3907	.1093
0.14	.0557	.4443	0.69	.2549	.2451	1.24	.3925	.1075
0.15	.0596	.4404	0.70	.2580	.2420	1.25	.3944	.1056
0.16	.0636	.4364	0.71	.2611	.2389	1.26	.3962	.1038
0.17	.0675	.4325	0.72	.2642	.2358	1.27	.3980	.1020
0.18	.0714	.4286	0.73	.2673	.2327	1.28	.3997	.1003
0.19	.0753	.4247	0.74	.2704	.2296	1.29	.4015	.0985
0.20	.0793	.4207	0.75	.2734	.2266	1.30	.4032	.0968
0.21	.0832	.4168	0.76	.2764	.2236	1.31	.4049	.0951
0.22	.0871	.4129	0.77	.2794	.2206	1.32	.4066	.0934
0.23	.0910	.4090	0.78	.2823	.2177	1.33	.4082	.0918
0.24	.0948	.4052	0.79	.2852	.2148	1.34	.4099	.0901
0.25	.0987	.4013	0.80	.2881	.2119	1.35	.4115	.0885
0.26	.1026	.3974	0.81	.2910	.2090	1.36	.4131	.0869
0.27	.1064	.3936	0.82	.2939	.2061	1.37	.4147	.0853
0.28	.1103	.3897	0.83	.2967	.2033	1.38	.4162•	.0838
0.29	.1141	.3859	0.84	.2995	.2005	1.39	.4177	.0823
0.30	.1179	.3821	0.85	.3023	.1977	1.40	.4192	.0808
0.31	.1217	.3783	0.86	.3051	.1949	1.41	.4207	.0793
0.32	.1255	.3745	0.87	.3078	.1922	1.42	.4222	.0778
0.33	.1293	.3707	0.88	.3106	.1894	1.43	.4236	.0764
0.34	.1331	.3669	0.89	.3133	.1867	1.44	.4251	.0749
0.35	.1368	.3632	0.90	.3159	.1841	1.45	.4265	.0735
0.36	.1406	.3594	0.91	.3186	.1814	1.46	.4279	.0721
0.37	.1443	.3557	0.92	.3212	.1788	1.47	.4292	.0708
0.38	.1480	.3520	0.93	.3238	.1762	1.48	.4306	.0694
0.39	.1517	.3483	0.94	.3264	.1736	1.49	.4319	.0681
0.40	.1554	.3446	0.95	.3289	.1711	1.50	.4332	.0668
0.41	.1591	.3409	0.96	.3315	.1685	1.51	.4345	.0655
0.42	.1628	.3372	0.97	.3340	.1660	1.52	.4357	.0643
0.43	.1664	.3336	0.98	.3365	.1635	1.53	.4370	.0630
0.44	.1700	.3300	0.99	.3389	.1611	1.54	.4382	.0618
0.45	.1736	.3264	1.00	.3413	.1587	1.55	.4394	.0606
0.46	.1772	.3228	1.01	.3438	.1562	1.56	.4406	.0594
0.47	.1808	.3192	1.02	.3461	.1539	1.57	.4418	.0582
0.48	.1844	.3156	1.03	.3485	.1515	1.58	.4429	.0571
0.49	.1879	.3121	1.04	.3508	.1492	1.59	.4441	.0559
0.50	.1915	.3085	1.05	.3531	.1469	1.60	.4452	.0548
0.51	.1950	.3050	1.06	.3554	.1446	1.61	.4463	.0537
0.52	.1985	.3015	1.07	.3577	.1423	1.62	.4474	.0526
0.53	.2019	.2981	1.08	.3599	.1401	1.63	.4484	.0516
0.54	.2054	.2946	1.09	.3621	.1379	1.64	.4495	.0505

TABLE D.3 (Continued)

z	⊿	⊿	z	⊿	⊿	z	⊿	⊿
1.65	.4505	.0495	2.22	.4868	.0132	2.79	.4974	.0026
1.66	.4515	.0485	2.23	.4871	.0129	2.80	.4974	.0026
1.67	.4525	.0475	2.24	.4875	.0125	2.81	.4975	.0025
1.68	.4535	.0465	2.25	.4878	.0122	2.82	.4976	.0024
1.69	.4545	.0455	2.26	.4881	.0119	2.83	.4977	.0023
1.70	.4554	.0446	2.27	.4884	.0116	2.84	.4977	.0023
1.71	.4564	.0436	2.28	.4887	.0113	2.85	.4978	.0022
1.72	.4573	.0427	2.29	.4890	.0110	2.86	.4979	.0021
1.73	.4582	.0418	2.30	.4893	.0107	2.87	.4979	.0021
1.74	.4591	.0409	2.31	.4896	.0104	2.88	.4980	.0020
1.75	.4599	.0401	2.32	.4898	.0102	2.89	.4981	.0019
1.76	.4608	.0392	2.33	.4901	.0099	2.90	.4981	.0019
1.77	.4616	.0384	2.34	.4904	.0096	2.91	.4982	.0018
1.78	.4625	.0375	2.35	.4906	.0094	2.92	.4982	.0018
1.79	.4633	.0367	2.36	.4909	.0091	2.93	.4983	.0017
1.80	.4641	.0359	2.37	.4911	.0089	2.94	.4984	.0016
1.81	.4649	.0351	2.38	.4913	.0087	2.95	.4984	.0016
1.82	.4656	.0344	2.39	.4916	.0084	2.96	.4985	.0015
1.83	.4664	.0336	2.40	.4918	.0082	2.97	.4985	.0015
1.84	.4671	.0329	2.41	.4920	.0080	2.98	.4986	.0014
1.85	.4678	.0322	2.42	.4922	.0078	2.99	.4986	.0014
1.86	.4686	.0314	2.43	.4925	.0075	3.00	.4987	.0013
1.87	.4693	.0307	2.44	.4927	.0073	3.01	.4987	.0013
1.88	.4699	.0301	2.45	.4929	.0071	3.02	.4987	.0013
1.89	.4706	.0294	2.46	.4931	.0069	3.03	.4988	.0012
1.90	.4713	.0287	2.47	.4932	.0068	3.04	.4988	.0012
1.91	.4719	.0281	2.48	.4934	.0066	3.05	.4989	.0011
1.92	.4726	.0274	2.49	.4936	.0064	3.06	.4989	.0011
1.93	.4732	.0268	2.50	.4938	.0062	3.07	.4989	.0011
1.94	.4738	.0262	2.51	.4940	.0060	3.08	.4990	.0010
1.95	.4744	.0256	2.52	.4941	.0059	3.09	.4990	.0010
1.96	.4750	.0250	2.53	.4943	.0057	3.10	.4990	.0010
1.97	.4756	.0244	2.54	.4945	.0055	3.11	.4991	.0009
1.98	.4761	.0239	2.55	.4946	.0054	3.12	.4991	.0009
1.99	.4767	.0233	2.56	.4948	.0052	3.13	.4991	.0009
2.00	.4772	.0228	2.57	.4949	.0051	3.14	.4992	.0008
2.01	.4778	.0222	2.58	.4951	.0049	3.15	.4992	.0008
2.02	.4783	.0217	2.59	.4952	.0048	3.16	.4992	.0008
2.03	.4788	.0212	2.60	.4953	.0047	3.17	.4992	.0008
2.04	.4793	.0207	2.61	.4955	.0045	3.18	.4993	.0007
2.05	.4798	.0202	2.62	.4956	.0044	3.19	.4993	.0007
2.06	.4803	.0197	2.63	.4957	.0043	3.20	.4993	.0007
2.07	.4808	.0192	2.64	.4959	.0041	3.21	.4993	.0007
2.08	.4812	.0188	2.65	.4960	.0040	3.22	.4994	.0006
2.09	.4817	.0183	2.66	.4961	.0039	3.23	.4994	.0006
2.10	.4821	.0179	2.67	.4962	.0038	3.24	.4994	.0006
2.11	.4826	.0174	2.68	.4963	.0037	3.25	.4994	.0006
2.12	.4830	.0170	2.69	.4964	.0036	3.30	.4995	.0005
2.13	.4834	.0166	2.70	.4965	.0035	3.35	.4996	.0004
2.14	.4838	.0162	2.71	.4966	.0034	3.40	.4997	.0003
2.15	.4842	.0158	2.72	.4967	.0033	3.45	.4997	.0003
2.16	.4846	.0154	2.73	.4968	.0032	3.50	.4998	.0002
2.17	.4850	.0150	2.74	.4969	.0031	3.60	.4998	.0002
2.18	.4854	.0146	2.75	.4970	.0030	3.70	.4999	.0001
2.19	.4857	.0143	2.76	.4971	.0029	3.80	.4999	.0001
2.20	.4861	.0139	2.77	.4972	.0028	3.90	.49995	.00005
2.21	.4864	.0136	2.78	.4973	.0027	4.00	.49997	.00003

APPENDIX E
GLOSSARY

Some of the most commonly used terms in engineering economy, both in this book and in general usage, are defined in the following pages.

Accelerated Cost Recovery System (ACRS). A new depreciation method given by the 1981 tax act and applicable for *all* assets placed in service on January 1, 1981 or later. In the ACRS method all depreciable assets have statutory recovery periods of 3, 5, 10, or 15 years for tax purposes. The percentage of first cost that can be deducted from taxable income for each year is specified for each class.

Accounts receivable. The total amount of credit extended to customers.

Accrued interest. Interest required to be paid on a bond since the last interest payment.

Administrative expense. The cost of operating the business at the management level, including officers' salaries, legal costs, etc.

Allowance for funds used during construction (AFDC). The cost of money invested in a plant while it is under construction. It is also known as the "interest lost during construction (ILDC)." This interest is capitalized and becomes part of the plant investment.

Amortization. The gradual recovery of an investment in a capitalized asset over a series of time periods by allocating part of the total cost to each period. It is also an IRS-approved tax deduction method similar to straight-line depreciation. It can also be used to refer to a payment plan to pay off a financial debt.

Annual report. The formal financial statement issued every year by a company to its stockholders. It contains information on assets, liabilities, earnings, net profits, etc.

Annuity. A series of equal annual payments extending over a period of years.

Annuity factor. The function of interest rate and time that specifies the amount of periodic annuity.

Annuity fund. A fund reserved to pay annuities.

Annuity fund factor. The function of interest rate and time that specifies the present worth of funds required for a given annuity plan.

Assets. Resources of any kind owned by a company and of value to that enterprise as a going concern. They can be classified as (1) current assets, e.g., cash, marketable securities, accounts receivable, raw materials, and inventories; (2) fixed assets, e.g., property, plant, and equipment; and (3) intangible assets, e.g., goodwill, patents, copyrights, leases, licenses, franchises, etc.

Balance sheet. A condensed statement of financial position of a company as of a specified moment of time. It shows the total assets, total liabilities, and stockholders' equity.

Bond. A certificate of indebtedness representing a long-term obligation of a specific value offering assured interest at an established rate on the par or face value. Bonds are usually issued with par values in multiples of $100 or $1,000. The company promises to pay the bondholders a specific rate (or amount) of interest for a specified length of time and to repay the principal at some specific maturity date. The interest payments are made annually, semiannually or quarterly.

Bond rating. An official opinion by an outside professional service, e.g., Moody's Investor Service or Standard & Poor's Corp., on the credit reputation of a bond issuer and the investment quality of its securities. The opinion is given in letter values, e.g., AAA or Baa, etc.

Book value. The recorded current value of an asset or property as shown on the accounting records of a company. It is calculated by writing off (i.e., subtracting) the accumulated depreciation, amortization, or depletion from the first cost.

Capital gain or capital loss. The gain or loss resulting from the sale of a capital asset. They can be defined as either short-term (12 months or less) or long-term (more than 12 months) depending on the time duration the asset is owned.

Capitalization. The total amount of various securities issued by a company, including bonds, debentures, preferred and common stocks, and surplus.

Capitalized cost. The present worth of a uniform series of periodic costs that continue over an infinite period of time.

Capital recovery. The process of regaining the net capital investment. Typically, this includes interest (or return) and depreciation.

Capital recovery factor. A factor used to compute the amount of money required at the end of each period for the purpose of capital recovery.

Carrying charge. The total annual costs, i.e., depreciation, return, taxes, insurance, and normal operating and maintenance costs associated with investment in a given project.

Cash flow. The net income (profit) plus depreciation, depletion, or amortization from a given project.

Compound amount. The future worth of a sum invested (or loaned) at compound interest.

Compound amount factor. A factor that gives the future worth at compounded interest when it is multiplied by the single sum or uniform series of payments.

Compounding. The mathematical process of periodically adding return to invested money and thereby increasing the principal upon which future return is based.

Debt. The portion of the capitalization of a company that includes bonds, long-term notes, debentures, and possibly long-term leases.

Debt ratio. The ratio of debt capital to total capitalization.

Deferred taxes. Taxes collected because of current business operations but not to be paid until some future time due to government tax regulations.

Depletion. A form of capital recovery that reflects a declining value of an asset as a result of a decrease in the quantity available. It is applicable to such natural resources as oil, gas, coal, or timber, etc.

Depreciation. A form of capital recovery applicable to a property with a useful life of two or more years for the purpose of recovering the first cost less net salvage value over its useful life.

Discounting. A mathematical process used to reduce a principal sum at some future time to its equivalent at the present time.

Earnings. The portion of the net income that may be distributed as dividends to the stockholders or kept as retained income.

Earnings value. The present worth of the future net earnings.

Effective interest rate: The actual value of annual interest rate calculated using compound interest rate.

Endowment. The fund developed to support a project or a sequence of donations or financial obligations.

Equity. The portion of the capitalization of a company that belongs to the owners. It includes common and preferred stocks and retained earnings.

Expected return. The profit anticipated from a business venture.

Expenditure. The spending of money for either expense or investment purposes.

Expense. Costs that are incurred in the operation and maintenance of the business and that are not capitalized. Expenses are paid directly from revenues and are deductible for tax purposes.

First Cost. The initial cost of a capitalized property that includes transportation, installation, preparation for service, and other relevant initial expenditures.

Fixed charge rate. The sum of annual investment related charges, given as a percentage of the original plant investment.

Future worth. The equivalent value at a given future date based on time value of money.

Goodwill. The established reputation of a company as an established well-known and well-operated business.

Incremental cost. The additional cost increase due to increasing the output from one level to another.

Indirect cost. Those costs that are not directly assignable to a particular project or operation, e.g., general and administrative expenses, pensions, professional services, etc.

Intangibles. The conditions or economic factors that cannot be expressed in quantitative terms, e.g., goodwill.

Interest. The cost for the use of capital.

Interest lost during construction (ILDC). *See* Allowance for funds used during construction.

Interest rate. The ratio of the interest payment to the principal for a given unit of time and usually given as a percentage of the principal.

Interest rate, nominal. The customary type of interest rate designation on an annual basis without considering compounding periods.

Internally generated funds. Funds obtained from retained earnings, depreciation and/or depletion, investment tax credit, and deferred taxes.

Investment (capital). The cost (or present value) of all the properties and funds required to establish and maintain the enterprise or project.

Iowa curves. Generally accepted retirement patterns generated by the Iowa State University in the 1930s for use by utilities in their group-property depreciation analysis. Presently, there are 28 such survivor curve types.

Lease. A contract under which the owner of property (the lessor) gives another party (the lessee) the right to use property, plan, or equipment for a stated period of time in return for a specified rental payment.

Levelizing. The process of converting a nonuniform series of annual payments to an equivalent uniform series.

Leverage. The potential to increase financial gains as a percentage of an investment or equity by operating or financing largely on borrowed funds.

Leveraging. The process of financing largely on borrowed funds.

Liabilities. All the claims of creditors against a company's assets, including accounts, wages, and salaries payable, accrued taxes payable, dividends payable, and long-term debt.

Long-term debt. Mortgage bonds, debentures, and notes that are due one year or more from the date of issuance.

Marginal cost. The cost of one additional unit of production, activity, or service.

Minimum attractive rate of return (MARR). The minimum acceptable rate of return. Normally, only those investment opportunities that yield a rate of return greater than the MARR are considered. The investment opportunities yielding less than the MARR are considered not worthwhile.

Mortgages. The long-term securities given for repayment of a debt usually connected with real property.

Net income. The income remaining after all expenses, including depreciation and interest expenses, and taxes have been paid. It is equal to dividends plus retained income (or earnings).

Net salvage value. The gross salvage (scrap) value of a property less the cost of removal.

Nominal interest. The number used to describe the annual interest rate.

Operating cost. The annual sum of operation expenses, including testing, inspection, selling, administration, property taxes, etc., and maintenance expenses. It is also known as the operation and maintenance cost.

Overhead cost. *See* Indirect cost.

Payoff period. The period of time required for a machine, facility, or other investment to generate enough net revenue (or savings in operating cost) to recover its investment costs.

Preferred stock. A class of stock with a claim on the company's earnings before payment made on the common stock and usually given priority over common stock if the company liquidates itself.

Present worth. The equivalent value at the present, based on the time value of money.

Present worth factor. A factor used to calculate the present worth in an economic analysis involving compound interest.

Profitability index. The rate of return calculated in an economical analysis by using the discounted cash flow method.

Property tax. An annual assessment made against the company's owned property by a local government agency. It is also known as the ad valorem tax.

Rate of return. The interest rate at which the present worth of cash flows on a project is zero. It is also used for the interest rate earned by an investment.

Replacement study. An economic analysis to compare a present property against a property proposed to replace the existing one.

Required return. The minimum return or profit necessary to justify an investment.

Retirement. The removal of some property from use.

Revenue. The money received from customers in payment for services or goods sold plus other various income.

Revenue requirement. The revenue that must be received to cover all annual costs.

Salvage value. The cost recovered or which could be recovered from a used property when removed, sold, or scrapped.

Sensitivity analysis. The study of the relative magnitude of the change in one or more elements of an engineering economy problem that will reverse a choice decision among alternatives.

Simple interest. Interest that is not compounded.

Sinking fund. A fund established by a series of equal annual payments to produce a desired amount at the end of certain time periods for a specific purpose, such as replacement of a property or retirement of a debt.

Sinking-fund factor. A factor used to determine the periodic deposit required to accumulate a specified future amount.

Study period. The period of time over which the pattern of annual costs for various alternatives is considered.

Sunk cost. A cost that is incurred, and will continue to be, due to a previous decision and that cannot be changed by present or future decisions. It is the unrecovered balance of an investment.

Taxable income. The portion of total revenue that remains after making all deductions, including expenses incurred, permitted by present laws and regulations.

Tax life. The property or asset life used for depreciation calculations.

Tax rate. The rate applied to taxable income that determines the amount of taxes owed.

Tax write-off. The portion of a given expenditure that can be deducted for federal income tax purposes during a year or series of years.

Time value of money. The change in the value of money over time as a result of its earning power.

Working capital. That portion of investment represented by current assets (assets that are not capitalized) less the current liabilities. The capital necessary, due to the time lag between expenditures and receipts, for the ongoing daily operation of the business.

REFERENCES

1. Ackoff, R. L., and Sasieni, M. W., *Fundamentals of Operations Research.* Wiley, New York, 1968.

2. Albrook, R. C., "Participative Management: Time for a Second Look." *Fortune Magazine,* **75**(5), 166–170 (1967).

3. *A Manual on User Benefit Analysis of Highway and Bus-Transit Improvements.* American Association of State Highway and Transportation Officials, Washington, D.C., 1977.

4. Amos, J. J., and Sarchet, B. R., *Management for Engineers.* Prentice-Hall, Englewood Cliffs, NJ, 1981.

5. ANSI Z94.5-1972, *American National Standards for Industrial Engineering Terminology for Engineering Economy.* American Society of Mechanical Engineers, New York, 1972.

6. Argyris, C., "Personality vs Organization." *Organizational Dynamics,* **3**(2), 2–17 (Fall 1971).

7. Argyris, C., *Understanding Organizational Behavior.* Dorsey, Homewood, IL, 1960.

8. Barish, N. N., and Kaplan, S., *Economic Analysis: For Engineering and Managerial Decision Making.* McGraw-Hill, New York, 1978.

9. Bayton, J. A., and Chapman, R. L., *Transformation of Scientists and Engineers into Managers.* N.A.S.A. Document SP-291, NASA, Washington, D.C., 1972.

10. Bekiroglu, H., and Gönen, T., "How Model Building Helped Cut Restaurant Losses." *Restaurant Business,* **76**(6), 129–130 (1977).

11. Bekiroglu, H., and Gönen, T., "Is There an Answer for Assembly Line Blues?" *Proceedings of the Midwest Annual Regional Conference of American Institute for Decision Sciences,* Chicago, 1979, pp. 153–156.

12. Bekiroglu, H., and Gönen, T., "Labor Turnover's Roots, Costs, and Some Potential Solutions." *Personnel Administrator,* **26**(7), 67–73, (1981).

13. Bekiroglu, H., and Gönen, T., "Motivation—The State of the Art." *Personnel Journal,* **56**(10), 561–562 (1977).

14. Blanchard, B. S., *Design and Manage to Life Cycle Cost*. M/A Press, Portland, OR, 1978.

15. Blanchard, B. S., *Engineering Organization and Management*. Prentice-Hall, Englewood Cliffs, NJ, 1976.

16. Blank, L., and Tarquin, A., *Engineering Economy*. McGraw-Hill, New York, 1983.

17. Bussey, L. E., *The Economic Analysis of Industrial Projects*. Prentice-Hall, Englewood Cliffs, NJ, 1978.

18. Bussey, L. E., and Stevens, G. T., "Net Present Value from Complex Cash Flow Streams by Simulation." *AIIE Transactions*, **3**(1), 81–89 (1971).

19. Canada, J. R., and White, J. A., *Capital Investment Decision Analysis for Management and Engineering*, Prentice-Hall, Englewood Cliffs, NJ, 1980.

20. Cleland, D. I., and King, W. R., *System Analysis and Project Management*. McGraw-Hill, New York, 1983.

21. Cleland, D. I., and Kocaoglu, D. F., *Engineering Management*. McGraw-Hill, New York, 1981.

22. Cronstedt, V., *Engineering Management and Administration*. McGraw-Hill, New York, 1961.

23. DeGarmo, E. P., Canada, J. R., and Sullivan, W. G., *Engineering Economy*. Macmillan. New York, 1979.

24. Department of the Navy, Naval Facilities Engineering Command, *Economic Analysis Handbook* Publication P-442, U.S. Government Printing Office, Washington, D.C., 1971.

25. EXECUCOM Systems Corporation, *IFPS User's Manual*. Release 7.0, 1.1, Austin, TX, 1982.

26. EXECUCOM System Corporation, *IFPS/Plus User's Manual*. Vol. 1 *Basic Modeling and Reporting*. Release 3.6, 1.6–1.9, Austin, TX, 1988.

27. Executive Office of the Present, the Office of Management and Budget Circular A-94, *Discount Rates to Be Used in Evaluating Time-Distributed Costs and Benefits*. U.S. Government Printing Office, Washington, D.C., March 27, 1972.

28. Fayol, H., *General and Industrial Management*. Pitman, London, 1949.

29. Fitch, W. C., Wolf, F. K., and Bissinger, B. H., *The Estimation of Depreciation*. Western Michigan University, Kalamazoo, MI, 1974.

30. Gönen, T., Anderson, P. M., and Bowen, D. W., "Energy and the Future." *Proceedings of the First World Hydrogen Energy Conference*, Miami Beach, FL, **3**(2C), 55–78 (1976).

31. Gönen, T., and Bekiroglu, H., "A Simulation of Operations of a Quick-Service Steak House Restaurant." *Proceedings of the 1977 Winter Simulation Conference*, Gaithersburg, MD, December 5–7, 1977, pp. 755–757.

32. Gönen, T., and Bekiroglu, H., "Some Views on Inflation and a Phillips Curve for the United States' Economy." *Proceedings of the Sixth Annual Regional Conference of American Institute for Decision Sciences*, Albany, New York, 1977, pp. 328–331.

33. Gönen, T., *Electric Power Distribution System Engineering*. McGraw-Hill, New York, 1986.

34. Gönen, T., and Eltouny, A. S., "Criteria for Industrialization Among Selected Nations." *Proceedings of the 1979 International Symposium of Engineering*, San Salvador, El Salvador, 1979, pp. 82–93.

35. Gönen, T., and B. L. Foote, "Application of the Multi-Objective Decision Theory to Distribution Systems Theory." *Proceedings of the Modeling and Simulation Conference*, Pittsburgh, PA, May 1–2, 1980, **II**(2), pp. 733–738.

36. Gönen, T., and Ponder, K., "Valuation, Life Analysis, and the IRS." *Industrial Engineering Journal*, **11**(5), 41–43 (1979).

37. Grant, E. L., Ireson, W. G., and Leavenworth, R. S., *Principles of Engineering Economy*, 7th ed. Wiley, New York, 1982.

38. Hershlag, Z. Y., *Turkey, The Challenge of Growth*. Brill, Lieden, Netherlands, 1968.

39. Hertz, D. B., "Investment Policies That Pay Off." *Harvard Business Review*, **46**(1), 96–108 (1968).

40. Hertz, D. B., "Risk Analysis in Capital Investment." *Harvard Business Review*, **42**(1), 95–106 (1964).

41. Herzberg, F., "One More Time: How Do You Motivate Employees?" *Harvard Business Review*, **46**(1), 53–62 (1968).

42. Hespos, R. F., and Stressmann, P. A., "Stochastic Decision Trees for the Analysis of Investment Decisions," *Management Science*, **9**(8), 244–259 (1966).

43. Hess, S. W., and Quigly, H. A., "Analysis of Risk in Investments Using Monte Carlo Technique." *Chemical Engineering Progress Symposium Series 42: Statistics and Numberical Methods in Chemical Engineering*, American Institute of Chemical Engineering, New York, 1963.

44. Hicks, T. G., *Successful Engineering Management*. McGraw-Hill, New York, 1966.

45. Hillier, F. S., *The Evaluation of Risky Interrelated Investments*. Amsterdam, North Holland, 1969.

46. Jeynes, P. H., *Profitability and Economic Choice*. Iowa State University Press, Ames, IA, 1969.

47. Karger, D. W., and Murdick, R. G., *Managing Engineering and Research*, 3rd ed. Industrial Press, New York, 1980.

48. Kazanowski, A. D., "A Standardized Approach to Cost-Effectiveness Evaluations," in J. M. English (ed.), *Cost Effectiveness*. Wiley, New York, 1968, pp. 113–150.

49. Kazonowski, A. D., "Some Cost-Effectiveness Evaluation Criteria," Appendix B in M. M. English (ed.), *Cost Effectiveness*. Wiley, New York, 1968.

50. Kocaoglu, D. F., "Engineering Management Programs as Aids in Moving from Technical Specialty to Technical Management." *Engineering Management International*, **2**(2), 33–47 (1984).

51. Likert, R., *The Human Organization*. McGraw-Hill, New York, 1967.

52. Lundborg, L. B., "Executive Survival Kit." *Industry Week*, **128**, May 26 (1980).

53. Magee, J. F., "Decision Trees for Decision Making." *Harvard Business Review*, **42**(4), 126–138 (1964).

54. Magee, J. F., "How to Use Decision Trees in Capital Investment." *Harvard Business Review*, **42**(5), 79–96 (1964).

55. Marston, A., Winfrey, R., and Hempstead, J. C., *Engineering Valuation and Depreciation*. Iowa State University Press, Ames, IA, 1953.

56. Maslow, A. H., "A Theory of Human Motivation." *Psychological Review*, **50**, 370–396 (1943).

57. McGregor, D., *The Human Side of Enterprise*. McGraw-Hill, New York, 1960.

58. Newman, D. G., *Engineering Economic Analysis*, 2nd ed. Engineering Press, San Jose, CA, 1983.

59. Oglesby, C. H., Bishop, A. B., and Willeke, G. E., "A Method for Decisions Among Freeway Location Alternatives Based on User and Community Consequences." Highway Research Record No. 305, Highway Research Board, Washington, D.C., 1970, pp. 1–14.

60. *Proposed Practices for Economic Analysis of River Basin Projects*. Report to the Federal Inter-Agency River Basin Committee, prepared by the Subcommittee on Benefits and Costs, U.S. Government Printing Office, Washington, D.C., 1950.

61. Raiffa, H., *Decision Analysis: Introductory Lectures on Choices Under Uncertainty*. Addison-Wesley, Reading, MA, 1968.

62. Riggs, J. L., *Essentials of Engineering Economics*. McGraw-Hill, New York, 1982.

63. Samuelson, P. A., *Economics*. McGraw-Hill, New York, 1970.

64. Shapiro, E., *Macroeconomic Analysis*. Harcourt Brace and World, New York, 1970.

65. Shannon, R. E., *Engineering Management*. Wiley, New York, 1980.

66. Smith, G., *Engineering Economy: Analysis of Capital Expenditures*, 4th ed. Iowa State University Press, Ames, IA, 1987.

67. Stermole, F. J., *Economic Evaluation and Investment Decision Methods*, 4th ed. Investment Evaluations Corporation, Golden, CO, 1982.

68. Subcommittee on the Priorities and Economy in Government of the United States Congress, *Benefit–Cost Analysis of Federal Programs*. U.S. Government Printing Office, Washington, D.C., 1973.

69. Terbough, G. D., *Business Investment Management*. Machinery and Allied Products Institute, Washington, D.C., 1967.

70. Terbough, G. D., *Dynamic Equipment Policy*. McGraw-Hill, New York, 1949.

71. Thuesen, H. G., Fabrycky, W. L., and Thuesen, G. J., *Engineering Economy*, 5th ed. Prentice-Hall, Englewood Cliffs, NJ, 1977.

72. Ullmann, J. E., Christman, D. A., and Holtje, B. (ed.), *Handbook of Engineering Management*. Wiley, New York, 1986.

73. *United States Code*. 1940 ed., Government Printing Office, Washington, D.C., 1940, p. 2964.

74. White, J. A., Agee, M. H., and Case, K. E., *Principals of Engineering Economics*. Wiley, New York, 1977.

75. Winfrey, R., *Depreciation of Group Properties*. Engineering Research Institute, Revised Bulletin 155, Iowa State University, Ames, IA, 1969.

76. Winfrey, R., *Statistical Analyses of Industrial Property Retirements*. Engineering Research Institute, Revised Bulletin 125, Iowa State University, Ames, IA, 1967.

INDEX

Accelerated cost recovery system (ACRS)
method, 218–231
Accounting:
  cost concepts, 15–17
  direct cost, 17
  financial accounting, 18
  fixed cost, 17
  future cost, 15–16
  indirect cost, 17
  life-cycle cost, 15–16
  opportunity cost, 15–16
  overhead cost, 17
  managerial accounting, 15, 17–18
  past cost, 15–16
  sunk cost, 16
  variable cost, 17
Accounting principles, 17–18
Acid-test ratio, *see* Liquidity ratios
ACRS, *see* Accelerated cost recovery system
(ACRS) method
Adjusted basis, 211
Ad valorem tax, *see* Income tax
After-tax cash flow, 245–248
After-tax replacement analysis, *see* Replacement
analysis
Albrook, *see* Motivation
Annual worth analysis, 117, 126
Argyris, *see* Motivation
Assets, 18

Balance sheet, 18–20

B/C analysis with multiple alternatives,
307–309
Benefit–cost analysis, 302, 304–307
Benefit–cost ratio benefit method, *see* Benefit–
cost analysis
Beta distribution, 326–328
Bonds:
  definition, 142
  valuation, 142–143
Book value, 203
Breakeven:
  definition, 184
  period, 184
  point, 184
Breakeven analysis:
  application, 188–189
  comments on, 187, 189–193
  definition, 184–185
  improved breakeven analysis, 189
Breakeven period, *see* Breakeven
Breakeven point, *see* Breakeven

Capacity utilization, 196–197
Capital budgeting, 355–367
  effects of, 361–365
  factors affecting, 365–366
  under risk and uncertainty, 366–367
Capital expenditure analysis, computer aided,
413–414
Capital gain, 225
Capitalized worth method, 123–126

Capital rationing, 357–360
Capital recovery, 127–133
Capital write-off, *see* Depreciation, expense
Cash flow:
  application, 21
  generation, 21
Cash flow diagram, 39–41
Certainty, 316–317
Combined effective tax rate, 248–250
Combined federal and state income taxes,
  248–252
Combined interest–deflation rate, 290–293
Combined interest–inflation rate, 289–290
Comparing investment alternatives methods:
  for annual worth analysis, 117–123
  for benefit/cost ratio analysis, 117, 301–314
  for capitalized worth method, 123–126
  for future worth analysis, 117, 134–140
  for payback period analysis, 117, 140,
    184–198
  for present worth analysis, 117–123
Complete uncertainty, decision making under,
  345–350
Compound interest factors:
  limits, 81–82
  relationships among, 71–75
Computer applications, examples, 418–425
Conditional alternatives, *see* Investment
  alternatives
Consumer price index (CPI), 287
Continuous compounding:
  definition, 92–93
  effective interest rates, 87–92
  interest formulas of, 93–105
Corporation federal income tax, *see* Income tax
Cost accounting:
  definition, 23
  indirect costs, 23
  period costs, 23
  product costs, 23
  production overhead, 23
Cost concepts, *see* Accounting
Cost-effectiveness analysis, 310–314
Cost of goods sold, 20–21
Cost-push inflation, 297
Criteria for ranking projects, some comments on,
  174–178
Current assets, 26–27
Current ratio, *see* Liquidity ratios

Debt analysis:
  debt-to-net-worth ratio, 28
  total-depth-to-equity ratio, 29
Decision-making process, 109–110

Decision tree analysis, 343–345
Declining-balance method, 210–214
Defender *vs.* challenger, *see* Replacement
  analysis
Deflation, 285
Demand-pull inflation, 297
Dependent alternatives, *see* Investment
  alternatives
Depletion, 231–232
Depreciation:
  accounting, 202–203
  ACRS method, 218–231
  charge, 202–203
  definition, 201
  expense, 202–203
  group properties, 232–233
  methods, 204–233
  modified ACRS method, 230–232
  reserve, 202
Depreciation accounting, *see* Depreciation
Depreciation charge, *see* Depreciation
Depreciation expense, *see* Depreciation
Depreciation methods, comparison of, *see*
  Depreciation
Depreciation reserve, *see* Depreciation
Direct cost, *see* Accounting
Discount rate, 118
Discounting, 118
  definition, 41
  levelizing, 61–62
  notation, 42
  single-payment compound amount factor, 42–45
  single-payment present worth factor, 45–49
  summary of discrete compounding, 63
  uniform-series capital recovery factor, 56–61
  uniform-series compound amount factor, 45–53
  uniform-series present worth factor, 54–56
  uniform-series sinking-fund factor, 53–54
Dominance criterion, 346
Do-nothing alternative, *see* Investment alternatives
Dumping, 195–196

Economic life, 115, 205
Effective interest rate, 87–92
Engineering economy, role of, 11
Engineering management:
  definition, 1–3
  functions of, 6–7
  motivation, 7
  transition, 4–5
  types of candidates, 5–6
Expected value, *see* Probability theory
Expenses, 21
Expensing, 231

Fair value, 201
Federal tax, *see* Income tax
Financial accounting, *see* Accounting
Financing public projects, *see* Public sector
 project evaluation
First cost, 203
Fixed cost, *see* Accounting
Future worth analysis, 117, 134–140

Geometric gradient series, 75–80
Glossary, 440–445
Group properties:
 depreciation, *see* Depreciation
 retirement patterns, 273–281

Half-year convention, 219
Hurwicz rule (or principle), 348–349

IFPS/Plus, 415–417
Implicit price index (IPI), 287
Income statement, 20
Income tax:
 corporation federal income tax, 242–244
 definition, 237–238
 individual federal income tax, 242–244
 types, 238
Income tax rates for corporations, 244–245
Incremental rate of return (ROR):
 analysis, 168–171
 by Smith's network diagram method,
  171–174
Independent alternative, *see* Investment
 alternatives
Indirect costs, *see* Cost accounting
Individual federal income tax, *see* Income tax
Infinite study period, *see* Capitalized worth
 method
Inflation:
 combined interest–inflation rate,
  289–290
 definition, 284–285
 effects, 288
 effects on calculations, 293–295
 methods, calculation, 288–289
Interest:
 purchasing power, 37
 time value, 37
Interest calculations:
 compound interest, 39
 simple interest, 38
Interest tables, 371–412
Internal Revenue Code of 1986, *see* Tax reform
 act of 1986
Inventory turnover ratio, *see* Liquidity ratios

Investment alternatives:
 conditional, 111
 dependent alternative, 111
 do-nothing alternative, 111
 independent alternative, 111
 mandatory, 112
 mutually exclusive, 111
Investment project types, 356–357
Investment tax credit, 231

KITA, *see* Motivation

Laplace rule (or principle), 346–347
Leadership, 9
Lease-or-buy analysis, 194–195
Leasing, replacement by, *see* Replacement
 analysis
Liabilities:
 current liabilities, 18
 long-term liabilities, 20
Life-cycle costing, 144–149
Likert, *see* Motivation
Limits of compound interest factors, 81–82
Liquidity ratios:
 acid-test ratio, 27
 current ratio, 27
 inventory turnover ratio, 28

Make-or-buy analysis, 193–194
Managerial accounting, *see* Accounting
Managerial skills:
 administrative, 11
 analytical, 11
 communication, 11
 decision making, 11
 entrepreneural, 11
 interpersonal, 10
 organizational, 11
 technical, 10
Mandatory alternative, *see* Investment
 alternatives
Market value, 201
Maslow, *see* Motivation
Maximax and minimum rules (or principles),
  347–348
Maximin and minimax rules (or principles), 347
Minimax regret rule, 349–350
Minimum attractive ROR (MARR), 112–114
Modified ACRS method, *see* Depreciation
Modified benefit cost analysis, 304–307
Monte-Carlo simulation, 338–342
Motivation:
 Albrook, 8
 Argyris, 8

Motivation: (*Continued*)
  KITA, 8
  Likert, 8
  Maslow, 7
  theory X, 7
  theory Y, 8
Multipurpose public projects, 309
Mutually exclusive alternatives, *see* Investment
  alternatives

Noncash expense, *see* Depreciation
Normal distribution, 328–337

Opportunity cost, *see* Accounting
Opportunity foregone, cost, 112
Optimum economic life, *see* Replacement
  analysis
Ordinary income, 225
Outsider viewpoint, 265
Overhead cost, *see* Accounting
Owners equity, 18–19

Past cost, *see* Accounting
Payback, *see* Breakeven
Payback period analysis, 117, 140, 184–198
Payoff matrix, 345
Payout, *see* Breakeven
Period cost, *see* Cost accounting
Personal property, 219
Present worth analysis, 117–123
Present worth of escalating series, 295–297
Price index, 286–287
Probability distributions, *see* Probability theory
Probability theory:
  expected value, 320–325
  introduction, 317–319
  probability distributions, 325–327
    beta distribution, 326–328
    normal distribution, 328–337
Product cost, *see* Cost accounting
Production overhead, *see* Cost accounting
Profitability ratios:
  coverage ratios, 31
  earning power, 31
  gross profit margin, 29
  net profit margin, 29
  operating margin, 29
  profitability, 29–30
  return on assets ratio, 30
  turnover ratio, 31
Profit margin, 195, 196
Property lives, types of, *see* Replacement
  analysis
Property taxes, *see* Income tax

Public sector project evaluation:
  benefit–cost analysis, 302, 304–307
  definition, 301–302
  financing, 303–304
  interest rate selection, 304
  with multiple alternatives, 307–309
  point of view, 302–303
Purchasing power, *see* Interest

Random normal deviates, table, 437
Random numbers, table, 436
Rate of return (ROR) analysis:
  definition, 158–159
  method, 159–164
  by multiple RORs, 166–168
  by trial-and-error, 164–166
Real property, 219
Recapture, 224–225
Recapture of investment tax credit, 225–227
Recovery period, 219–220
Recovery property, 218–219
Relationships among compound interest factors,
  71–75
Replacement, reasons for, *see* Replacement
  analysis
Replacement analysis:
  after tax, 268–273
  defender *vs.* challenger, 261–264
  group properties, 273–281
  leasing, 265–268
  optimum economic life, 259–261
  outsider viewpoint, 265
  property lives, types of, 256–257
  reasons for replacement, 257–259
Replacement value, 201
Revenues, 21
Risk, 316–317
Risk analysis, 23–26

Sales taxes, *see* Income tax
Salvage value, 203
Savage principles, *see* Minimax regret rule
Sensitivity analysis, 197–198
Simple interest, *see* Interest calculations
Sinking-fund method, 214–216
Smith's network diagram method, *see* Incremen-
  tal rate of return (ROR)
Standardized normal distribution function, areas
  under, 438–439
Stocks:
  definition, 143
  valuation, 143
Straight-line method, 204–208
Structural inflation, 297

Study period, 114–117
Sum-of-years, digits method, 208–210
Sunk cost, 264–265

Tax reform act of 1986, 227–230, 239
Theory X, *see* Motivation
Theory Y, *see* Motivation
Time value of money, *see* Interest

sensitivity analysis for, 337–338
Units of production method, 218
Useful life, *see* Economic life

Value-added tax, 238
Value to owner, 201
Variable cost, *see* Accounting
Variance, *see* Probability theory

Working capital, 26